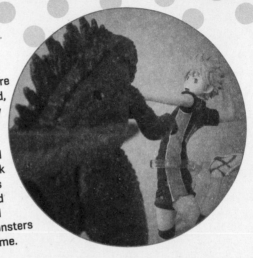

Whether it's a living creature or a structure of some kind, giant things are inherently exciting. As you look at them, you can just feel your stomach squirm and drop. When I used to work in an office, my desk was on the sixth floor. I would look out the window and pretend to see giant monsters walking past it all the time.

HARUICHI FURUDATE began his manga career when he was 25 years old with the one-shot *Ousama Kid* (King Kid), which won an honorable mention for the 14th Jump Treasure Newcomer Manga Prize. His first series, *Kiben Gakuha, Yotsuya Sensei no Kaidan* (Philosophy School, Yotsuya Sensei's Ghost Stories), was serialized in Weekly Shonen Jump in 2010. In 2012, he began serializing *Haikyu!!* in Weekly Shonen Jump, where it became his most popular work to date.

HAIKYU!!
VOLUME 13
SHONEN JUMP Manga Edition

Story and Art by
HARUICHI FURUDATE

Translation **1** **ADRIENNE BECK**
Touch-Up Art & Lettering **2** **ERIKA TERRIQUEZ**
Design **3** **YUKIKO WHITLEY**
Editor **4** **MARLENE FIRST**

HAIKYU!! © 2012 by Haruichi Furudate
All rights reserved.
First published in Japan in 2012 by SHUEISHA Inc., Tokyo.
English translation rights arranged by SHUEISHA Inc.

The stories, characters and incidents mentioned
in this publication are entirely fictional.

No portion of this book may be reproduced or transmitted
in any form or by any means without written permission
from the copyright holders.

Printed in the U.S.A.

Published by VIZ Media, LLC
P.O. Box 77010
San Francisco, CA 94107

10 9 8 7 6 5 4 3 2 1
First printing, July 2017

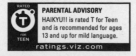
PARENTAL ADVISORY
HAIKYU!! is rated T for Teen
and is recommended for ages
13 and up for mild language.
ratings.viz.com

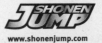
www.shonenjump.com

www.viz.com

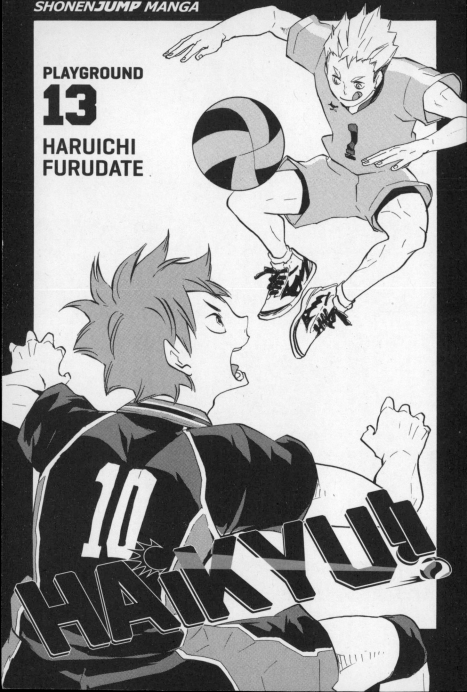

PLAYGROUND

13

HARUICHI FURUDATE

HAIKYU!!

Karasuno High School Volleyball Club

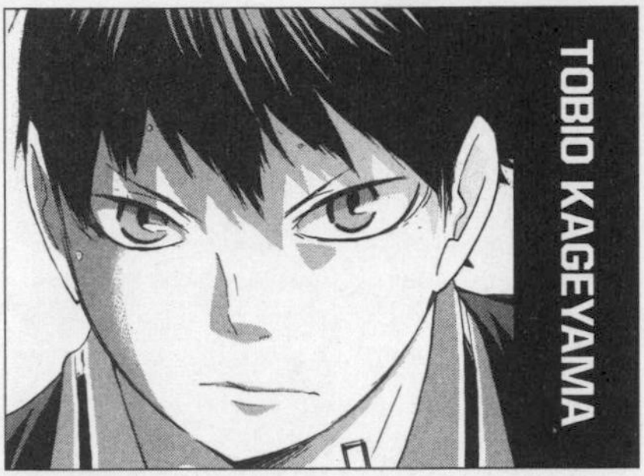
TOBIO KAGEYAMA

1ST YEAR / SETTER
His instincts and athletic talent are so good that he's like a "king" who rules the court. Demanding and egocentric.

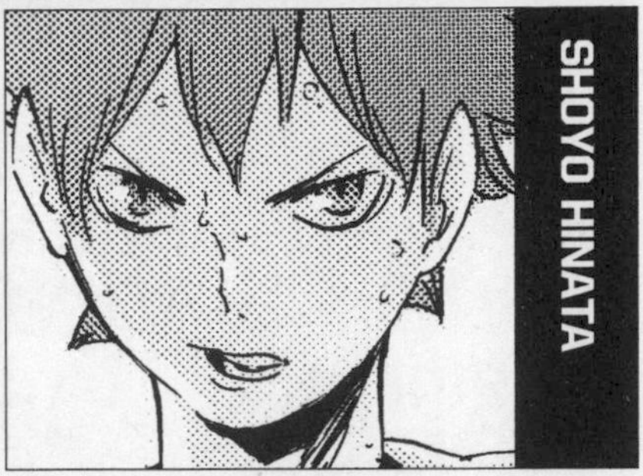
SHOYO HINATA

1ST YEAR / MIDDLE BLOCKER
Even though he doesn't have the best body type for volleyball, he is super athletic. Gets nervous easily.

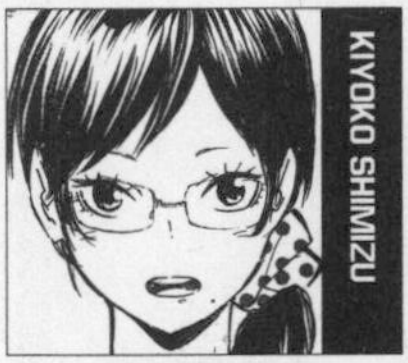
KIYOKO SHIMIZU

3RD YEAR
MANAGER

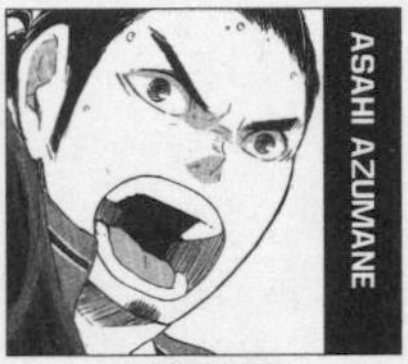
ASAHI AZUMANE

3RD YEAR
WING SPIKER

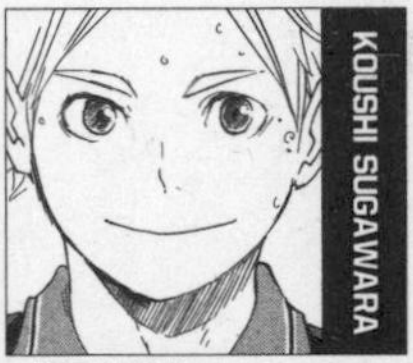
KOUSHI SUGAWARA

3RD YEAR (VICE CAPTAIN)
SETTER

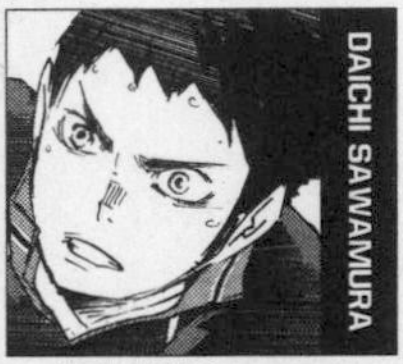
DAICHI SAWAMURA

3RD YEAR (CAPTAIN)
WING SPIKER

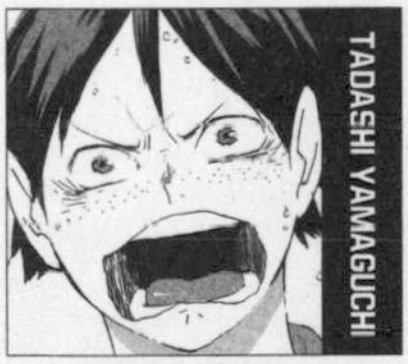
TADASHI YAMAGUCHI

1ST YEAR
MIDDLE BLOCKER

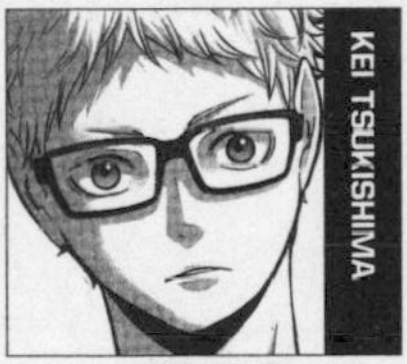
KEI TSUKISHIMA

1ST YEAR
MIDDLE BLOCKER

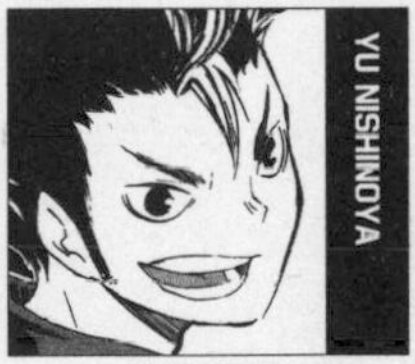
YU NISHINOYA

2ND YEAR
LIBERO

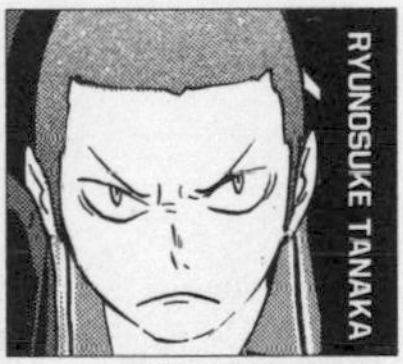
RYUNOSUKE TANAKA

2ND YEAR
WING SPIKER

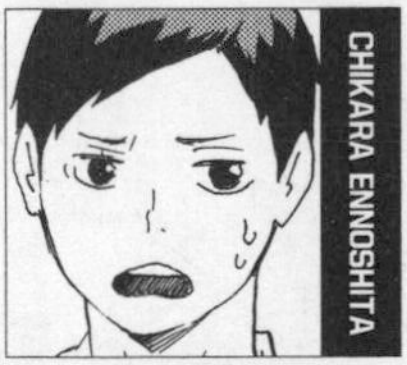
CHIKARA ENNOSHITA

2ND YEAR
WING SPIKER

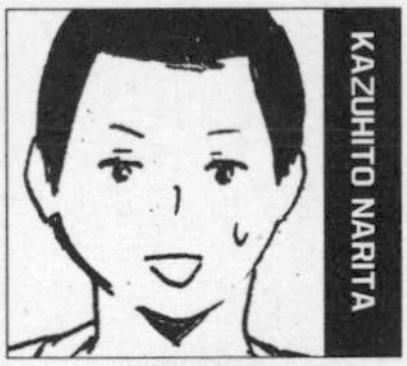
KAZUHITO NARITA

2ND YEAR
MIDDLE BLOCKER

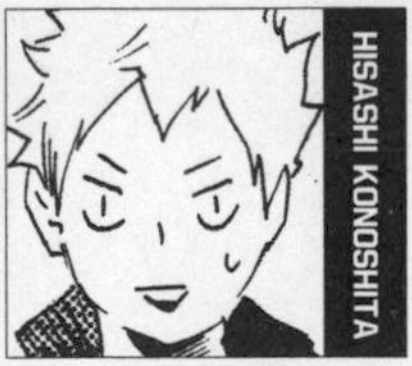
HISASHI KONOSHITA

2ND YEAR
WING SPIKER

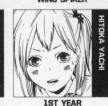

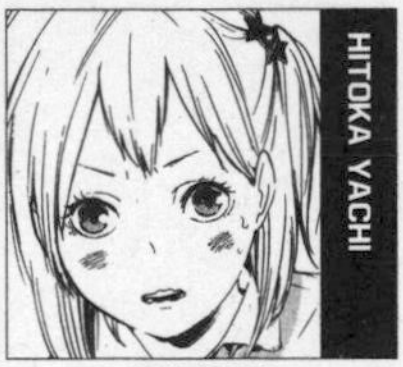
HITOKA YACHI

1ST YEAR
MANAGER

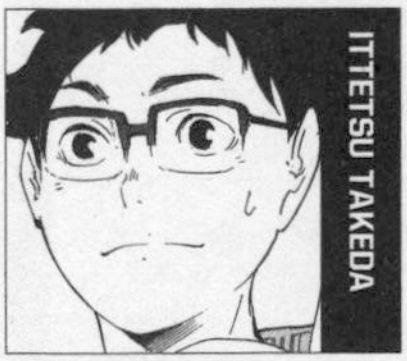
ITTETSU TAKEDA

ADVISER

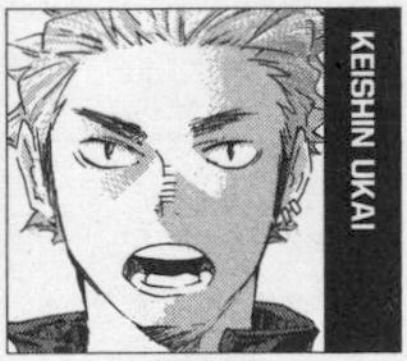
KEISHIN UKAI

COACH

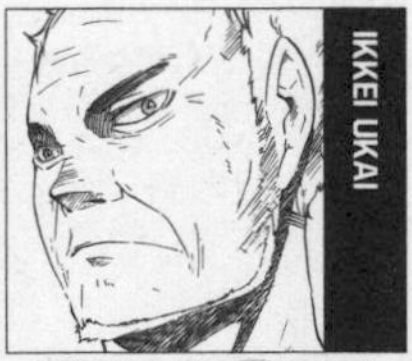
IKKEI UKAI

FORMER HEAD COACH

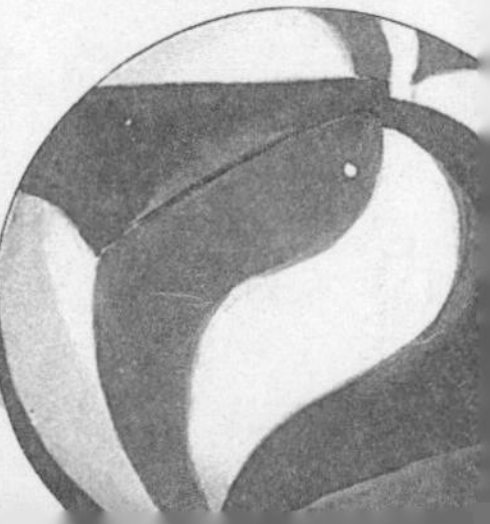

CHARACTERS

MIYAGI PREFECTURE SPRING TOURNAMENT QUALIFIER TOURNAMENT ARC

SHIRATORIZAWA

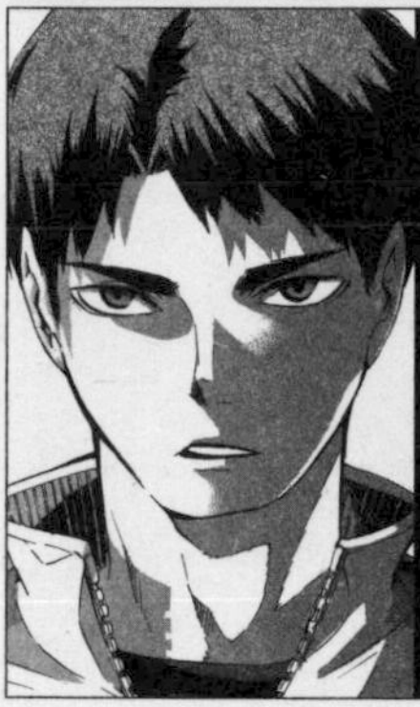

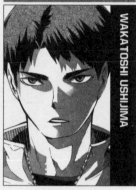

WAKATOSHI USHIJIMA

3RD YEAR
WING SPIKER

DATE TECH

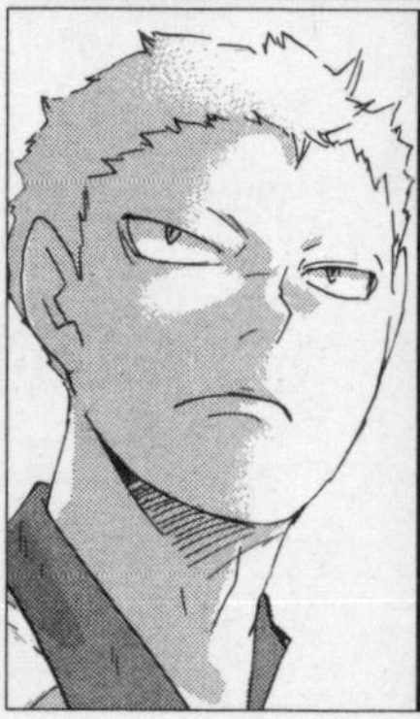

TAKANOBU AONE

2ND YEAR
MIDDLE BLOCKER

AOBA JOHSAI

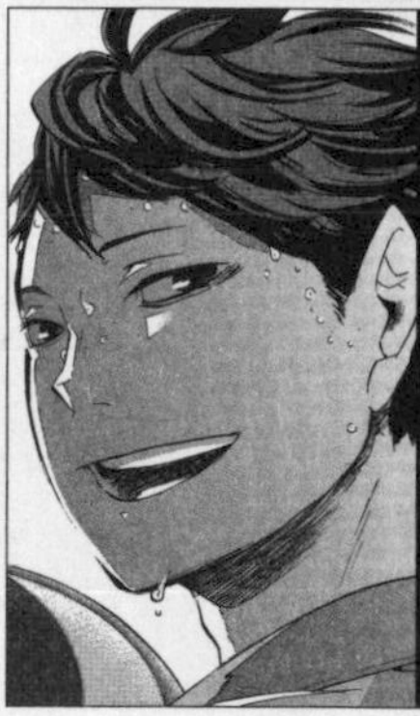

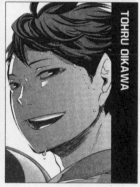

TOHRU OIKAWA

3RD YEAR
SETTER

KARASUNO'S MAJOR RIVALS

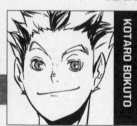

FUKURODANI (Tokyo)

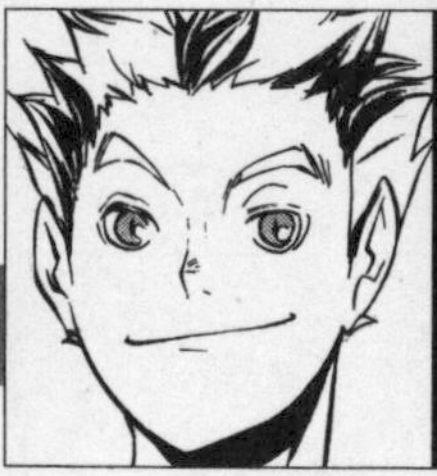

KOTARO BOKUTO

3RD YEAR
WING SPIKER

NEKOMA (Tokyo)

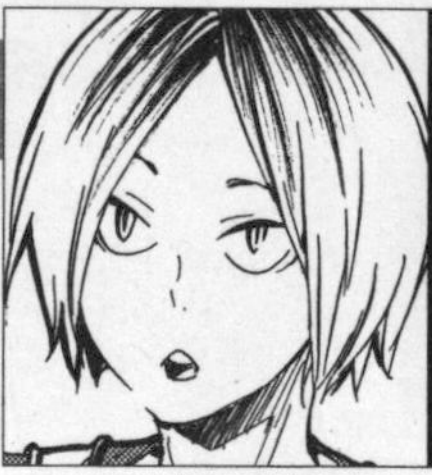

KENMA KOZUME

2ND YEAR
SETTER

Ever since he saw the legendary player known as "the Little Giant" compete at the national volleyball finals, Shoyo Hinata has been aiming to be the best volleyball player ever! He decides to join the volleyball club at his middle school and gets to play in an official tournament during his third year. His team is crushed by a team led by volleyball prodigy Tobio Kageyama, also known as "the King of the Court." Swearing revenge on Kageyama, Hinata graduates middle school and enters Karasuno High School, the school where the Little Giant played. However, upon joining the club, he finds out that Kageyama is there too! The two of them bicker constantly, but they bring out the best in each other's talents and become a powerful combo! Eliminated from the Inter-High Qualifiers, the Karasuno team sets their sights on the Spring Tournament. They travel to Tokyo for a weeklong training camp with Nekoma and a bunch of other Tokyo powerhouse teams. Armed with an arsenal of new weapons, Karasuno heads to the Spring Tournament preliminaries! They easily win their first game but struggle against Kakugawa Academy's 6'7" goliath, Hyakuzawa, in the second round! Karasuno is overwhelmed at first, but with the help of everything they've learned at the training camp, they come out victorious and earn a spot in the Qualifier Tournament! Which team will they go up against next...?

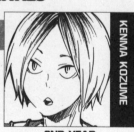

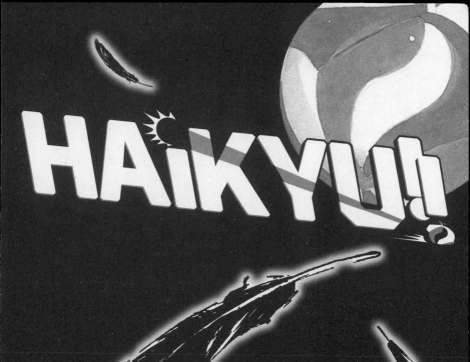

HAIKYU!!

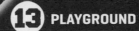

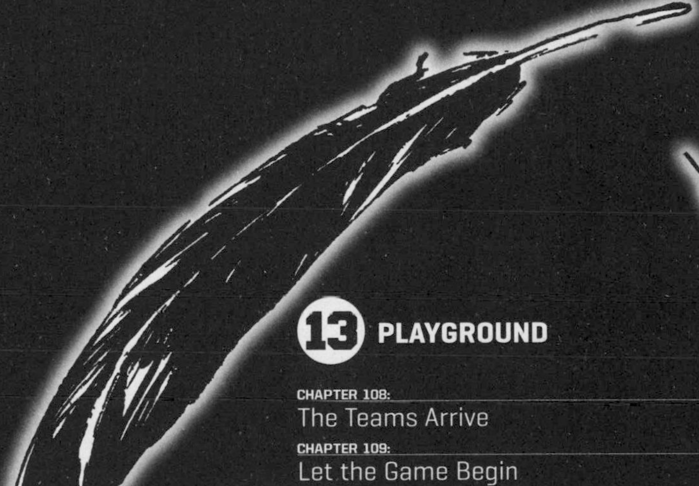

13 PLAYGROUND

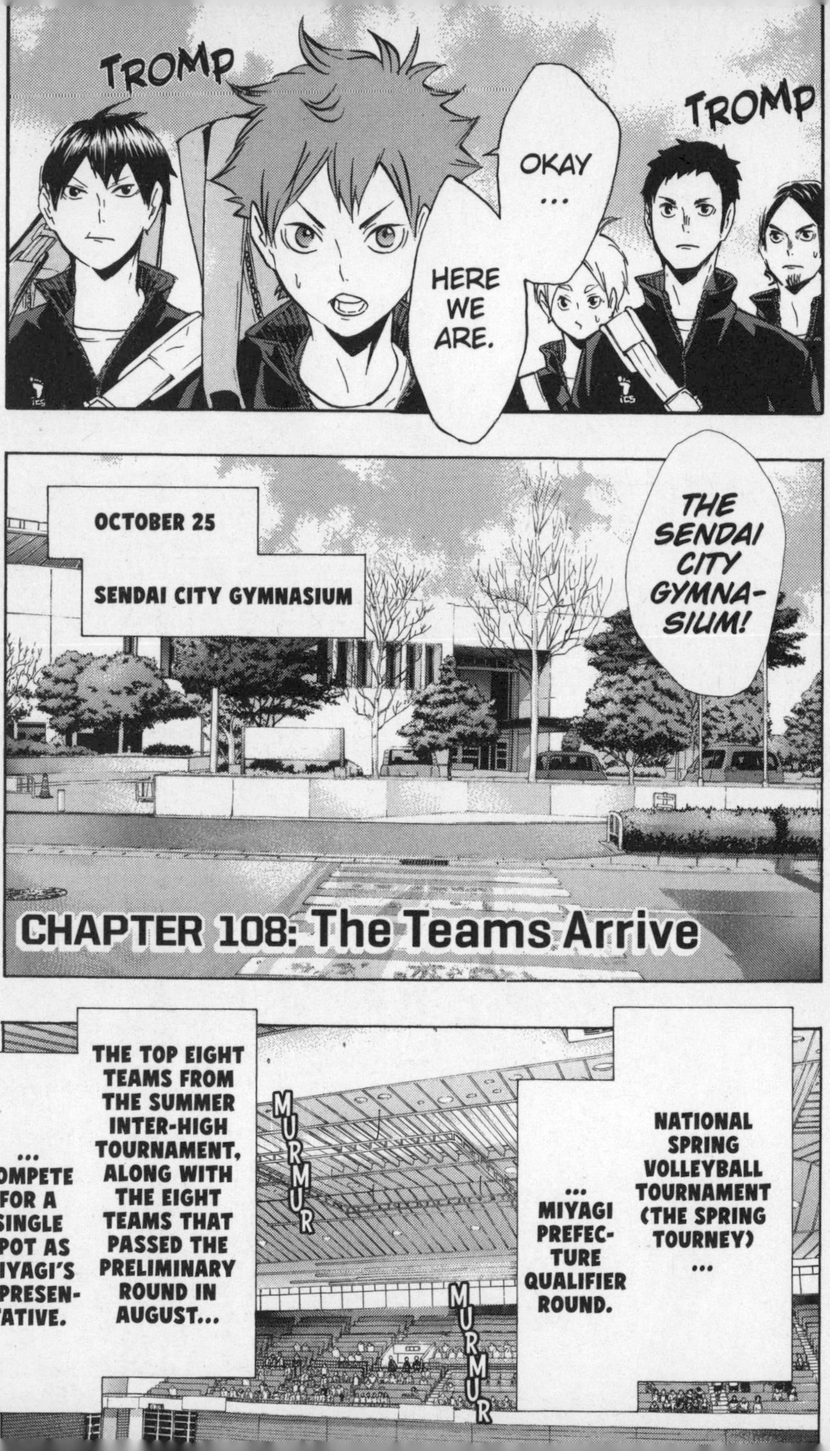
TROMP
OKAY ...
HERE WE ARE.
TROMP
THE SENDAI CITY GYMNA-SIUM!
OCTOBER 25
SENDAI CITY GYMNASIUM
CHAPTER 108: The Teams Arrive
NATIONAL SPRING VOLLEYBALL TOURNAMENT (THE SPRING TOURNEY) ...
... MIYAGI PREFEC-TURE QUALIFIER ROUND.
MURMUR
MURMUR
THE TOP EIGHT TEAMS FROM THE SUMMER INTER-HIGH TOURNAMENT, ALONG WITH THE EIGHT TEAMS THAT PASSED THE PRELIMINARY ROUND IN AUGUST...
... COMPETE FOR A SINGLE SPOT AS MIYAGI'S REPRESEN-TATIVE.

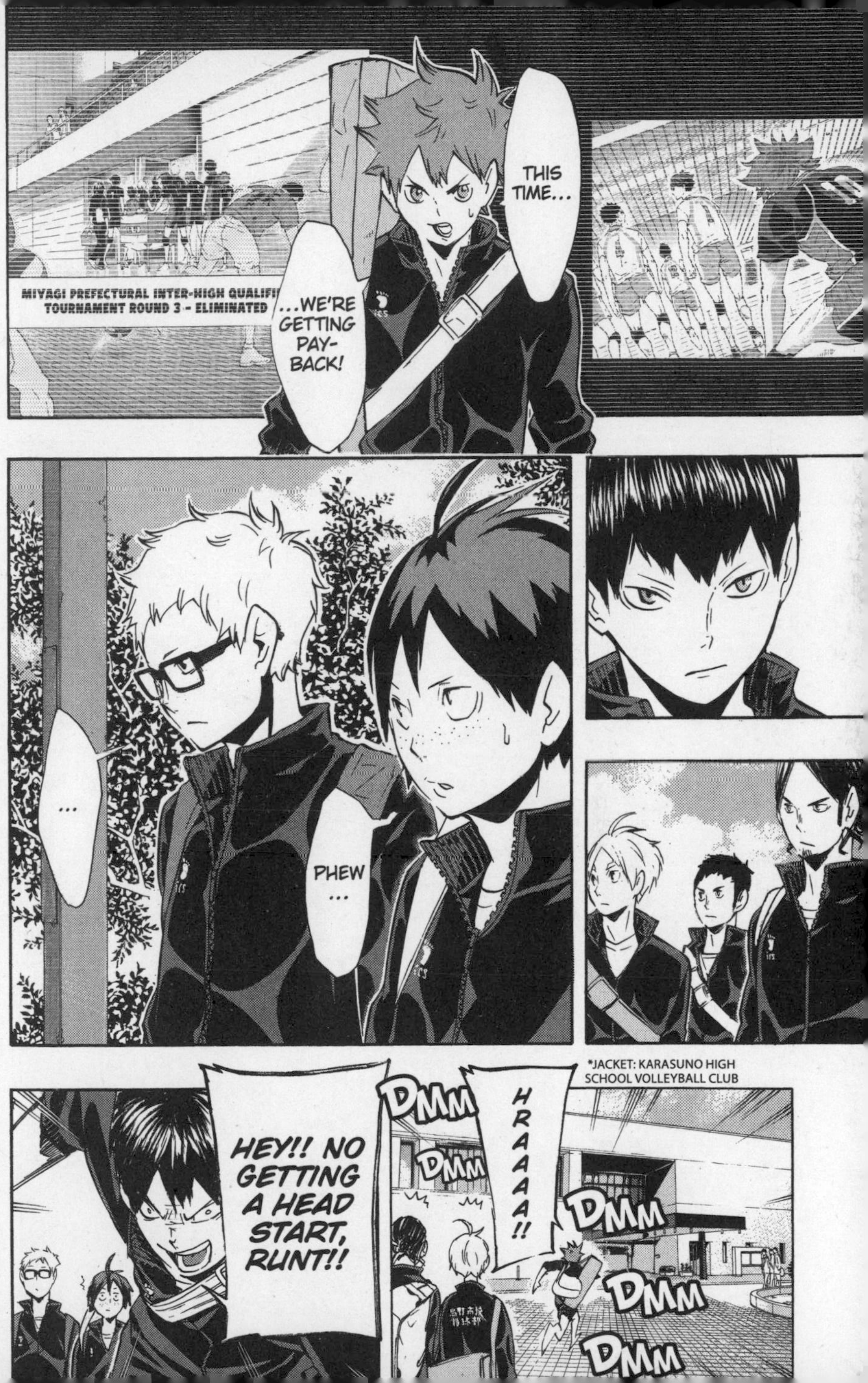
THIS TIME...
...WE'RE GETTING PAY-BACK!
MIYAGI PREFECTURAL INTER-HIGH QUALIFI
TOURNAMENT ROUND 3 – ELIMINATED
PHEW...
...
DMM
HRAAAAA!!
DMM
DMM
DMM
DMM
*JACKET: KARASUNO HIGH SCHOOL VOLLEYBALL CLUB
HEY!! NO GETTING A HEAD START, RUNT!!

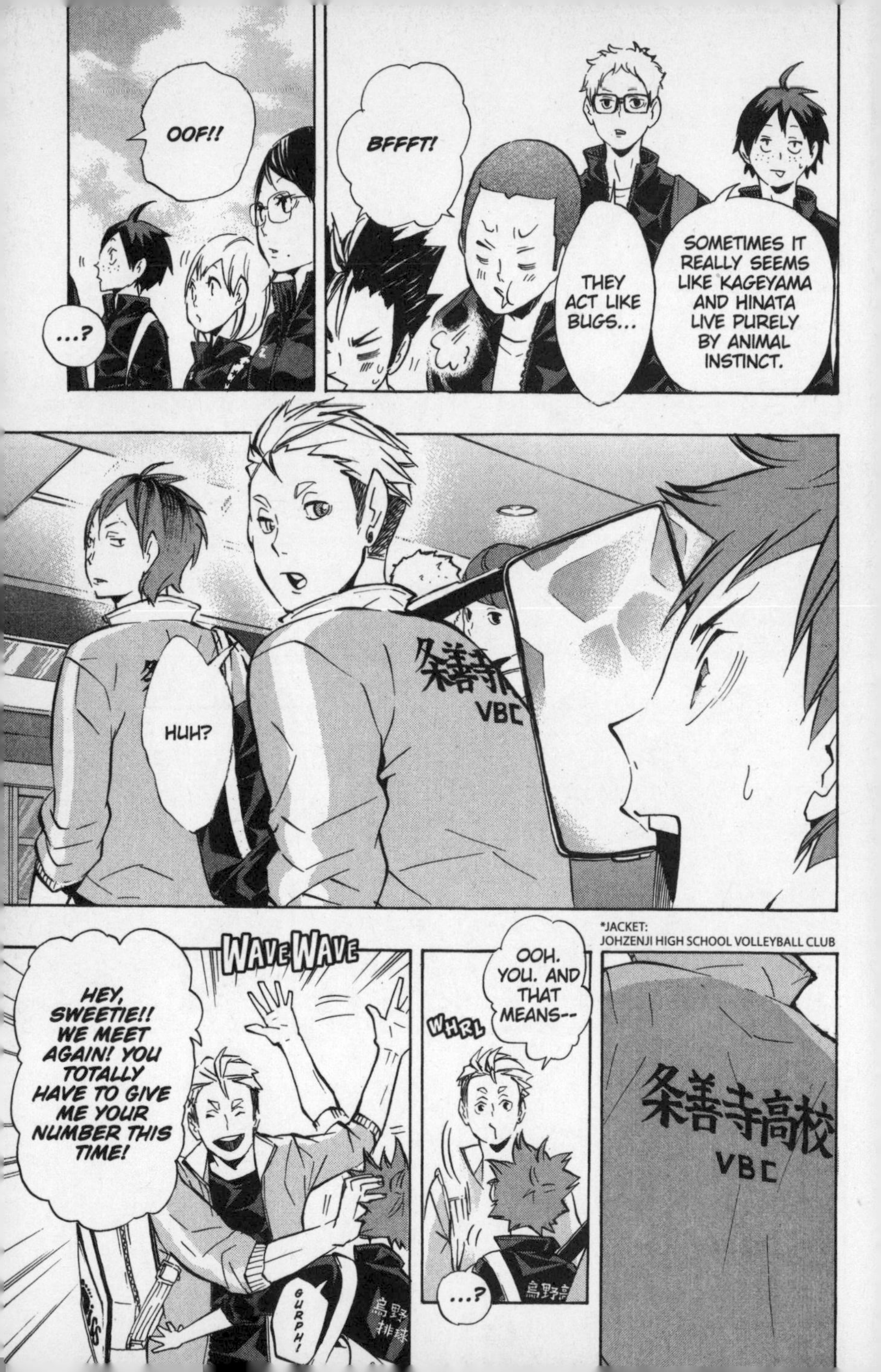
BFFFT!
SOMETIMES IT REALLY SEEMS LIKE KAGEYAMA AND HINATA LIVE PURELY BY ANIMAL INSTINCT.
THEY ACT LIKE BUGS...
OOF!!
...?
HUH?
条善寺
VBC
条善寺高校
VBC
OOH. YOU. AND THAT MEANS--
WHRL
...?
烏野高
WAVE WAVE
HEY, SWEETIE!! WE MEET AGAIN! YOU TOTALLY HAVE TO GIVE ME YOUR NUMBER THIS TIME!
GURPH!
烏野排球
*JACKET: JOHZENJI HIGH SCHOOL VOLLEYBALL CLUB

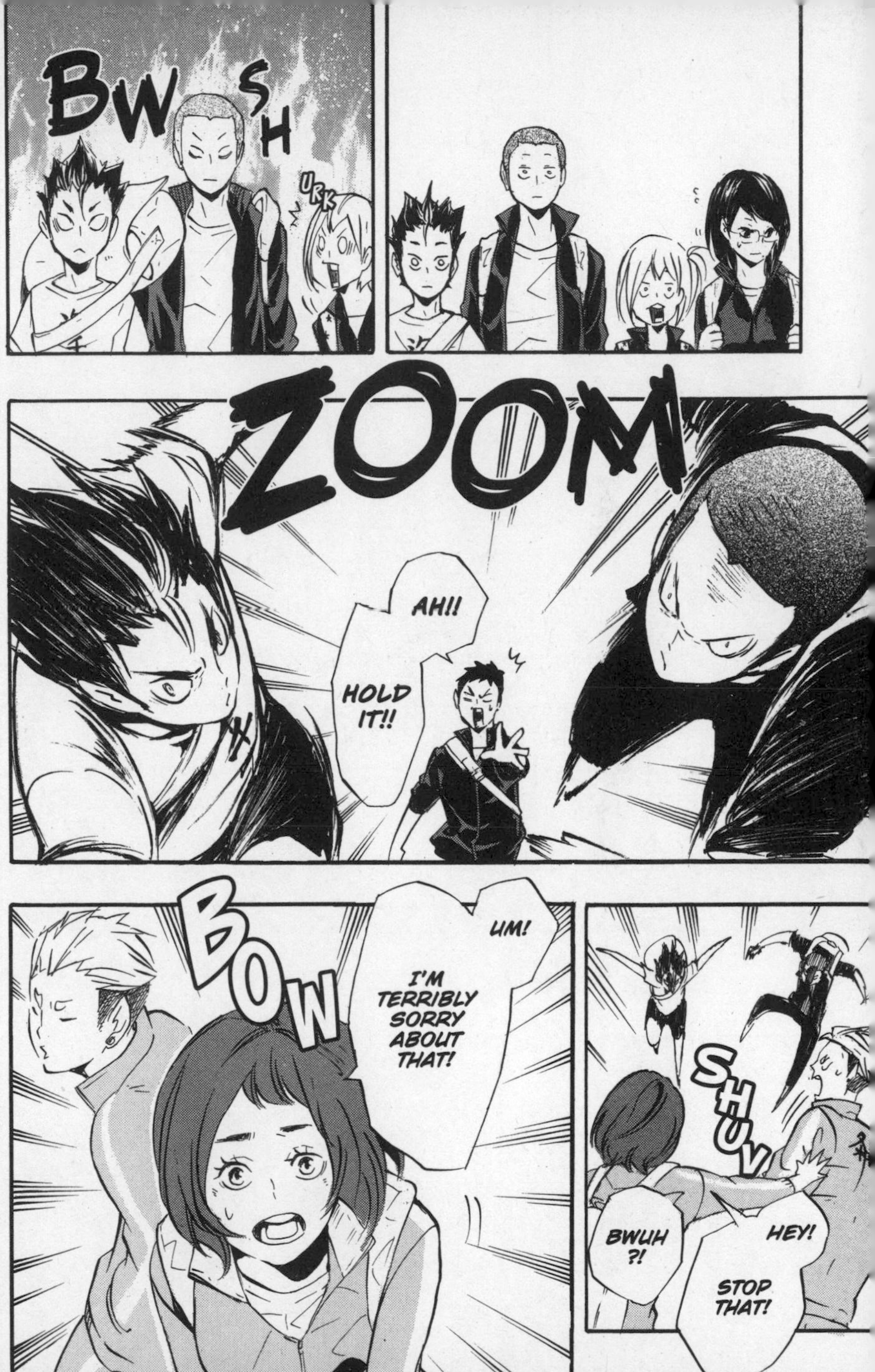
BWSH
URK
ZOOM
AH!!
HOLD IT!!
SHUV
HEY!
STOP THAT!
BWUH ?!
BOW
UM!
I'M TERRIBLY SORRY ABOUT THAT!

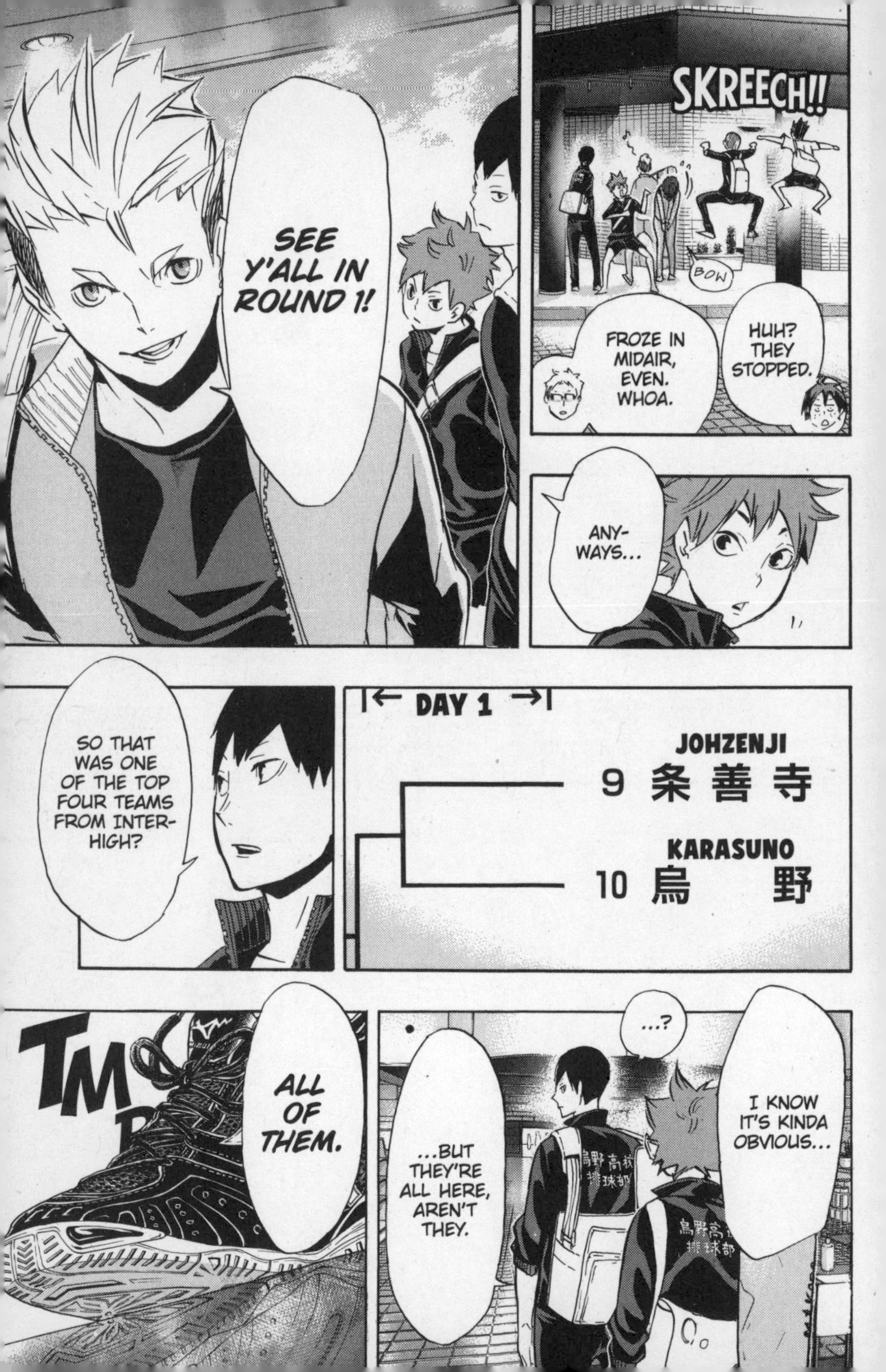
SKREECH!!
BOW
HUH? THEY STOPPED.
FROZE IN MIDAIR, EVEN. WHOA.
ANY-WAYS...
SEE Y'ALL IN ROUND 1!
DAY 1
JOHZENJI
9 条善寺
KARASUNO
10 烏 野
SO THAT WAS ONE OF THE TOP FOUR TEAMS FROM INTER-HIGH?
I KNOW IT'S KINDA OBVIOUS...
...?
...BUT THEY'RE ALL HERE, AREN'T THEY.
ALL OF THEM.
TMP

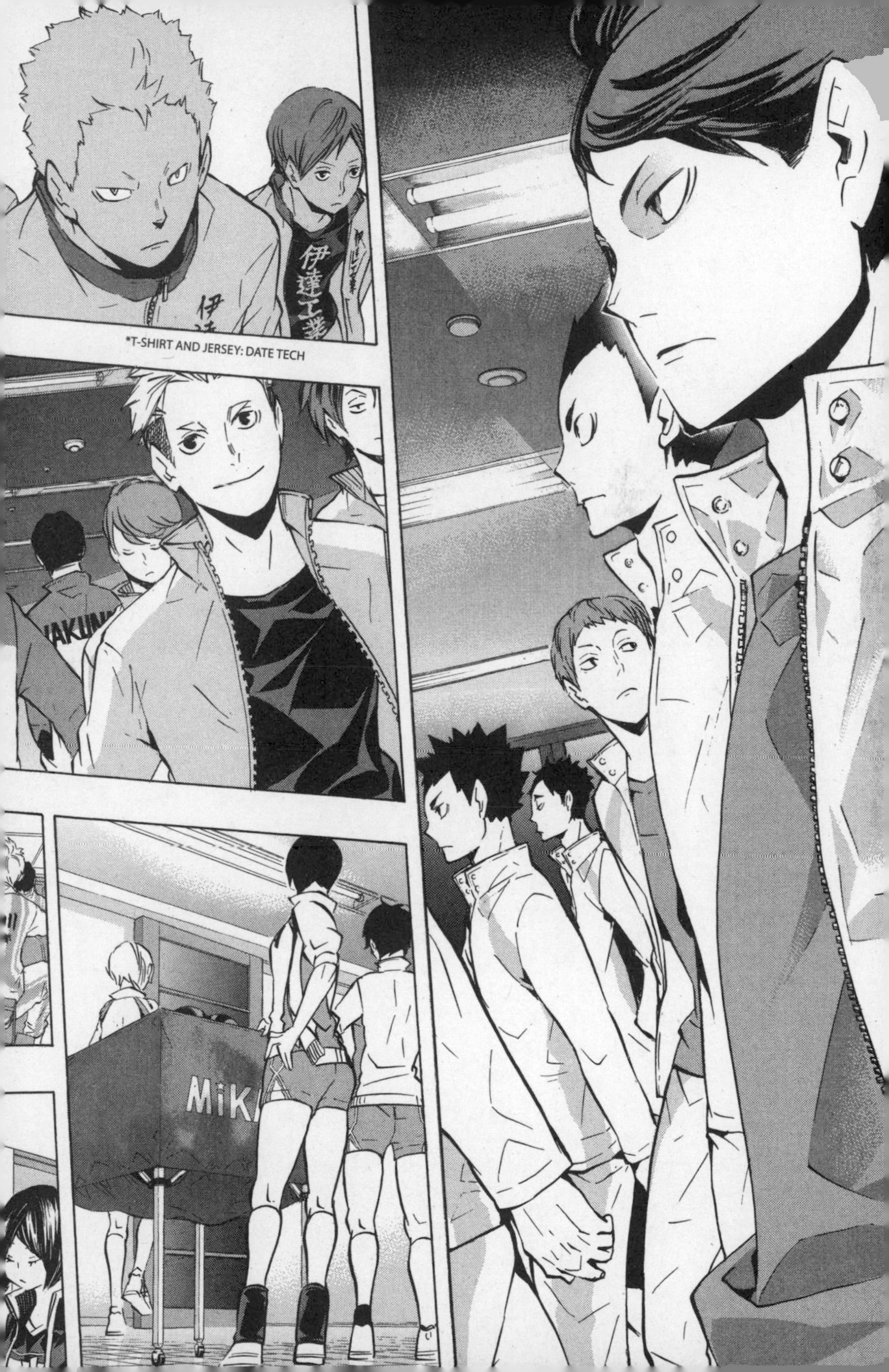
伊達工業
*T-SHIRT AND JERSEY: DATE TECH
MiKA

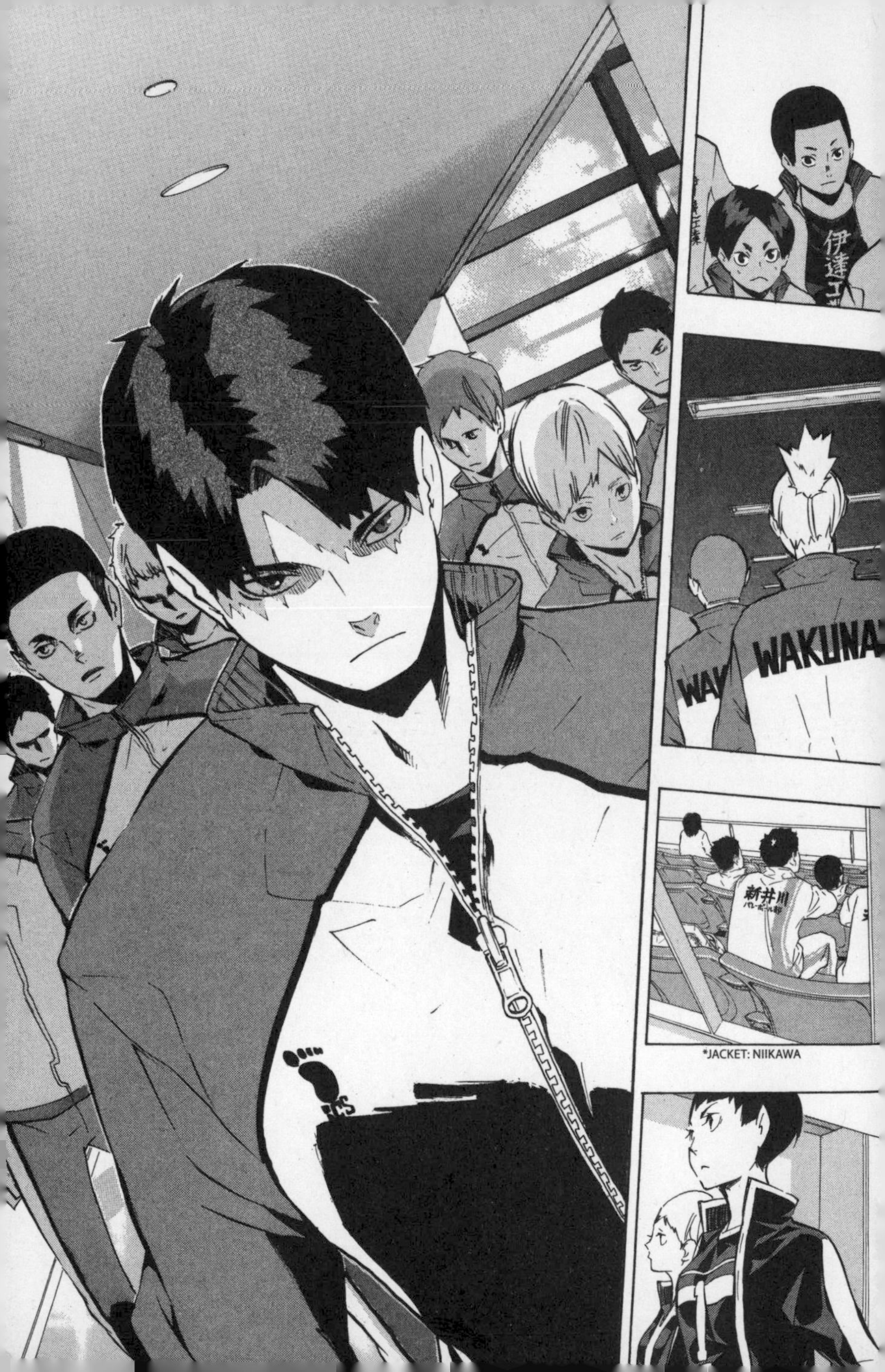
WAKUNA
WAK
新井川
*JACKET: NIIKAWA

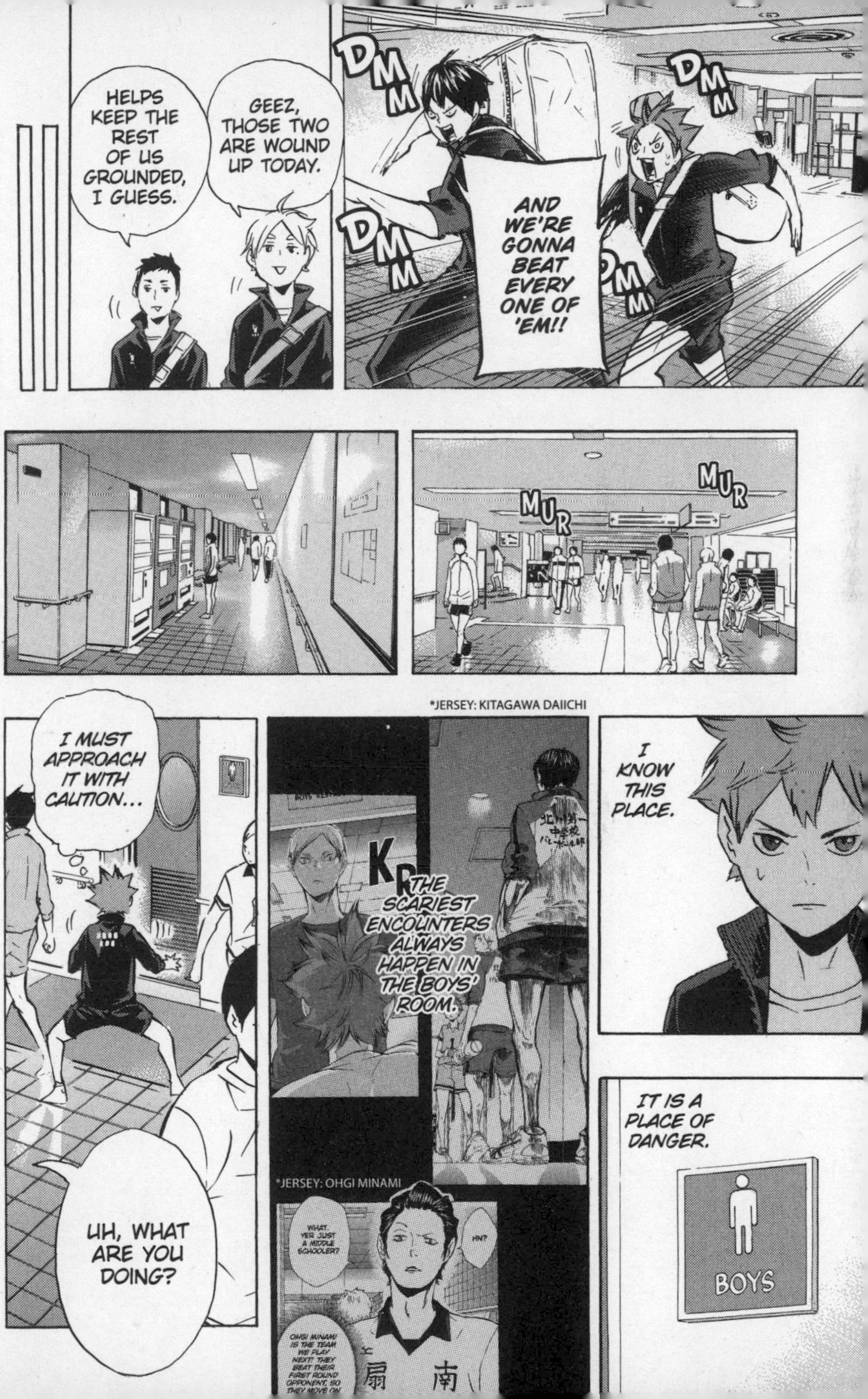
DMM
DMM
AND WE'RE GONNA BEAT EVERY ONE OF 'EM!!
DMM
DMM
GEEZ, THOSE TWO ARE WOUND UP TODAY.
HELPS KEEP THE REST OF US GROUNDED, I GUESS.
MUR
MUR
I KNOW THIS PLACE.
IT IS A PLACE OF DANGER.
BOYS
*JERSEY: KITAGAWA DAIICHI
KR
THE SCARIEST ENCOUNTERS ALWAYS HAPPEN IN THE BOYS' ROOM.
*JERSEY: OHGI MINAMI
HN?
WHAT. YER JUST A MIDDLE SCHOOLER?
OHGI MINAMI IS THE TEAM WE PLAY NEXT! THEY BEAT THEIR FIRST ROUND OPPONENT, SO THEY MOVE ON
I MUST APPROACH IT WITH CAUTION...
UH, WHAT ARE YOU DOING?

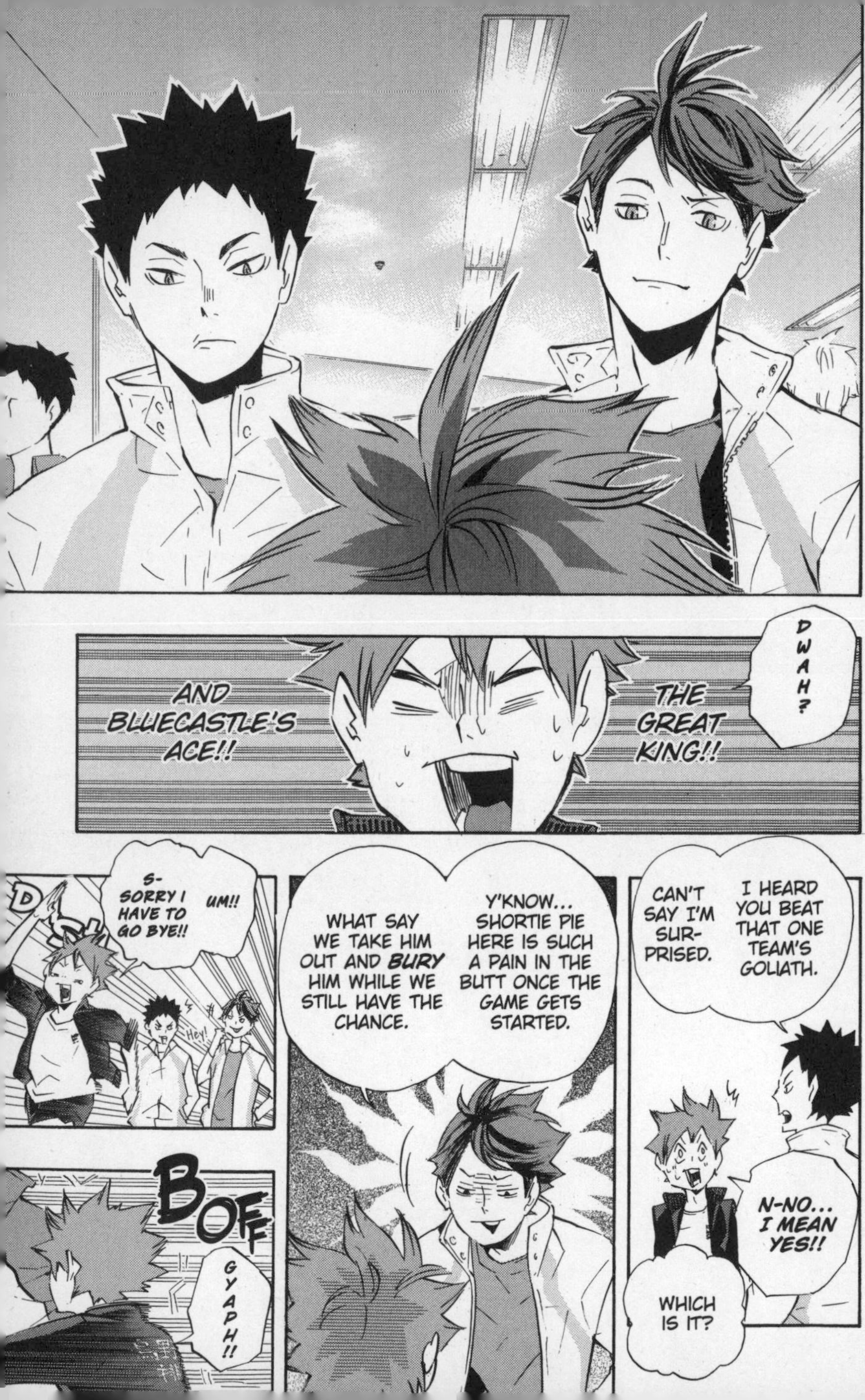
DWAH?
THE GREAT KING!!
AND BLUECASTLE'S ACE!!
I HEARD YOU BEAT THAT ONE TEAM'S GOLIATH.
CAN'T SAY I'M SURPRISED.
N-NO... I MEAN YES!!
WHICH IS IT?
Y'KNOW... SHORTIE PIE HERE IS SUCH A PAIN IN THE BUTT ONCE THE GAME GETS STARTED.
WHAT SAY WE TAKE HIM OUT AND BURY HIM WHILE WE STILL HAVE THE CHANCE.
UM!!
S-SORRY I HAVE TO GO BYE!!
Hey!
BOFF
GYAPH!!

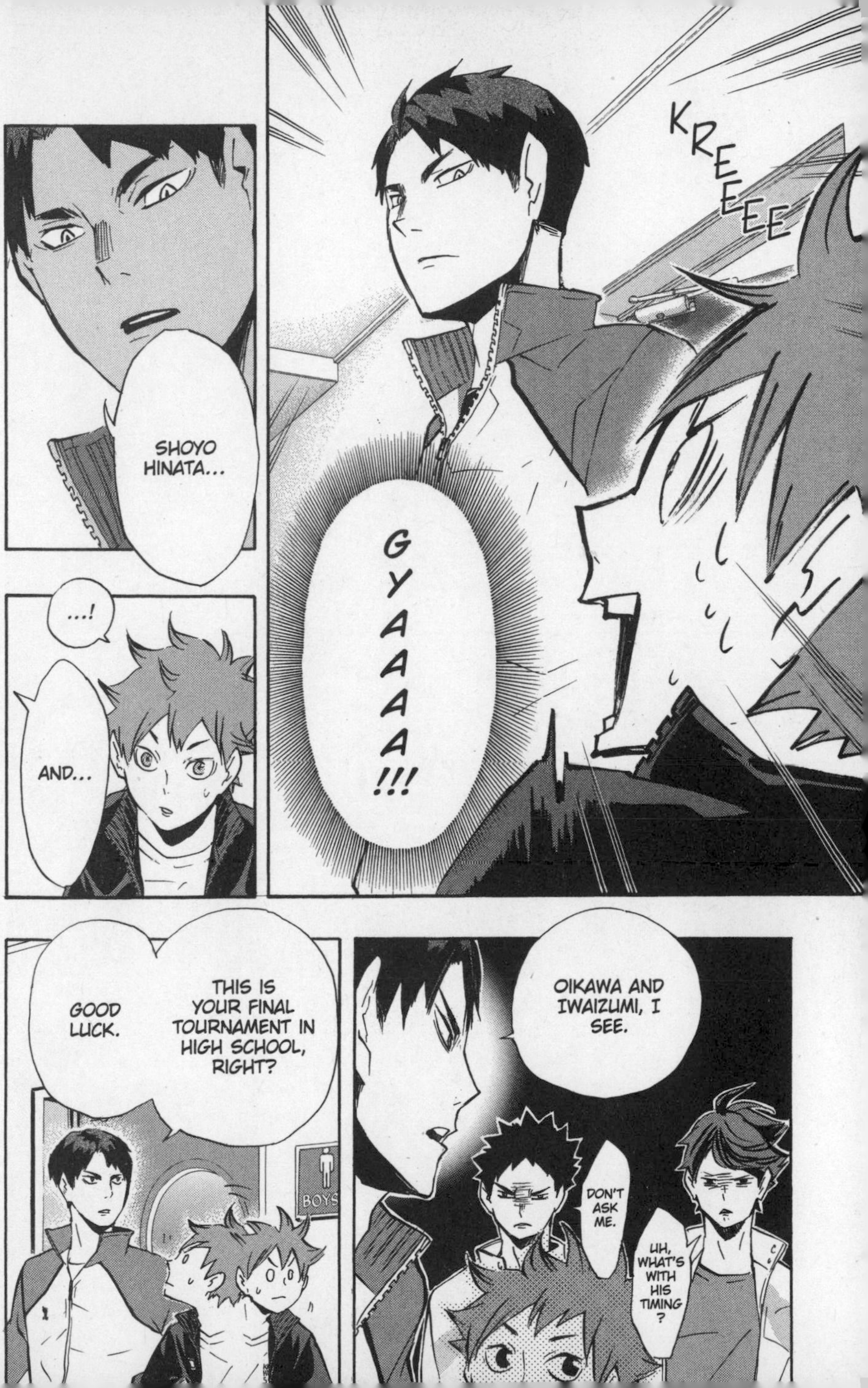
KREEEEE
GYAAAAA!!!
SHOYO HINATA...
...!
AND...
OIKAWA AND IWAIZUMI, I SEE.
UH, WHAT'S WITH HIS TIMING?
DON'T ASK ME.
THIS IS YOUR FINAL TOURNAMENT IN HIGH SCHOOL, RIGHT?
GOOD LUCK.
BOYS

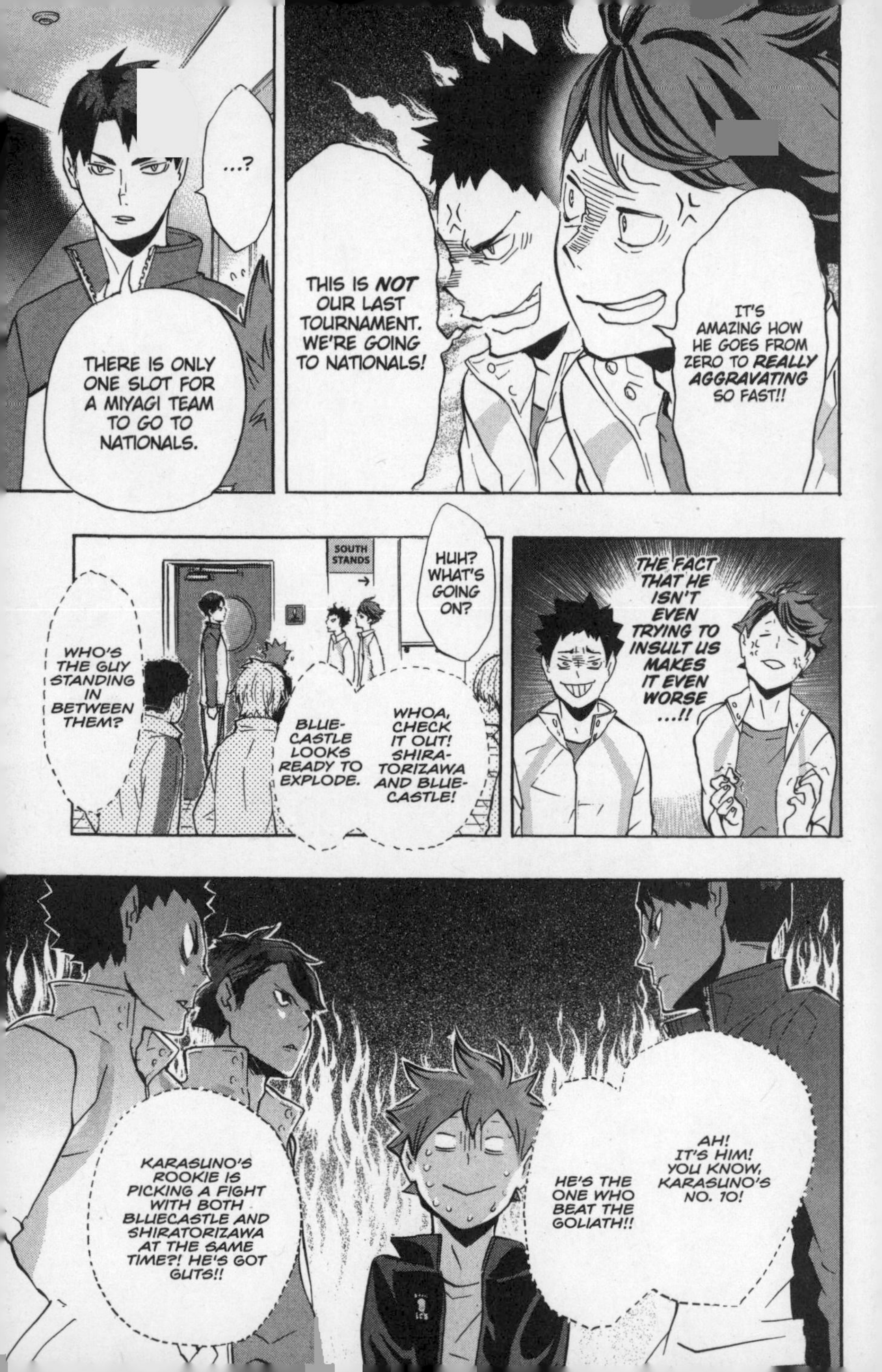
THIS IS NOT OUR LAST TOURNAMENT. WE'RE GOING TO NATIONALS!
IT'S AMAZING HOW HE GOES FROM ZERO TO REALLY AGGRAVATING SO FAST!!
...?
THERE IS ONLY ONE SLOT FOR A MIYAGI TEAM TO GO TO NATIONALS.
THE FACT THAT HE ISN'T EVEN TRYING TO INSULT US MAKES IT EVEN WORSE...!!
SOUTH STANDS
HUH? WHAT'S GOING ON?
WHOA, CHECK IT OUT! SHIRATORIZAWA AND BLUE-CASTLE!
BLUE-CASTLE LOOKS READY TO EXPLODE.
WHO'S THE GUY STANDING IN BETWEEN THEM?
AH! IT'S HIM! YOU KNOW, KARASUNO'S NO. 10!
HE'S THE ONE WHO BEAT THE GOLIATH!!
KARASUNO'S ROOKIE IS PICKING A FIGHT WITH BOTH BLUECASTLE AND SHIRATORIZAWA AT THE SAME TIME?! HE'S GOT GUTS!!

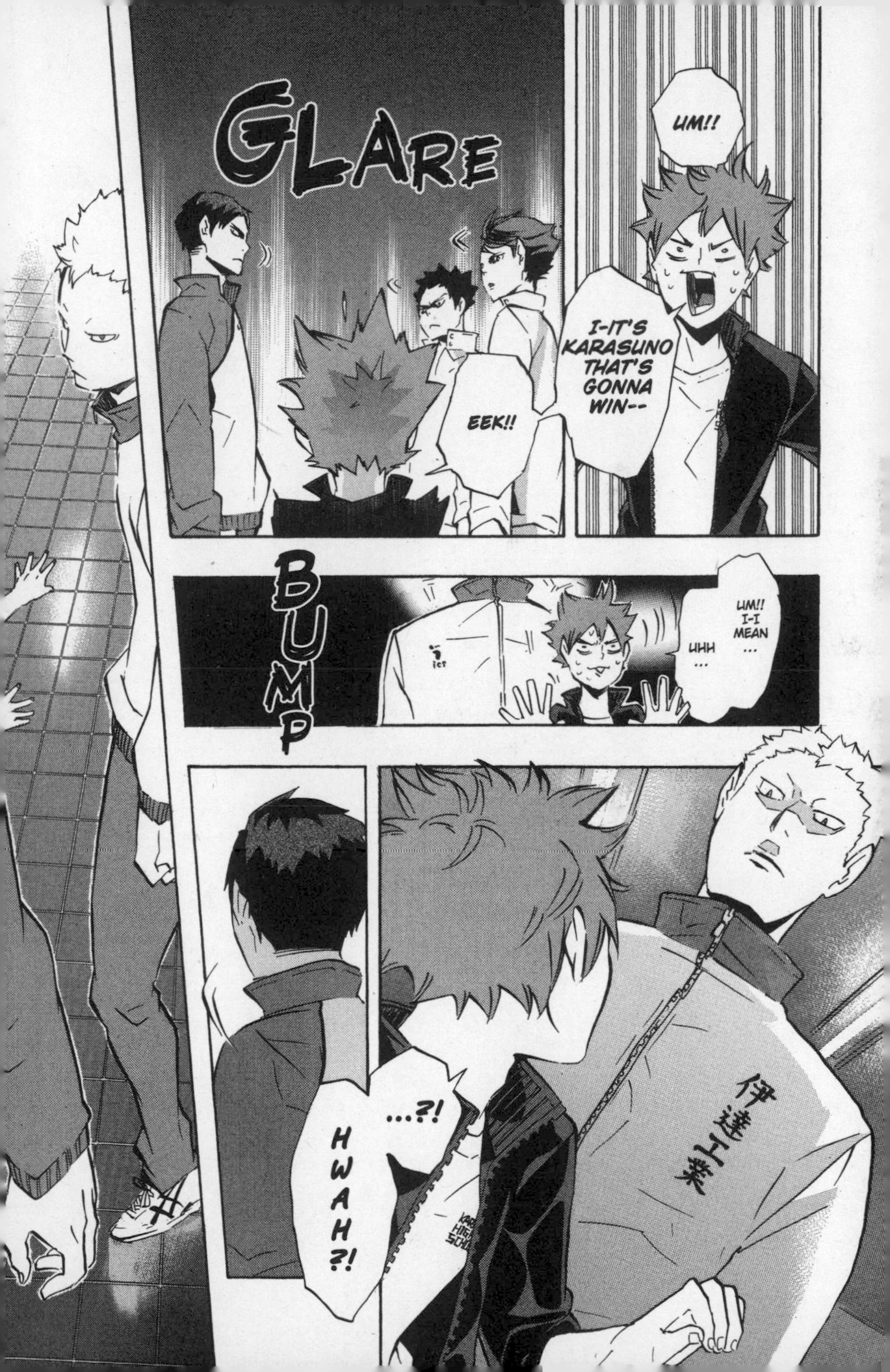
UM!!
I-IT'S KARASUNO THAT'S GONNA WIN--
GLARE
EEK!!
UM!! I-I MEAN ...
UHH ...
BUMP
...?!
HWAH?!
伊達工業

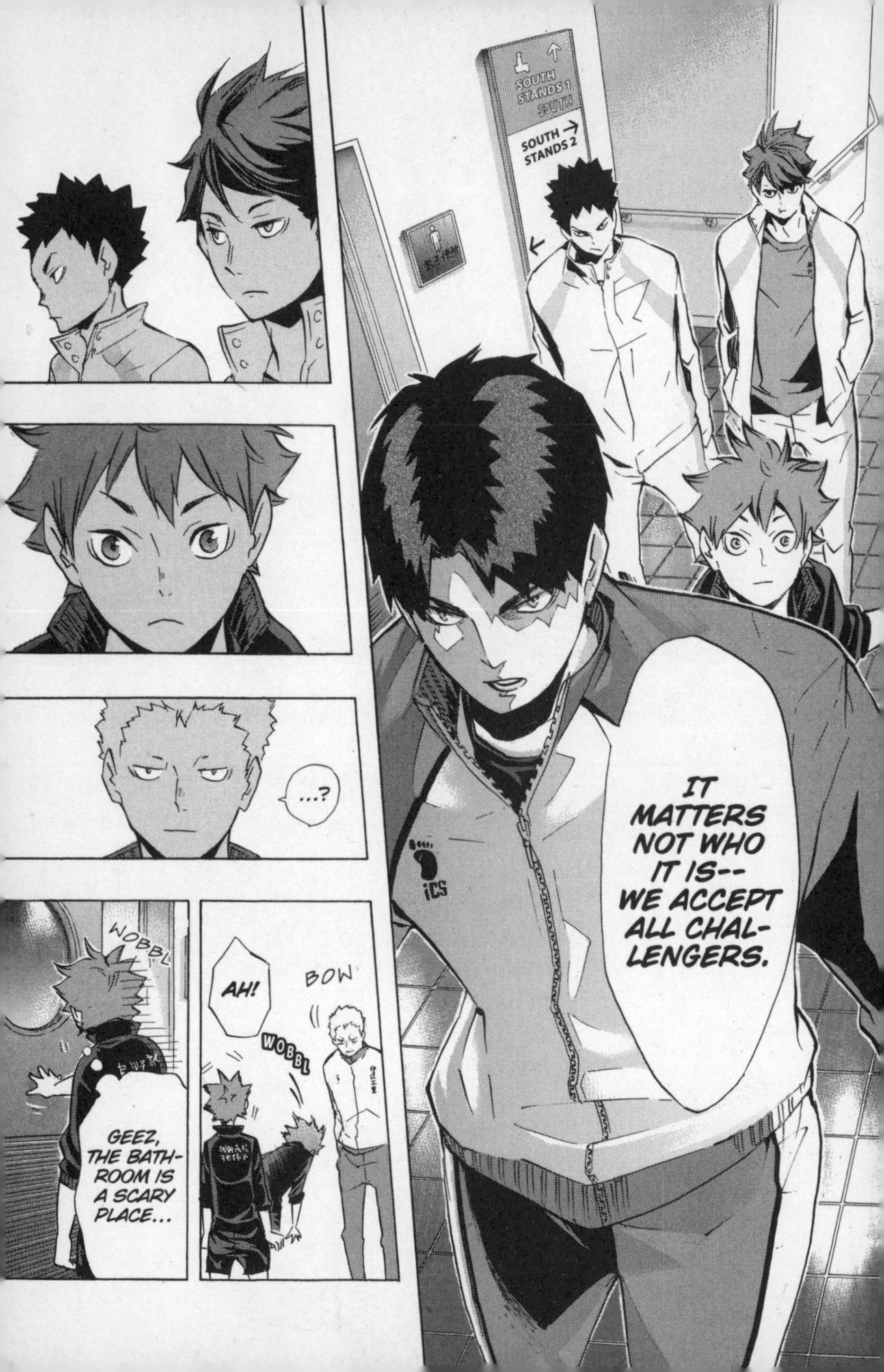
SOUTH STANDS 1
SOUTH
SOUTH STANDS 2
IT MATTERS NOT WHO IT IS-- WE ACCEPT ALL CHAL-LENGERS.
...?
AH!
BOW
WOBBL
WOBBL
GEEZ, THE BATH-ROOM IS A SCARY PLACE...

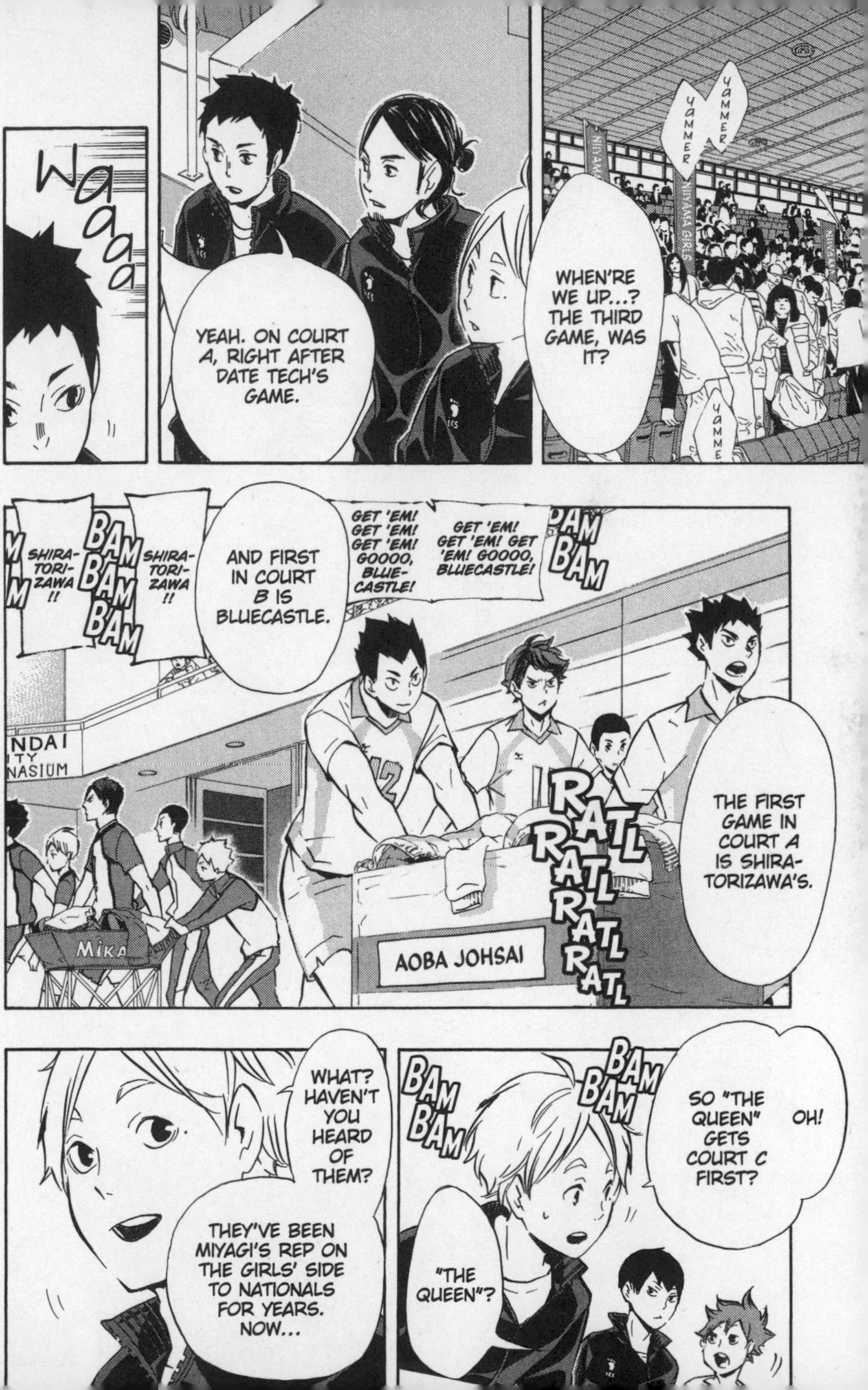
YAMMER
YAMMER
WHEN'RE WE UP...? THE THIRD GAME, WAS IT?
YAMME
YEAH. ON COURT A, RIGHT AFTER DATE TECH'S GAME.
Waaaa
BAM BAM
THE FIRST GAME IN COURT A IS SHIRA-TORIZAWA'S.
RATL RATL RATL RATL RATL
AOBA JOHSAI
GET 'EM! GET 'EM! GET 'EM! GOOOO, BLUECASTLE!
GET 'EM! GET 'EM! GET 'EM! GOOOO, BLUE-CASTLE!
AND FIRST IN COURT B IS BLUECASTLE.
SHIRA-TORI-ZAWA !!
BAM BAM BAM
SHIRA-TORI-ZAWA !!
MIKA
OH!
SO "THE QUEEN" GETS COURT C FIRST?
BAM BAM
BAM BAM
"THE QUEEN"?
WHAT? HAVEN'T YOU HEARD OF THEM?
THEY'VE BEEN MIYAGI'S REP ON THE GIRLS' SIDE TO NATIONALS FOR YEARS. NOW...

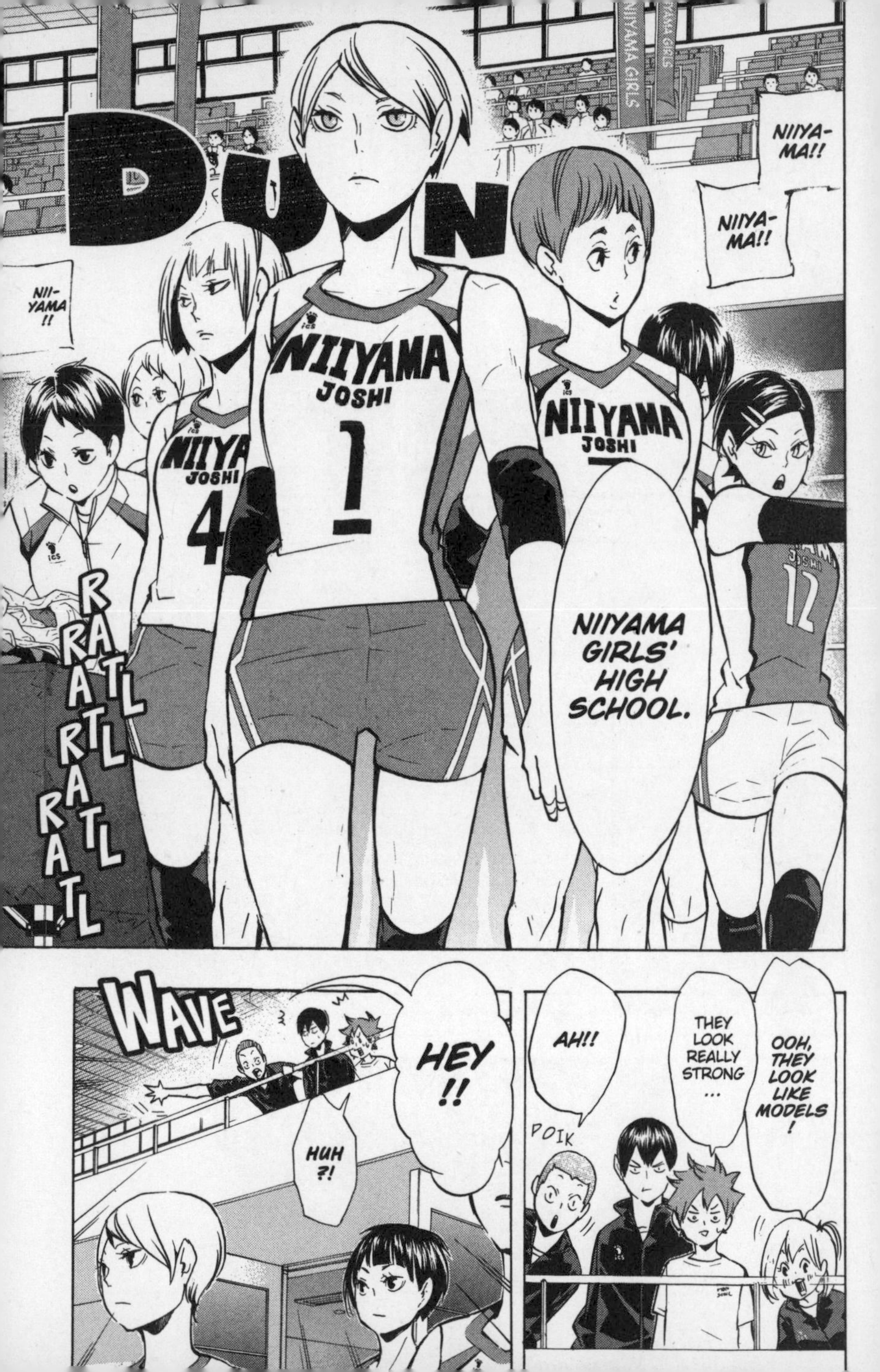
NIIYAMA GIRLS
NIIYA-MA!!
NIIYA-MA!!
DUN
NII-YAMA !!
NIIYAMA GIRLS' HIGH SCHOOL.
RATTL RATTL RATTL RATTL
OOH, THEY LOOK LIKE MODELS!
THEY LOOK REALLY STRONG...
AH!!
POIK
HEY !!
WAVE
HUH ?!

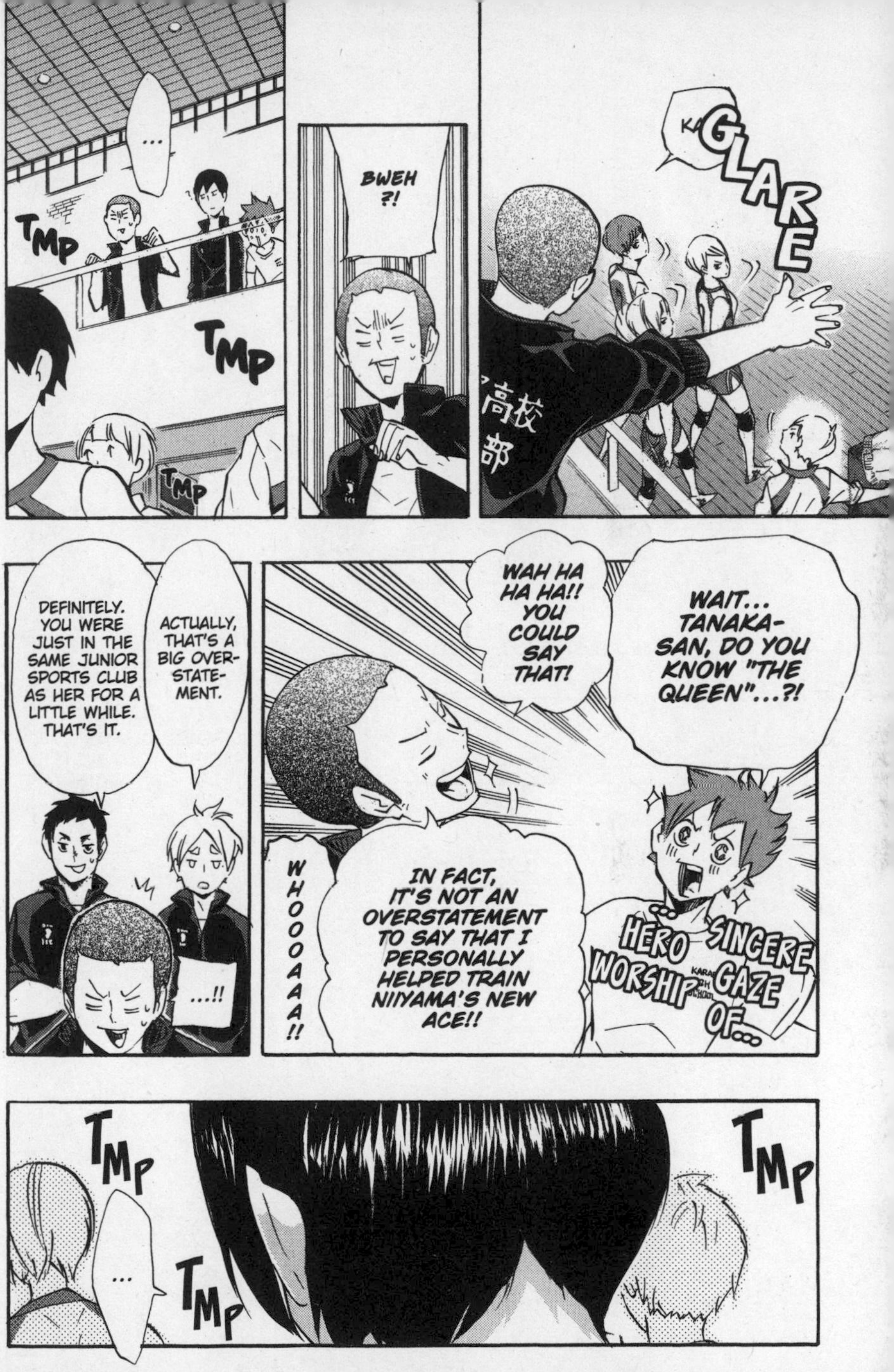
KA
GLARE
BWEH ?!
...
TMP
TMP
TMP
WAIT... TANAKA-SAN, DO YOU KNOW "THE QUEEN"...?!
SINCERE GAZE OF...
HERO WORSHIP
WAH HA HA HA!! YOU COULD SAY THAT!
IN FACT, IT'S NOT AN OVERSTATEMENT TO SAY THAT I PERSONALLY HELPED TRAIN NIIYAMA'S NEW ACE!!
WHOOOOAAA!!
ACTUALLY, THAT'S A BIG OVER-STATE-MENT.
DEFINITELY. YOU WERE JUST IN THE SAME JUNIOR SPORTS CLUB AS HER FOR A LITTLE WHILE. THAT'S IT.
...!!
TMP
TMP
...
TMP

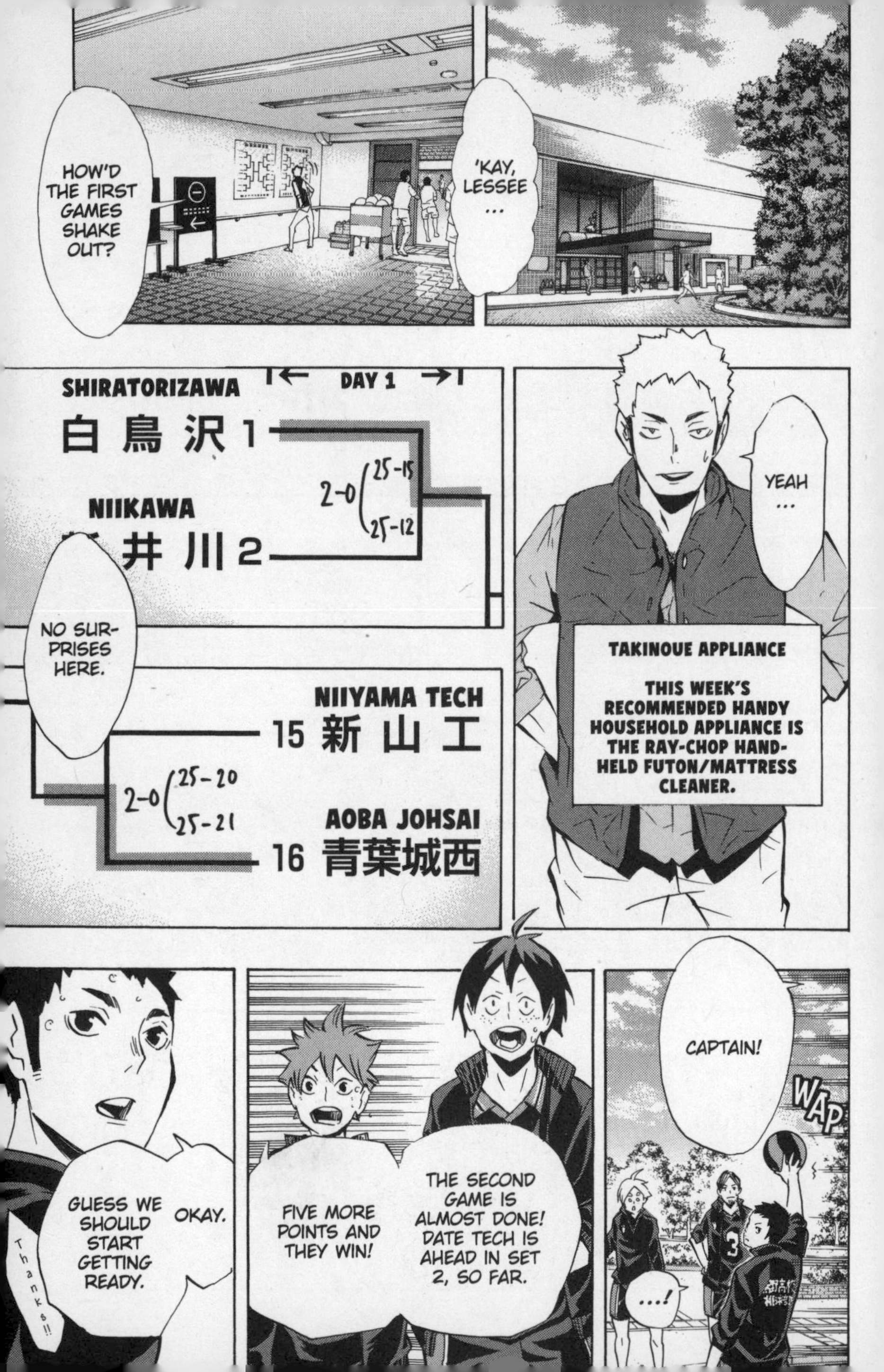
'KAY, LESSEE ...
HOW'D THE FIRST GAMES SHAKE OUT?
YEAH ...
TAKINOUE APPLIANCE
THIS WEEK'S RECOMMENDED HANDY HOUSEHOLD APPLIANCE IS THE RAY-CHOP HAND-HELD FUTON/MATTRESS CLEANER.
DAY 1
SHIRATORIZAWA
白鳥沢 1
2-0 (25-15 25-12
NIIKAWA
井川 2
NO SUR-PRISES HERE.
NIIYAMA TECH
15 新山工
2-0 (25-20 25-21
AOBA JOHSAI
16 青葉城西
CAPTAIN!
WAP
...!
THE SECOND GAME IS ALMOST DONE! DATE TECH IS AHEAD IN SET 2, SO FAR.
FIVE MORE POINTS AND THEY WIN!
OKAY.
GUESS WE SHOULD START GETTING READY.
Thanks!!

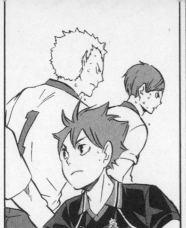

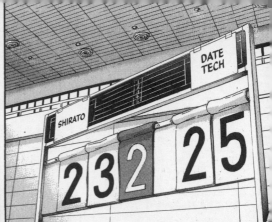

SHIRATO	DATE TECH
23 2	25

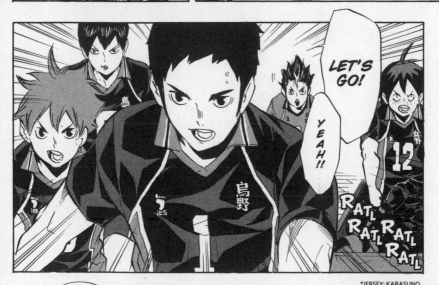

LET'S GO!

YEAH!!

RATL RATL RATL RATL RATL RATL

*JERSEY: KARASUNO

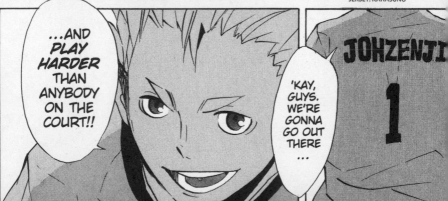

...AND *PLAY HARDER* THAN ANYBODY ON THE COURT!!

'KAY, GUYS. WE'RE GONNA GO OUT THERE...

JOHZENJI

1

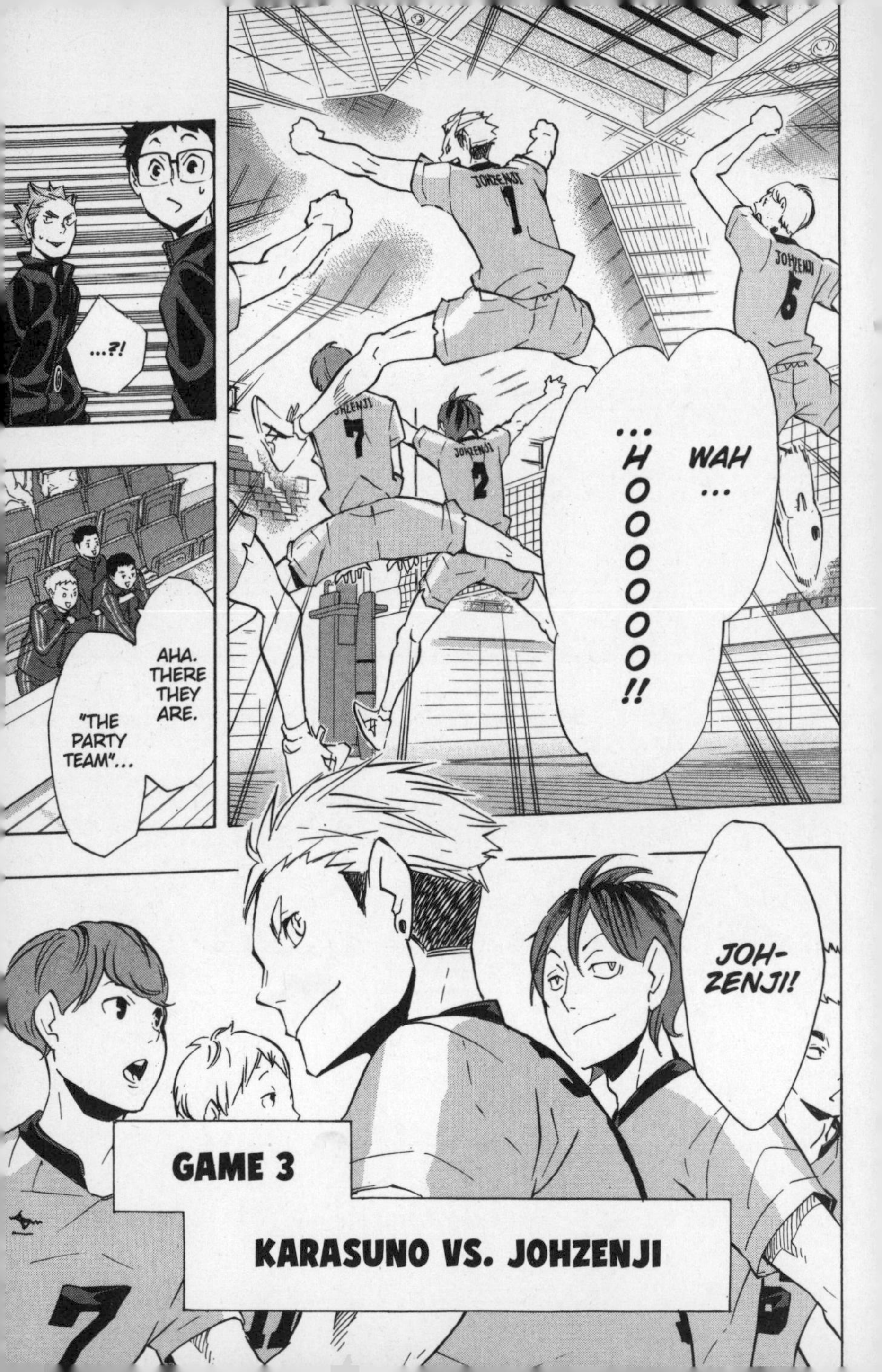
WAH...
...HOOOOOO!!
...?!
AHA. THERE THEY ARE.
"THE PARTY TEAM"...
JOH-ZENJI!
GAME 3
KARASUNO VS. JOHZENJI

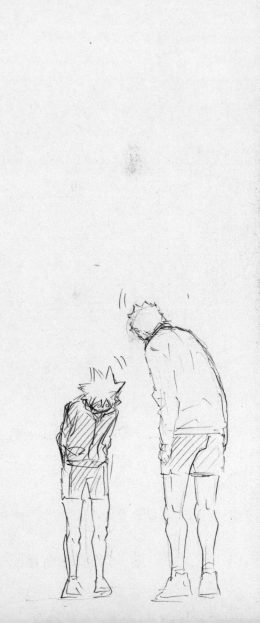

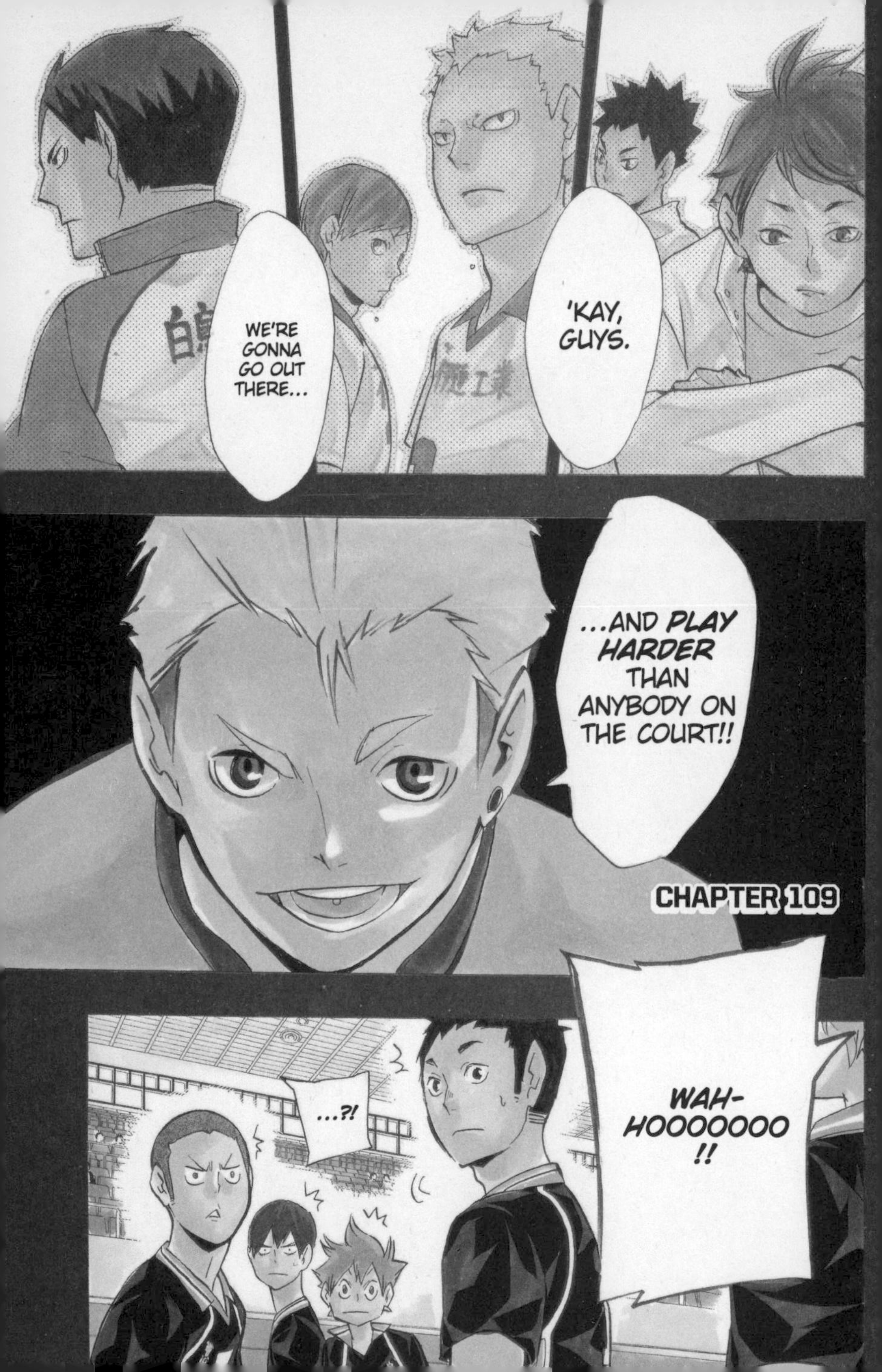
'KAY, GUYS.
WE'RE GONNA GO OUT THERE...
...AND PLAY HARDER THAN ANYBODY ON THE COURT!!
CHAPTER 109
WAH-HOOOOOOO!!
...?!

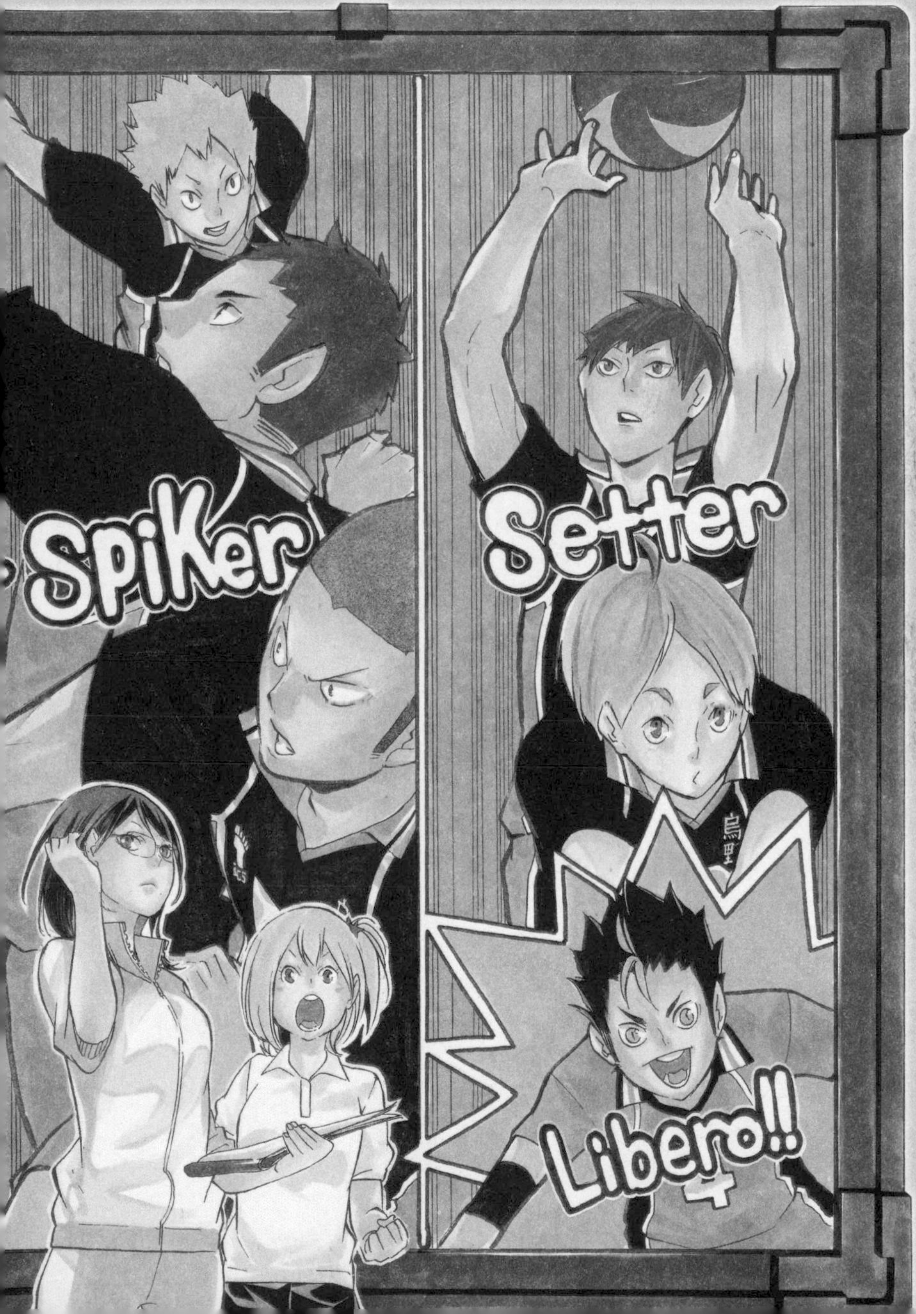
Setter
Libero!!
Spiker

CHAPTER 109: Let the Game Begin

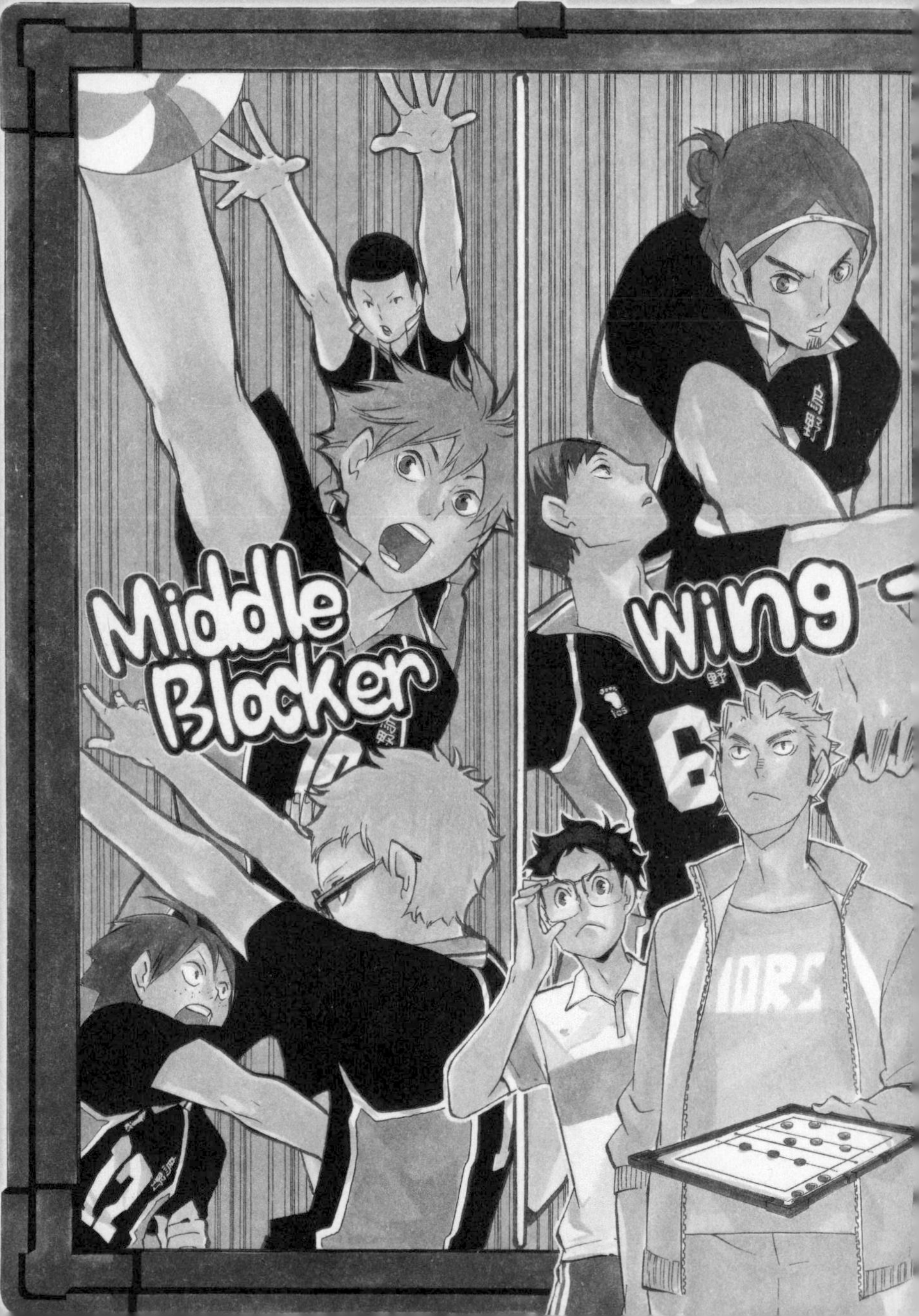
Middle Blocker
Wing

HAIKYU!!

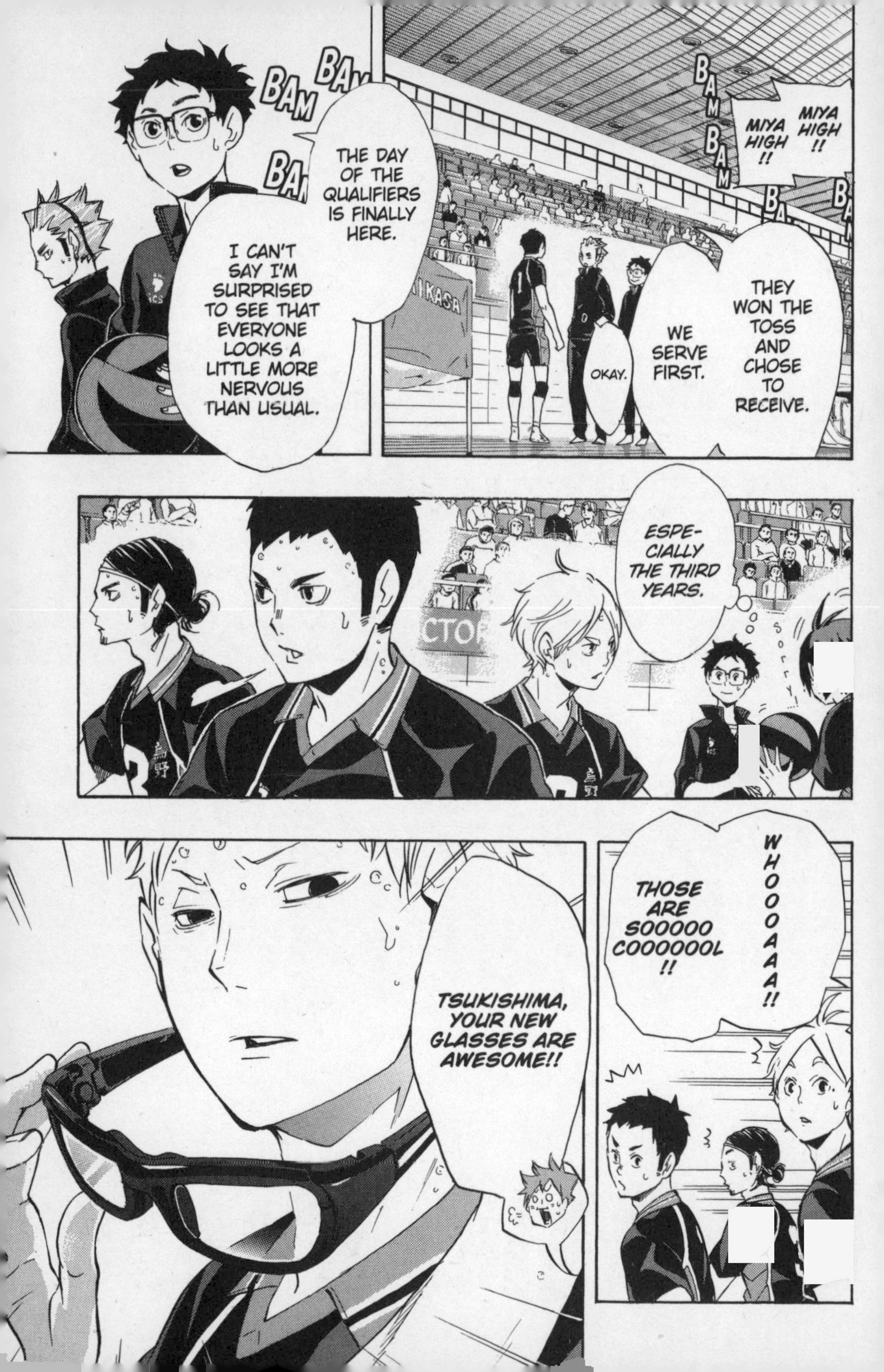
BAM
BAM
MIYA HIGH!!
MIYA HIGH!!
BAM
THEY WON THE TOSS AND CHOSE TO RECEIVE.
WE SERVE FIRST.
OKAY.
BAM
BAM
BAM
THE DAY OF THE QUALIFIERS IS FINALLY HERE.
I CAN'T SAY I'M SURPRISED TO SEE THAT EVERYONE LOOKS A LITTLE MORE NERVOUS THAN USUAL.
ESPECIALLY THE THIRD YEARS.
Sorry..!
WHOOOOAAAA!!
THOSE ARE SOOOOO COOOOOOL!!
TSUKISHIMA, YOUR NEW GLASSES ARE AWESOME!!

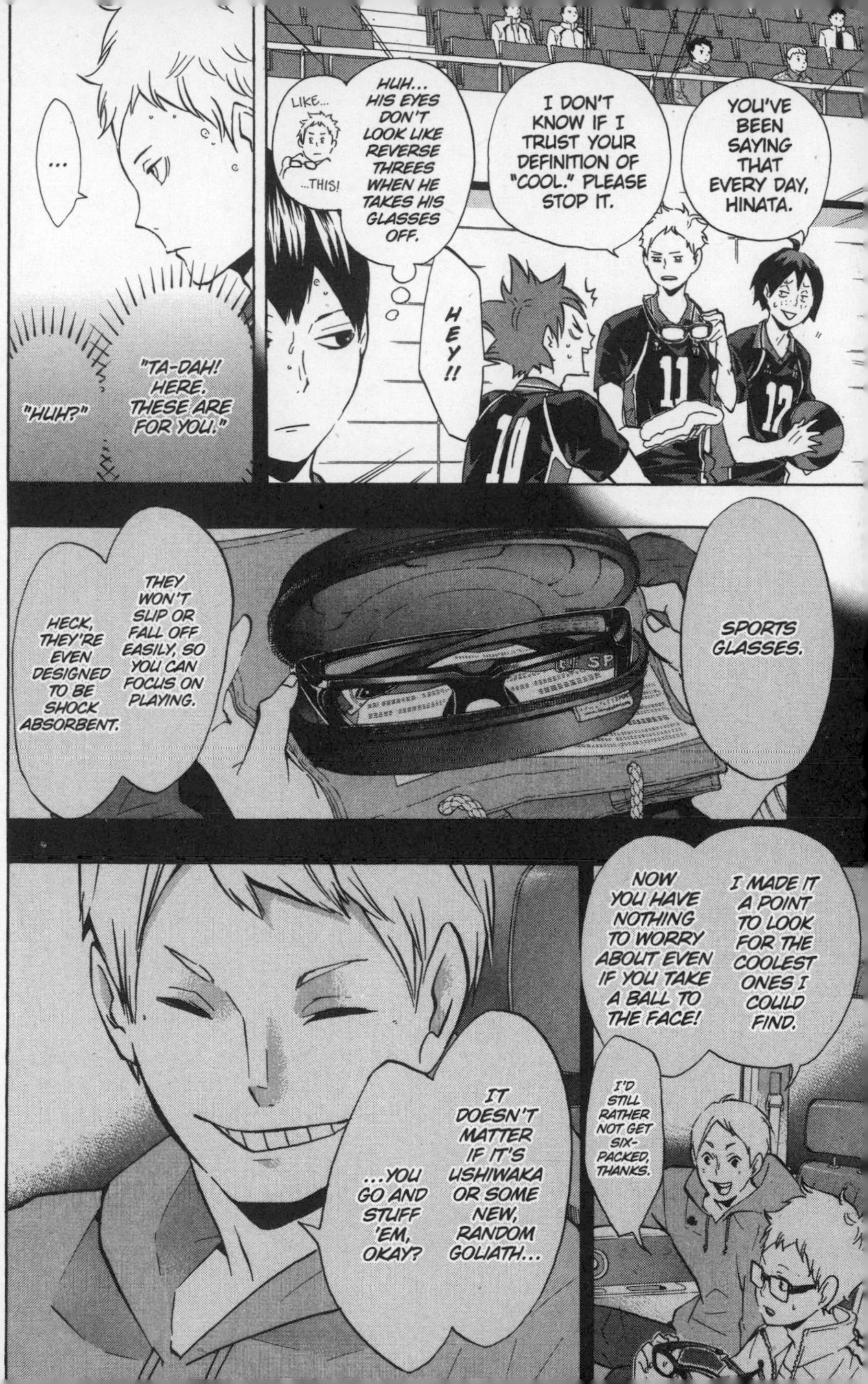
YOU'VE BEEN SAYING THAT EVERY DAY, HINATA.
I DON'T KNOW IF I TRUST YOUR DEFINITION OF "COOL." PLEASE STOP IT.
HUH... HIS EYES DON'T LOOK LIKE REVERSE THREES WHEN HE TAKES HIS GLASSES OFF.
LIKE...
...THIS!
HEY!!
...
"TA-DAH! HERE. THESE ARE FOR YOU."
"HUH?"
SPORTS GLASSES.
THEY WON'T SLIP OR FALL OFF EASILY, SO YOU CAN FOCUS ON PLAYING.
HECK, THEY'RE EVEN DESIGNED TO BE SHOCK ABSORBENT.
I MADE IT A POINT TO LOOK FOR THE COOLEST ONES I COULD FIND.
NOW YOU HAVE NOTHING TO WORRY ABOUT EVEN IF YOU TAKE A BALL TO THE FACE!
I'D STILL RATHER NOT GET SIX-PACKED, THANKS.
IT DOESN'T MATTER IF IT'S USHIWAKA OR SOME NEW, RANDOM GOLIATH...
...YOU GO AND STUFF 'EM, OKAY?

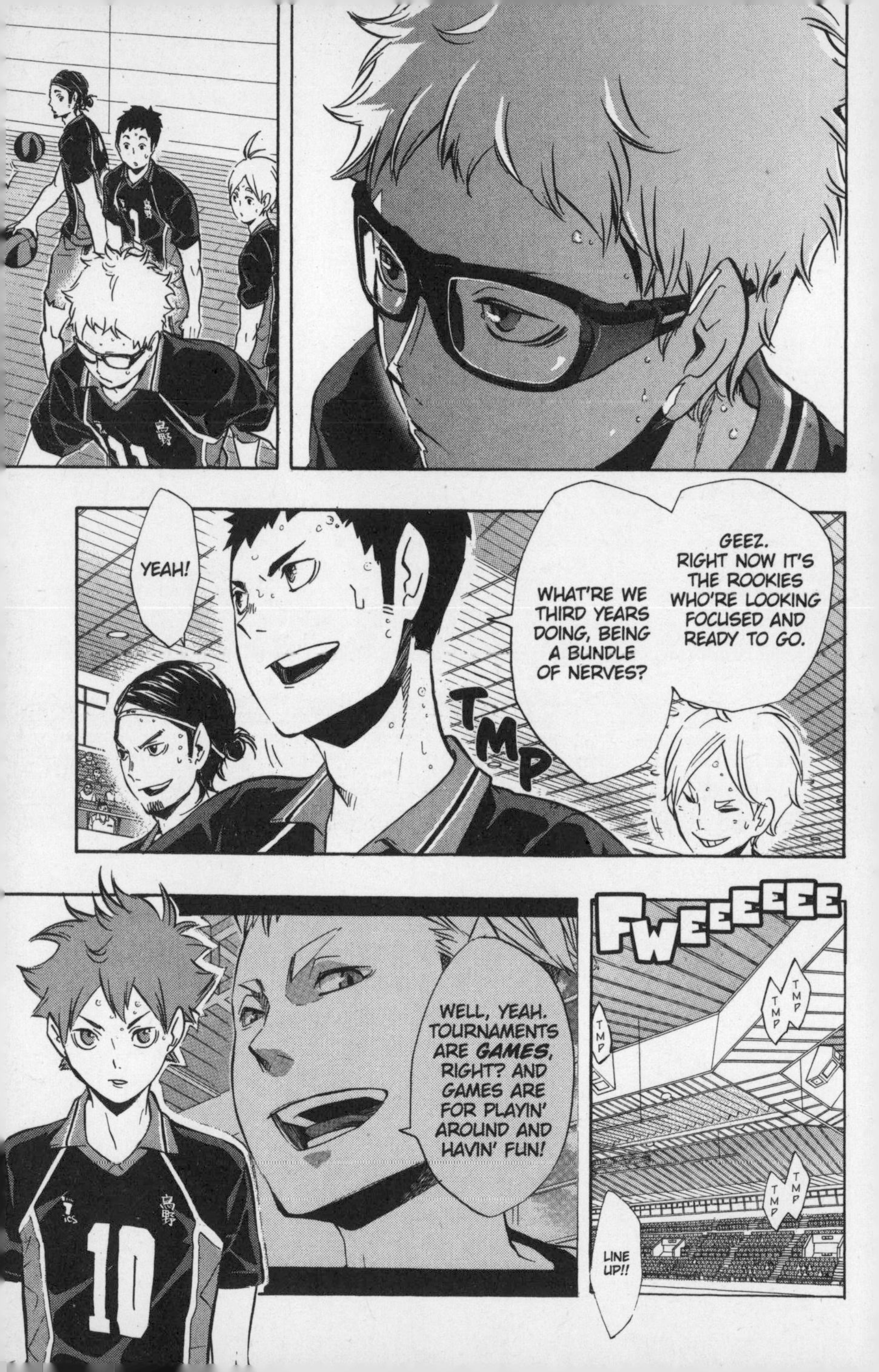
GEEZ. RIGHT NOW IT'S THE ROOKIES WHO'RE LOOKING FOCUSED AND READY TO GO.
WHAT'RE WE THIRD YEARS DOING, BEING A BUNDLE OF NERVES?
TMP
YEAH!
FWEEEEEE
TMP
TMP
TMP
TMP
TMP
LINE UP!!
WELL, YEAH. TOURNAMENTS ARE *GAMES*, RIGHT? AND GAMES ARE FOR PLAYIN' AROUND AND HAVIN' FUN!

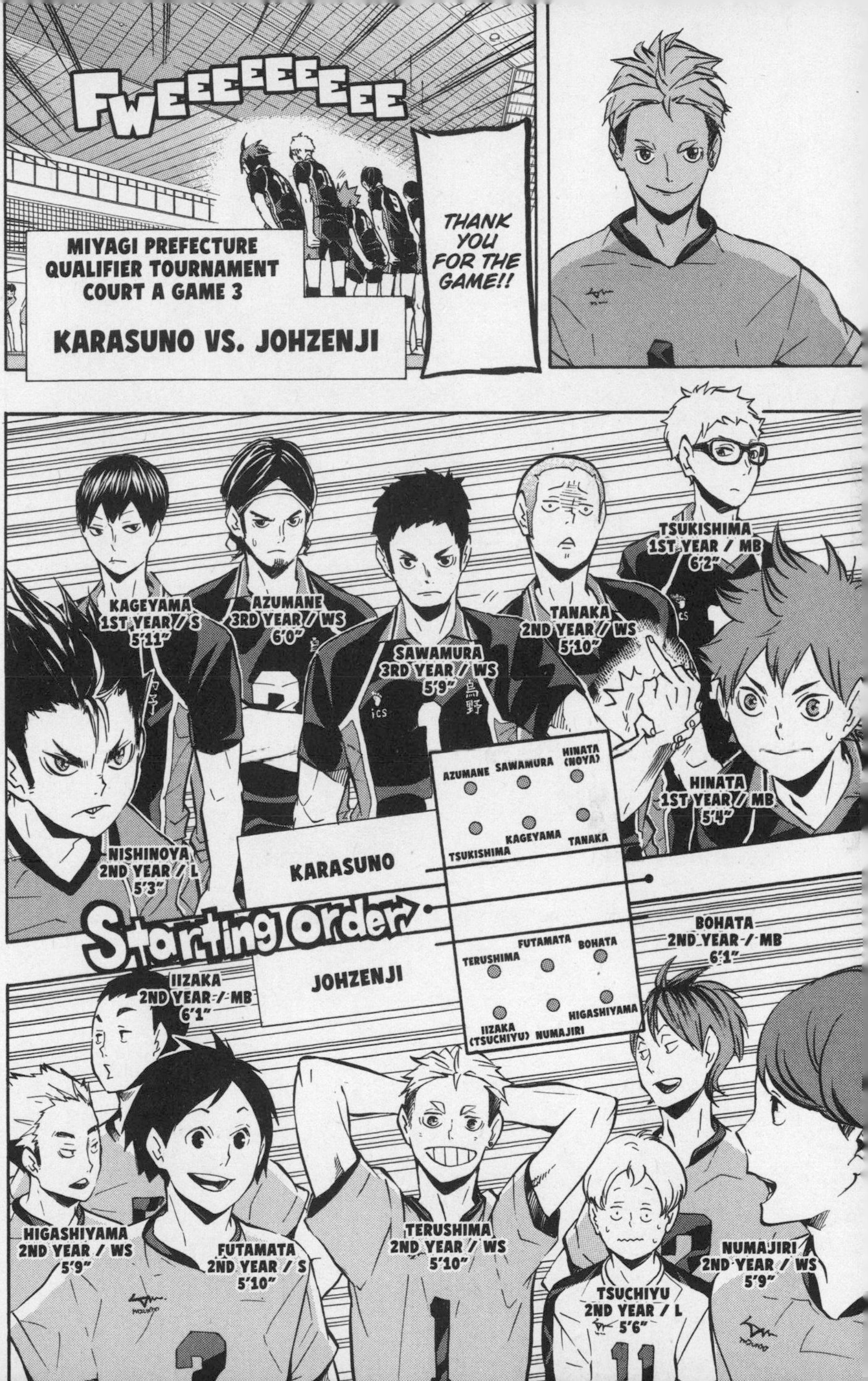
FWEEEEEEEEE
THANK YOU FOR THE GAME!!
MIYAGI PREFECTURE QUALIFIER TOURNAMENT COURT A GAME 3
KARASUNO VS. JOHZENJI
TSUKISHIMA 1ST YEAR / MB 6'2"
TANAKA 2ND YEAR / WS 5'10"
SAWAMURA 3RD YEAR / WS 5'9"
AZUMANE 3RD YEAR / WS 6'0"
KAGEYAMA 1ST YEAR / S 5'11"
HINATA 1ST YEAR / MB 5'4"
NISHINOYA 2ND YEAR / L 5'3"
Starting Order
KARASUNO
AZUMANE
SAWAMURA
HINATA (NOYA)
TSUKISHIMA
KAGEYAMA
TANAKA
JOHZENJI
TERUSHIMA
FUTAMATA
BOHATA
IIZAKA (TSUCHIYU)
NUMAJIRI
HIGASHIYAMA
BOHATA 2ND YEAR / MB 6'1"
IIZAKA 2ND YEAR / MB 6'1"
NUMAJIRI 2ND YEAR / WS 5'9"
TSUCHIYU 2ND YEAR / L 5'6"
TERUSHIMA 2ND YEAR / WS 5'10"
FUTAMATA 2ND YEAR / S 5'10"
HIGASHIYAMA 2ND YEAR / WS 5'9"

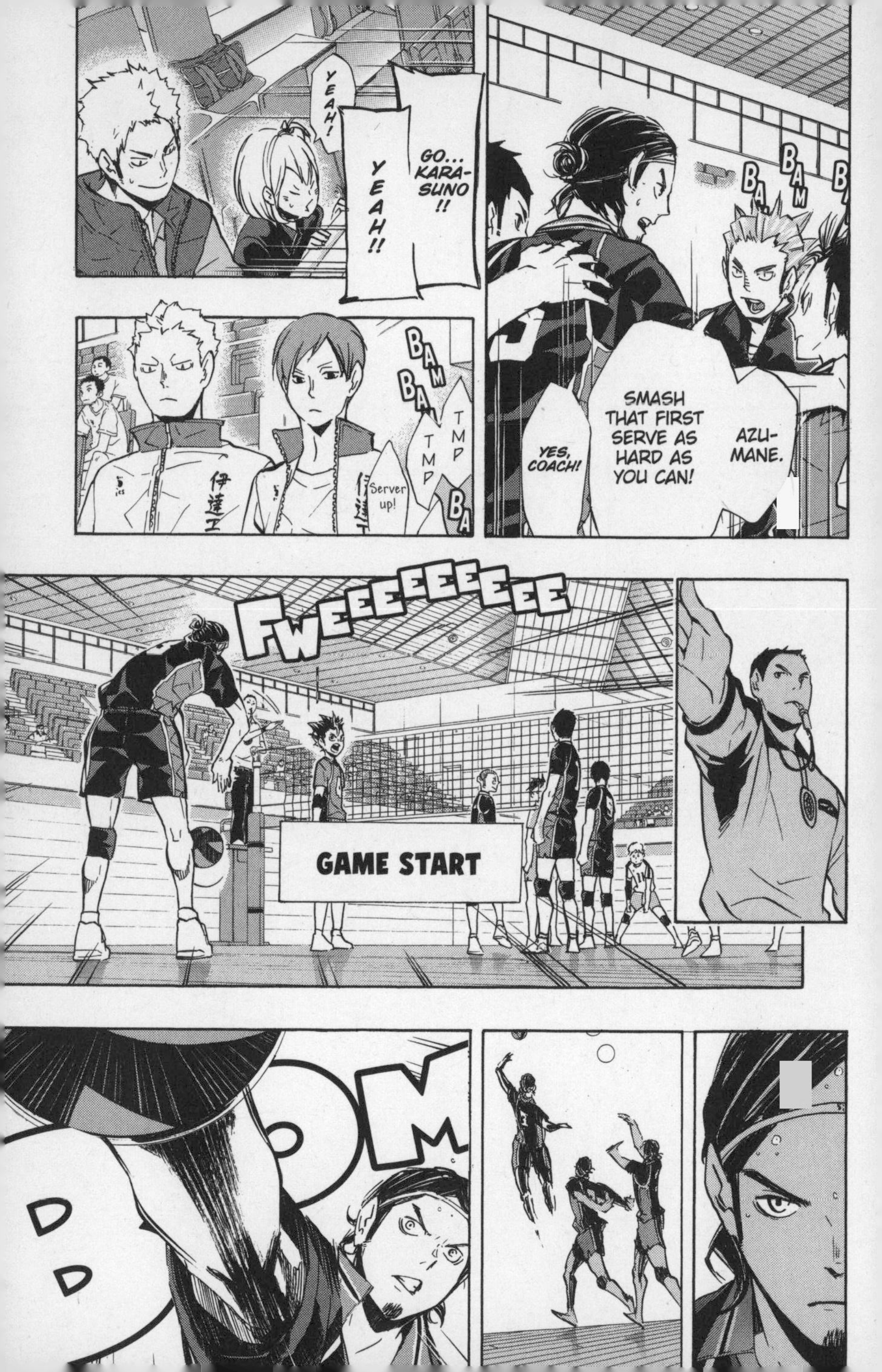
BAM BAM B
AZUMANE.
SMASH THAT FIRST SERVE AS HARD AS YOU CAN!
YES, COACH!
GO... KARASUNO!!
YEAH!!
YEAH!
BAM BAM
TMP TMP
Server up!
BA
FWEEEEEEEEE
GAME START

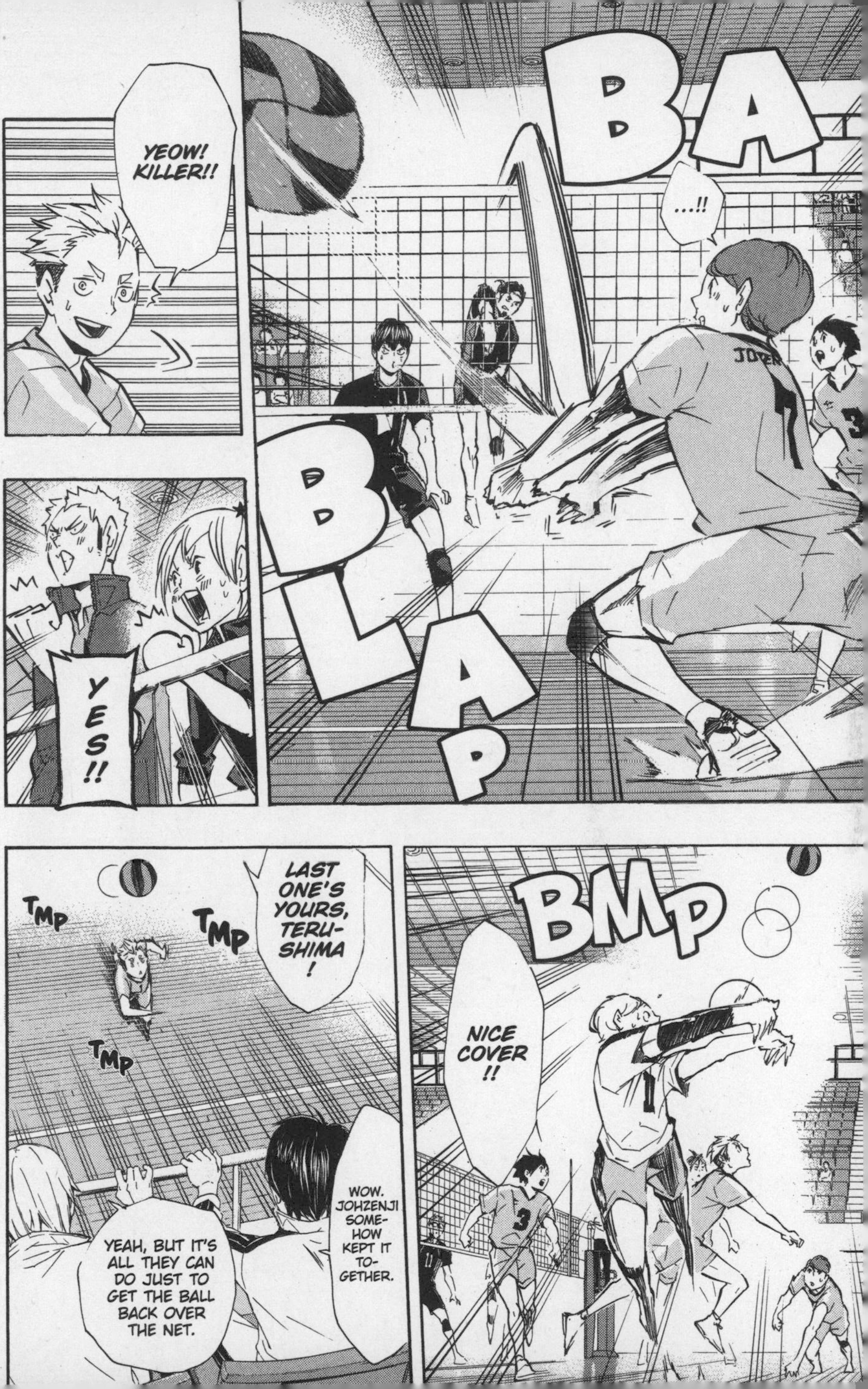
BA
...!!
BLAP
YEOW! KILLER!!
YES!!
BMP
NICE COVER!!
LAST ONE'S YOURS, TERUSHIMA!
TMP
TMP
TMP
WOW. JOHZENJI SOMEHOW KEPT IT TOGETHER.
YEAH, BUT IT'S ALL THEY CAN DO JUST TO GET THE BALL BACK OVER THE NET.

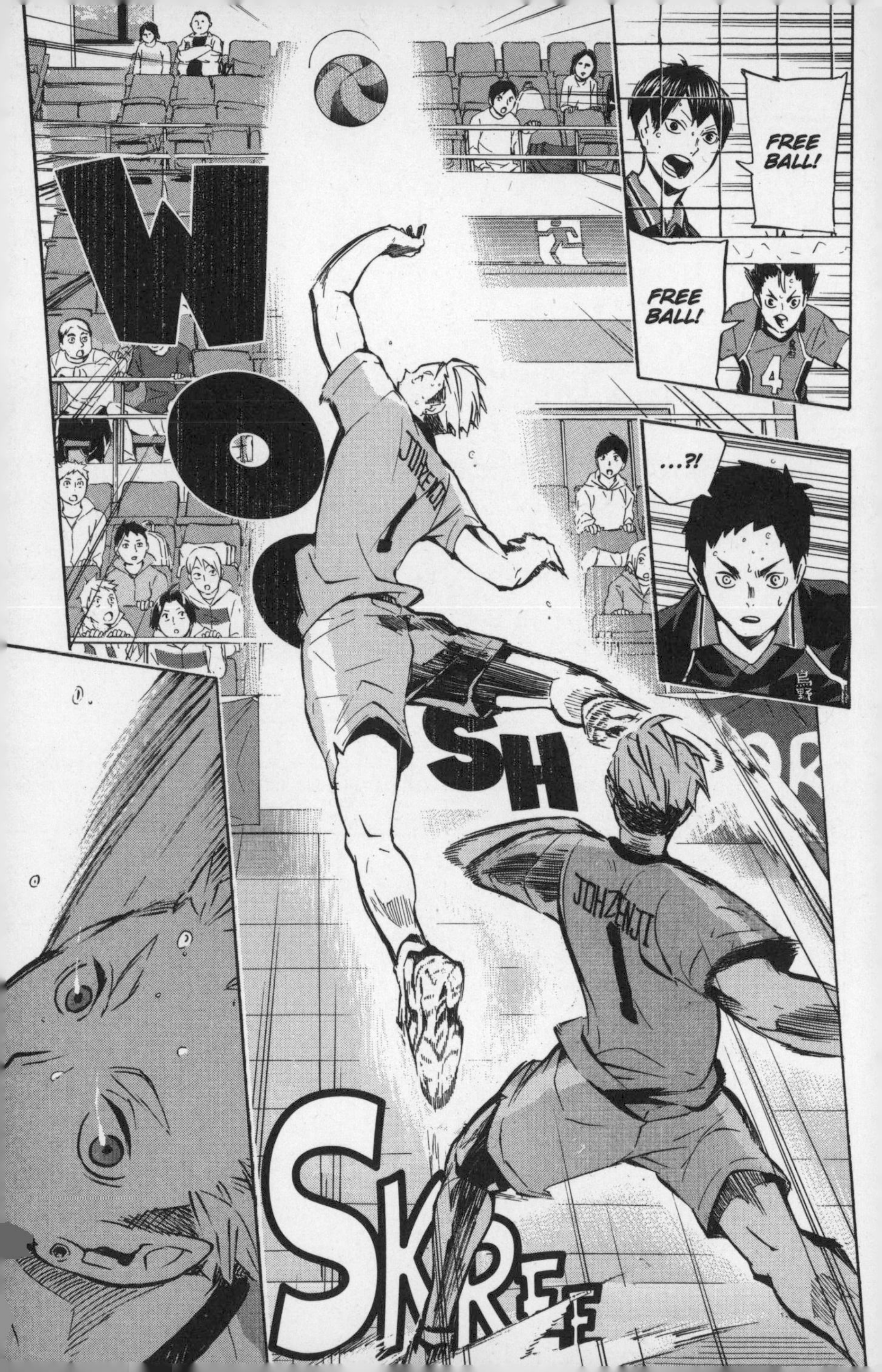
FREE BALL!
FREE BALL!
...?!
WOO
SH
SKREE

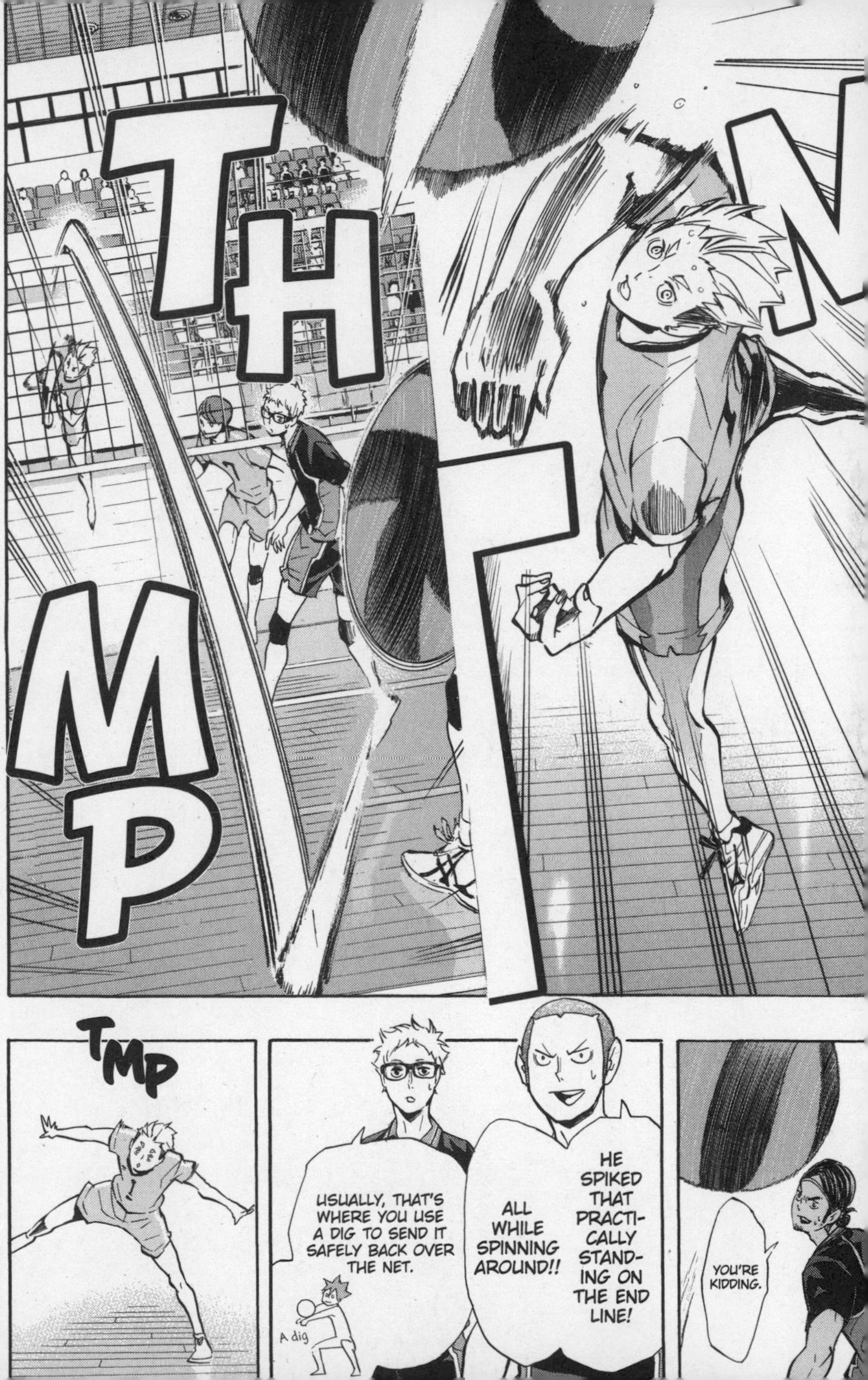
THMP
YOU'RE KIDDING.
HE SPIKED THAT PRACTI-CALLY STAND-ING ON THE END LINE!
ALL WHILE SPINNING AROUND!!
USUALLY, THAT'S WHERE YOU USE A DIG TO SEND IT SAFELY BACK OVER THE NET.
A dig
TMP

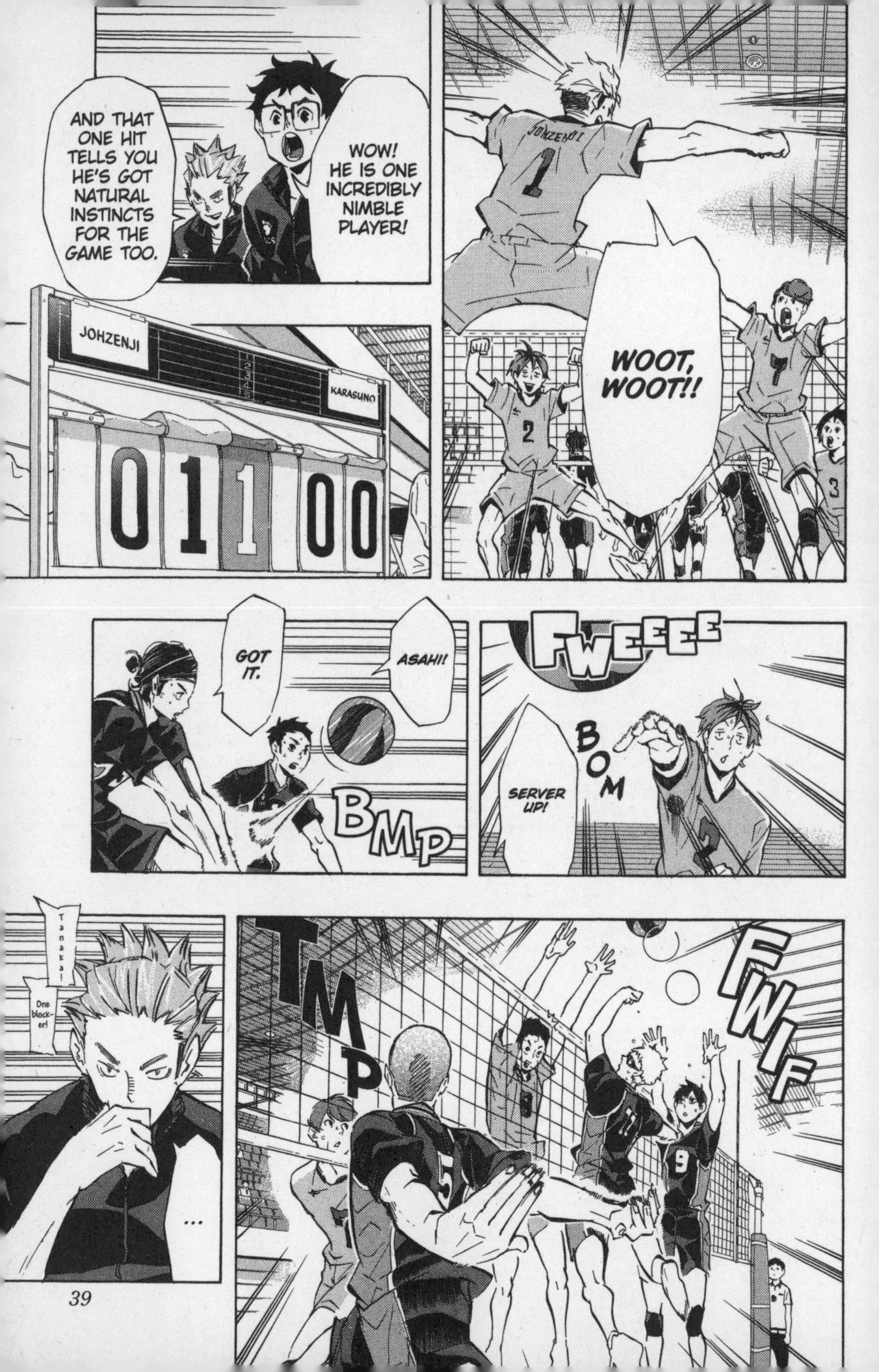
WOOT, WOOT!!
WOW! HE IS ONE INCREDIBLY NIMBLE PLAYER!
AND THAT ONE HIT TELLS YOU HE'S GOT NATURAL INSTINCTS FOR THE GAME TOO.
JOHZENJI
KARASUNO
FWEEEE
SERVER UP!
BOM
ASAHI!
GOT IT.
BMP
FWIF
TMP
Tanaka!
One blocker!
...

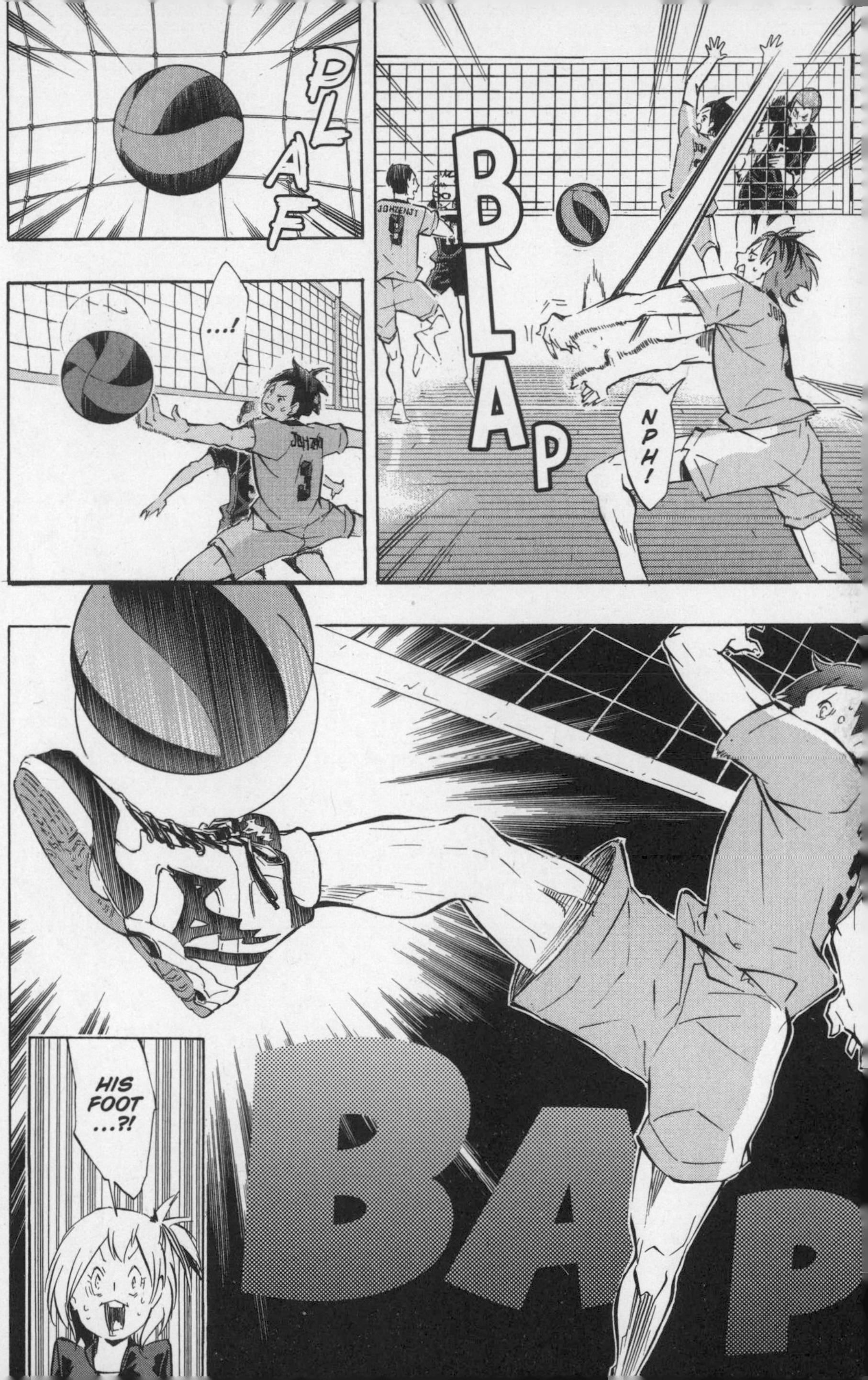
BLAP
NPH!
PLAF
...!
BAP
HIS FOOT ...?!

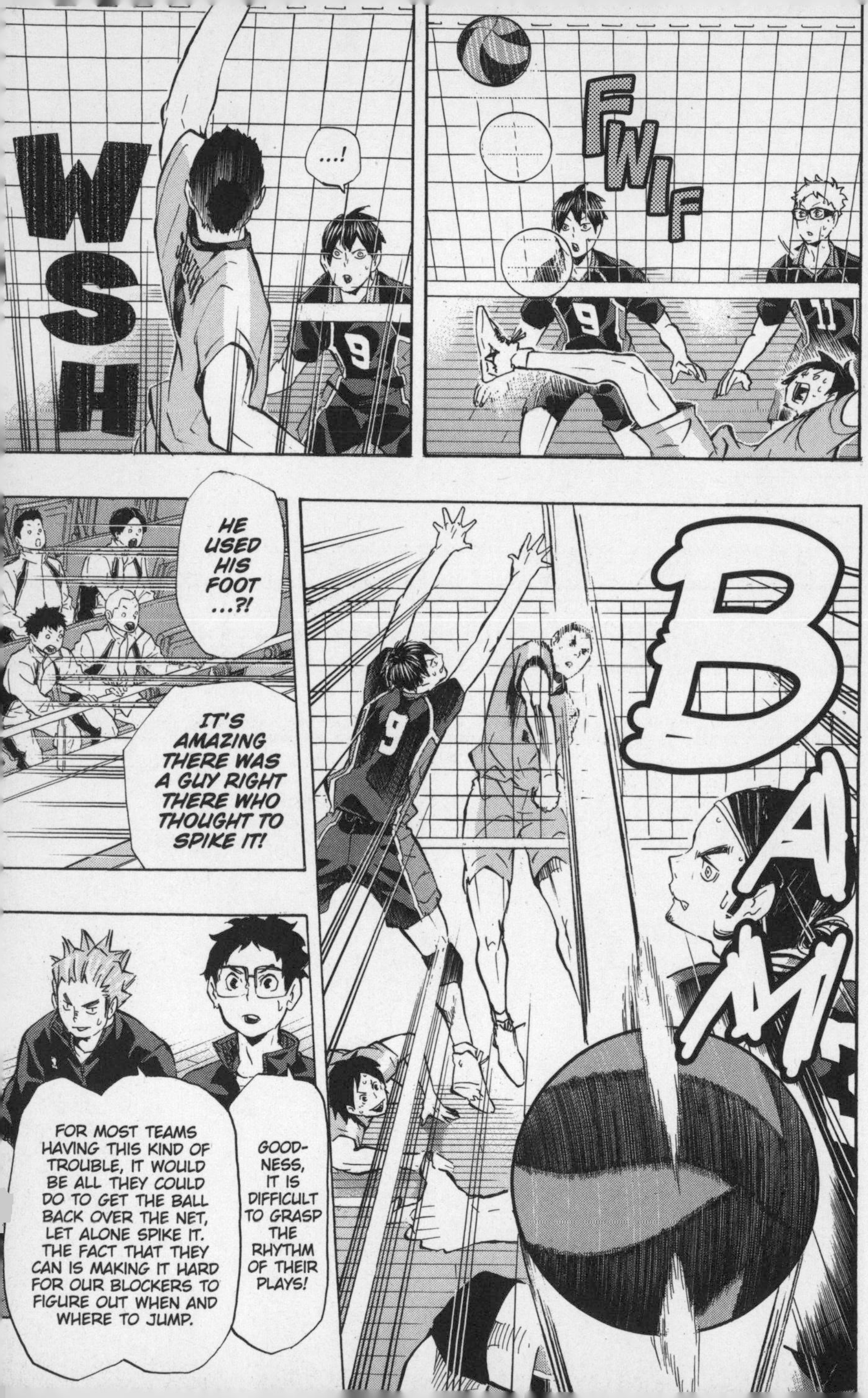
FWIF
...!
WSH
BAM
HE USED HIS FOOT ...?!
IT'S AMAZING THERE WAS A GUY RIGHT THERE WHO THOUGHT TO SPIKE IT!
GOOD-NESS, IT IS DIFFICULT TO GRASP THE RHYTHM OF THEIR PLAYS!
FOR MOST TEAMS HAVING THIS KIND OF TROUBLE, IT WOULD BE ALL THEY COULD DO TO GET THE BALL BACK OVER THE NET, LET ALONE SPIKE IT. THE FACT THAT THEY CAN IS MAKING IT HARD FOR OUR BLOCKERS TO FIGURE OUT WHEN AND WHERE TO JUMP.

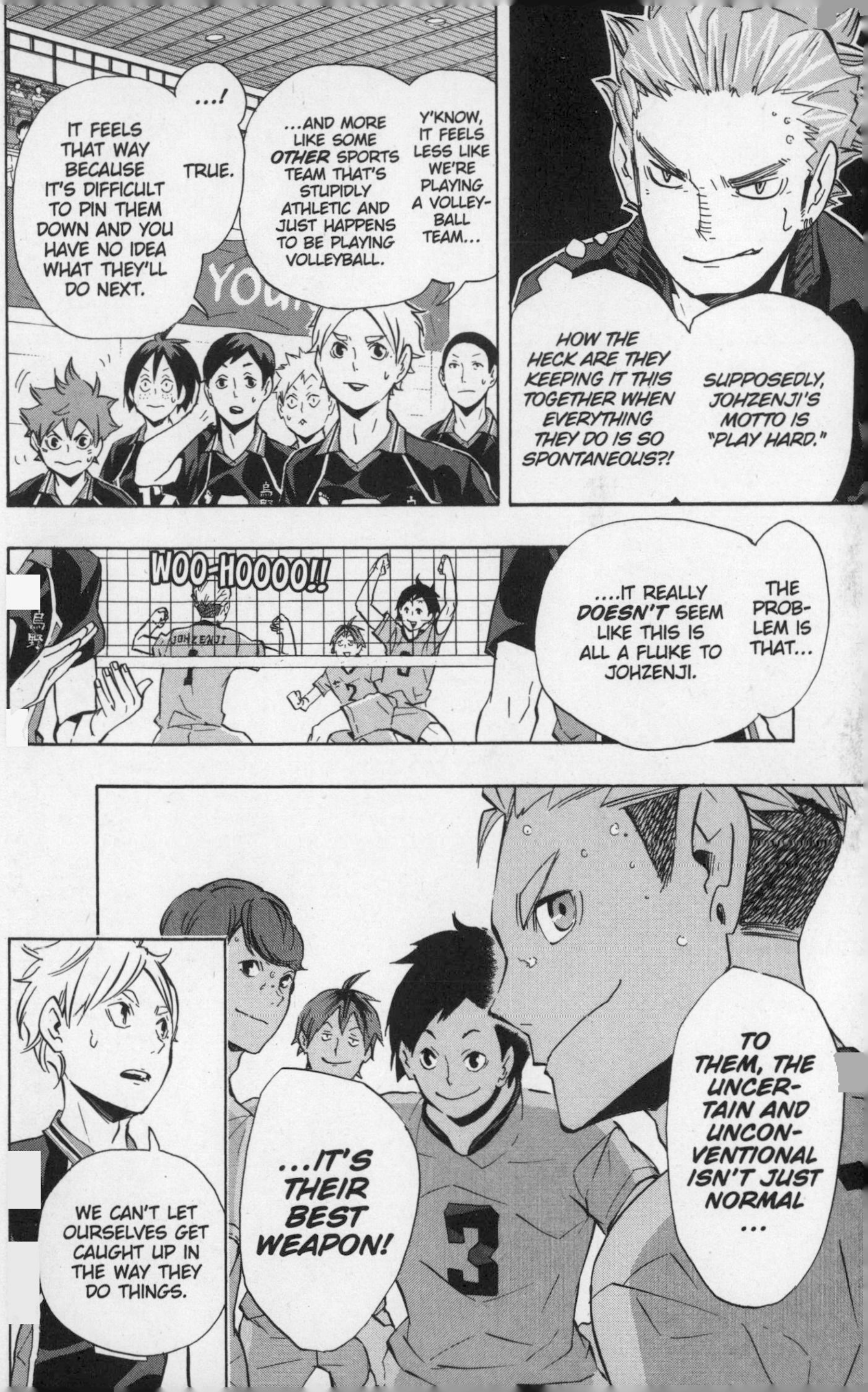
SUPPOSEDLY, JOHZENJI'S MOTTO IS "PLAY HARD."
HOW THE HECK ARE THEY KEEPING IT THIS TOGETHER WHEN EVERYTHING THEY DO IS SO SPONTANEOUS?!
Y'KNOW, IT FEELS LESS LIKE WE'RE PLAYING A VOLLEY-BALL TEAM...
...AND MORE LIKE SOME OTHER SPORTS TEAM THAT'S STUPIDLY ATHLETIC AND JUST HAPPENS TO BE PLAYING VOLLEYBALL.
...!
TRUE.
IT FEELS THAT WAY BECAUSE IT'S DIFFICULT TO PIN THEM DOWN AND YOU HAVE NO IDEA WHAT THEY'LL DO NEXT.
THE PROB-LEM IS THAT...
....IT REALLY DOESN'T SEEM LIKE THIS IS ALL A FLUKE TO JOHZENJI.
WOO-HOOOO!!
TO THEM, THE UNCER-TAIN AND UNCON-VENTIONAL ISN'T JUST NORMAL ...
...IT'S THEIR BEST WEAPON!
WE CAN'T LET OURSELVES GET CAUGHT UP IN THE WAY THEY DO THINGS.

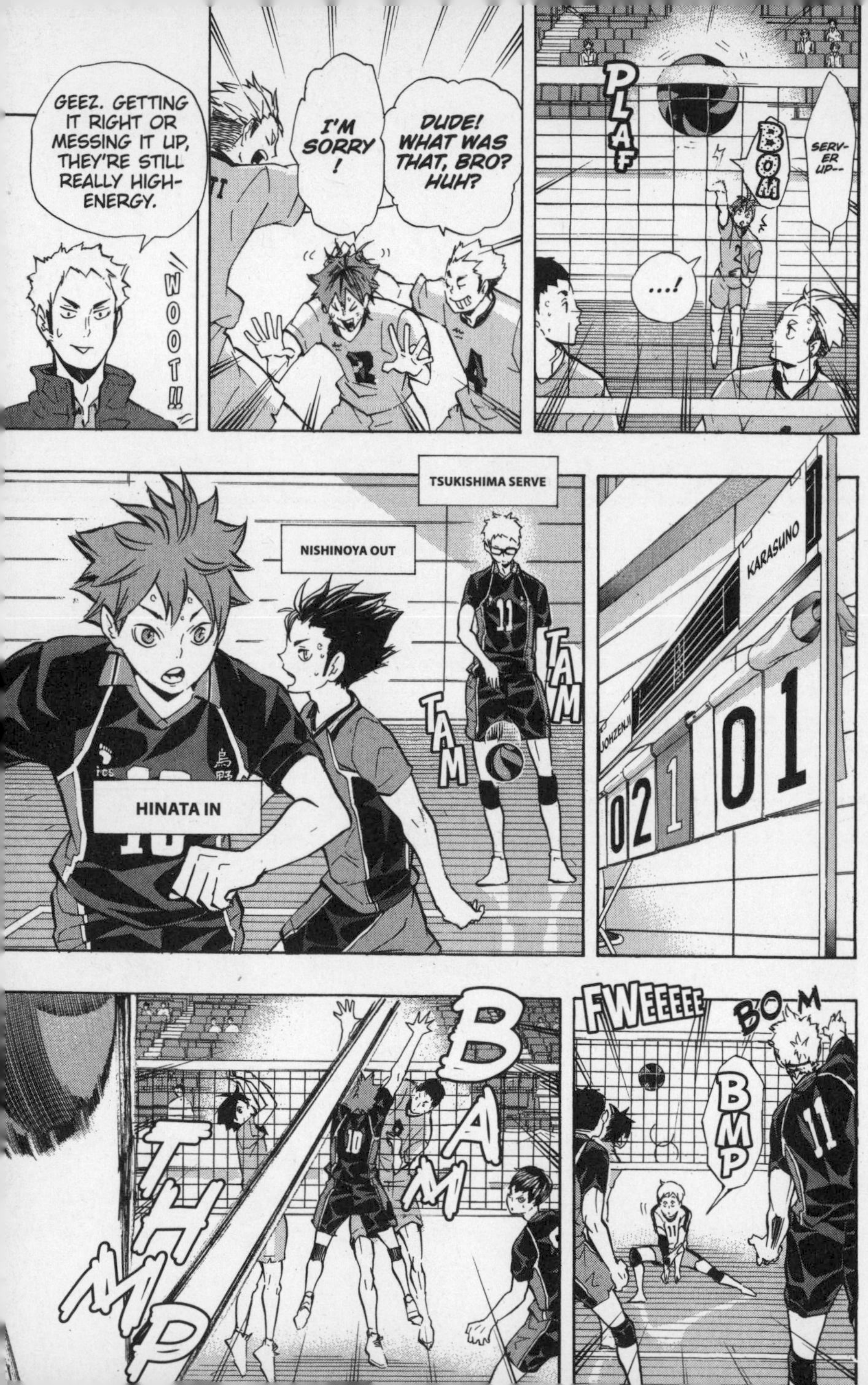
SERV-ER UP--
BOM
PLAF
...!
DUDE! WHAT WAS THAT, BRO? HUH?
I'M SORRY!
GEEZ. GETTING IT RIGHT OR MESSING IT UP, THEY'RE STILL REALLY HIGH-ENERGY.
WOOT!!
KARASUNO
JOHZENJI
02 1 01
TSUKISHIMA SERVE
NISHINOYA OUT
TAM
TAM
HINATA IN
FWEEEEE
BOM
BMP
BAM
THMP

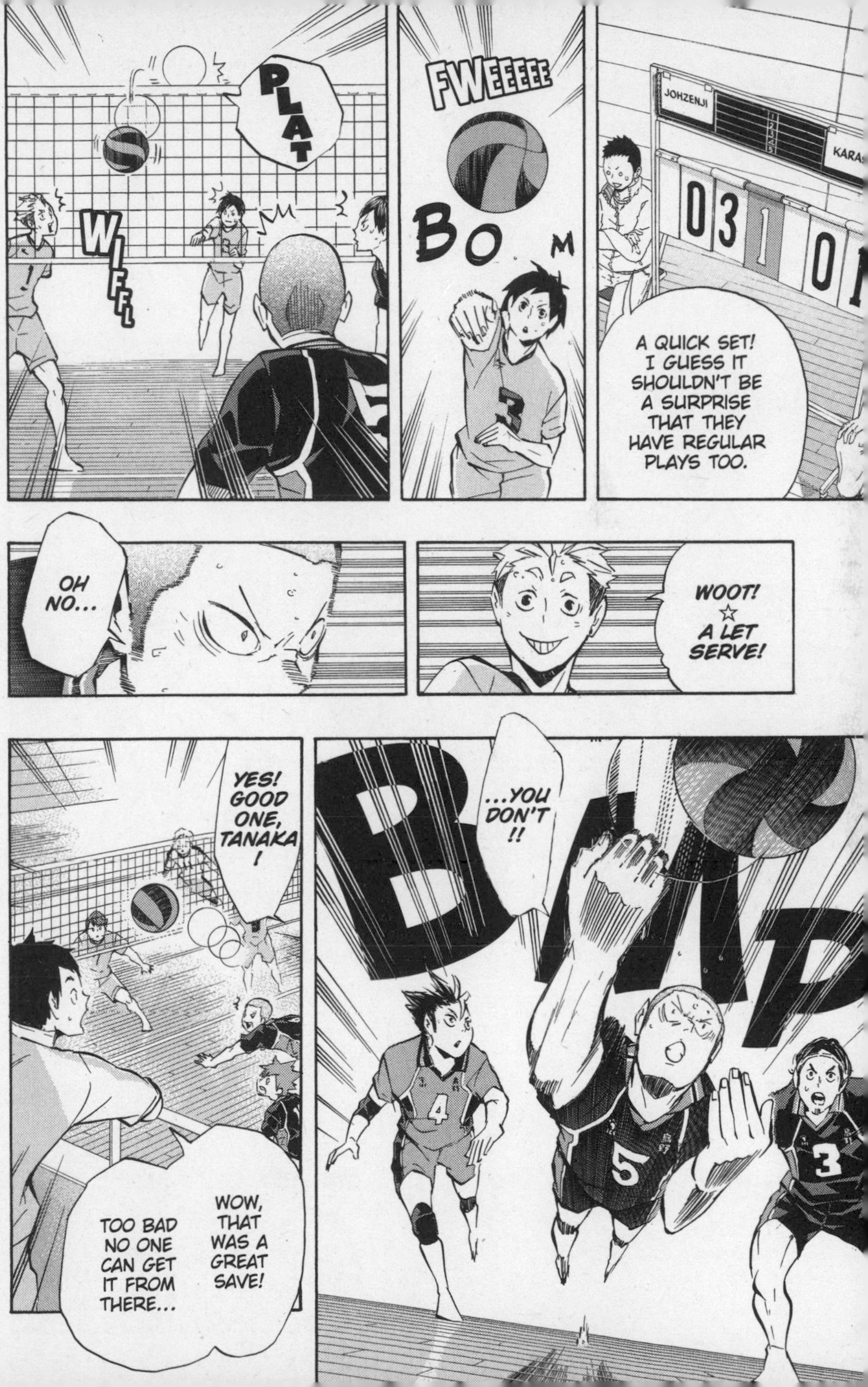
JOHZENJI
A QUICK SET! I GUESS IT SHOULDN'T BE A SURPRISE THAT THEY HAVE REGULAR PLAYS TOO.
FWEEEEE
BOM
PLAT
WIFFL
WOOT! ☆ A LET SERVE!
OH NO...
...YOU DON'T!!
YES! GOOD ONE, TANAKA!
WOW, THAT WAS A GREAT SAVE!
TOO BAD NO ONE CAN GET IT FROM THERE...

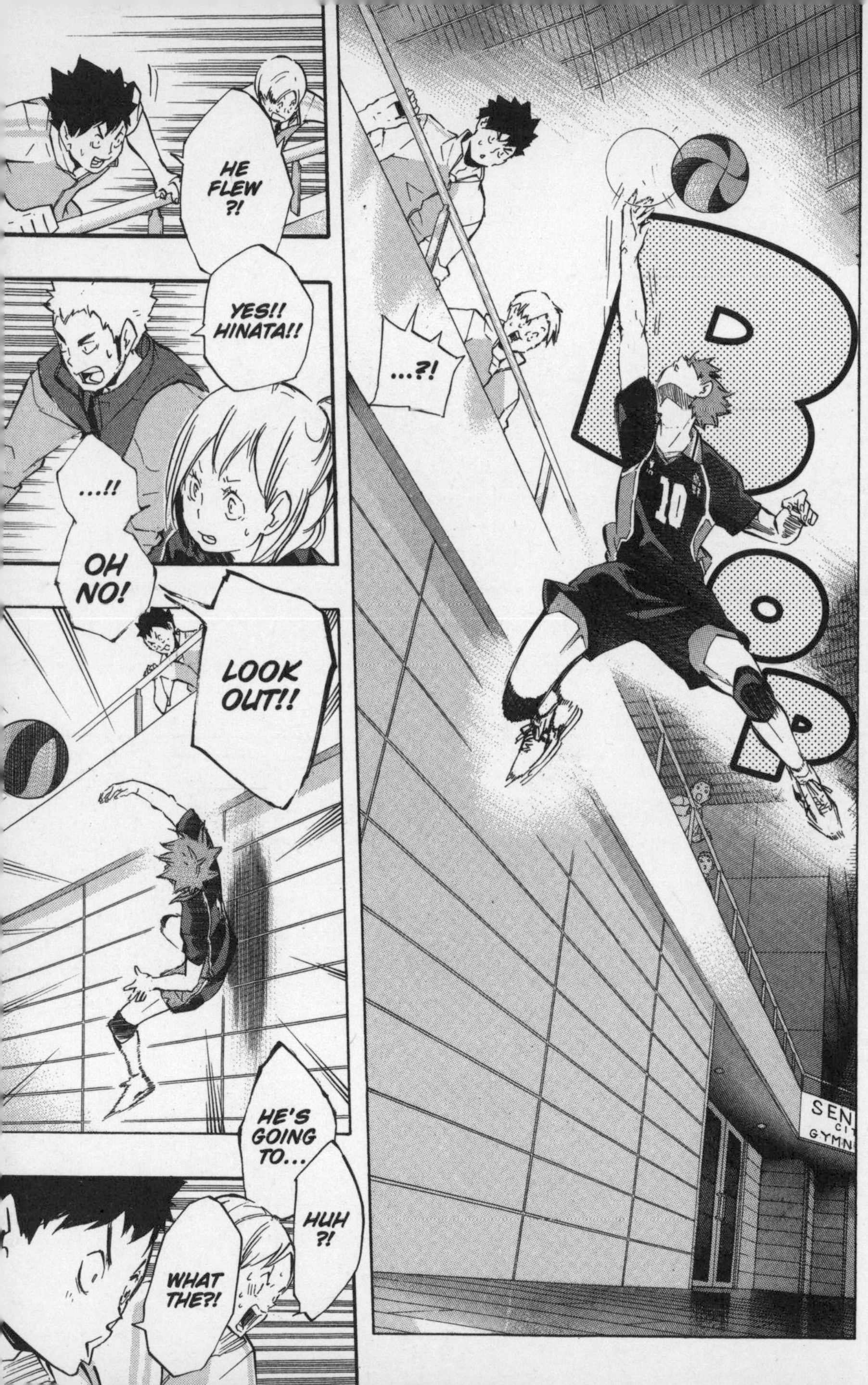
...?!
HE FLEW ?!
YES!! HINATA!!
...!!
OH NO!
LOOK OUT!!
HE'S GOING TO...
HUH ?!
WHAT THE?!

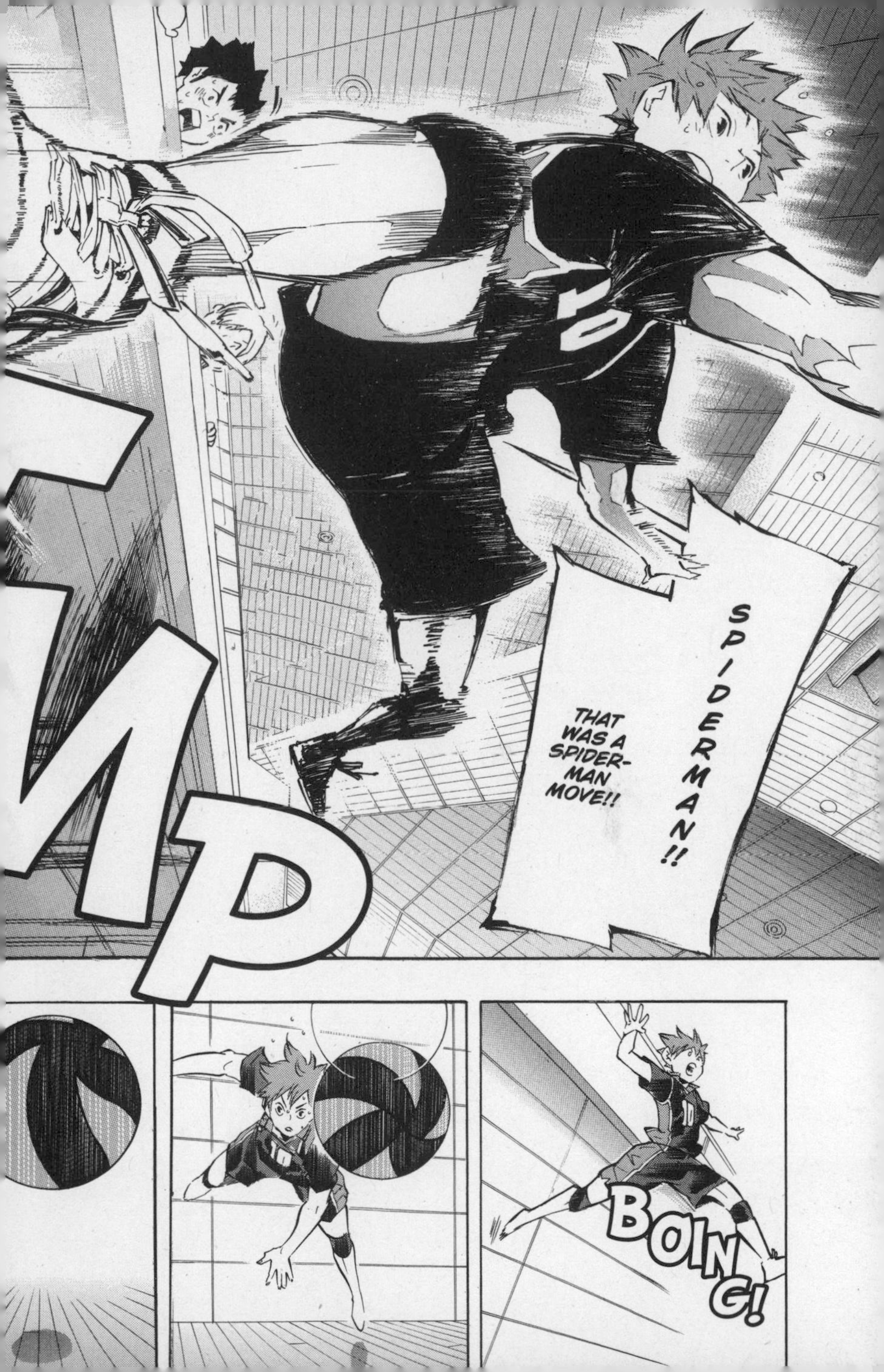
SPIDERMAN!!
THAT WAS A SPIDER-MAN MOVE!!
BOING!

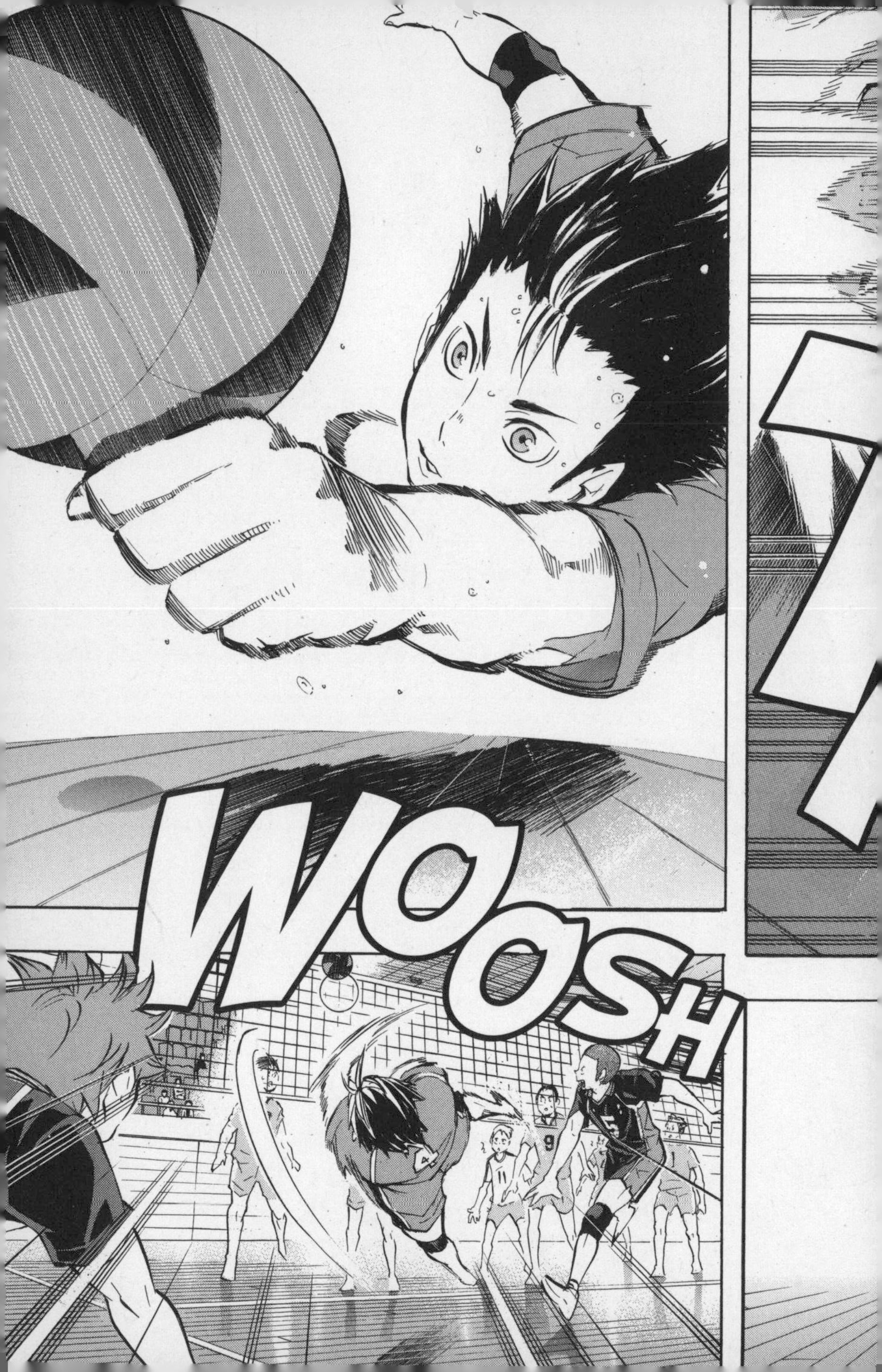
WOOSH

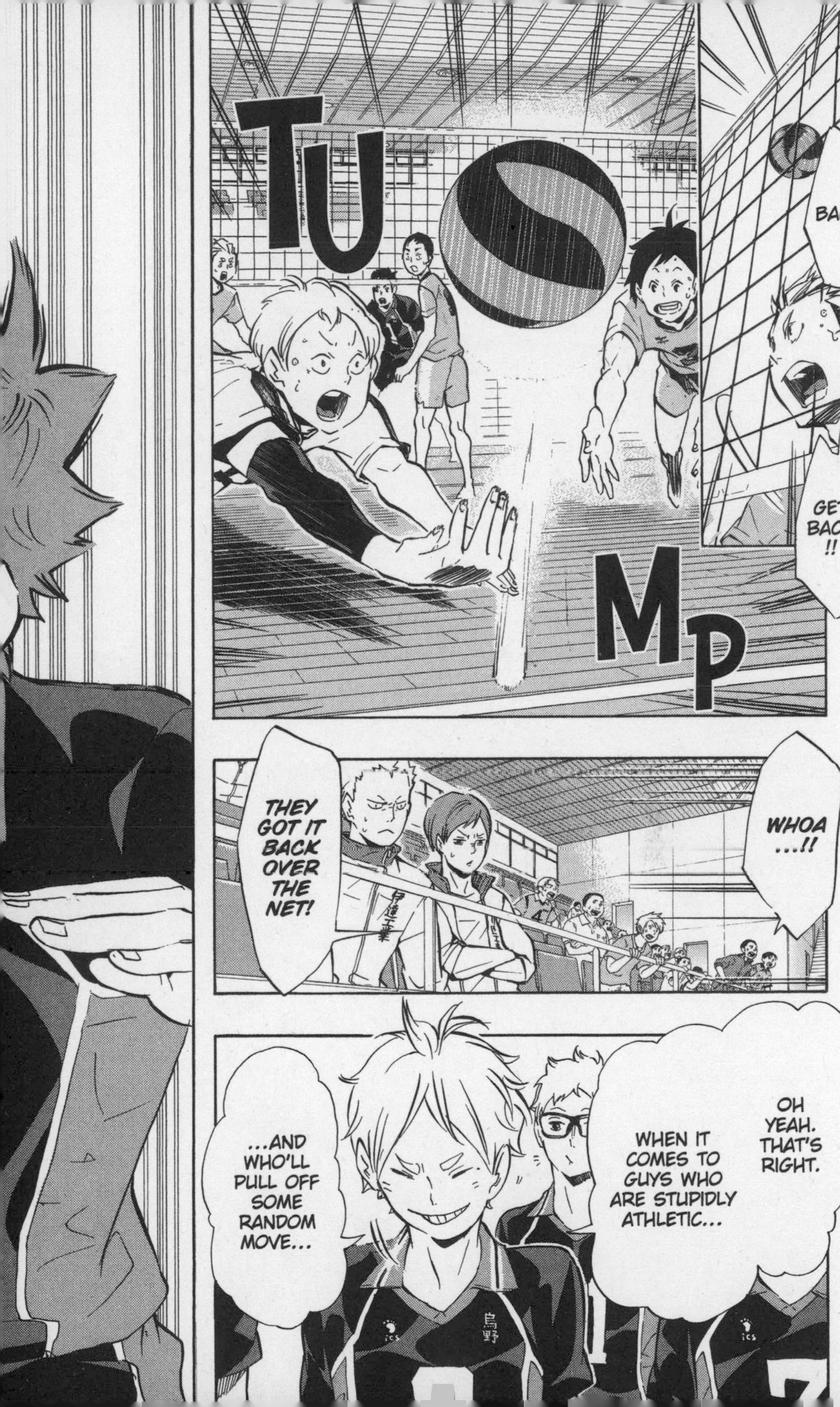
BACK!!
GET BACK!!
TUMP
WHOA...!!
THEY GOT IT BACK OVER THE NET!
OH YEAH. THAT'S RIGHT.
WHEN IT COMES TO GUYS WHO ARE STUPIDLY ATHLETIC...
...AND WHO'LL PULL OFF SOME RANDOM MOVE...

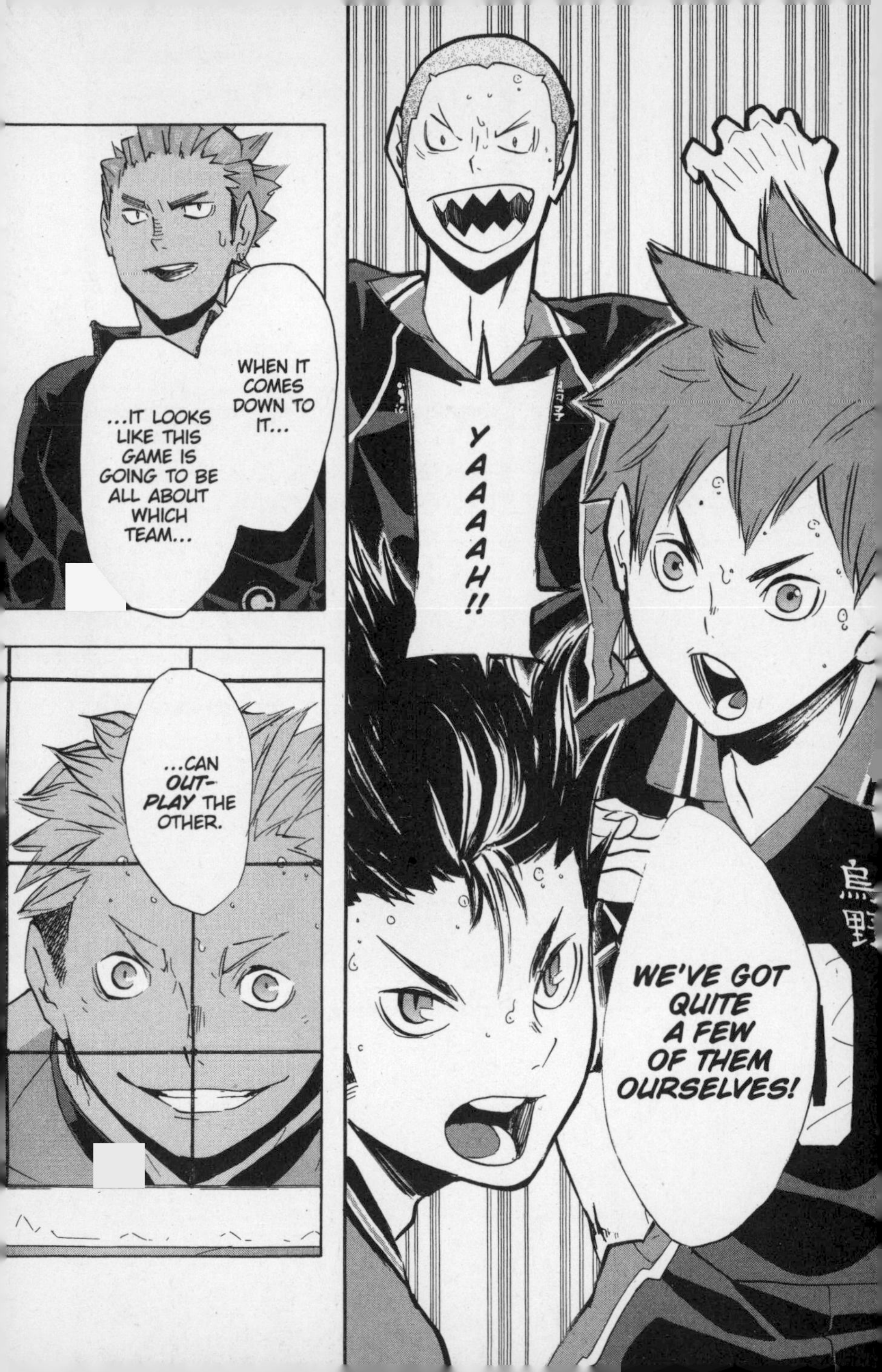
YAAAAAH!!
WE'VE GOT QUITE A FEW OF THEM OURSELVES!
WHEN IT COMES DOWN TO IT...
...IT LOOKS LIKE THIS GAME IS GOING TO BE ALL ABOUT WHICH TEAM...
...CAN OUT-PLAY THE OTHER.

WHEN I WAS STILL A STUDENT, I ALWAYS WISHED I COULD PULL OFF SOMETHING LIKE THAT IN A GAME. I DIDN'T GET THE CHANCE TO BACK THEN, SO I'M HAPPY I GOT THE OPPORTUNITY TO DRAW SOMETHING LIKE IT IN THIS STORY.

→

I ALWAYS WANTED TO TRY THIS...
WALL
WALL

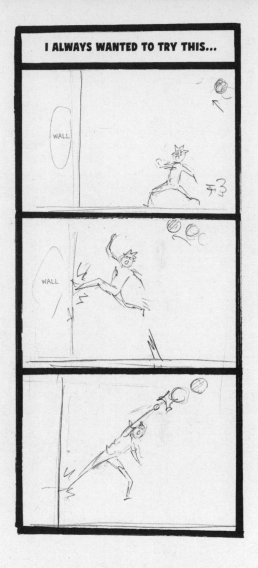

↑ LOOKING AT IT FROM THE SIDE, IT DOES LOOK LIKE A PRETTY COMMON SPIDERMAN POSE.

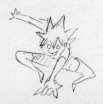

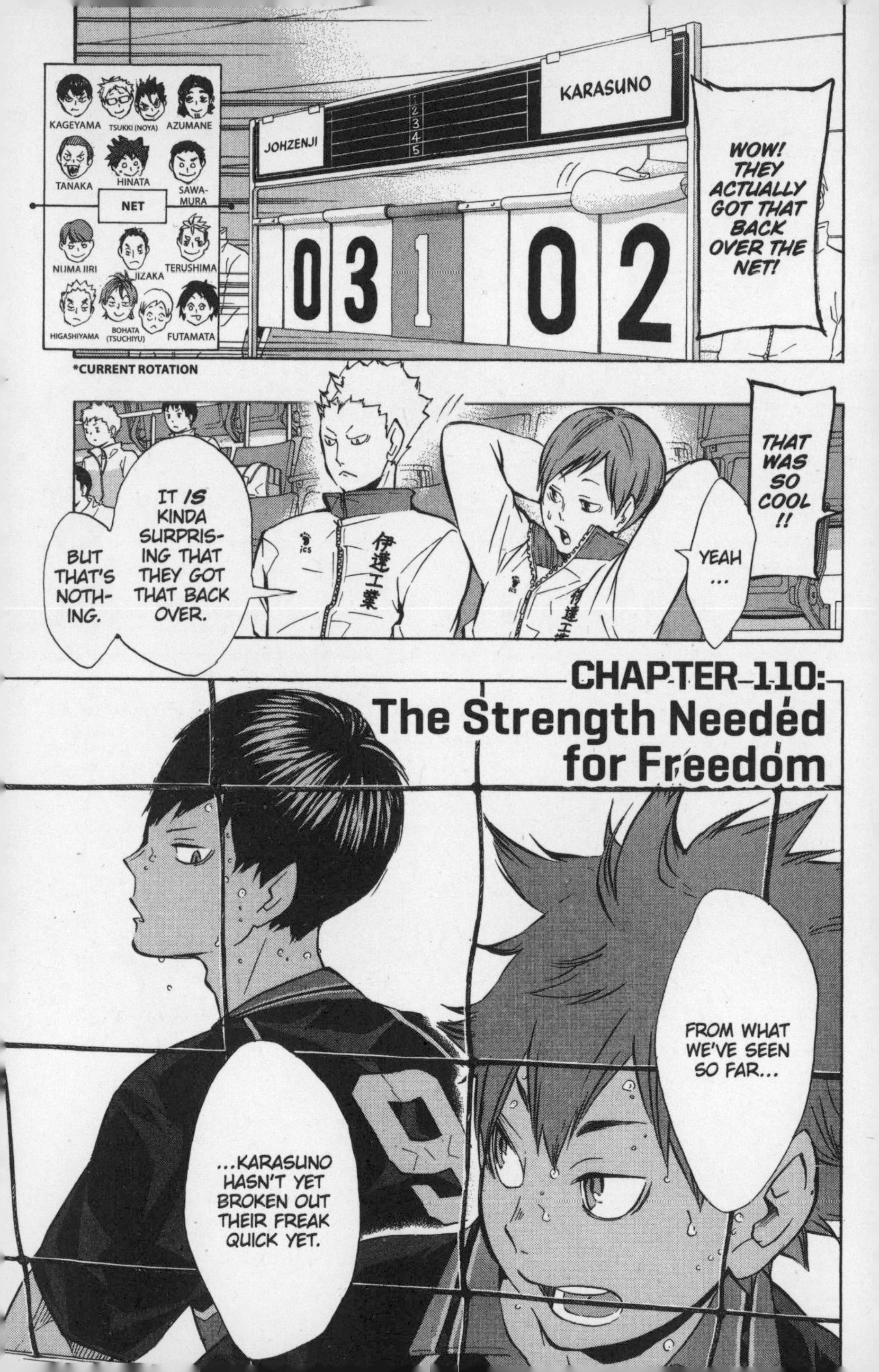
WOW! THEY ACTUALLY GOT THAT BACK OVER THE NET!
KARASUNO
JOHZENJI
03 1 02
KAGEYAMA
TSUKKI (NOYA)
AZUMANE
TANAKA
HINATA
SAWAMURA
NET
NUMAJIRI
IIZAKA
TERUSHIMA
HIGASHIYAMA
BOHATA (TSUCHIYU)
FUTAMATA
*CURRENT ROTATION
THAT WAS SO COOL!!
YEAH...
IT *IS* KINDA SURPRISING THAT THEY GOT THAT BACK OVER.
BUT THAT'S NOTHING.
CHAPTER 110:
The Strength Needed for Freedom
FROM WHAT WE'VE SEEN SO FAR...
...KARASUNO HASN'T YET BROKEN OUT THEIR FREAK QUICK YET.

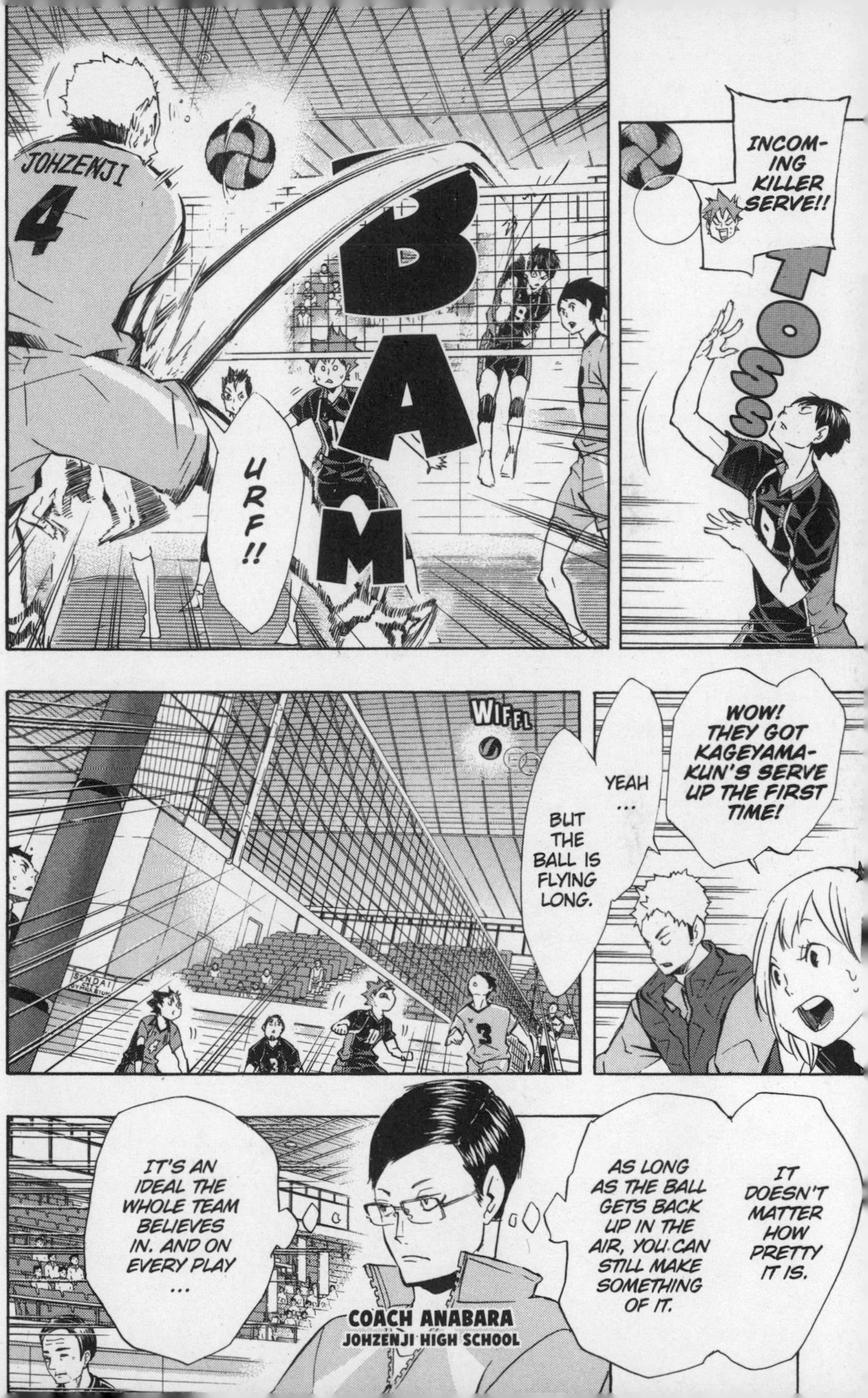
INCOMING KILLER SERVE!!
TOSS
JOHZENJI
4
BAM
URF!!
WOW! THEY GOT KAGEYAMA-KUN'S SERVE UP THE FIRST TIME!
YEAH ...
BUT THE BALL IS FLYING LONG.
WIFFL
IT DOESN'T MATTER HOW PRETTY IT IS.
AS LONG AS THE BALL GETS BACK UP IN THE AIR, YOU CAN STILL MAKE SOMETHING OF IT.
IT'S AN IDEAL THE WHOLE TEAM BELIEVES IN. AND ON EVERY PLAY ...
COACH ANABARA
JOHZENJI HIGH SCHOOL

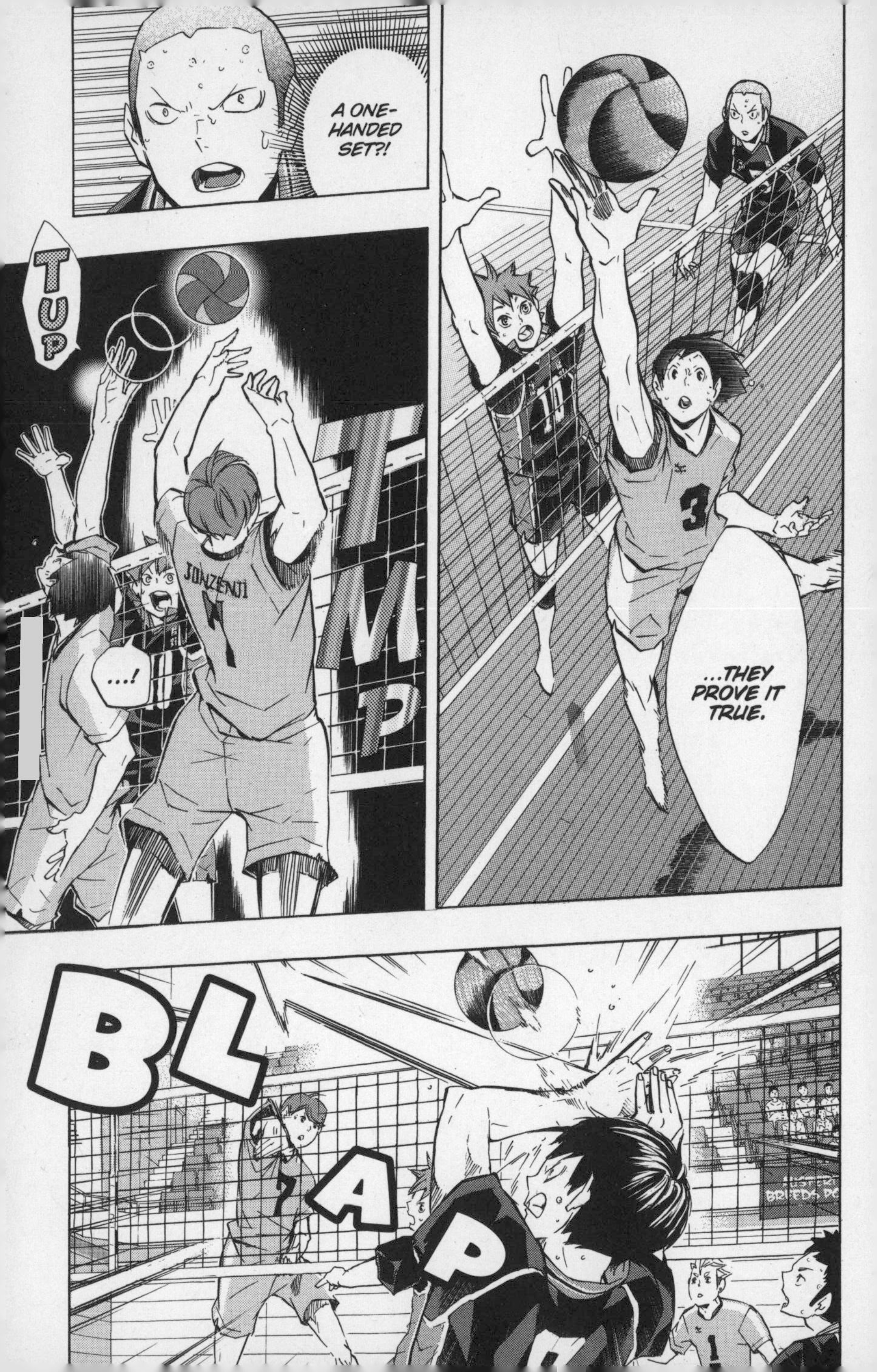
...THEY PROVE IT TRUE.
A ONE-HANDED SET?!
TUP
TMP
....!
BLAP

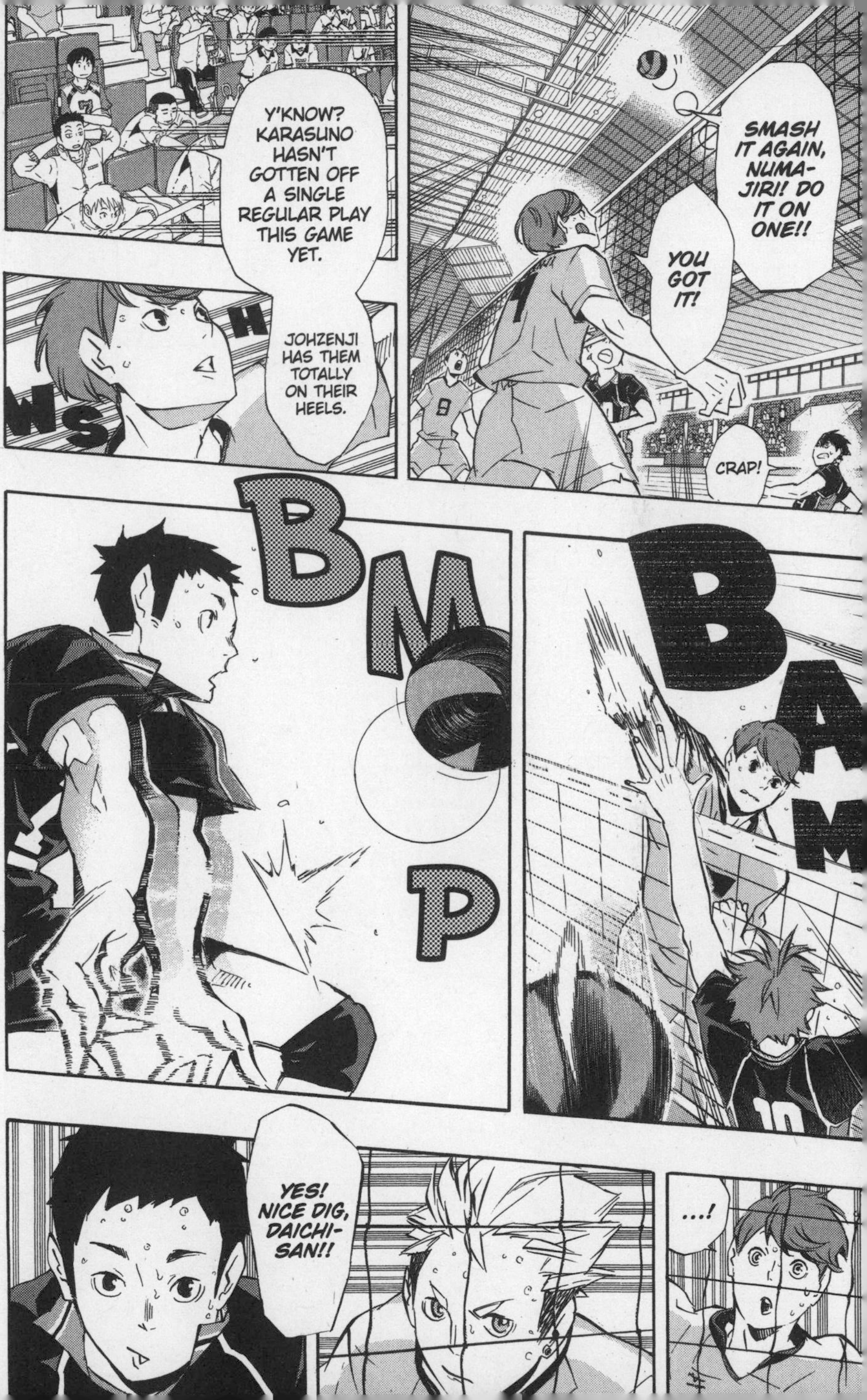
SMASH IT AGAIN, NUMA-JIRI! DO IT ON ONE!!
YOU GOT IT!
CRAP!
Y'KNOW? KARASUNO HASN'T GOTTEN OFF A SINGLE REGULAR PLAY THIS GAME YET.
JOHZENJI HAS THEM TOTALLY ON THEIR HEELS.
BAM
BMP
...!
YES! NICE DIG, DAICHI-SAN!!

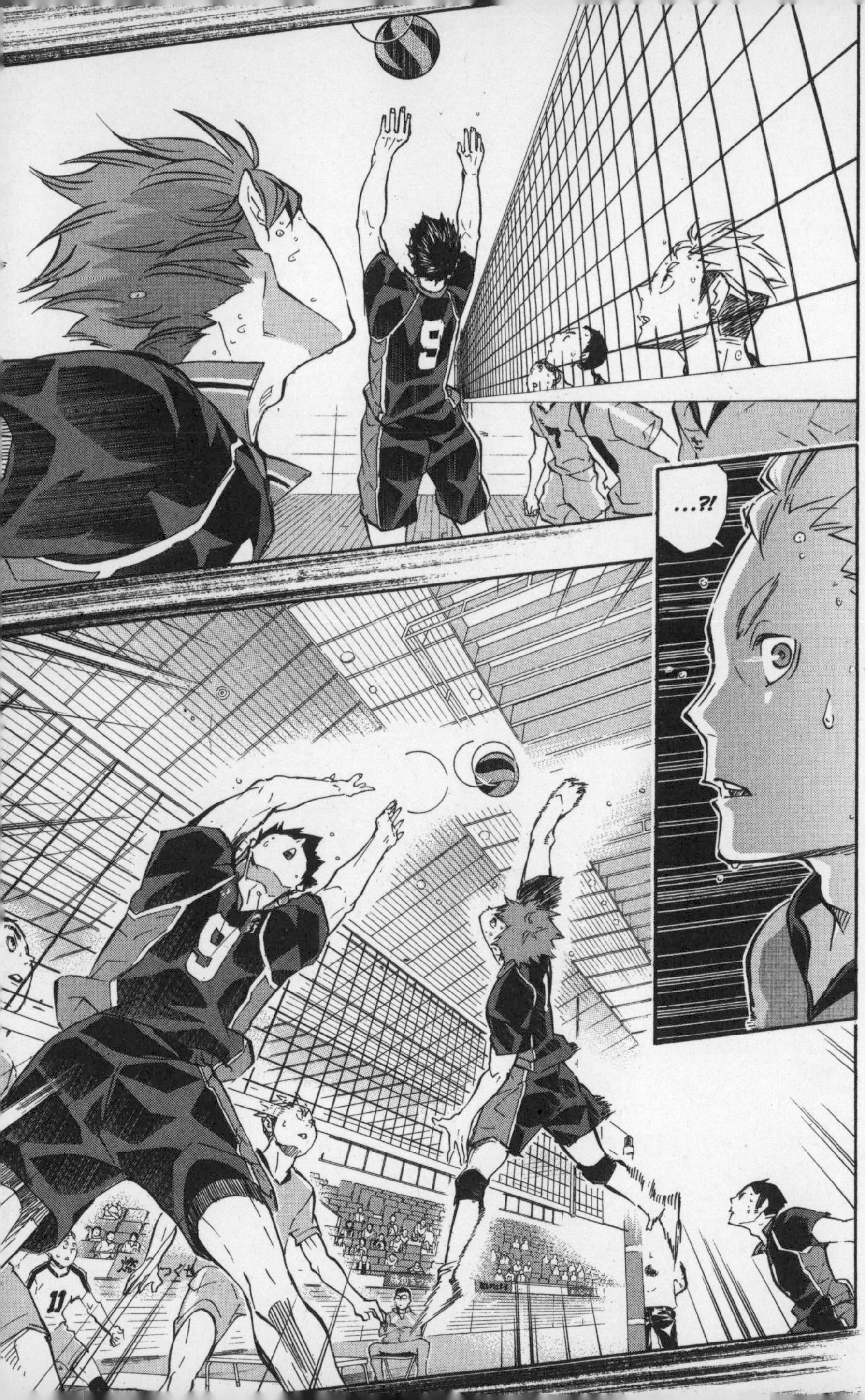
...?!
燃 つくせ

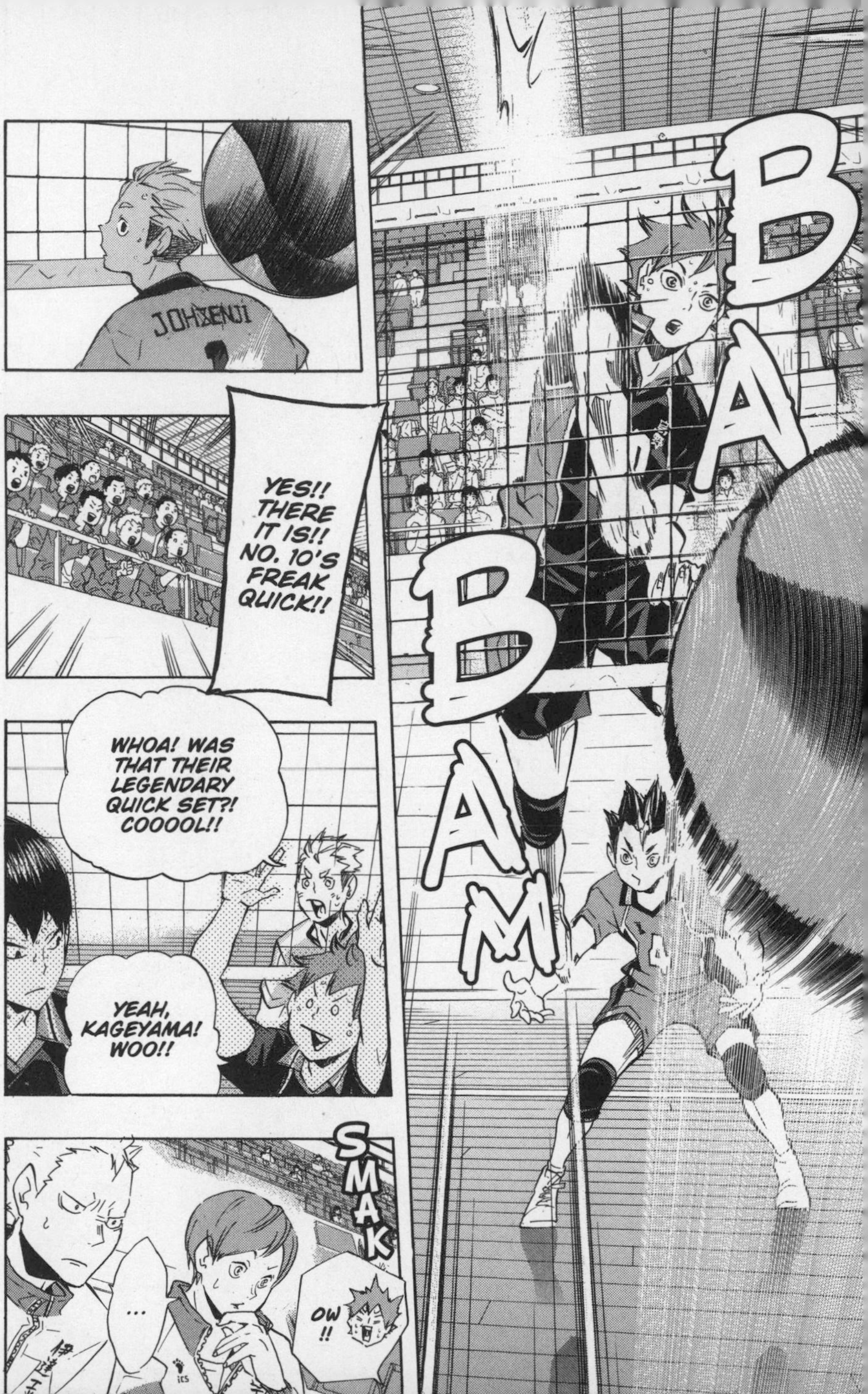
BA
BAM
JOHZENJI
YES!! THERE IT IS!! NO. 10'S FREAK QUICK!!
WHOA! WAS THAT THEIR LEGENDARY QUICK SET?! COOOOL!!
YEAH, KAGEYAMA! WOO!!
SMAK
OW !!
...

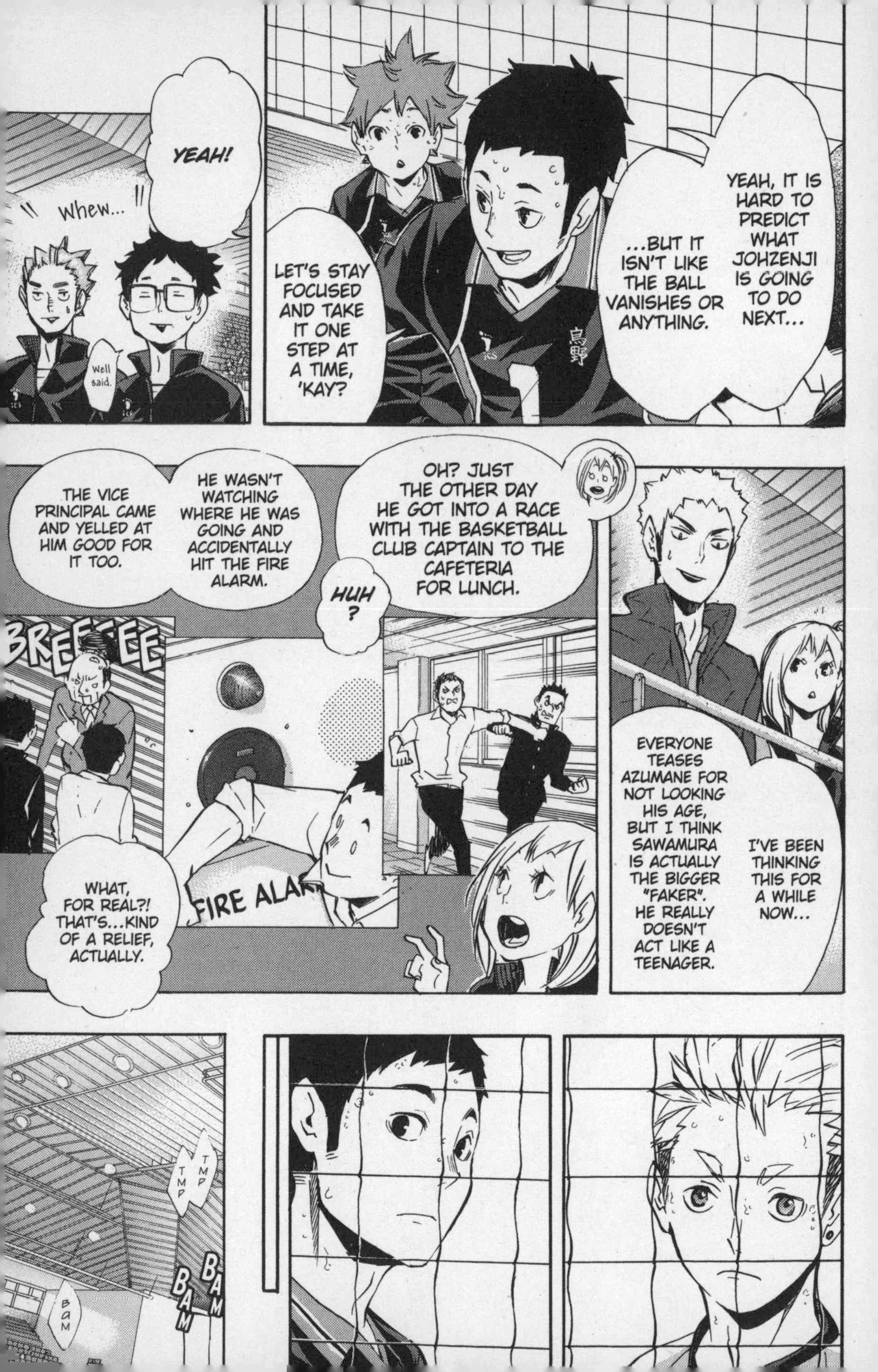
YEAH, IT IS HARD TO PREDICT WHAT JOHZENJI IS GOING TO DO NEXT...
...BUT IT ISN'T LIKE THE BALL VANISHES OR ANYTHING.
LET'S STAY FOCUSED AND TAKE IT ONE STEP AT A TIME, 'KAY?
YEAH!
Whew...
Well said.
I'VE BEEN THINKING THIS FOR A WHILE NOW...
EVERYONE TEASES AZUMANE FOR NOT LOOKING HIS AGE, BUT I THINK SAWAMURA IS ACTUALLY THE BIGGER "FAKER". HE REALLY DOESN'T ACT LIKE A TEENAGER.
OH? JUST THE OTHER DAY HE GOT INTO A RACE WITH THE BASKETBALL CLUB CAPTAIN TO THE CAFETERIA FOR LUNCH.
HUH?
HE WASN'T WATCHING WHERE HE WAS GOING AND ACCIDENTALLY HIT THE FIRE ALARM.
THE VICE PRINCIPAL CAME AND YELLED AT HIM GOOD FOR IT TOO.
BREEEEE
FIRE ALA
WHAT, FOR REAL?! THAT'S...KIND OF A RELIEF, ACTUALLY.
TMP TMP
BAM BAM BAM
Bam

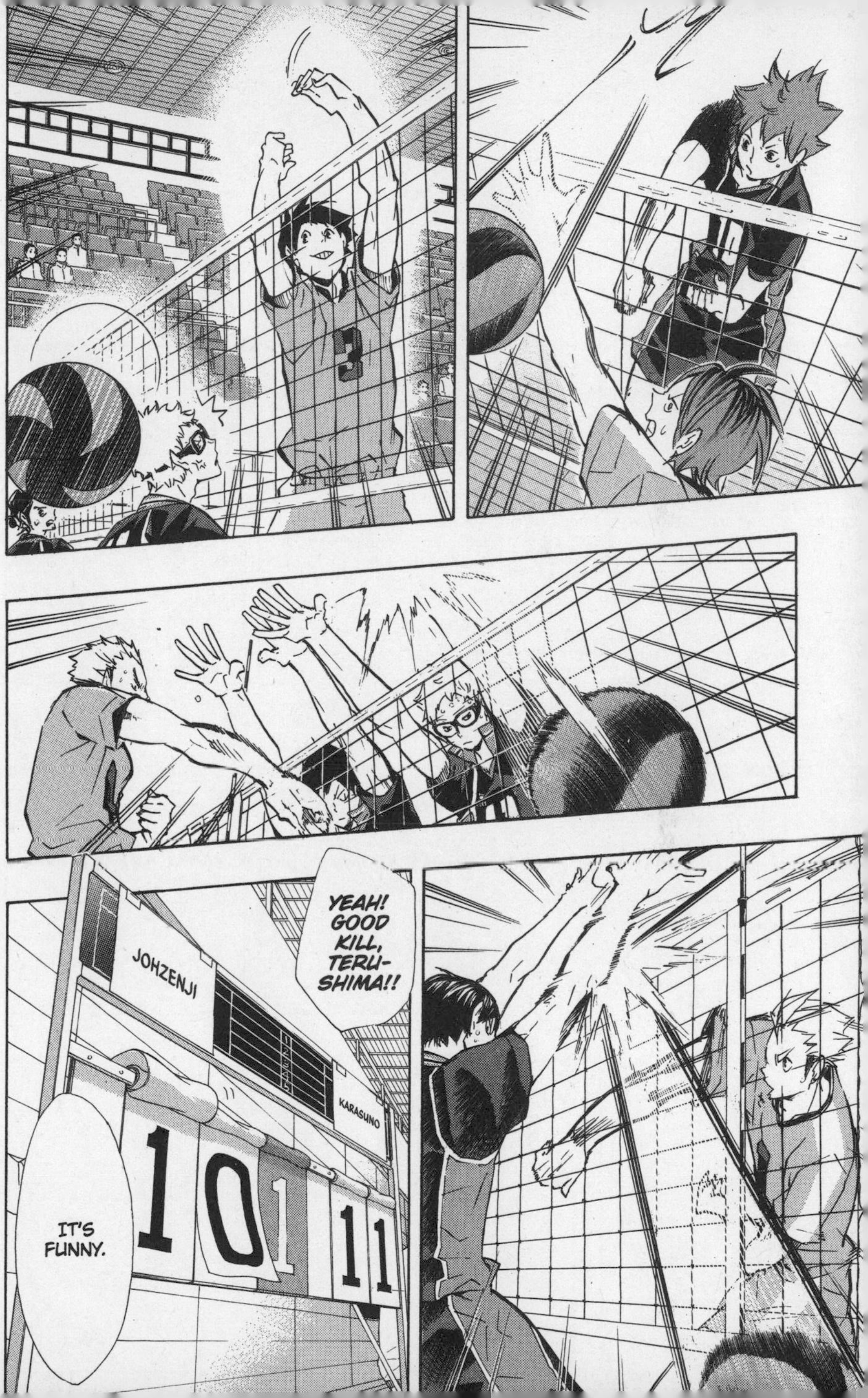
YEAH! GOOD KILL, TERU-SHIMA!!
JOHZENJI
KARASUNO
10 11
IT'S FUNNY.

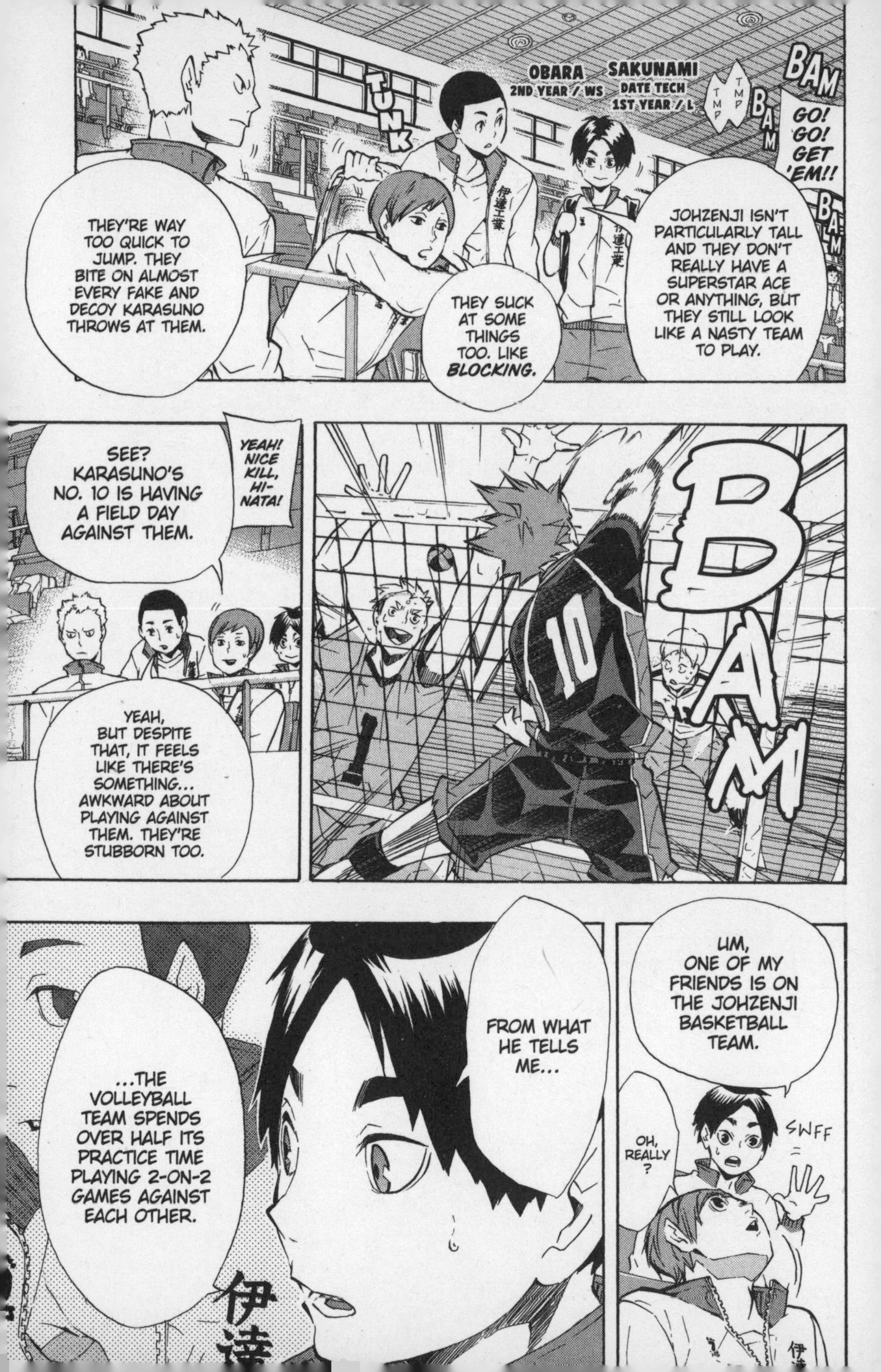
BAM
BAM
BAM
GO! GO! GET 'EM!!
TMP TMP
SAKUNAMI DATE TECH 1ST YEAR / L
OBARA 2ND YEAR / WS
JOHZENJI ISN'T PARTICULARLY TALL AND THEY DON'T REALLY HAVE A SUPERSTAR ACE OR ANYTHING, BUT THEY STILL LOOK LIKE A NASTY TEAM TO PLAY.
THEY SUCK AT SOME THINGS TOO. LIKE *BLOCKING.*
TUNK
THEY'RE WAY TOO QUICK TO JUMP. THEY BITE ON ALMOST EVERY FAKE AND DECOY KARASUNO THROWS AT THEM.
BAM
YEAH! NICE KILL, HI-NATA!
SEE? KARASUNO'S NO. 10 IS HAVING A FIELD DAY AGAINST THEM.
YEAH, BUT DESPITE THAT, IT FEELS LIKE THERE'S SOMETHING... AWKWARD ABOUT PLAYING AGAINST THEM. THEY'RE STUBBORN TOO.
UM, ONE OF MY FRIENDS IS ON THE JOHZENJI BASKETBALL TEAM.
OH, REALLY?
SWFF
FROM WHAT HE TELLS ME...
...THE VOLLEYBALL TEAM SPENDS OVER HALF ITS PRACTICE TIME PLAYING 2-ON-2 GAMES AGAINST EACH OTHER.

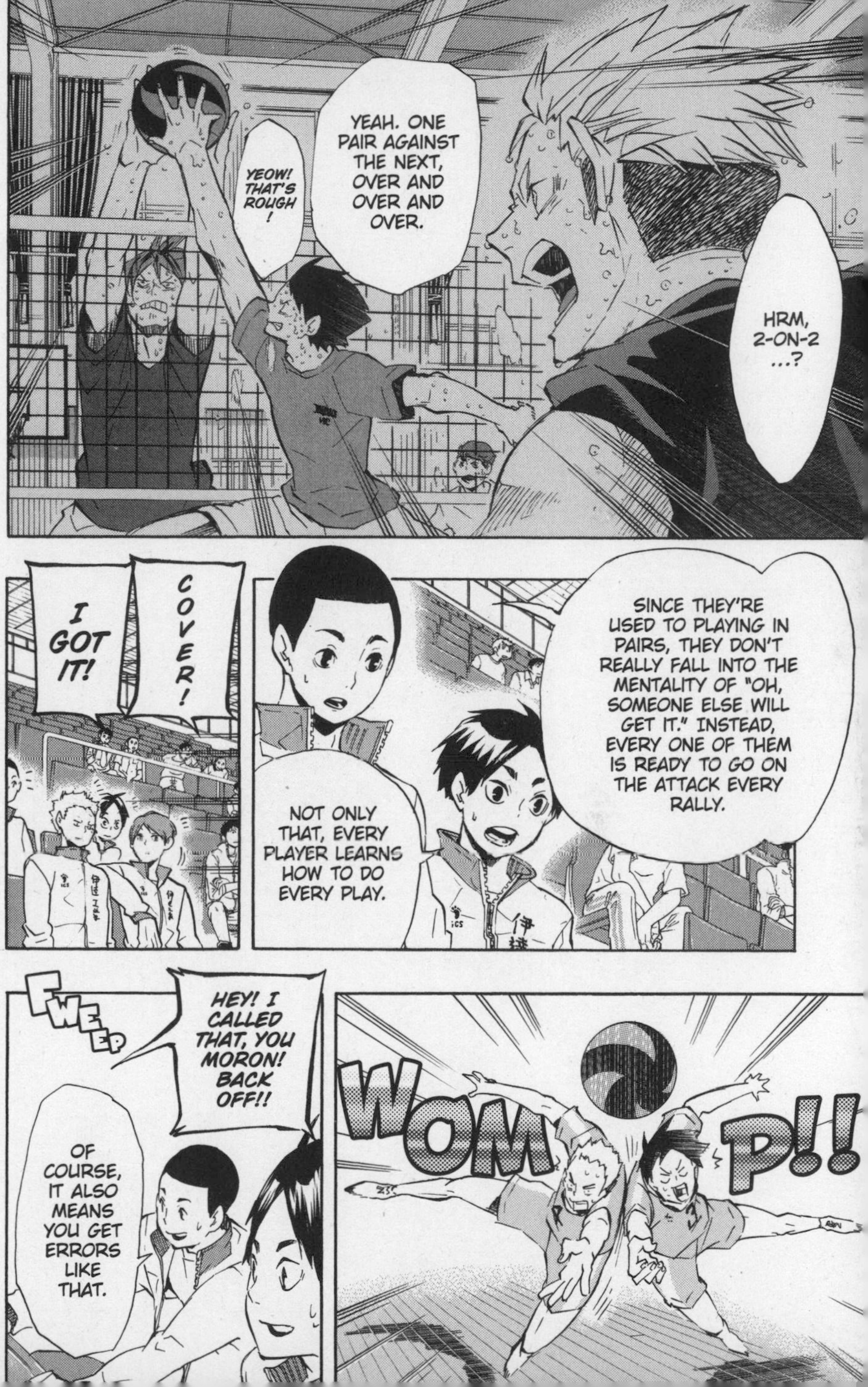
HRM, 2-ON-2 ...?
YEAH. ONE PAIR AGAINST THE NEXT, OVER AND OVER AND OVER.
YEOW! THAT'S ROUGH!
SINCE THEY'RE USED TO PLAYING IN PAIRS, THEY DON'T REALLY FALL INTO THE MENTALITY OF "OH, SOMEONE ELSE WILL GET IT." INSTEAD, EVERY ONE OF THEM IS READY TO GO ON THE ATTACK EVERY RALLY.
NOT ONLY THAT, EVERY PLAYER LEARNS HOW TO DO EVERY PLAY.
COVER!
I GOT IT!
WOMP!!
FWEEP
HEY! I CALLED THAT, YOU MORON! BACK OFF!!
OF COURSE, IT ALSO MEANS YOU GET ERRORS LIKE THAT.

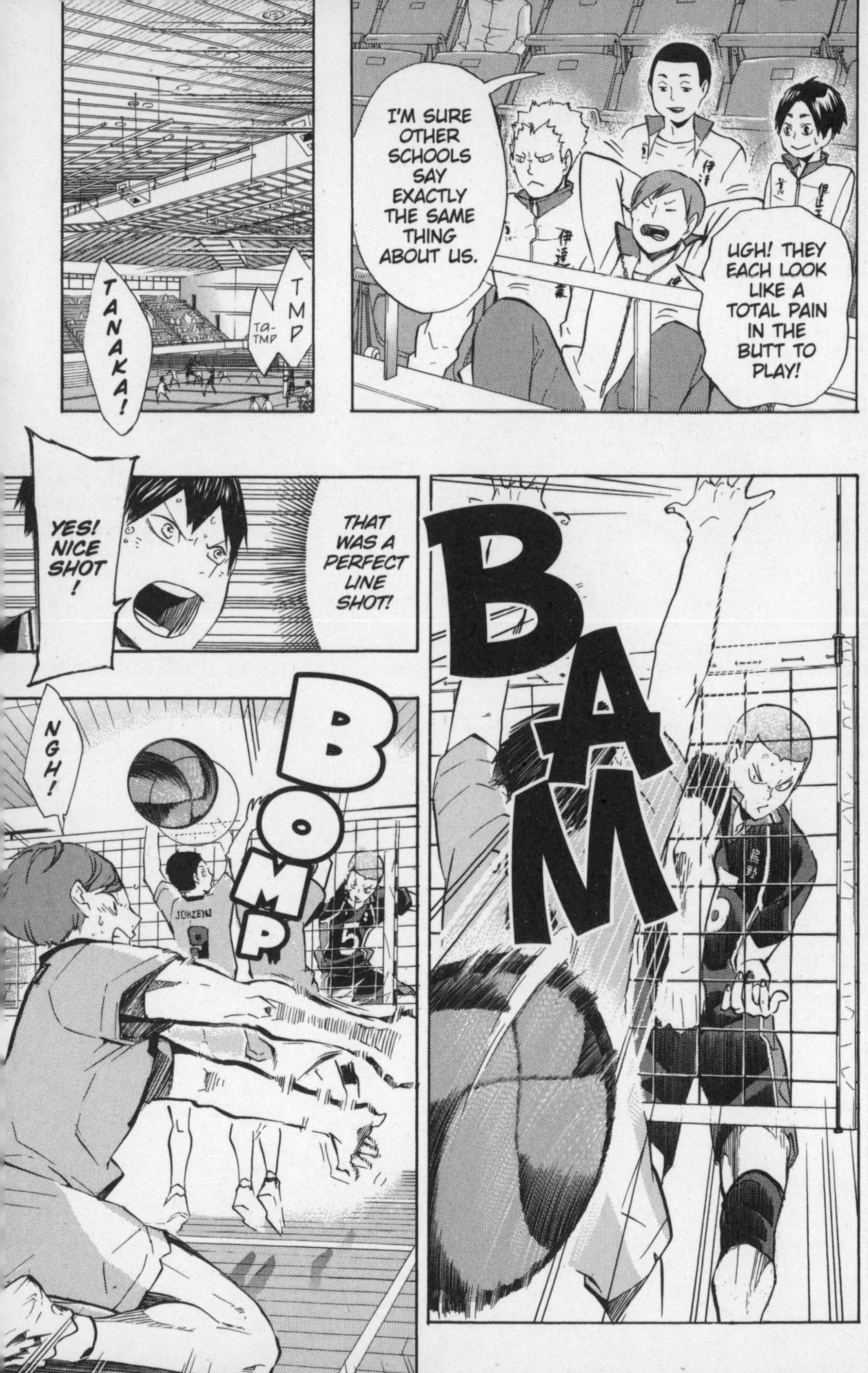
UGH! THEY EACH LOOK LIKE A TOTAL PAIN IN THE BUTT TO PLAY!
I'M SURE OTHER SCHOOLS SAY EXACTLY THE SAME THING ABOUT US.
TMP
TA-TMP
TANAKA!
BAM
THAT WAS A PERFECT LINE SHOT!
YES! NICE SHOT!
BOMP
NGH!
JOHZENJI

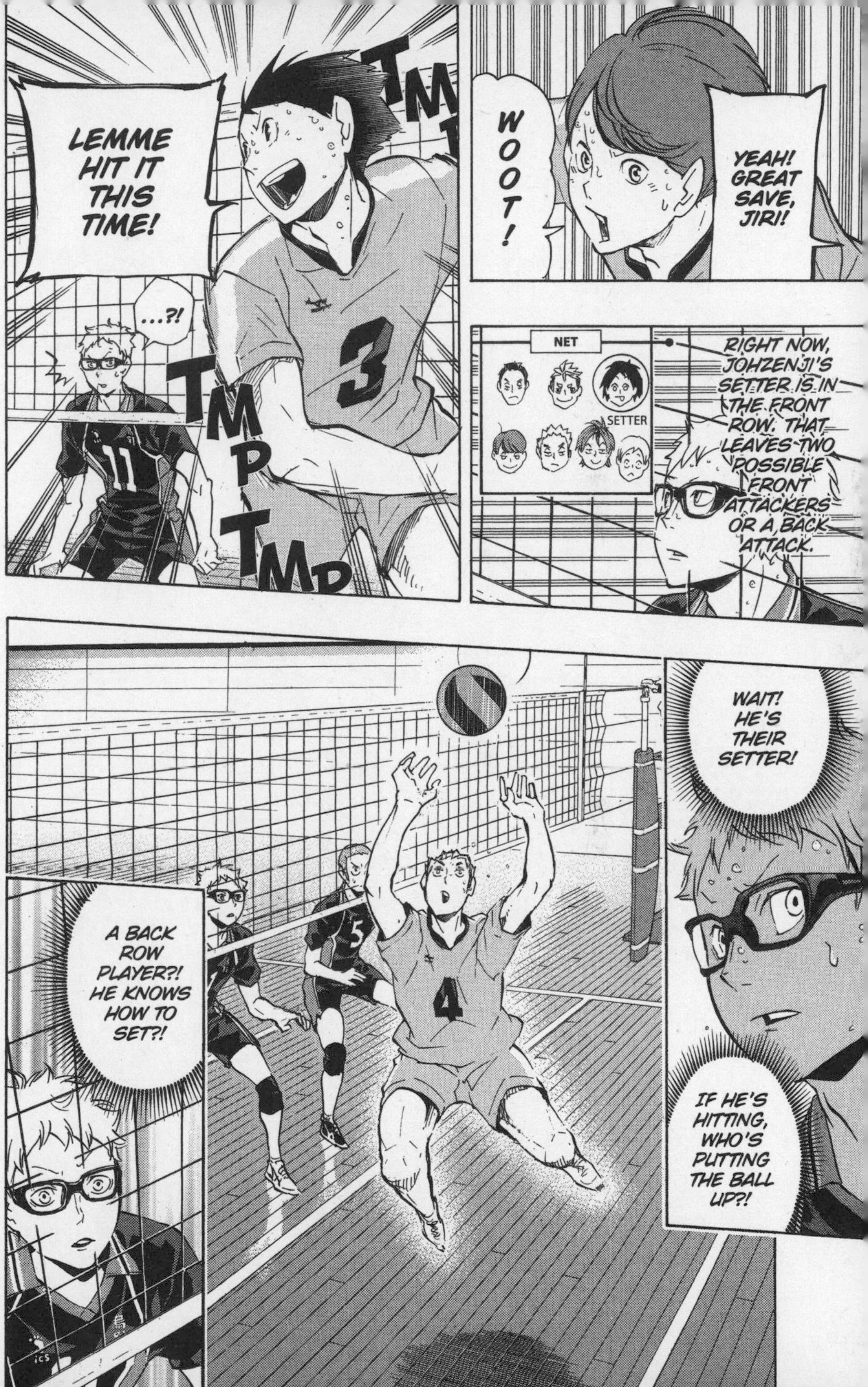
YEAH! GREAT SAVE, JIRI!
WOOT!
NET
SETTER
RIGHT NOW, JOHZENJI'S SETTER IS IN THE FRONT ROW. THAT LEAVES TWO POSSIBLE FRONT ATTACKERS OR A BACK ATTACK.
TMP
LEMME HIT IT THIS TIME!
...?!
TMP
TMP
WAIT! HE'S THEIR SETTER!
IF HE'S HITTING, WHO'S PUTTING THE BALL UP?!
A BACK ROW PLAYER?! HE KNOWS HOW TO SET?!

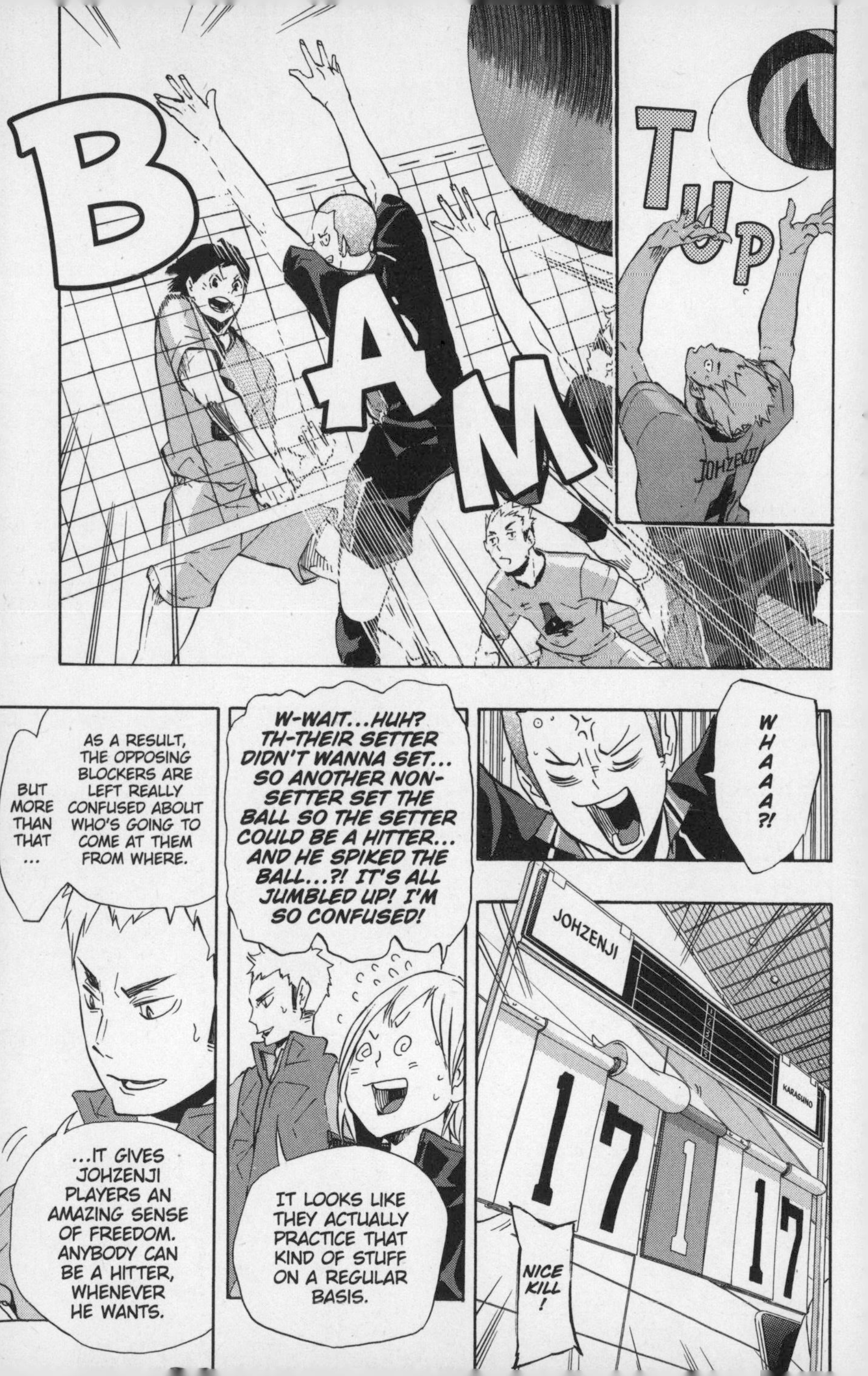
TUP
BAM
WHAAAA?!
JOHZENJI
KARASUNO
NICE KILL!
W-WAIT...HUH? TH-THEIR SETTER DIDN'T WANNA SET... SO ANOTHER NON-SETTER SET THE BALL SO THE SETTER COULD BE A HITTER... AND HE SPIKED THE BALL...?! IT'S ALL JUMBLED UP! I'M SO CONFUSED!
IT LOOKS LIKE THEY ACTUALLY PRACTICE THAT KIND OF STUFF ON A REGULAR BASIS.
AS A RESULT, THE OPPOSING BLOCKERS ARE LEFT REALLY CONFUSED ABOUT WHO'S GOING TO COME AT THEM FROM WHERE.
BUT MORE THAN THAT...
...IT GIVES JOHZENJI PLAYERS AN AMAZING SENSE OF FREEDOM. ANYBODY CAN BE A HITTER, WHENEVER HE WANTS.

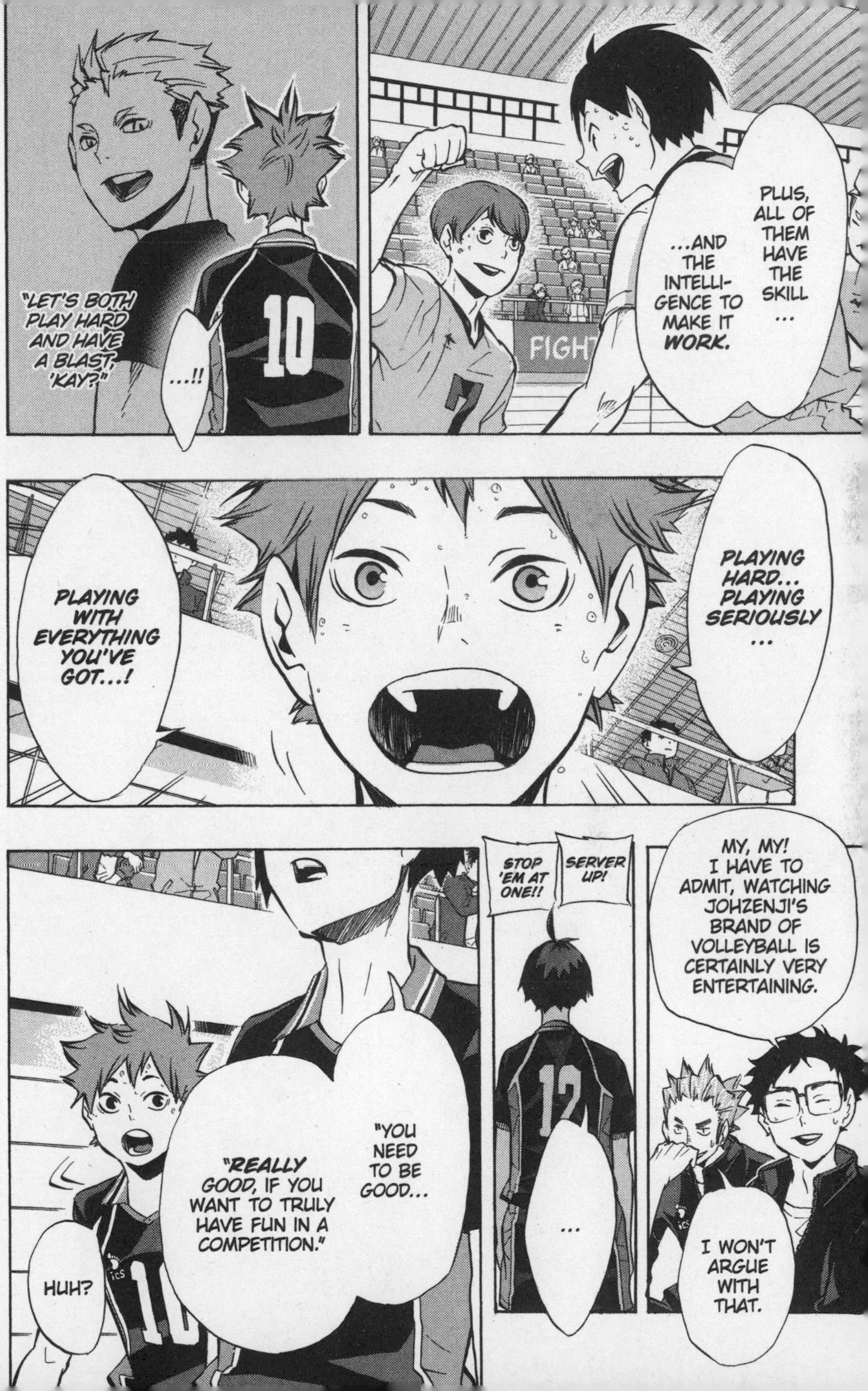
PLUS, ALL OF THEM HAVE THE SKILL...
...AND THE INTELLIGENCE TO MAKE IT *WORK.*
"LET'S BOTH PLAY HARD AND HAVE A BLAST, 'KAY?"
...!!
PLAYING HARD... PLAYING SERIOUSLY...
PLAYING WITH EVERYTHING YOU'VE GOT...!
MY, MY! I HAVE TO ADMIT, WATCHING JOHZENJI'S BRAND OF VOLLEYBALL IS CERTAINLY VERY ENTERTAINING.
I WON'T ARGUE WITH THAT.
SERVER UP!
STOP 'EM AT ONE!!
...
"YOU NEED TO BE GOOD...
"*REALLY* GOOD, IF YOU WANT TO TRULY HAVE FUN IN A COMPETITION."
HUH?

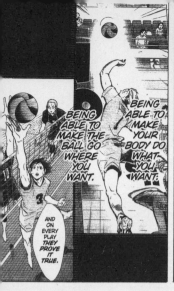

BEING ABLE TO MAKE THE BALL GO WHERE YOU WANT.

BEING ABLE TO MAKE YOUR BODY DO WHAT YOU WANT.

AND ON EVERY PLAY THEY PROVE IT TRUE.

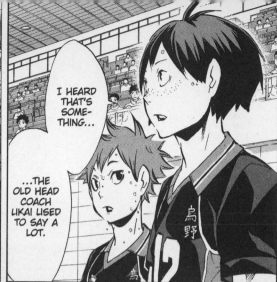

I HEARD THAT'S SOME-THING...

...THE OLD HEAD COACH UKAI USED TO SAY A LOT.

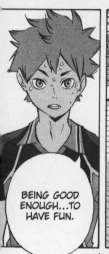

BEING GOOD ENOUGH...TO HAVE FUN.

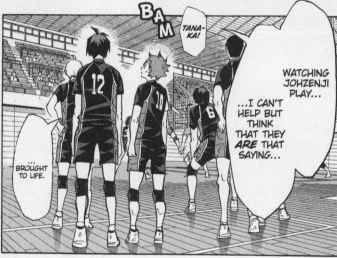

BAM

TANA-KA!

WATCHING JOHZENJI PLAY...

...I CAN'T HELP BUT THINK THAT THEY ARE THAT SAYING...

...BROUGHT TO LIFE.

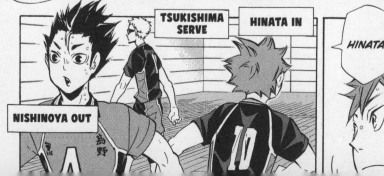

TSUKISHIMA SERVE

HINATA IN

NISHINOYA OUT

HINATA!

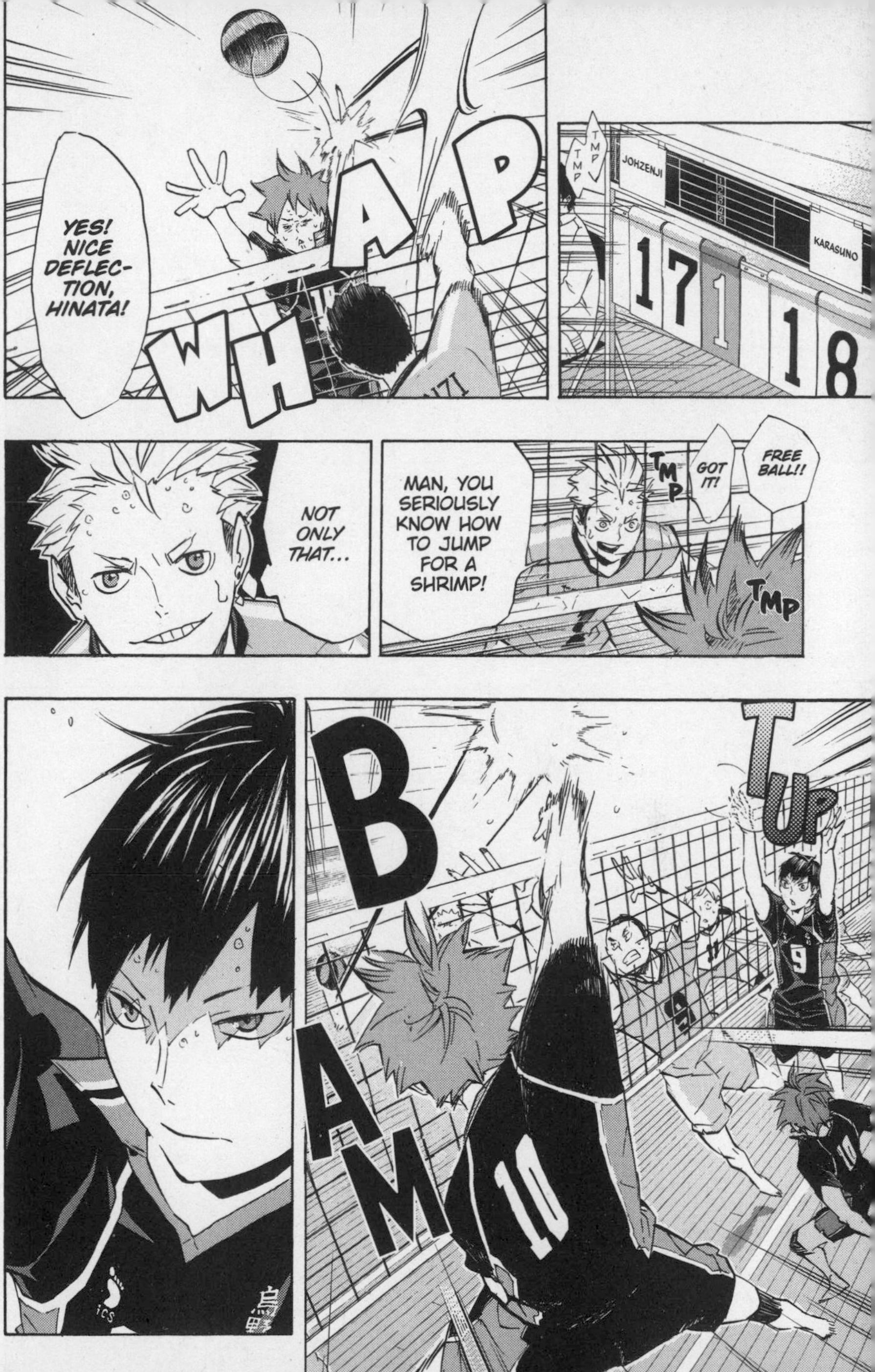
TMP TMP
JOHZENJI
KARASUNO
17
1
1
18
WHAP
YES! NICE DEFLECTION, HINATA!
FREE BALL!!
GOT IT!
TMP TMP
MAN, YOU SERIOUSLY KNOW HOW TO JUMP FOR A SHRIMP!
TMP
NOT ONLY THAT...
TUP
BAM

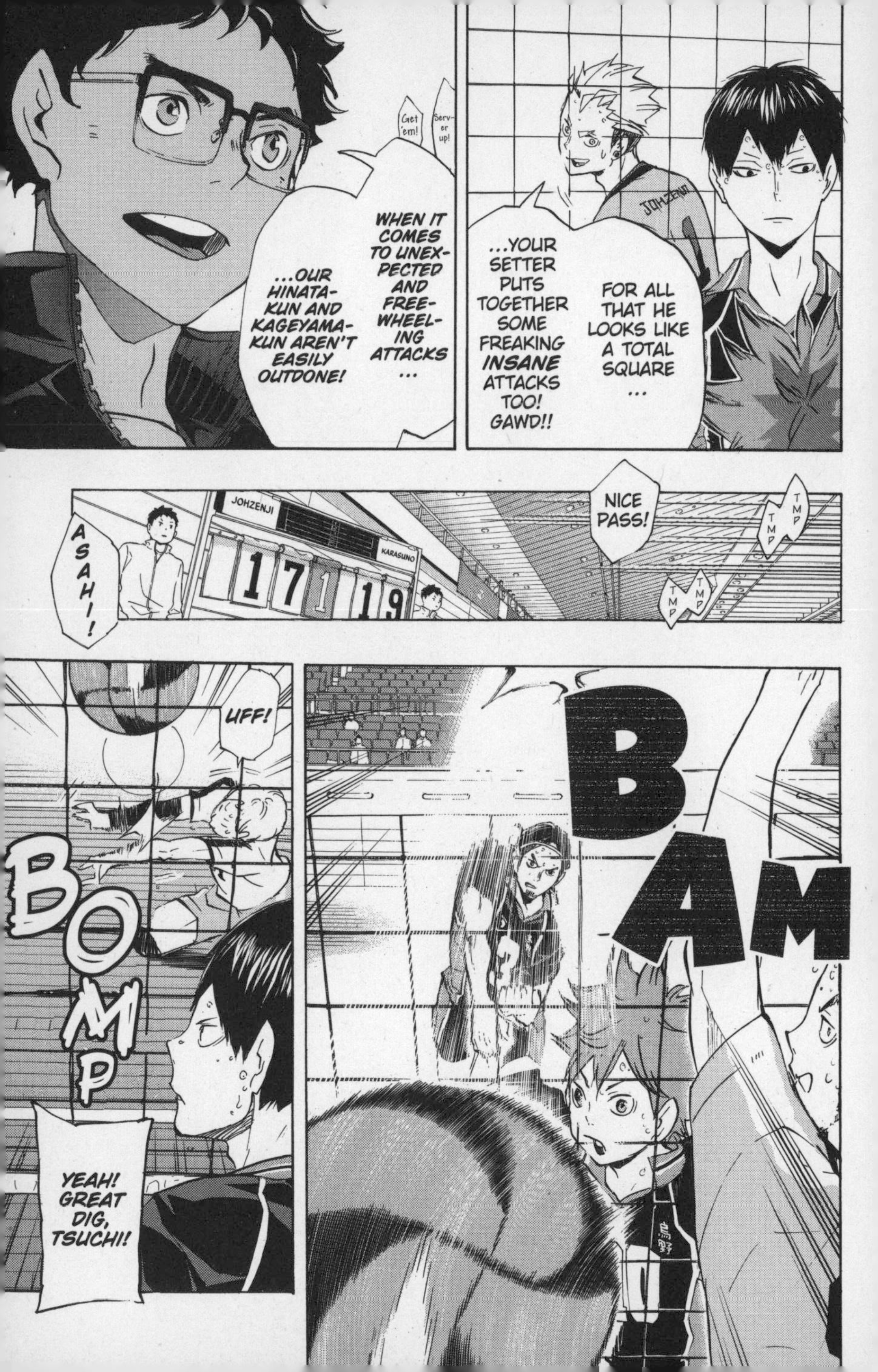
FOR ALL THAT HE LOOKS LIKE A TOTAL SQUARE ...
...YOUR SETTER PUTS TOGETHER SOME FREAKING INSANE ATTACKS TOO! GAWD!!
Serv-er up!
Get 'em!
WHEN IT COMES TO UNEXPECTED AND FREE-WHEELING ATTACKS ...
...OUR HINATA-KUN AND KAGEYAMA-KUN AREN'T EASILY OUTDONE!
TMP TMP
TMP TMP
NICE PASS!
JOHZENJI
KARASUNO
17 1 1 19
ASAHI!
BAM
UFF!
BOMP
YEAH! GREAT DIG, TSUCHI!

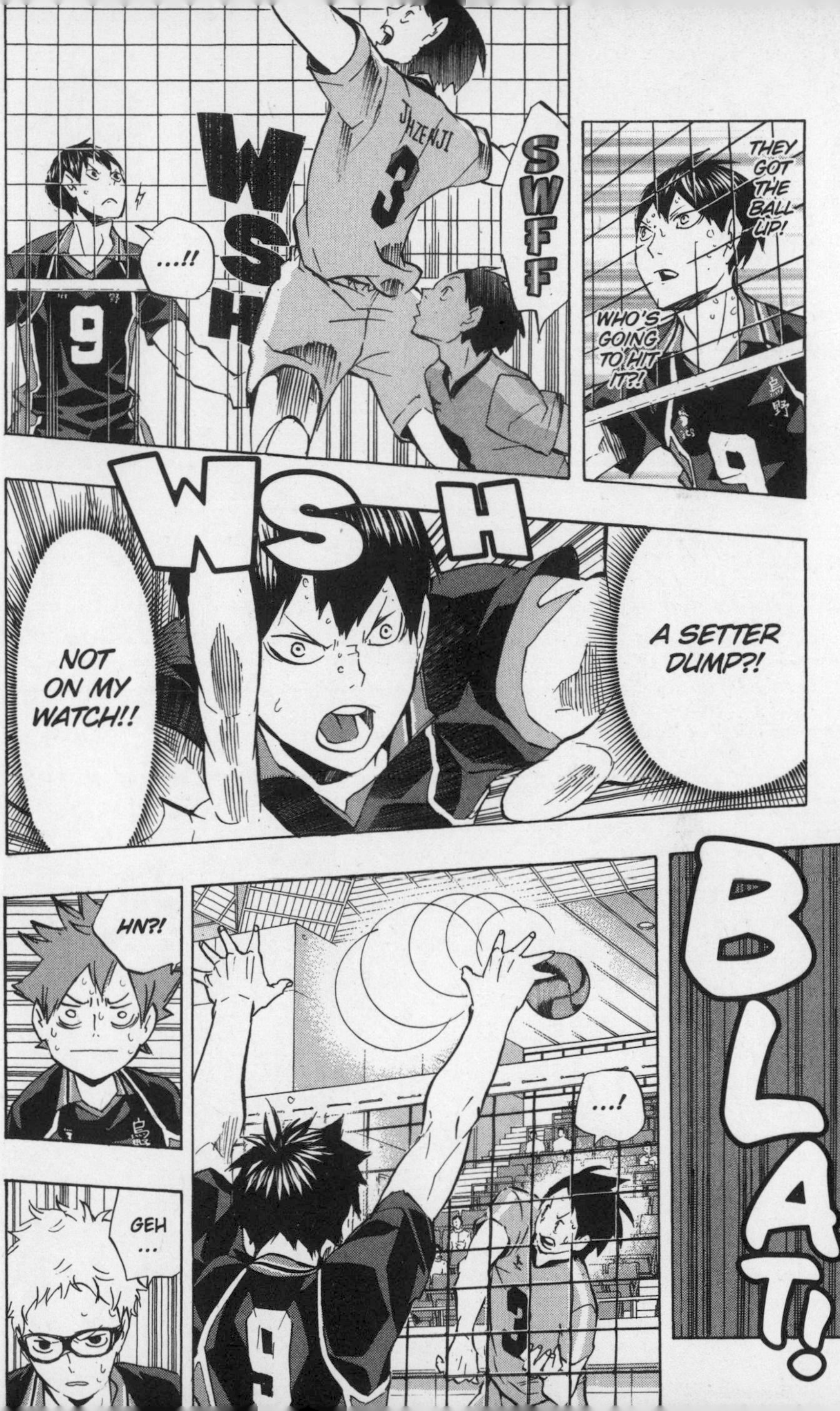
THEY GOT THE BALL UP!
WHO'S GOING TO HIT IT?!
SWFF
WSH
...!!
WSH
A SETTER DUMP?!
NOT ON MY WATCH!!
BLAT!
...!
HN?!
GEH ...

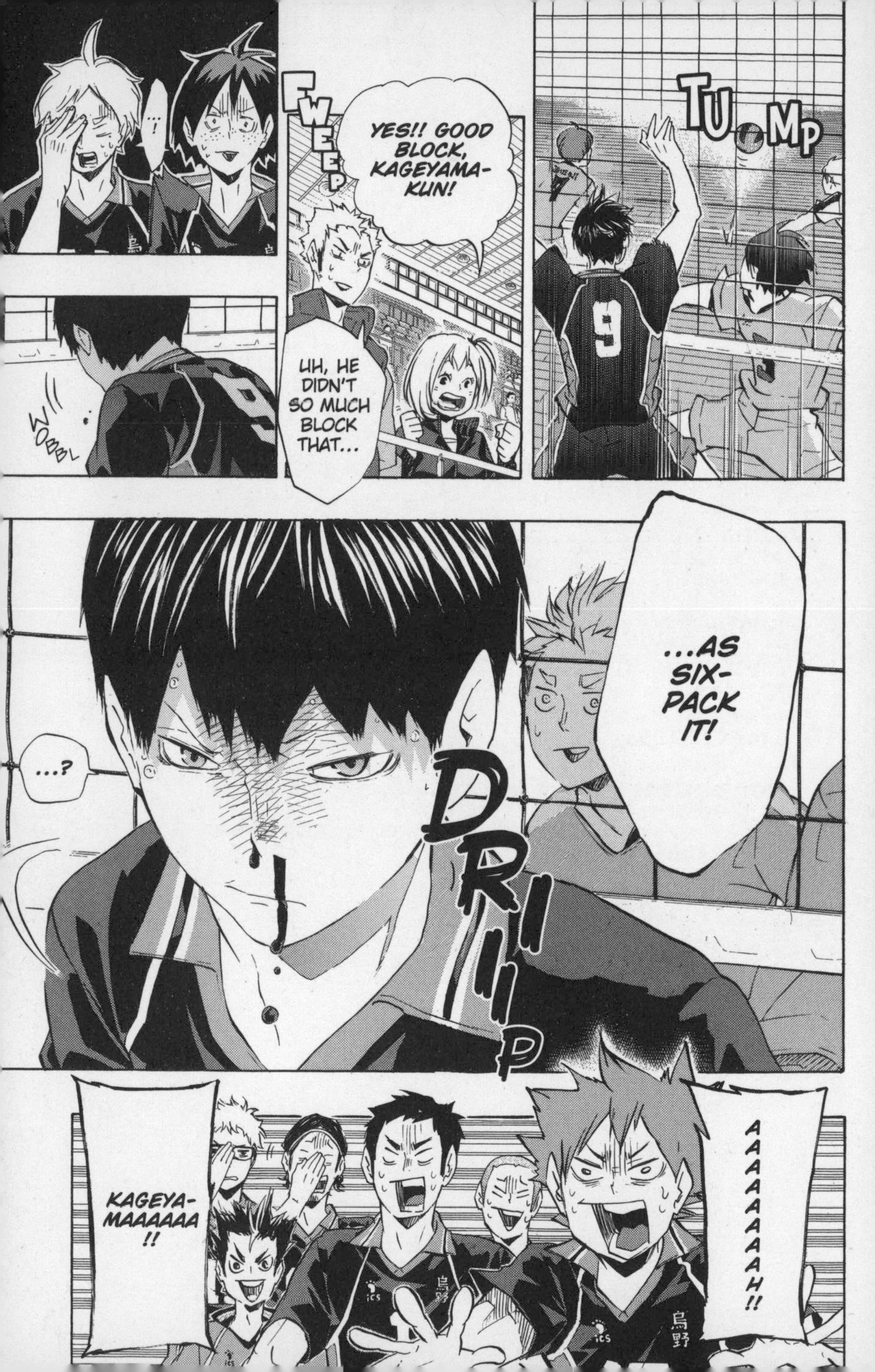
TUMP
FWEEP
YES!! GOOD BLOCK, KAGEYAMA-KUN!
UH, HE DIDN'T SO MUCH BLOCK THAT...
...!
WOBBL
...AS SIX-PACK IT!
DRIIIP
...?
AAAAAAAAAAH!!
KAGEYA-MAAAAAA!!

YUJI TERUSHIMA

JOHZENJI HIGH SCHOOL
CLASS 2-7

POSITION:
WING SPIKER

HEIGHT: 5'10"

WEIGHT: 147 LBS.
(AS OF APRIL, 2ND YEAR OF HIGH SCHOOL)

BIRTHDAY: APRIL 18

FAVORITE FOOD:
THOSE SAUSAGE-IN-A-BUN THINGS...

CURRENT WORRY:
THE BREADS AND SANDWICHES AT THE SCHOOL CAFETERIA DON'T SEEM AS GOOD AS THEY USED TO BE FOR SOME REASON...

ABILITY PARAMETERS
(5-POINT SCALE)

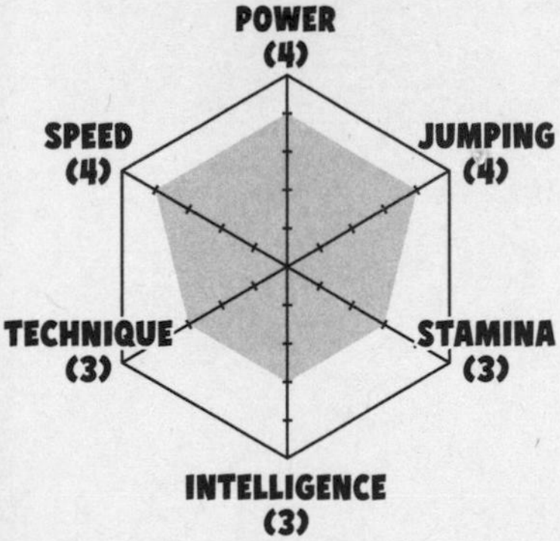

POWER (4)
JUMPING (4)
STAMINA (3)
INTELLIGENCE (3)
TECHNIQUE (3)
SPEED (4)

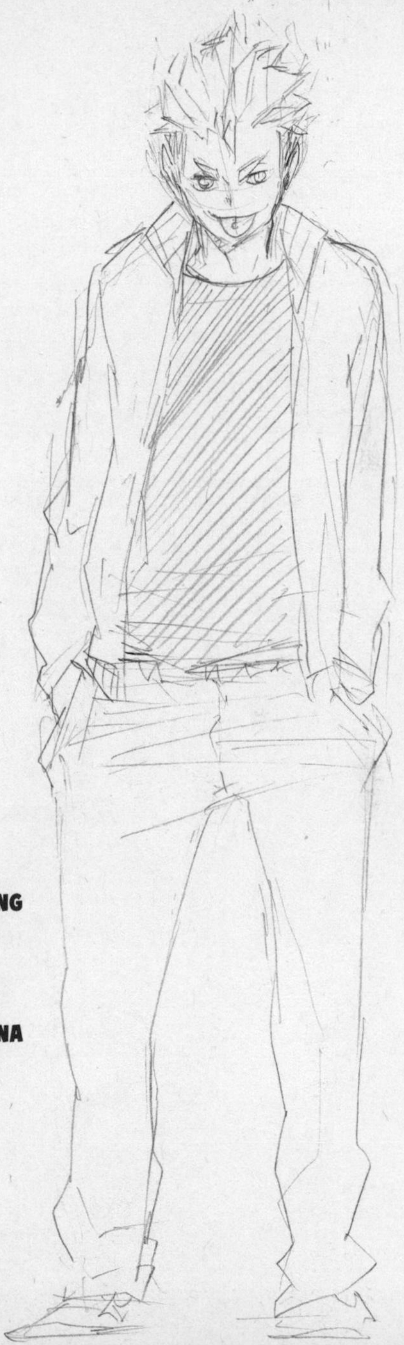

CHAPTER 111: Inexperienced

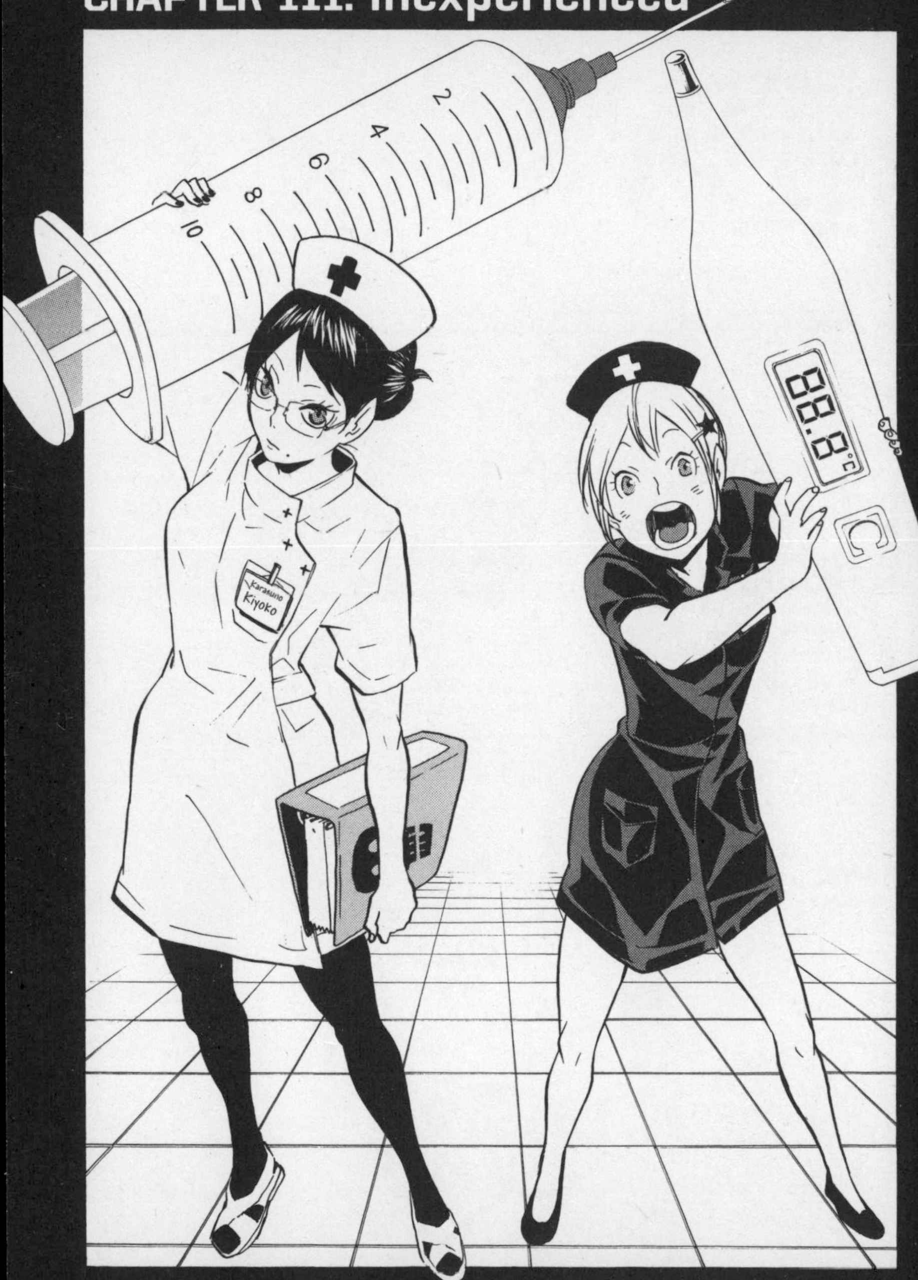
2
4
6
8
10
Karasuno
Kiyoko
88.8°C
C

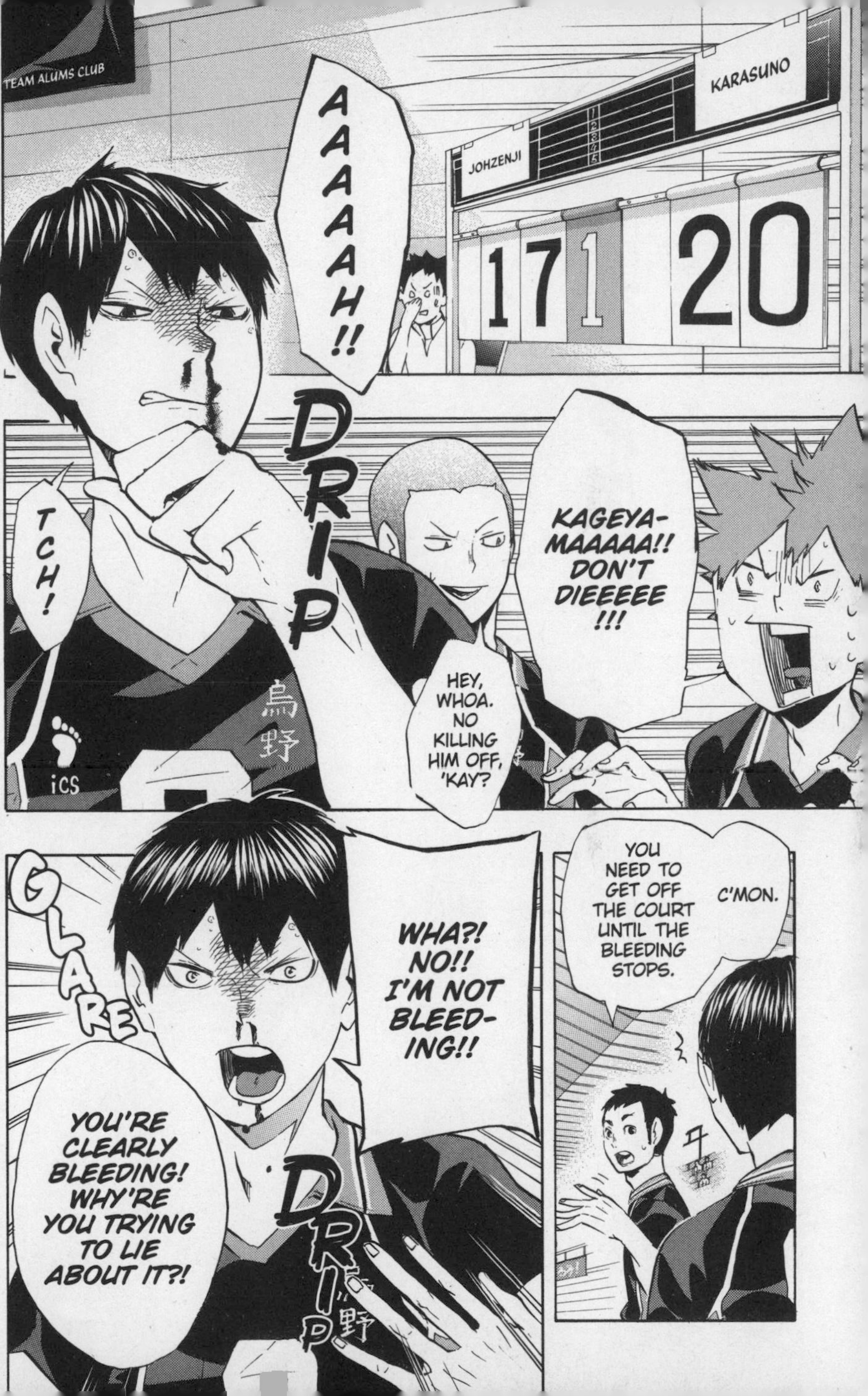
TEAM ALUMS CLUB
KARASUNO
JOHZENJI
17 1 20
AAAAAH!!
DRIP
KAGEYA-MAAAAA!! DON'T DIEEEEE!!!
HEY, WHOA. NO KILLING HIM OFF, 'KAY?
TCH!
C'MON.
YOU NEED TO GET OFF THE COURT UNTIL THE BLEEDING STOPS.
WHA?! NO!! I'M NOT BLEED-ING!!
GLARE
YOU'RE CLEARLY BLEEDING! WHY'RE YOU TRYING TO LIE ABOUT IT?!
DRIP

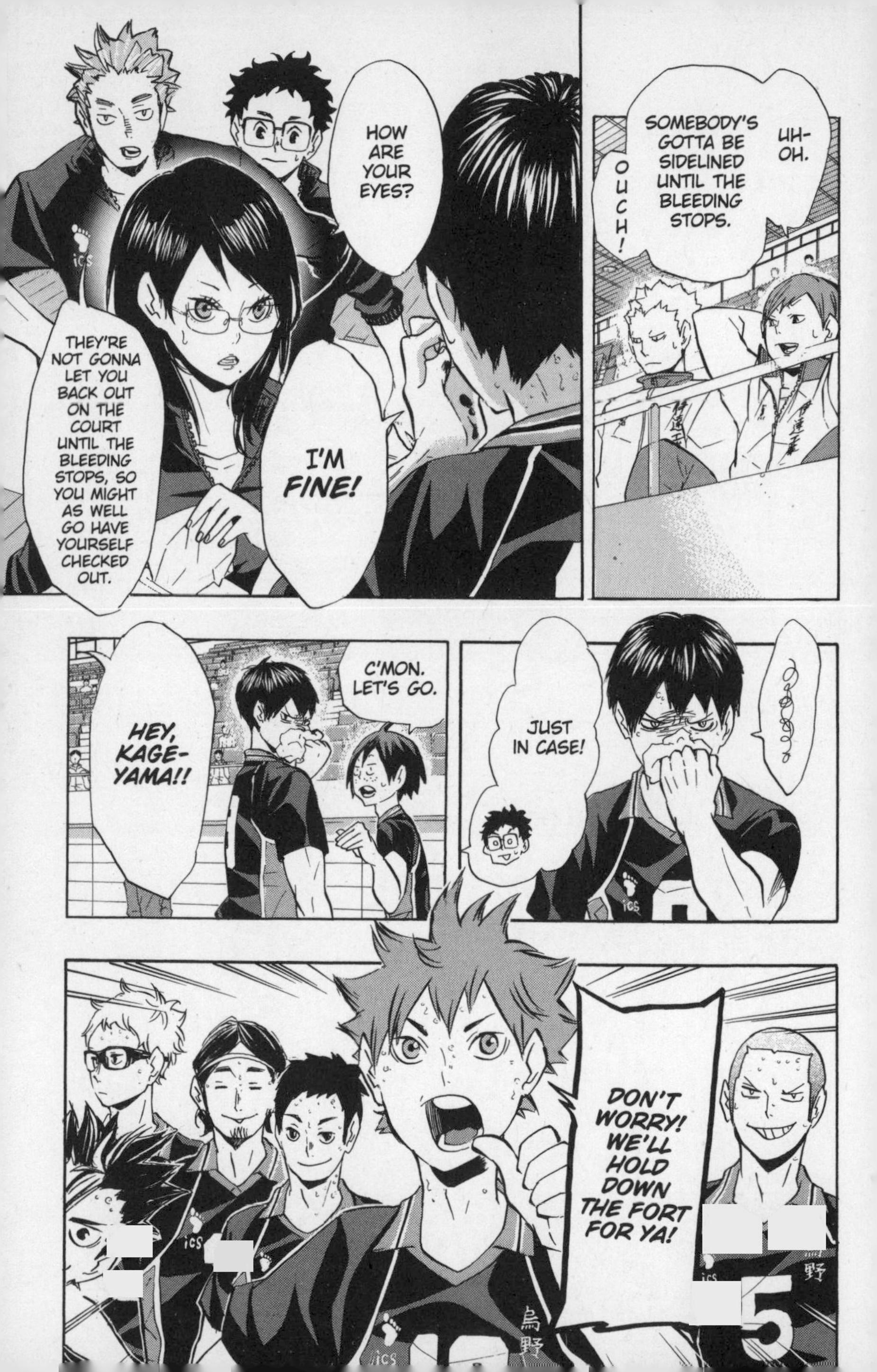
UH-OH.
SOMEBODY'S GOTTA BE SIDELINED UNTIL THE BLEEDING STOPS.
OUCH!
HOW ARE YOUR EYES?
I'M FINE!
THEY'RE NOT GONNA LET YOU BACK OUT ON THE COURT UNTIL THE BLEEDING STOPS, SO YOU MIGHT AS WELL GO HAVE YOURSELF CHECKED OUT.
JUST IN CASE!
C'MON. LET'S GO.
HEY, KAGE-YAMA!!
DON'T WORRY! WE'LL HOLD DOWN THE FORT FOR YA!

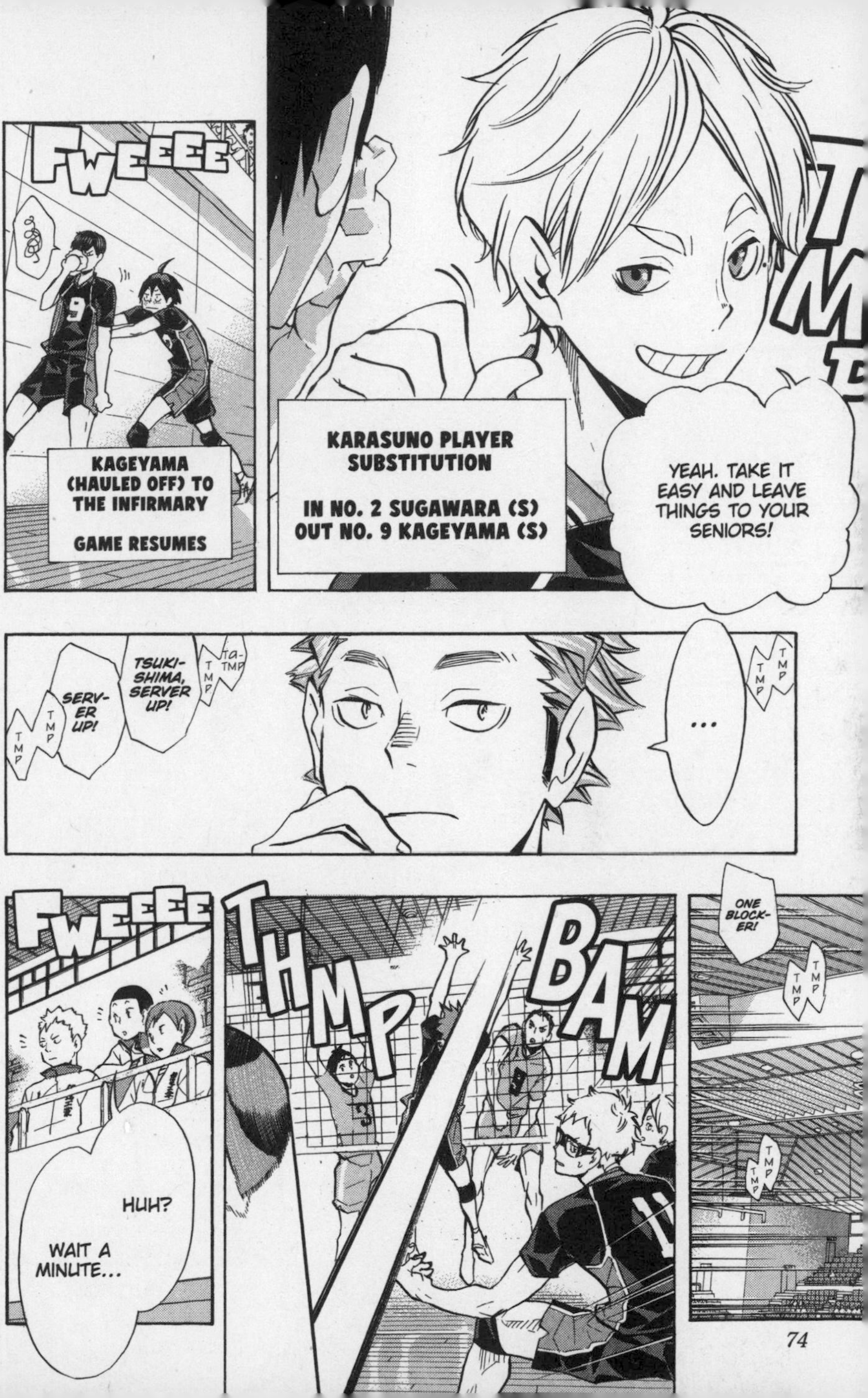
KARASUNO PLAYER SUBSTITUTION
IN NO. 2 SUGAWARA (S) OUT NO. 9 KAGEYAMA (S)
YEAH. TAKE IT EASY AND LEAVE THINGS TO YOUR SENIORS!
FWEEEE
KAGEYAMA (HAULED OFF) TO THE INFIRMARY
GAME RESUMES
TMP TMP
...
TA-TMP TMP
TSUKI-SHIMA, SERVER UP!
SERV-ER UP!
TMP TMP
ONE BLOCK-ER!
TMP TMP
TMP TMP
BAM
THMP
FWEEEE
HUH?
WAIT A MINUTE...

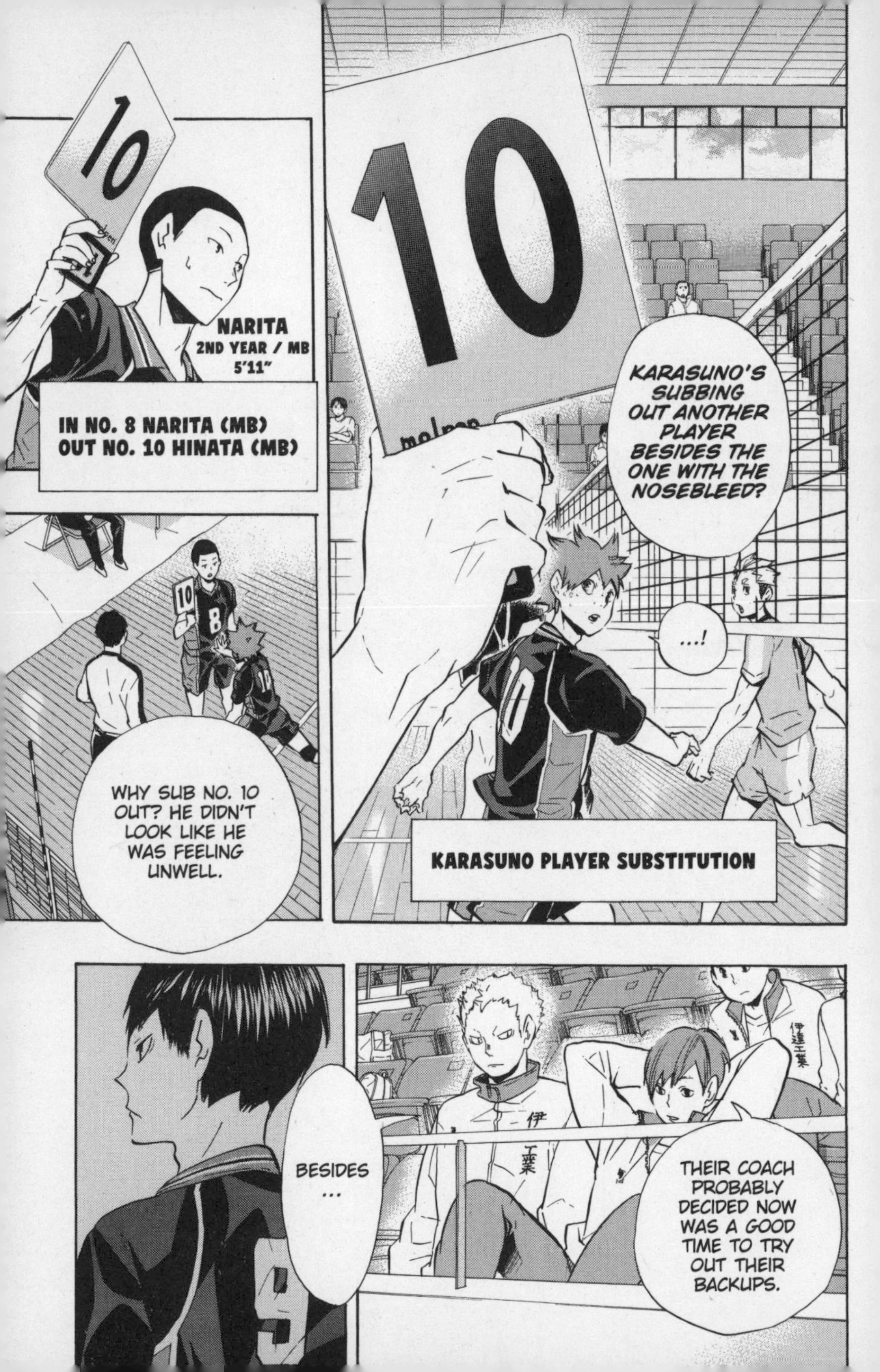
KARASUNO'S SUBBING OUT ANOTHER PLAYER BESIDES THE ONE WITH THE NOSEBLEED?
...!
KARASUNO PLAYER SUBSTITUTION
NARITA
2ND YEAR / MB
5'11"
IN NO. 8 NARITA (MB)
OUT NO. 10 HINATA (MB)
WHY SUB NO. 10 OUT? HE DIDN'T LOOK LIKE HE WAS FEELING UNWELL.
THEIR COACH PROBABLY DECIDED NOW WAS A GOOD TIME TO TRY OUT THEIR BACKUPS.
BESIDES...

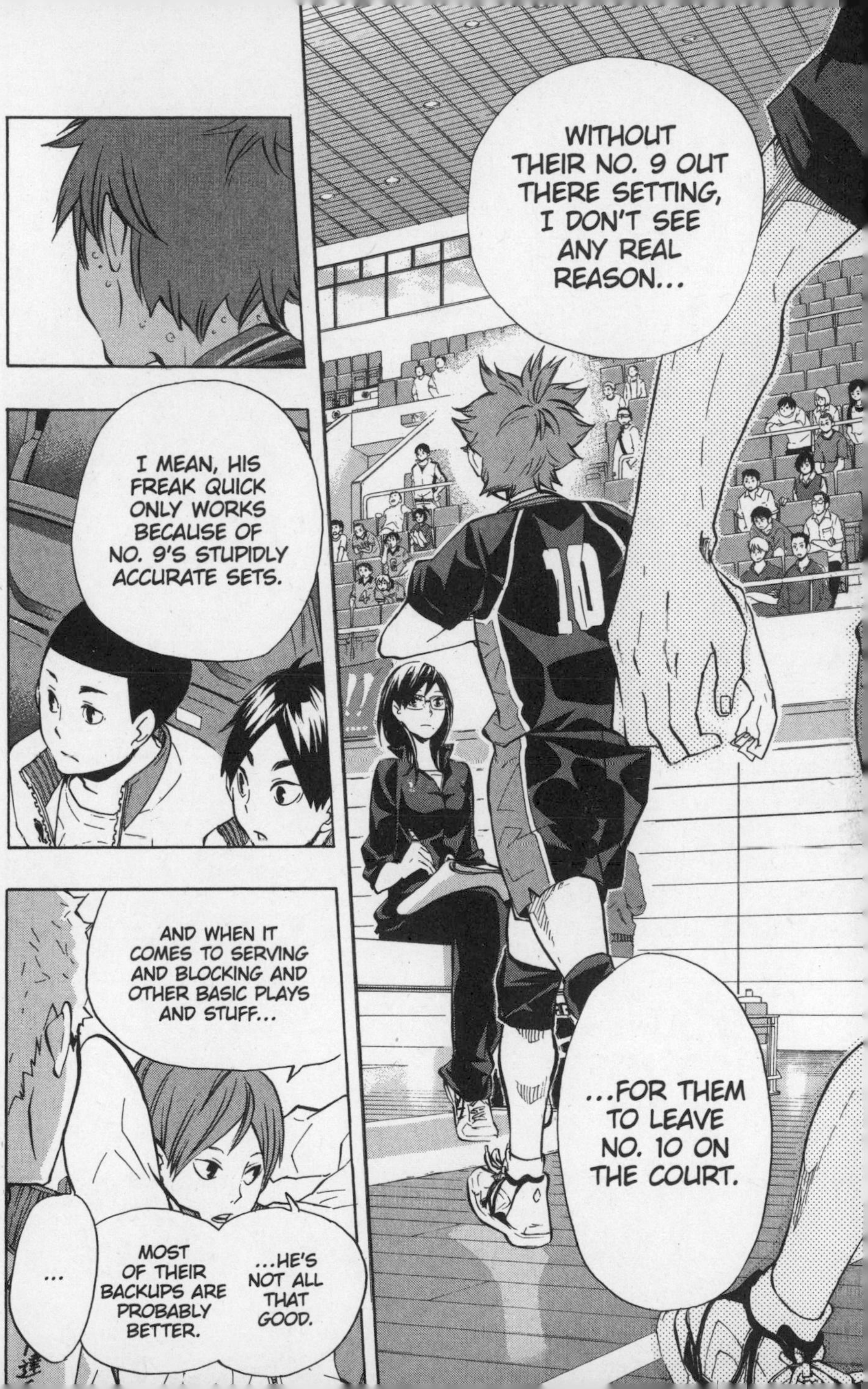
WITHOUT THEIR NO. 9 OUT THERE SETTING, I DON'T SEE ANY REAL REASON...
...FOR THEM TO LEAVE NO. 10 ON THE COURT.
I MEAN, HIS FREAK QUICK ONLY WORKS BECAUSE OF NO. 9'S STUPIDLY ACCURATE SETS.
AND WHEN IT COMES TO SERVING AND BLOCKING AND OTHER BASIC PLAYS AND STUFF...
...HE'S NOT ALL THAT GOOD.
MOST OF THEIR BACKUPS ARE PROBABLY BETTER.
...

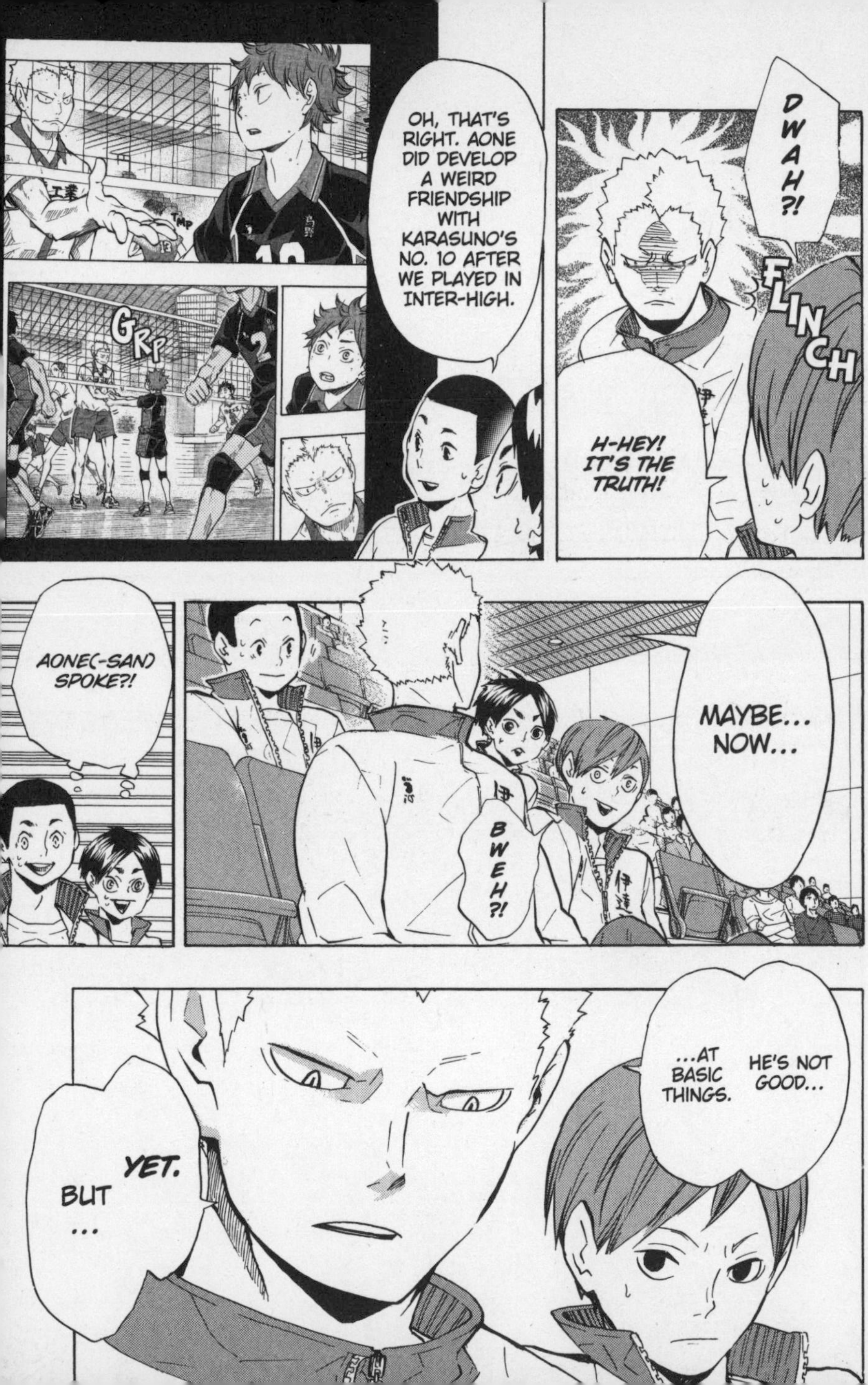
OH, THAT'S RIGHT. AONE DID DEVELOP A WEIRD FRIENDSHIP WITH KARASUNO'S NO. 10 AFTER WE PLAYED IN INTER-HIGH.
TMP
GRP
DWAH?!
FLINCH
H-HEY! IT'S THE TRUTH!
MAYBE... NOW...
BWEH?!
AONE(-SAN) SPOKE?!
HE'S NOT GOOD...
...AT BASIC THINGS.
BUT ...
YET.

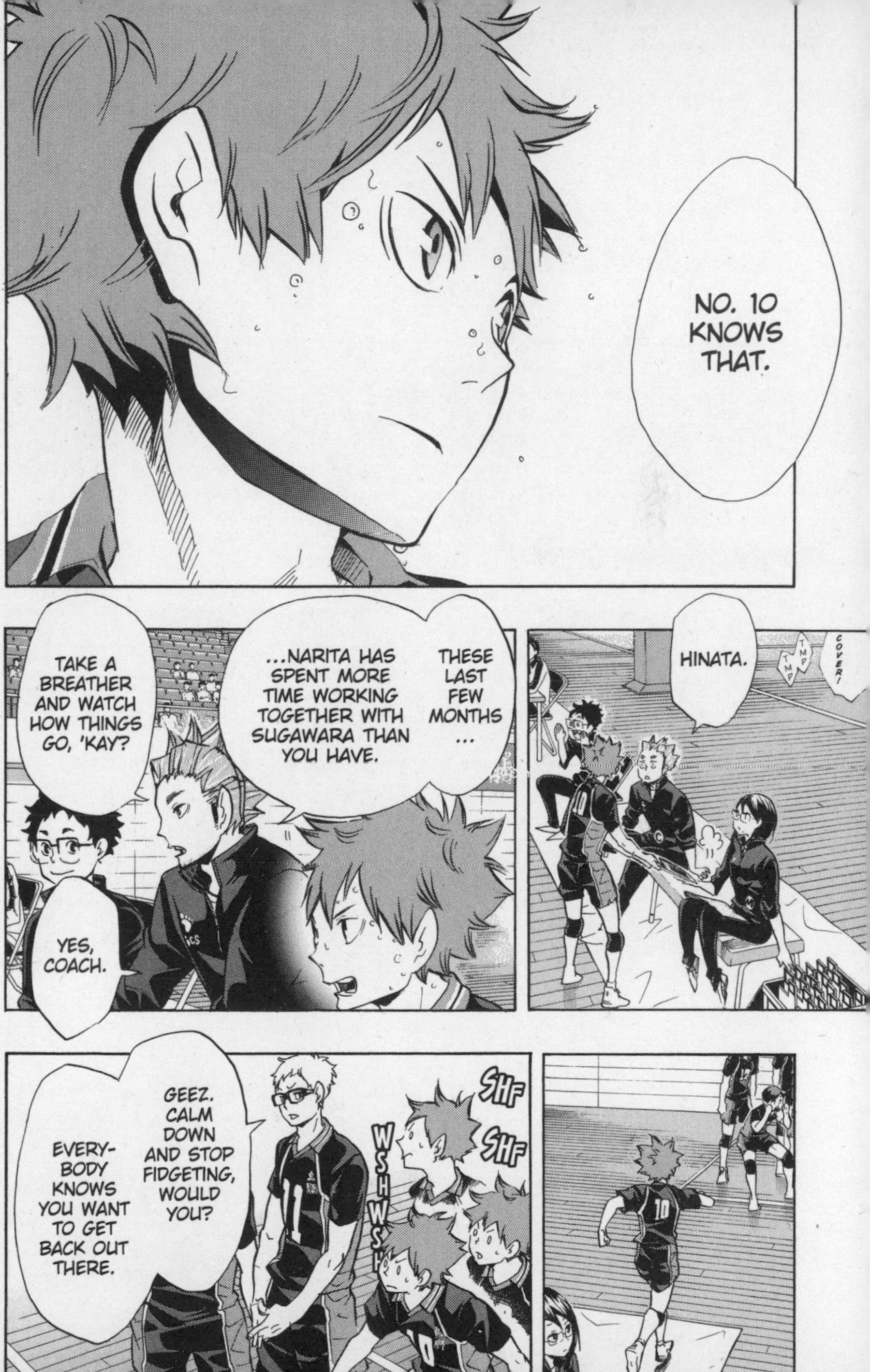
NO. 10 KNOWS THAT.
HINATA.
TMP TMP
COVER!
THESE LAST FEW MONTHS ...
...NARITA HAS SPENT MORE TIME WORKING TOGETHER WITH SUGAWARA THAN YOU HAVE.
TAKE A BREATHER AND WATCH HOW THINGS GO, 'KAY?
YES, COACH.
SHF
SHF
WSHWSH
GEEZ. CALM DOWN AND STOP FIDGETING, WOULD YOU?
EVERY-BODY KNOWS YOU WANT TO GET BACK OUT THERE.

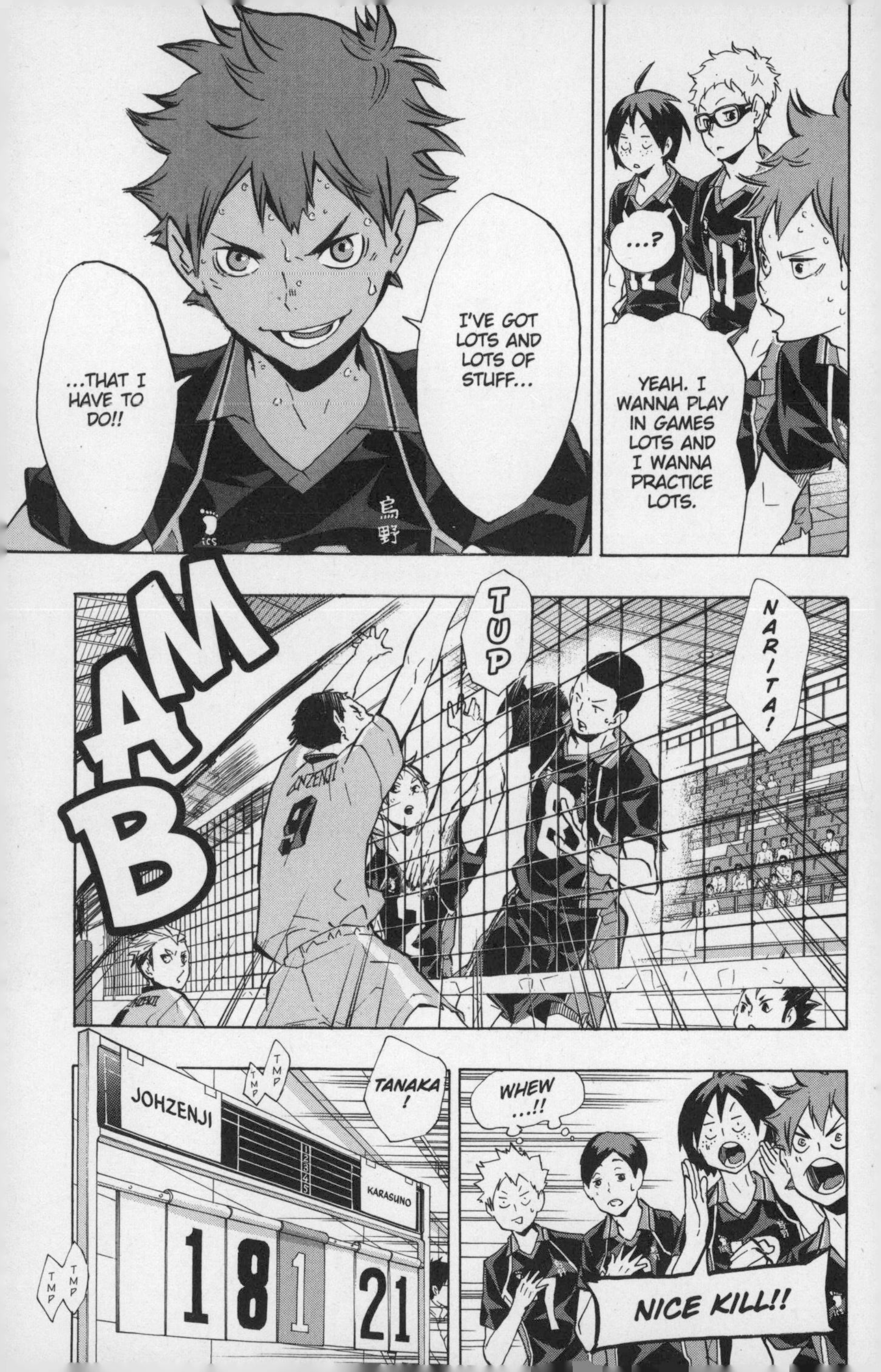

...?
YEAH. I WANNA PLAY IN GAMES LOTS AND I WANNA PRACTICE LOTS.
I'VE GOT LOTS AND LOTS OF STUFF...
...THAT I HAVE TO DO!!
NARITA!
TUP
BAM
WHEW ...!!
NICE KILL!!
TANAKA!
TMP TMP
JOHZENJI
KARASUNO
18 1 21
TMP TMP

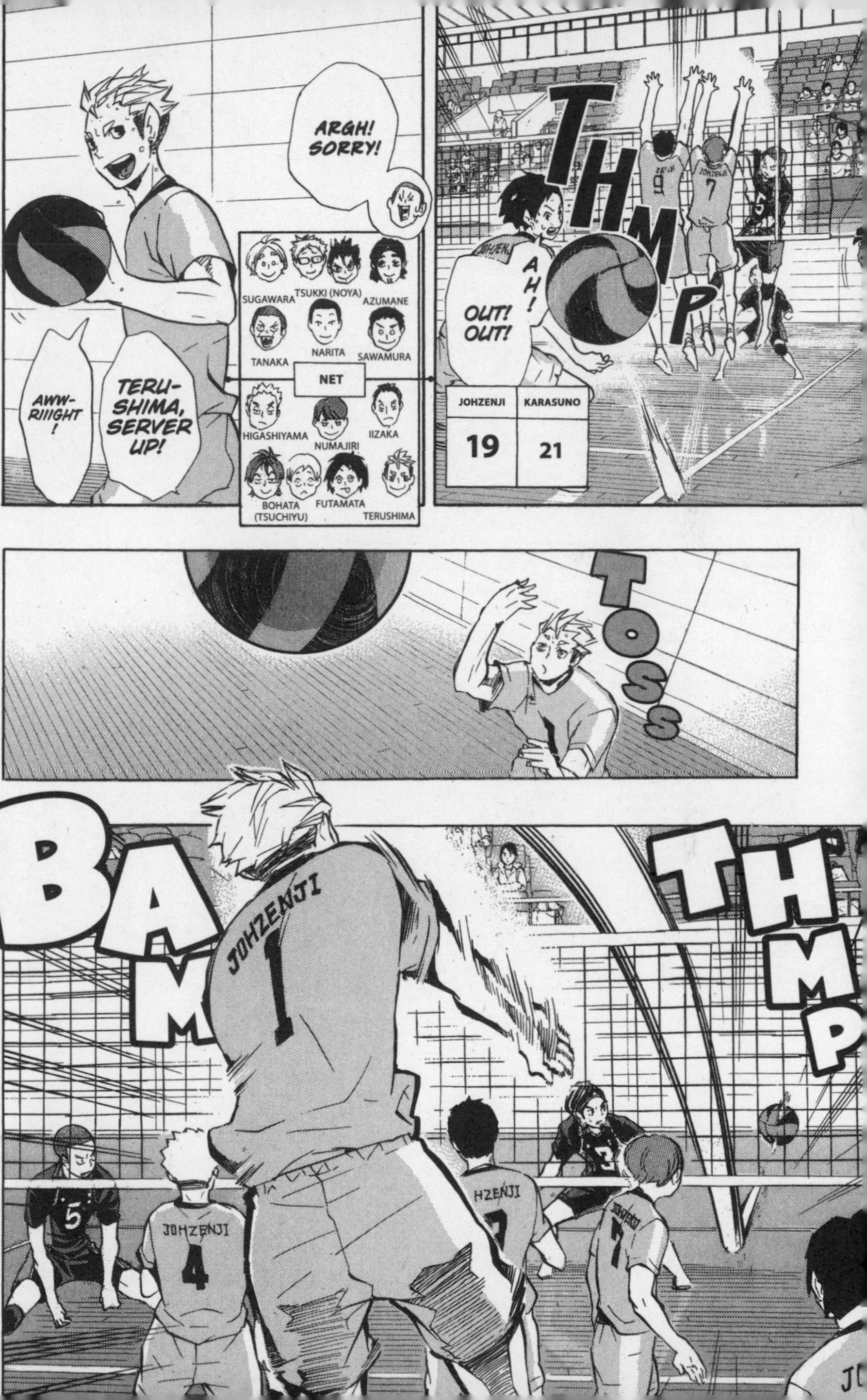
THMP
AH!
OUT! OUT!
JOHZENJI 19
KARASUNO 21
ARGH! SORRY!
SUGAWARA
TSUKKI (NOYA)
AZUMANE
TANAKA
NARITA
SAWAMURA
NET
HIGASHIYAMA
NUMAJIRI
IIZAKA
BOHATA (TSUCHIYU)
FUTAMATA
TERUSHIMA
TERU-SHIMA, SERVER UP!
AWW-RIIIGHT!
TOSS
BAM
THMP

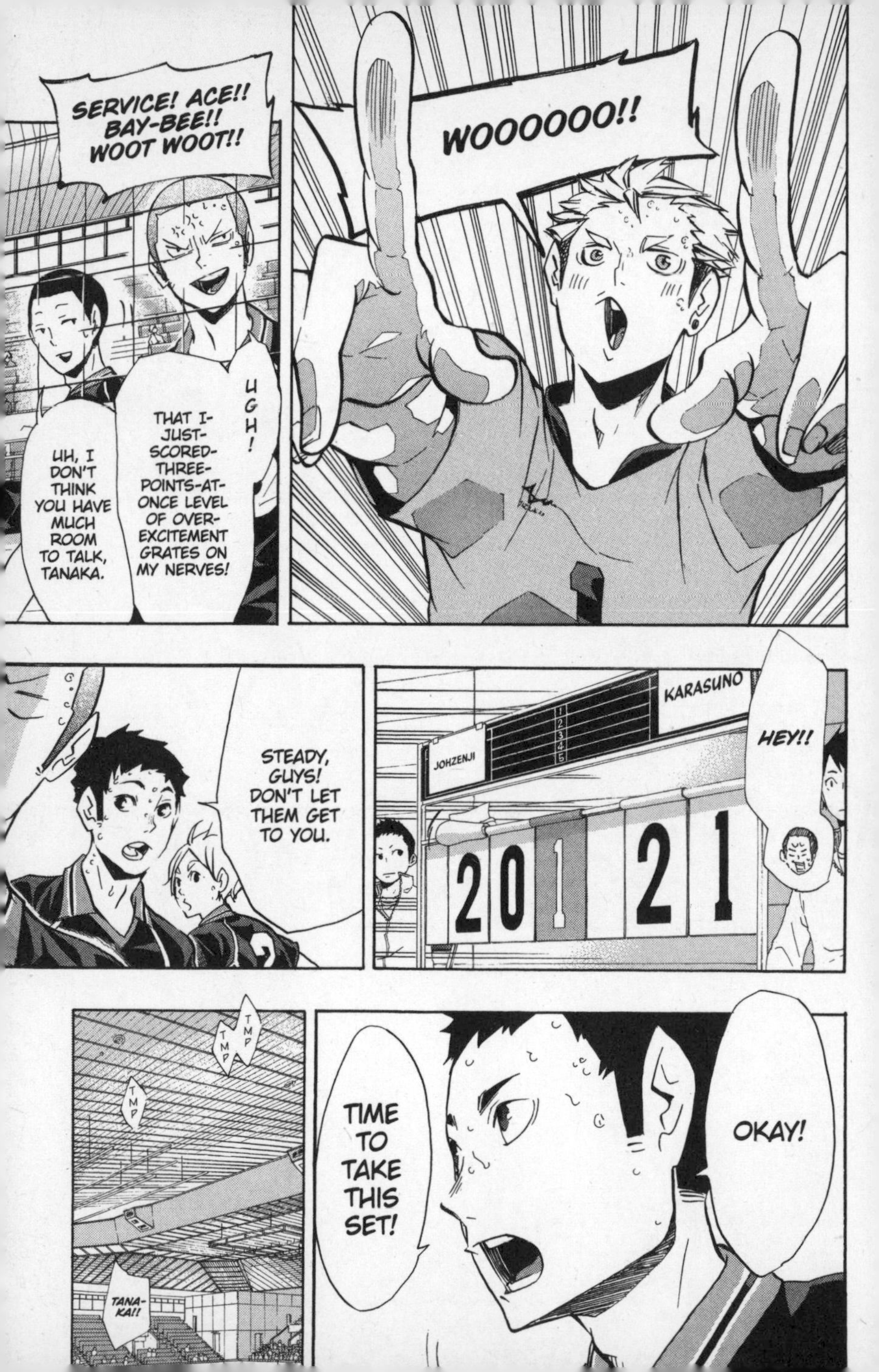
WOOOOOO!!
SERVICE! ACE!! BAY-BEE!! WOOT WOOT!!
UGH!
THAT I-JUST-SCORED-THREE-POINTS-AT-ONCE LEVEL OF OVER-EXCITEMENT GRATES ON MY NERVES!
UH, I DON'T THINK YOU HAVE MUCH ROOM TO TALK, TANAKA.
HEY!!
KARASUNO
JOHZENJI
STEADY, GUYS! DON'T LET THEM GET TO YOU.
OKAY!
TIME TO TAKE THIS SET!
TMP TMP
TMP
TANA-KA!!

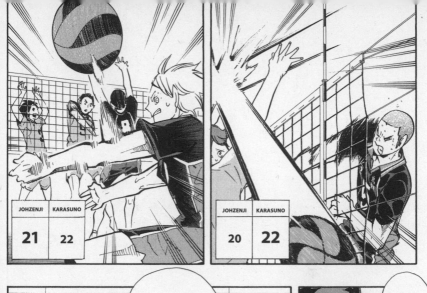

JOHZENJI	KARASUNO
21	22

JOHZENJI	KARASUNO
20	22

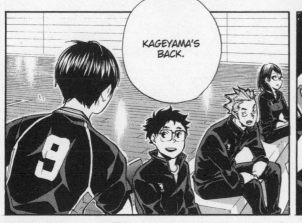

KAGEYAMA'S BACK.

OH!

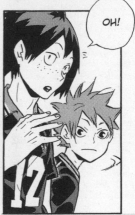

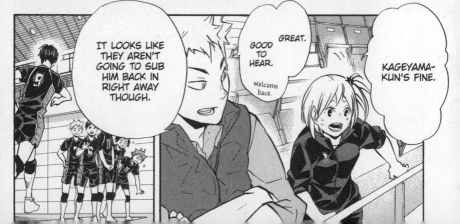

IT LOOKS LIKE THEY AREN'T GOING TO SUB HIM BACK IN RIGHT AWAY THOUGH.

GREAT.

GOOD TO HEAR.

Welcome back.

KAGEYAMA-KUN'S FINE.

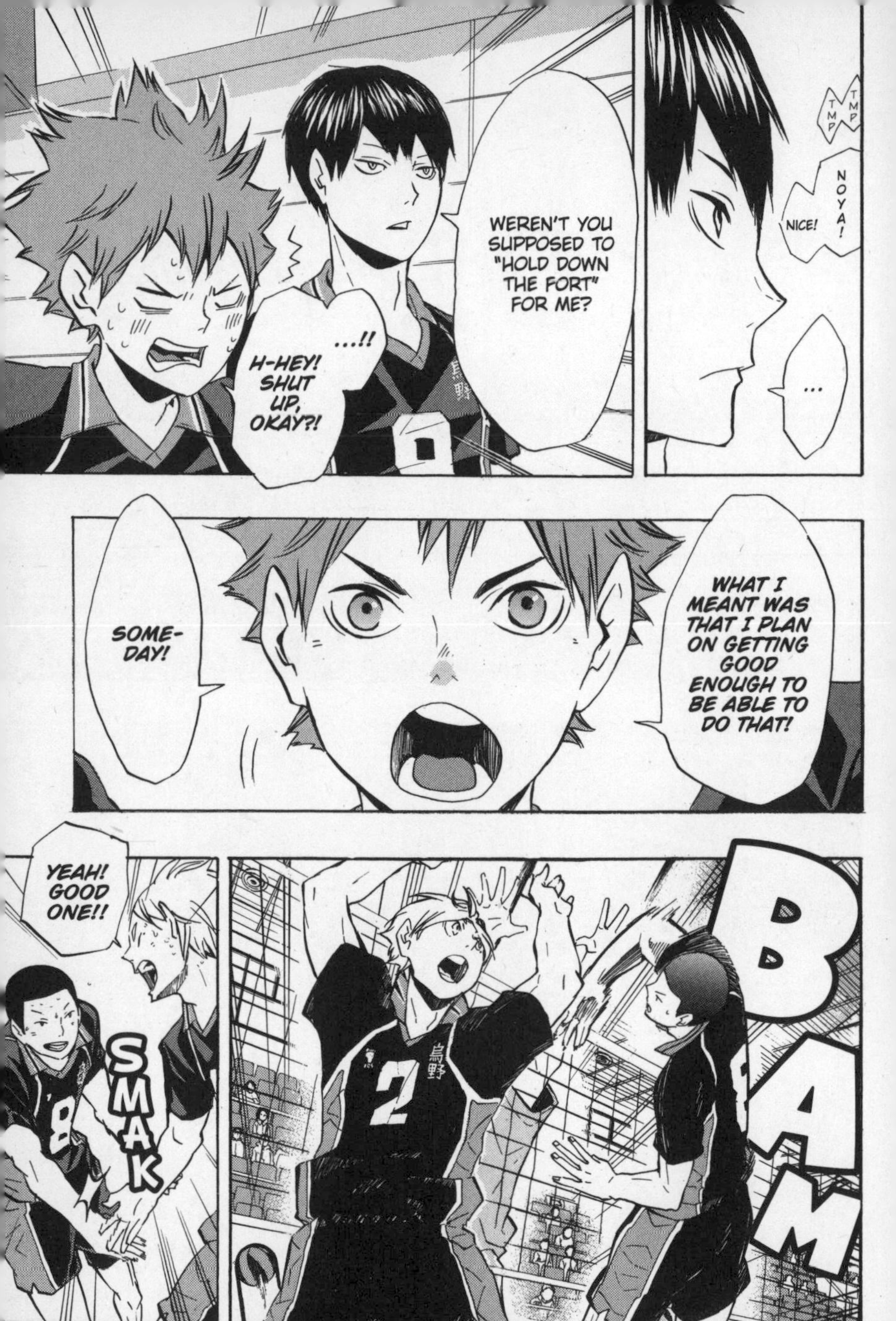
TMP TMP
NOYA!
NICE!
...
WEREN'T YOU SUPPOSED TO "HOLD DOWN THE FORT" FOR ME?
...!!
H-HEY! SHUT UP, OKAY?!
WHAT I MEANT WAS THAT I PLAN ON GETTING GOOD ENOUGH TO BE ABLE TO DO THAT!
SOME-DAY!
BAM
YEAH! GOOD ONE!!
SMAK

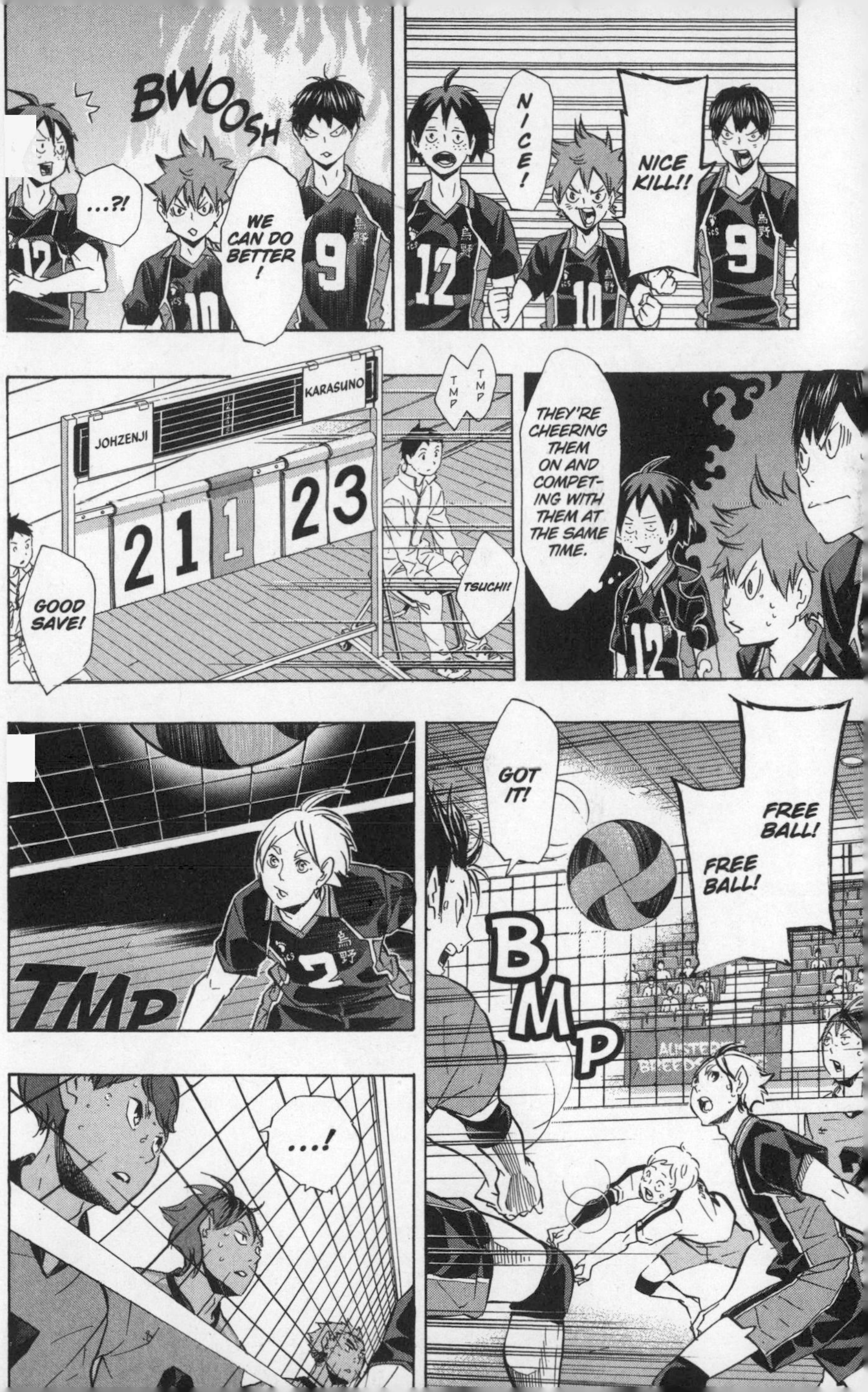
NICE KILL!!
NICE!
BWOOSH
WE CAN DO BETTER!
...?!
THEY'RE CHEERING THEM ON AND COMPETING WITH THEM AT THE SAME TIME.
TMP
TMP
KARASUNO
JOHZENJI
21
1
23
TSUCHI!
GOOD SAVE!
FREE BALL!
FREE BALL!
GOT IT!
BMP
TMP
...!

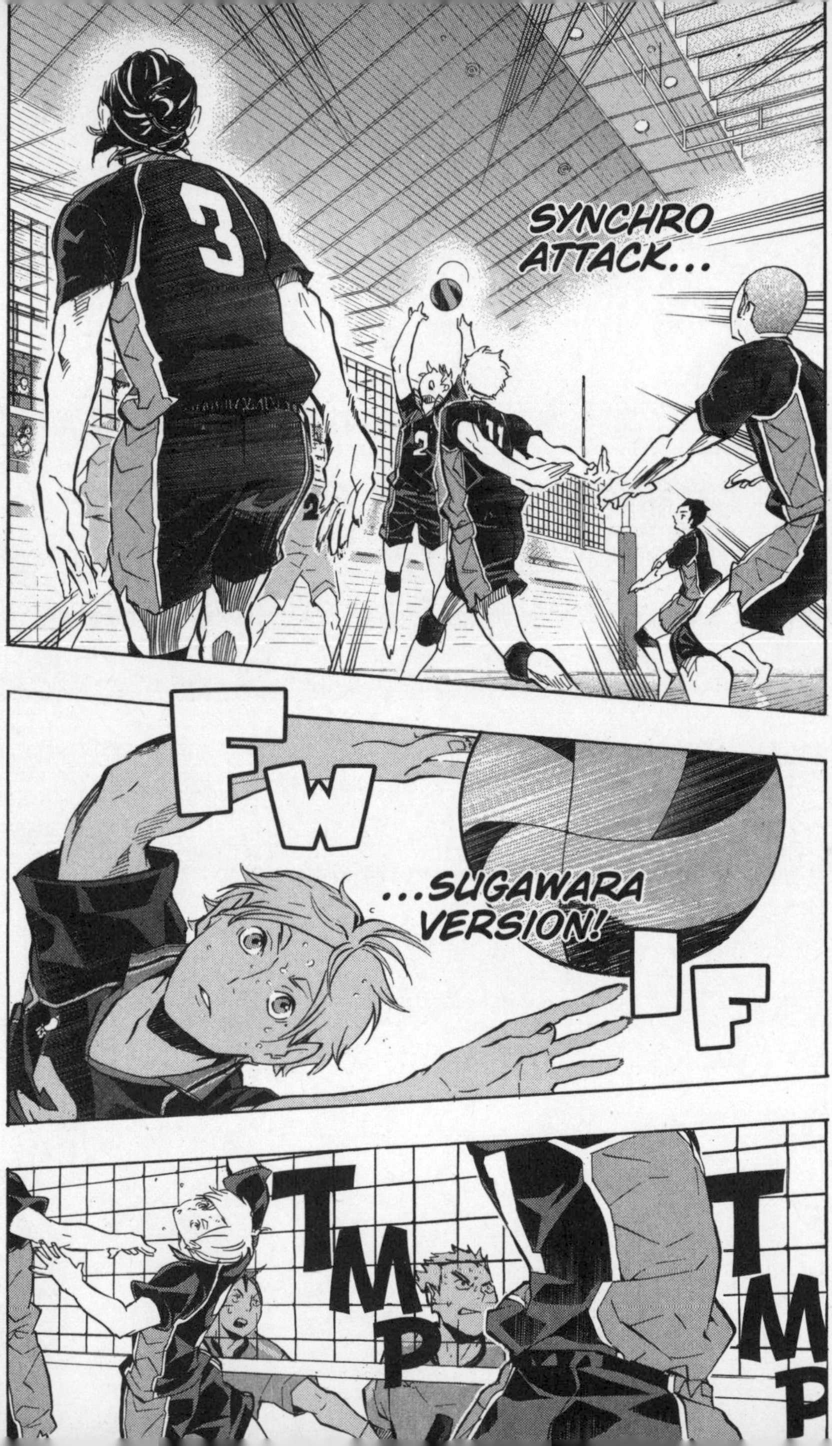
SYNCHRO ATTACK...
FWIF
...SUGAWARA VERSION!
TMP
TMP

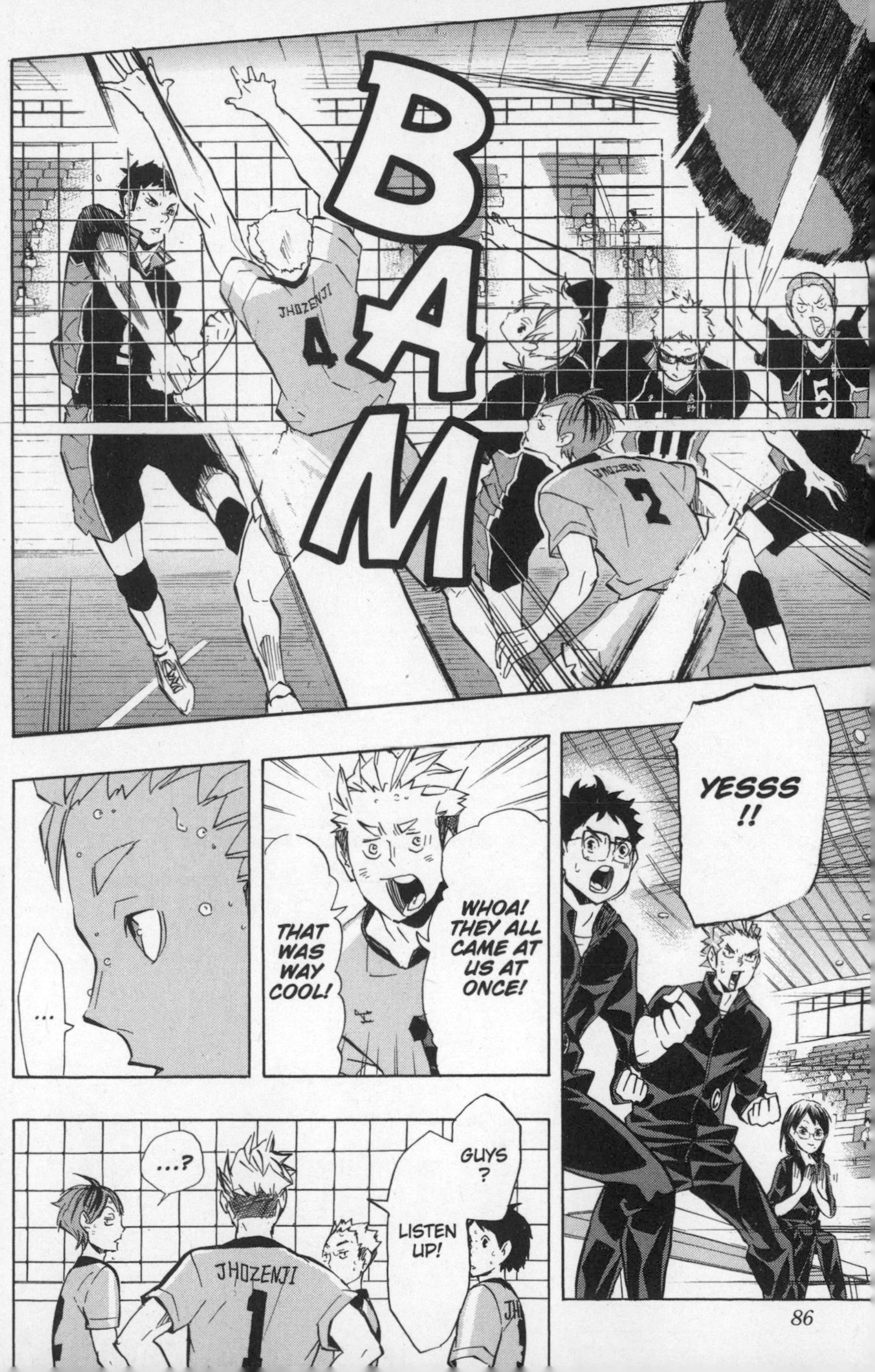
BAM
YESSS !!
WHOA! THEY ALL CAME AT US AT ONCE!
THAT WAS WAY COOL!
...
GUYS ?
LISTEN UP!
...?
JHOZENJI
JHOZENJI
JHOZENJI
JHOZENJI

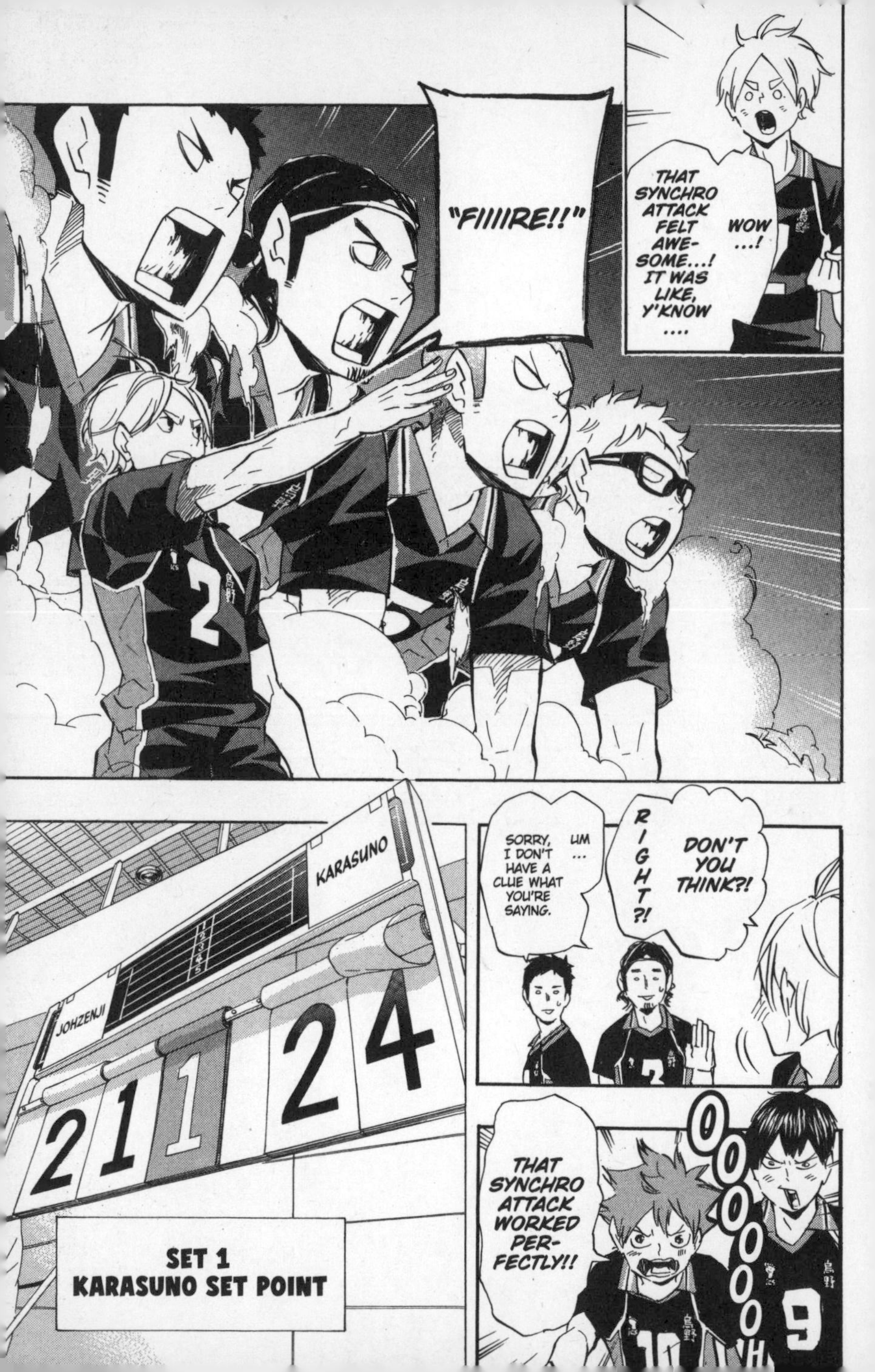
WOW ...!
THAT SYNCHRO ATTACK FELT AWE-SOME...! IT WAS LIKE, Y'KNOW ....
"FIIIIRE!!"
DON'T YOU THINK?!
RIGHT?!
UM ...
SORRY, I DON'T HAVE A CLUE WHAT YOU'RE SAYING.
OOOOOOO
THAT SYNCHRO ATTACK WORKED PER-FECTLY!!
KARASUNO
JOHZENJI
21
1
24
SET 1
KARASUNO SET POINT

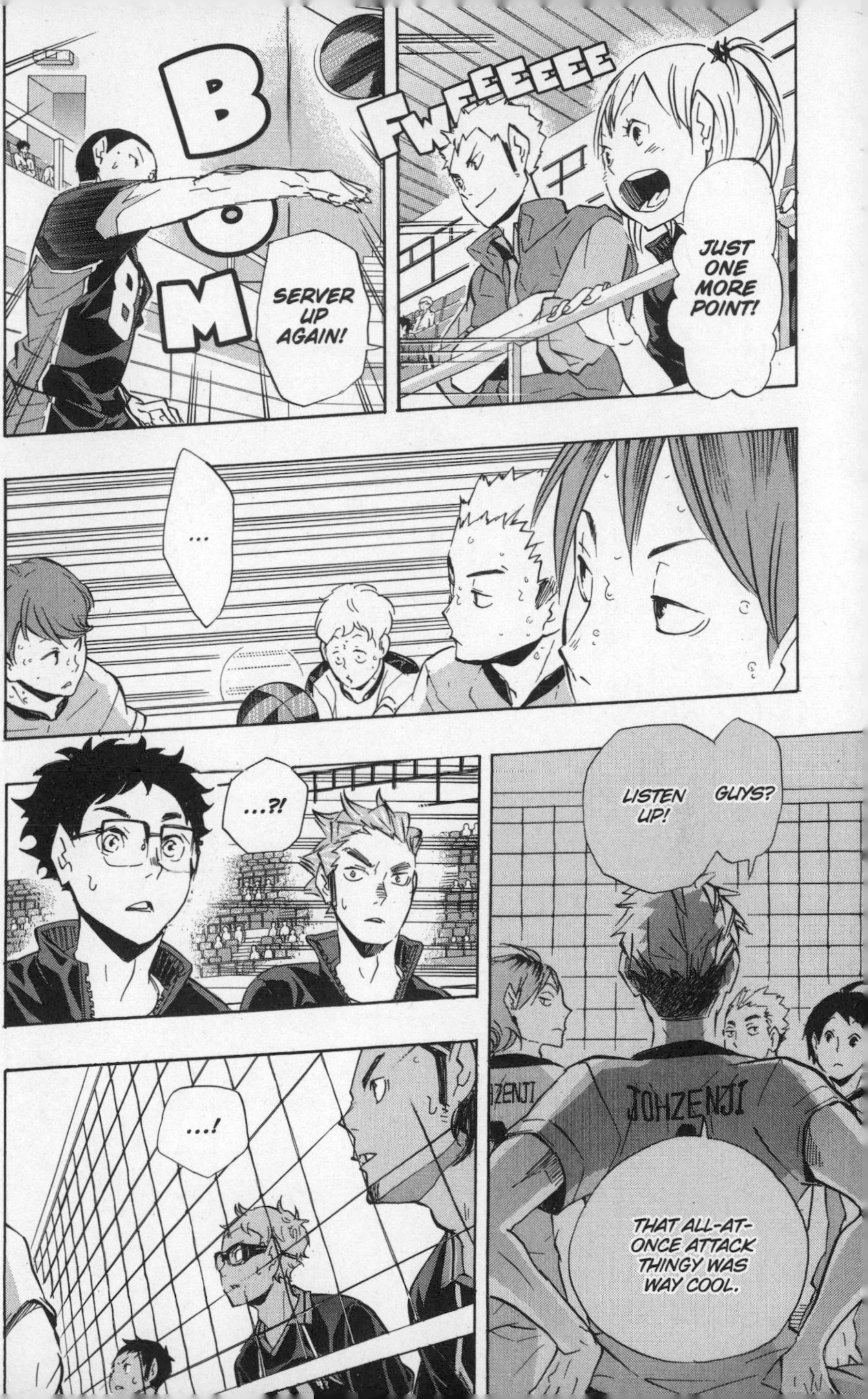
FWEEEEEE
JUST ONE MORE POINT!
BOOM
SERVER UP AGAIN!
...
GUYS?
LISTEN UP!
JOHZENJI
JOHZENJI
THAT ALL-AT-ONCE ATTACK THINGY WAS WAY COOL.
...?!
...!

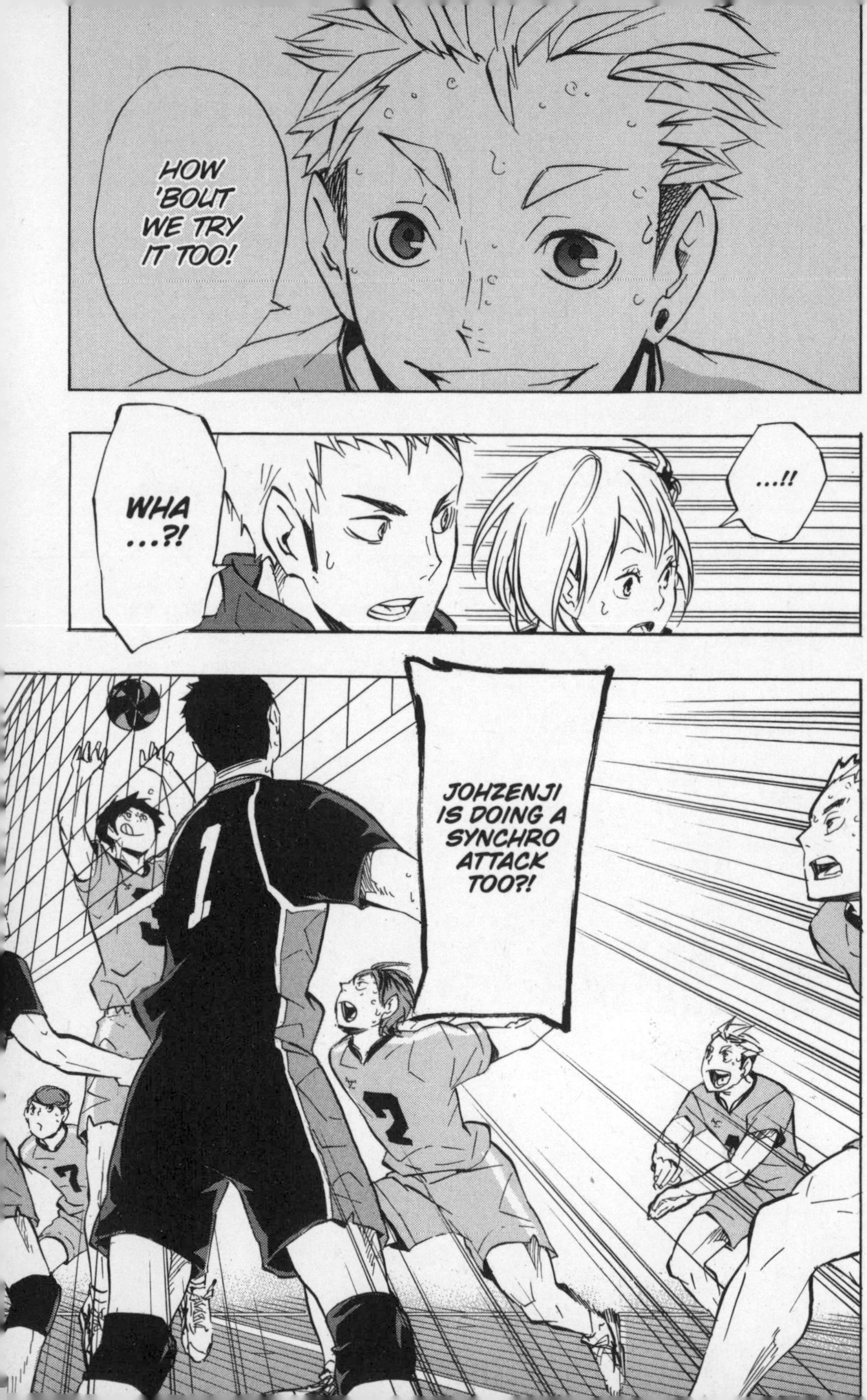
HOW 'BOUT WE TRY IT TOO!
...!!
WHA...?!
JOHZENJI IS DOING A SYNCHRO ATTACK TOO?!

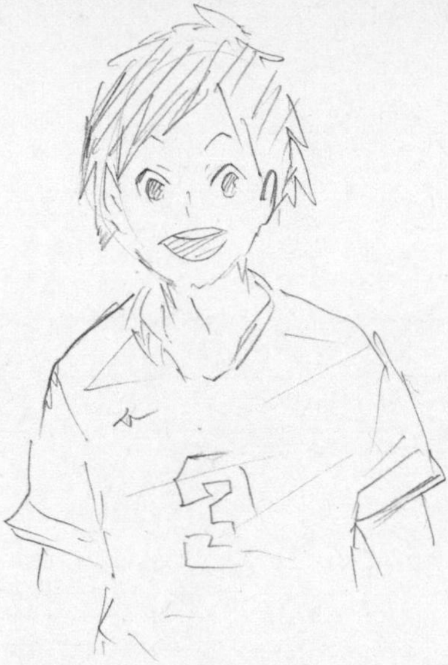

TAKEHARU FUTAMATA

JOHZENJI HIGH SCHOOL
CLASS 2-1

POSITION:
SETTER

HEIGHT: 5'10"

WEIGHT: 144 LBS.
(AS OF APRIL, 2ND YEAR
OF HIGH SCHOOL)

ABILITY PARAMETERS
(5-POINT SCALE)

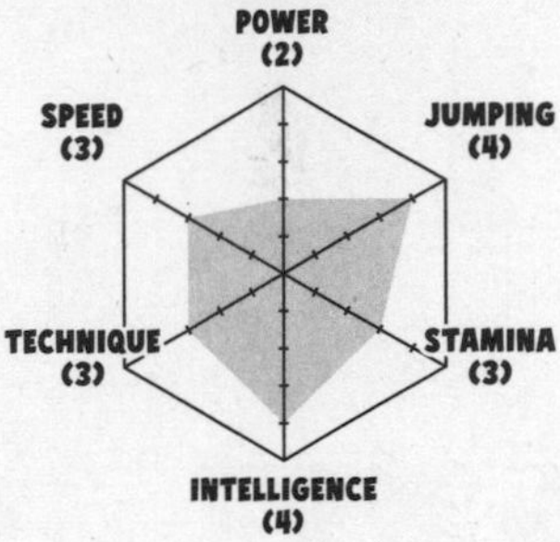
POWER (2)
JUMPING (4)
STAMINA (3)
INTELLIGENCE (4)
TECHNIQUE (3)
SPEED (3)

RINTARO NUMAJIRI

JOHZENJI HIGH SCHOOL
CLASS 2-3

POSITION:
WING SPIKER

HEIGHT: 5'9"

WEIGHT: 143 LBS.
(AS OF APRIL, 2ND YEAR
OF HIGH SCHOOL)

ABILITY PARAMETERS
(5-POINT SCALE)

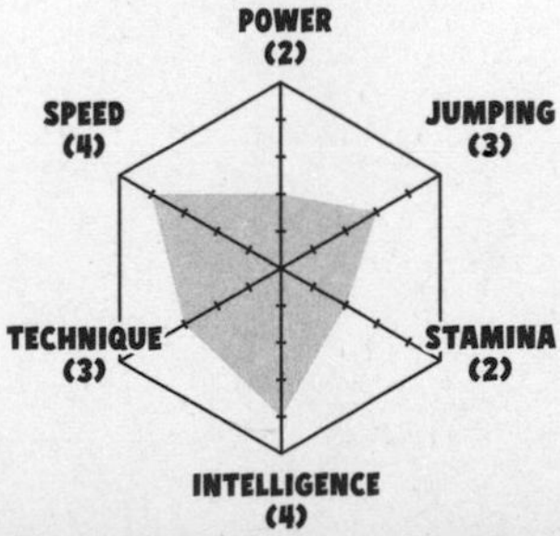
POWER (2)
JUMPING (3)
STAMINA (2)
INTELLIGENCE (4)
TECHNIQUE (3)
SPEED (4)

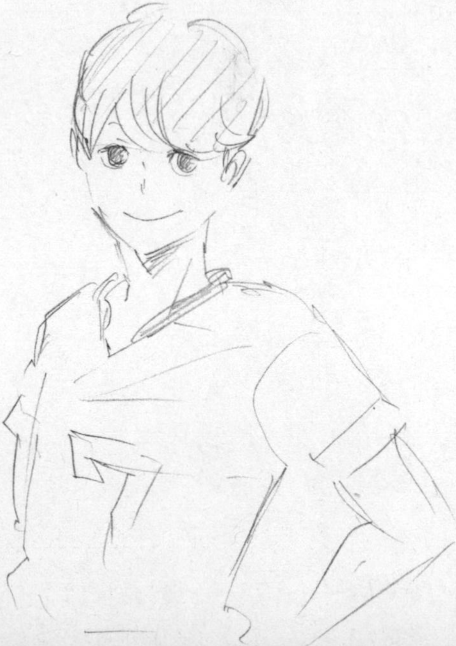

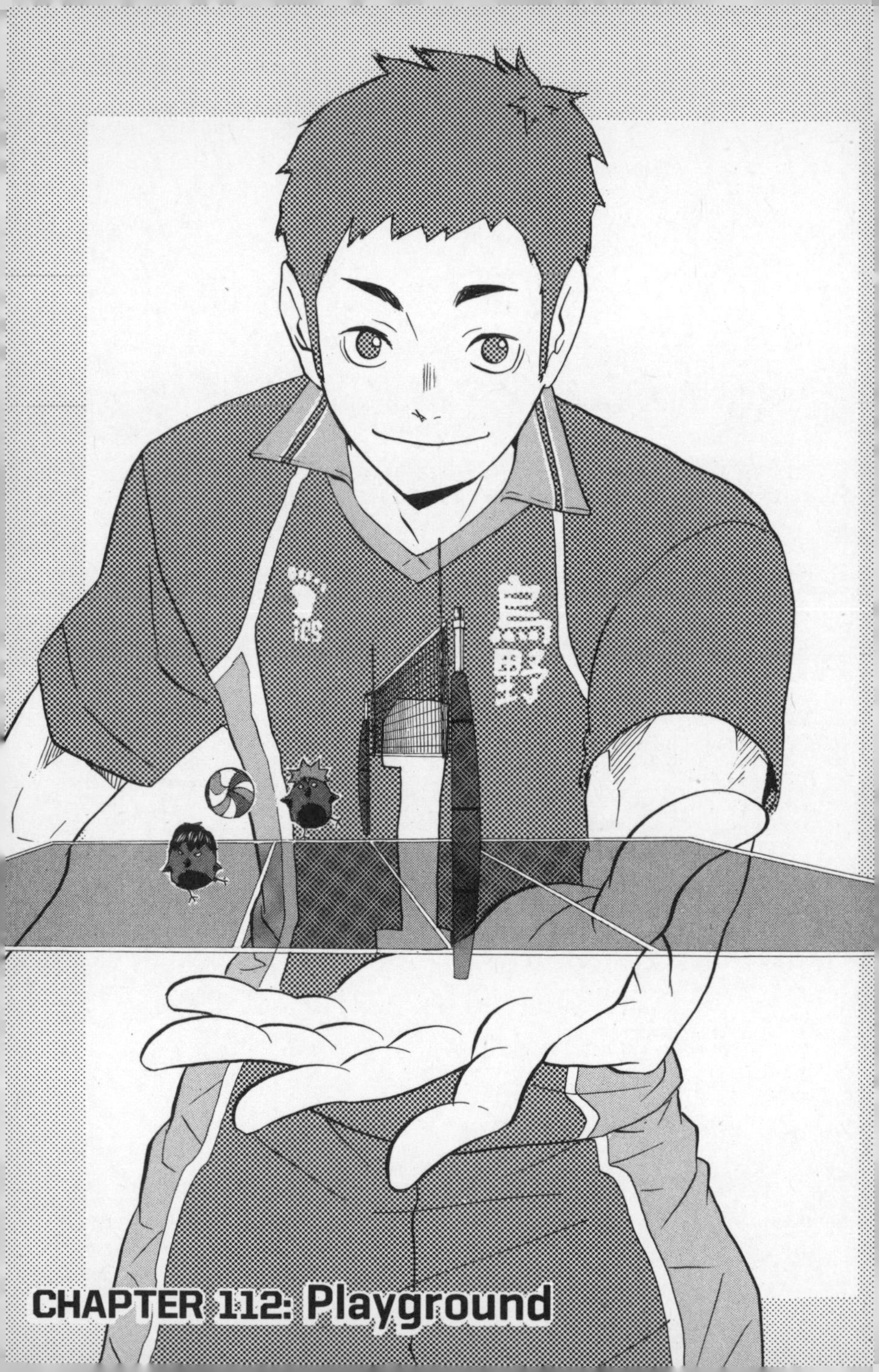
烏野

CHAPTER 112: Playground

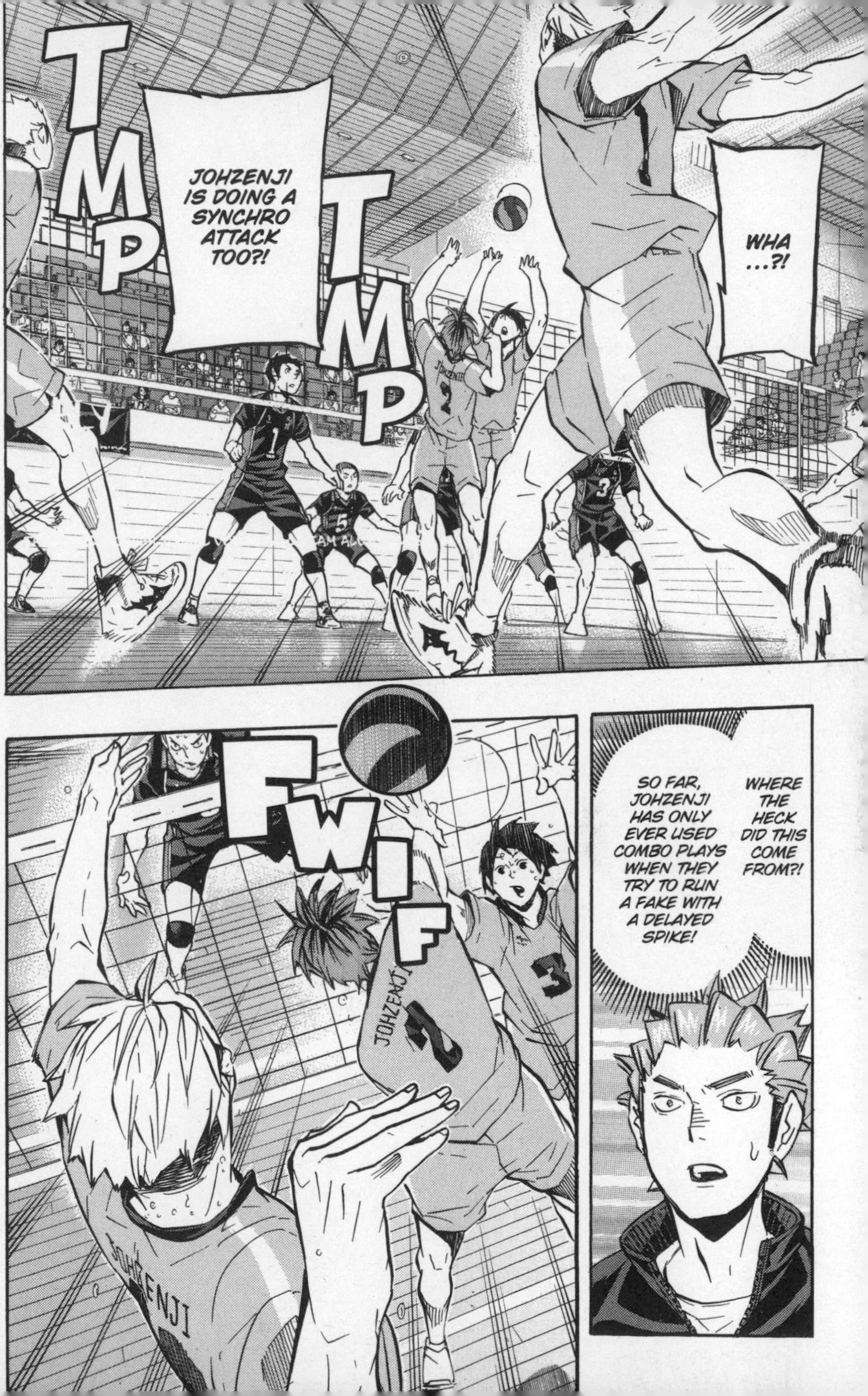
WHA ...?!
TMP
JOHZENJI IS DOING A SYNCHRO ATTACK TOO?!
TMP
WHERE THE HECK DID THIS COME FROM?!
SO FAR, JOHZENJI HAS ONLY EVER USED COMBO PLAYS WHEN THEY TRY TO RUN A FAKE WITH A DELAYED SPIKE!
FWIF

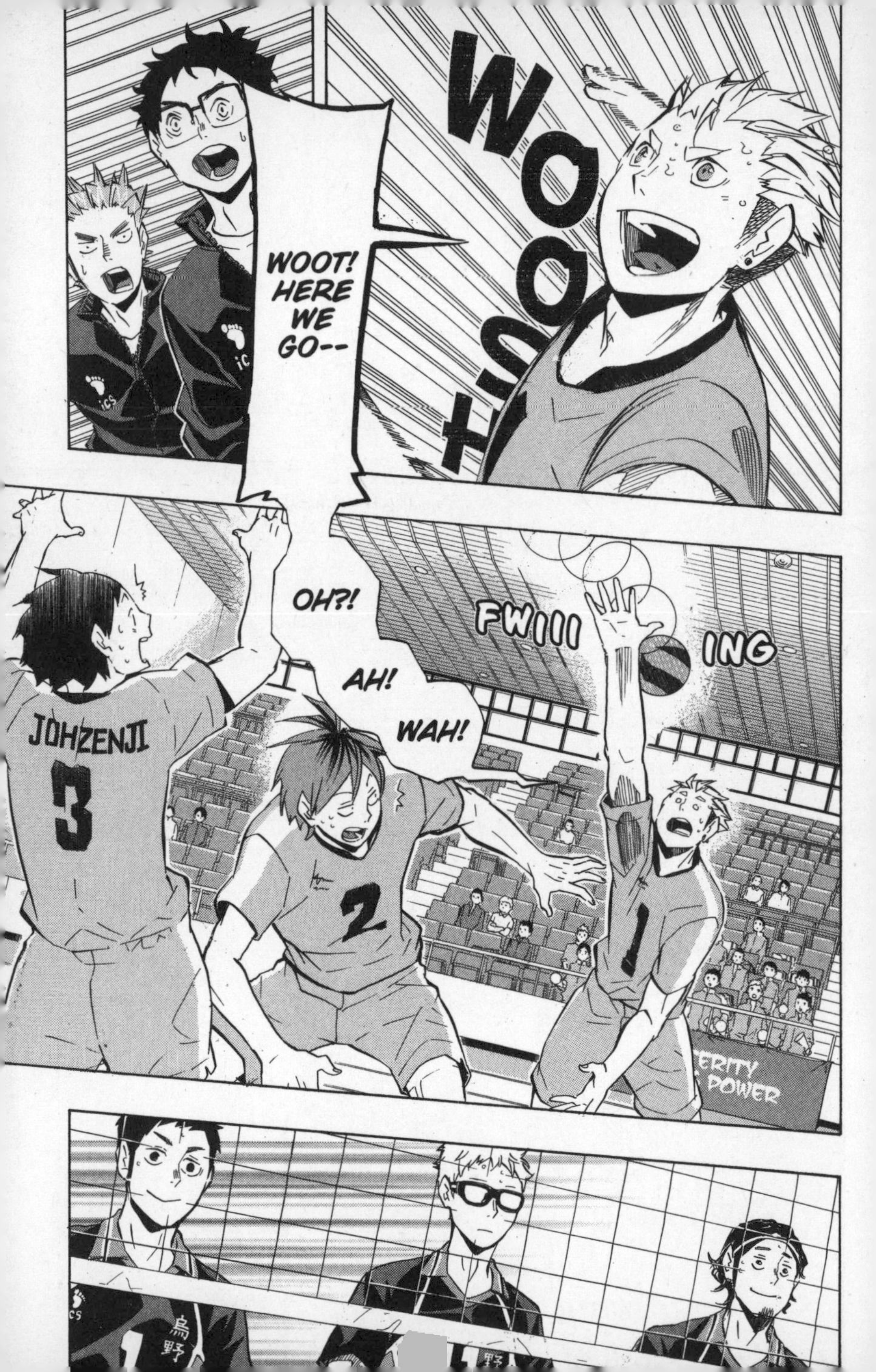
WOOOT
WOOT! HERE WE GO--
FWIII ING
OH?!
AH!
WAH!
JOHZENJI

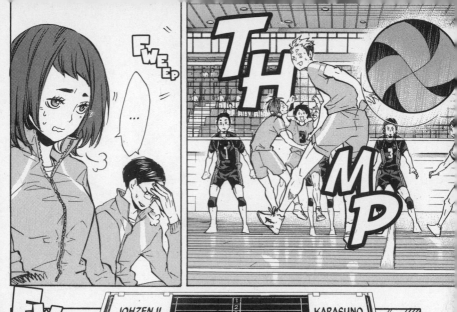

...

FWEEP

TH
M
P

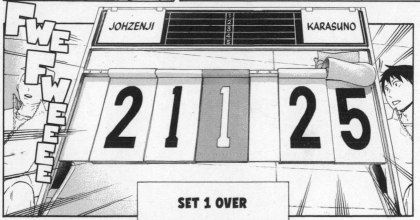

FWE FWEEE

		1		
JOHZENJI		2		KARASUNO
		3		
		4		
		5		

2 1 1 25

SET 1 OVER

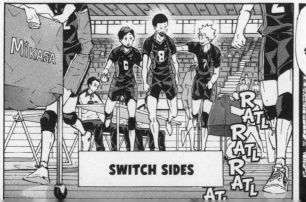

MIKASA

SWITCH SIDES

RATL
RATL
RATL
ATL

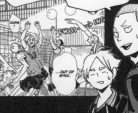

WE STILL DO THAT SOMETIMES.

NOW THAT LOOKS FAMILIAR. WE DERPED LIKE THAT MORE THAN ONCE.

OOPS

FWIII

...OUT OF SYNC.

NG

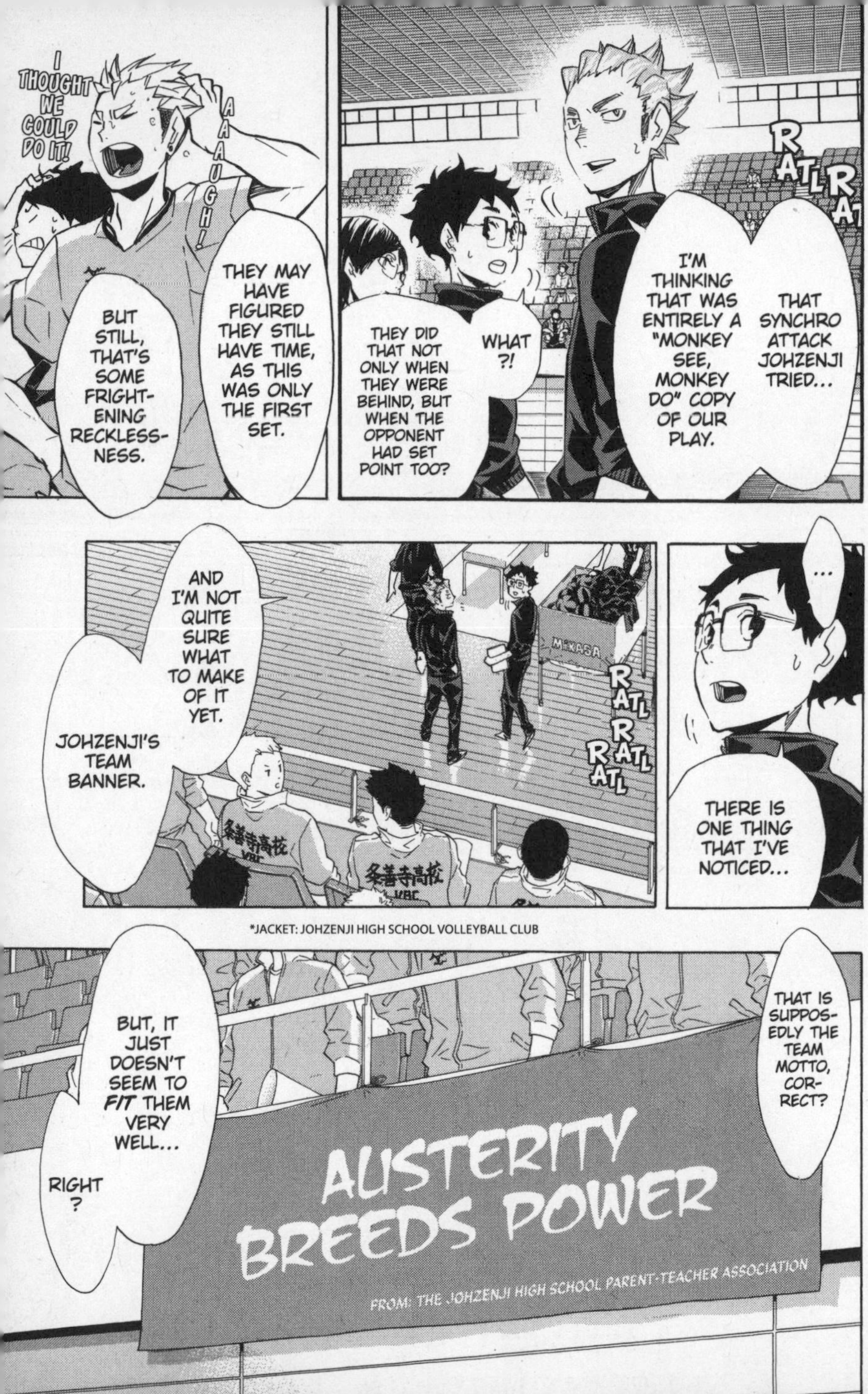
THAT SYNCHRO ATTACK JOHZENJI TRIED...
I'M THINKING THAT WAS ENTIRELY A "MONKEY SEE, MONKEY DO" COPY OF OUR PLAY.
RATL RATL
WHAT ?!
THEY DID THAT NOT ONLY WHEN THEY WERE BEHIND, BUT WHEN THE OPPONENT HAD SET POINT TOO?
I THOUGHT WE COULD DO IT!
AAAAUGH!
THEY MAY HAVE FIGURED THEY STILL HAVE TIME, AS THIS WAS ONLY THE FIRST SET.
BUT STILL, THAT'S SOME FRIGHT-ENING RECKLESS-NESS.
...
THERE IS ONE THING THAT I'VE NOTICED...
AND I'M NOT QUITE SURE WHAT TO MAKE OF IT YET.
JOHZENJI'S TEAM BANNER.
RATL RATL RATL
MIKASA
条善寺高校
条善寺高校
THAT IS SUPPOS-EDLY THE TEAM MOTTO, COR-RECT?
BUT, IT JUST DOESN'T SEEM TO *FIT* THEM VERY WELL...
RIGHT ?
AUSTERITY BREEDS POWER
FROM: THE JOHZENJI HIGH SCHOOL PARENT-TEACHER ASSOCIATION
*JACKET: JOHZENJI HIGH SCHOOL VOLLEYBALL CLUB

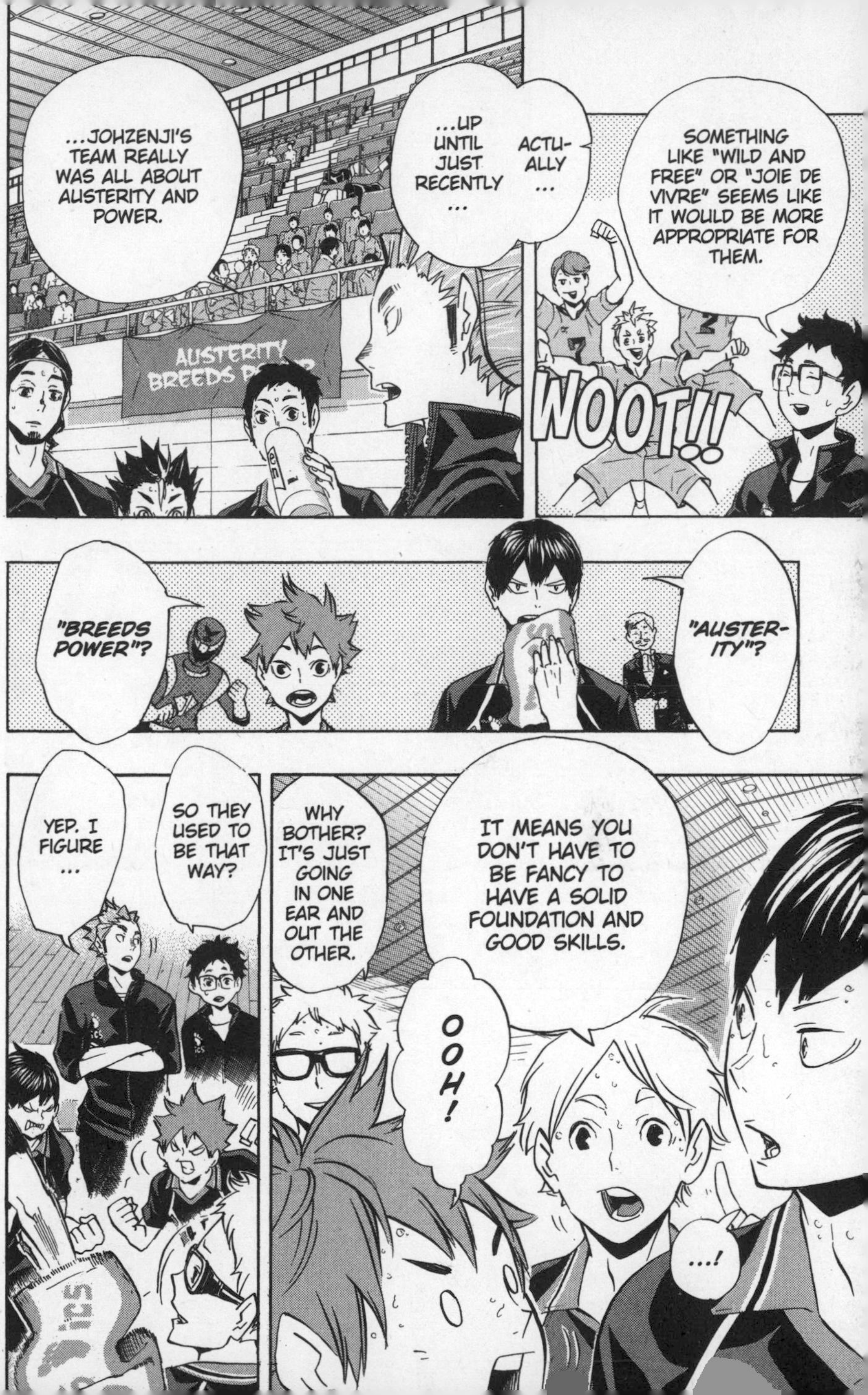
SOMETHING LIKE "WILD AND FREE" OR "JOIE DE VIVRE" SEEMS LIKE IT WOULD BE MORE APPROPRIATE FOR THEM.
WOOT!!
ACTU-ALLY ...
...UP UNTIL JUST RECENTLY ...
...JOHZENJI'S TEAM REALLY WAS ALL ABOUT AUSTERITY AND POWER.
AUSTERITY
BREEDS
"AUSTER-ITY"?
"BREEDS POWER"?
IT MEANS YOU DON'T HAVE TO BE FANCY TO HAVE A SOLID FOUNDATION AND GOOD SKILLS.
WHY BOTHER? IT'S JUST GOING IN ONE EAR AND OUT THE OTHER.
OOH!
...!
SO THEY USED TO BE THAT WAY?
YEP. I FIGURE ...

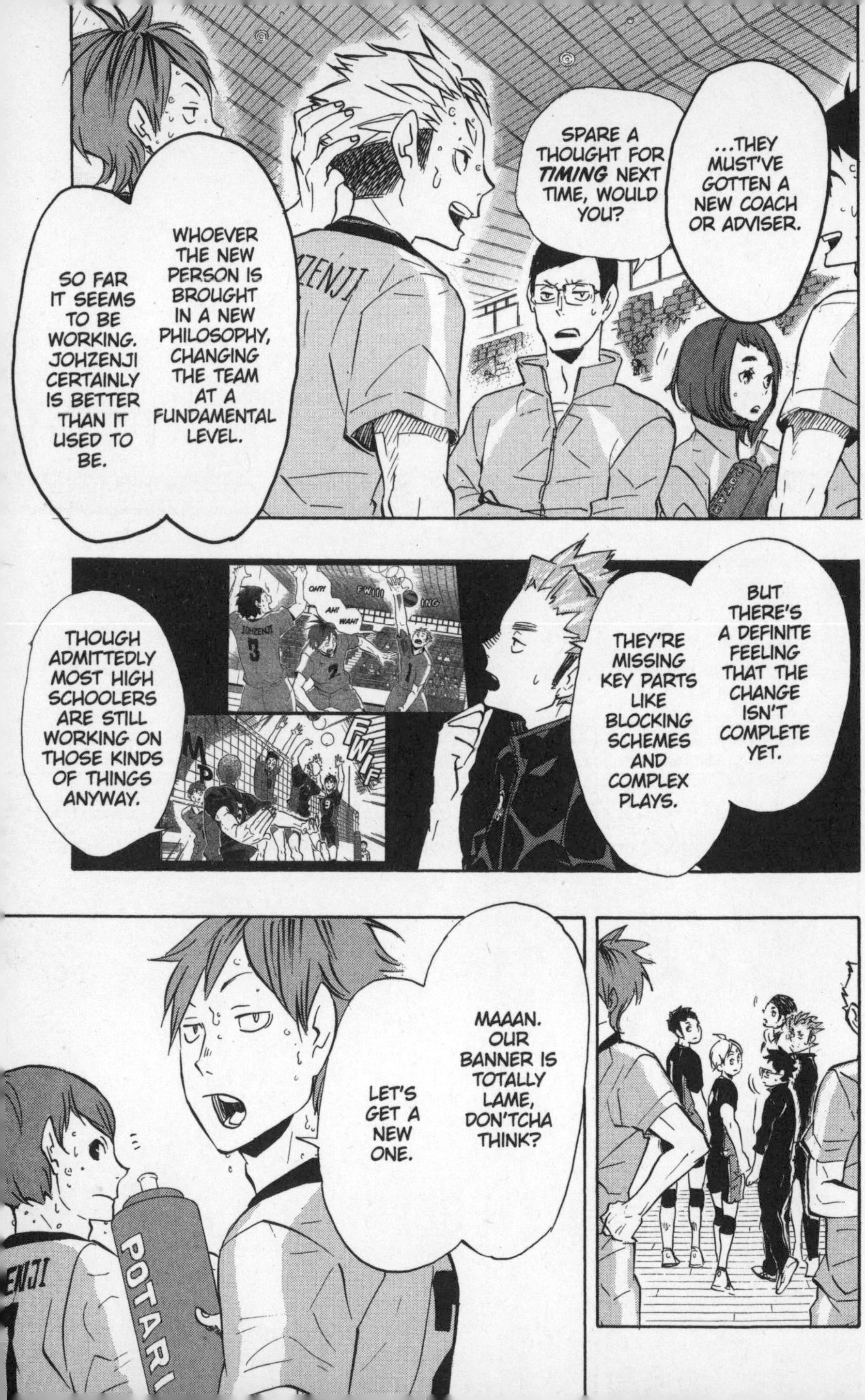
...THEY MUST'VE GOTTEN A NEW COACH OR ADVISER.
SPARE A THOUGHT FOR *TIMING* NEXT TIME, WOULD YOU?
WHOEVER THE NEW PERSON IS BROUGHT IN A NEW PHILOSOPHY, CHANGING THE TEAM AT A FUNDAMENTAL LEVEL.
SO FAR IT SEEMS TO BE WORKING. JOHZENJI CERTAINLY IS BETTER THAN IT USED TO BE.
BUT THERE'S A DEFINITE FEELING THAT THE CHANGE ISN'T COMPLETE YET.
THEY'RE MISSING KEY PARTS LIKE BLOCKING SCHEMES AND COMPLEX PLAYS.
FWIF
MP
THOUGH ADMITTEDLY MOST HIGH SCHOOLERS ARE STILL WORKING ON THOSE KINDS OF THINGS ANYWAY.
MAAAN. OUR BANNER IS TOTALLY LAME, DON'TCHA THINK?
LET'S GET A NEW ONE.
POTARI

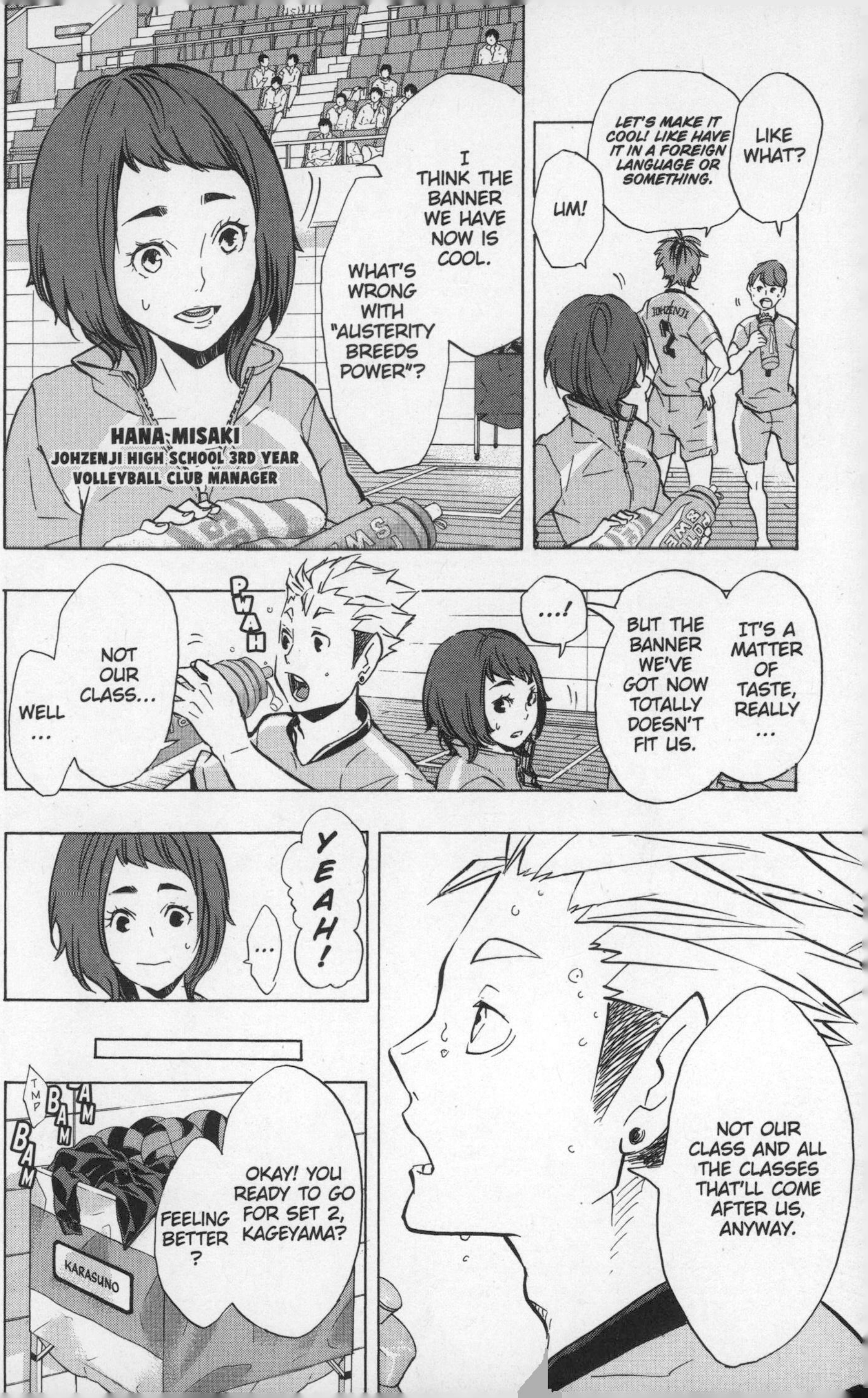
LIKE WHAT?
LET'S MAKE IT COOL! LIKE HAVE IT IN A FOREIGN LANGUAGE OR SOMETHING.
UM!
JOHZENJI
I THINK THE BANNER WE HAVE NOW IS COOL.
WHAT'S WRONG WITH "AUSTERITY BREEDS POWER"?
HANA MISAKI
JOHZENJI HIGH SCHOOL 3RD YEAR
VOLLEYBALL CLUB MANAGER
IT'S A MATTER OF TASTE, REALLY...
BUT THE BANNER WE'VE GOT NOW TOTALLY DOESN'T FIT US.
...!
PWAH
NOT OUR CLASS...
WELL...
NOT OUR CLASS AND ALL THE CLASSES THAT'LL COME AFTER US, ANYWAY.
YEAH!
...
OKAY! YOU READY TO GO FOR SET 2, KAGEYAMA?
FEELING BETTER?
BAM BAM BAM
TMP
KARASUNO

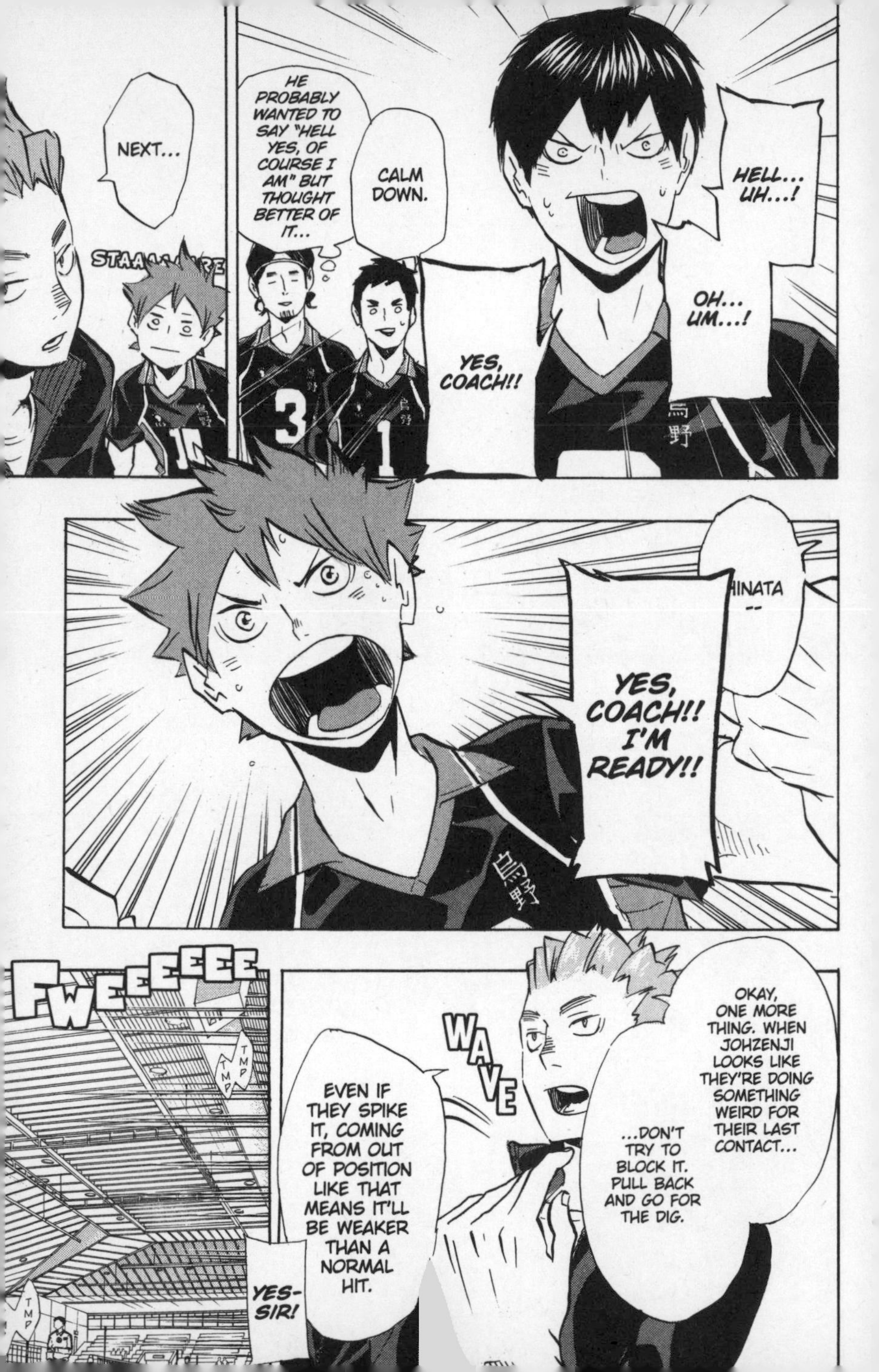
HELL... UH...!
OH... UM...!
YES, COACH!!
CALM DOWN.
HE PROBABLY WANTED TO SAY "HELL YES, OF COURSE I AM" BUT THOUGHT BETTER OF IT...
NEXT...
HINATA --
YES, COACH!! I'M READY!!
OKAY, ONE MORE THING. WHEN JOHZENJI LOOKS LIKE THEY'RE DOING SOMETHING WEIRD FOR THEIR LAST CONTACT...
...DON'T TRY TO BLOCK IT. PULL BACK AND GO FOR THE DIG.
WAVE
EVEN IF THEY SPIKE IT, COMING FROM OUT OF POSITION LIKE THAT MEANS IT'LL BE WEAKER THAN A NORMAL HIT.
YES-SIR!
FWEEEEEE
TMP TMP
TMP

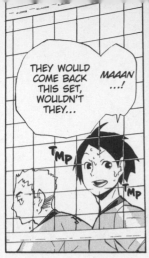

THEY WOULD COME BACK THIS SET, WOULDN'T THEY...

MAAAN ...!

TMP

TMP

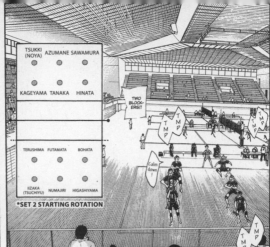

TSUKKI (NOYA)	AZUMANE	SAWAMURA
KAGEYAMA	TANAKA	HINATA

TERUSHIMA	FUTAMATA	BOHATA
IIZAKA (TSUCHIYU)	NUMAJIRI	HIGASHIYAMA

*SET 2 STARTING ROTATION

TWO BLOCK-ERS!!

TMP

Calm down!

TMP

TMP

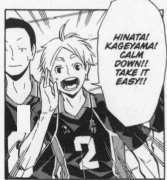

HINATA! KAGEYAMA! CALM DOWN!! TAKE IT EASY!!

2

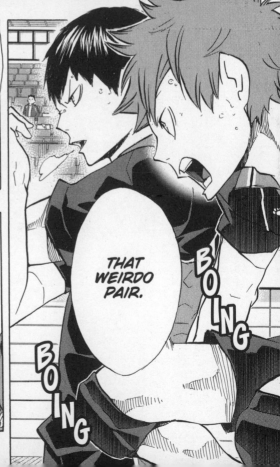

THAT WEIRDO PAIR.

BOING

BOING

BOING

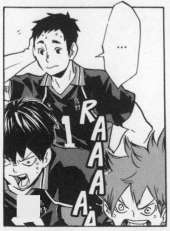

...

RAAAA
A

1

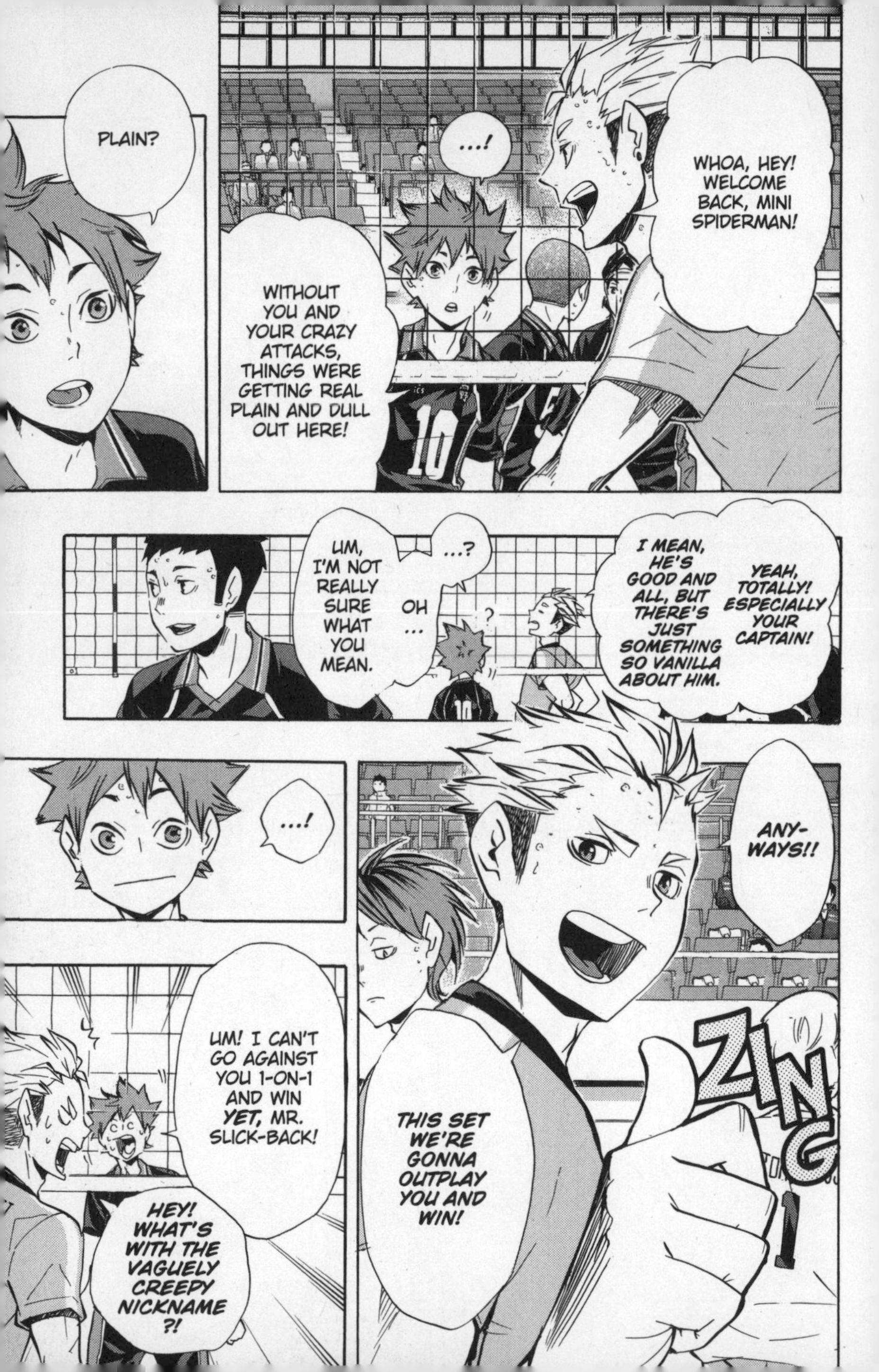
WHOA, HEY! WELCOME BACK, MINI SPIDERMAN!
...!
WITHOUT YOU AND YOUR CRAZY ATTACKS, THINGS WERE GETTING REAL PLAIN AND DULL OUT HERE!
PLAIN?
YEAH, TOTALLY! ESPECIALLY YOUR CAPTAIN!
I MEAN, HE'S GOOD AND ALL, BUT THERE'S JUST SOMETHING SO VANILLA ABOUT HIM.
...?
OH ...
UM, I'M NOT REALLY SURE WHAT YOU MEAN.
ANY-WAYS!!
THIS SET WE'RE GONNA OUTPLAY YOU AND WIN!
ZING
...!
UM! I CAN'T GO AGAINST YOU 1-ON-1 AND WIN YET, MR. SLICK-BACK!
HEY! WHAT'S WITH THE VAGUELY CREEPY NICKNAME ?!

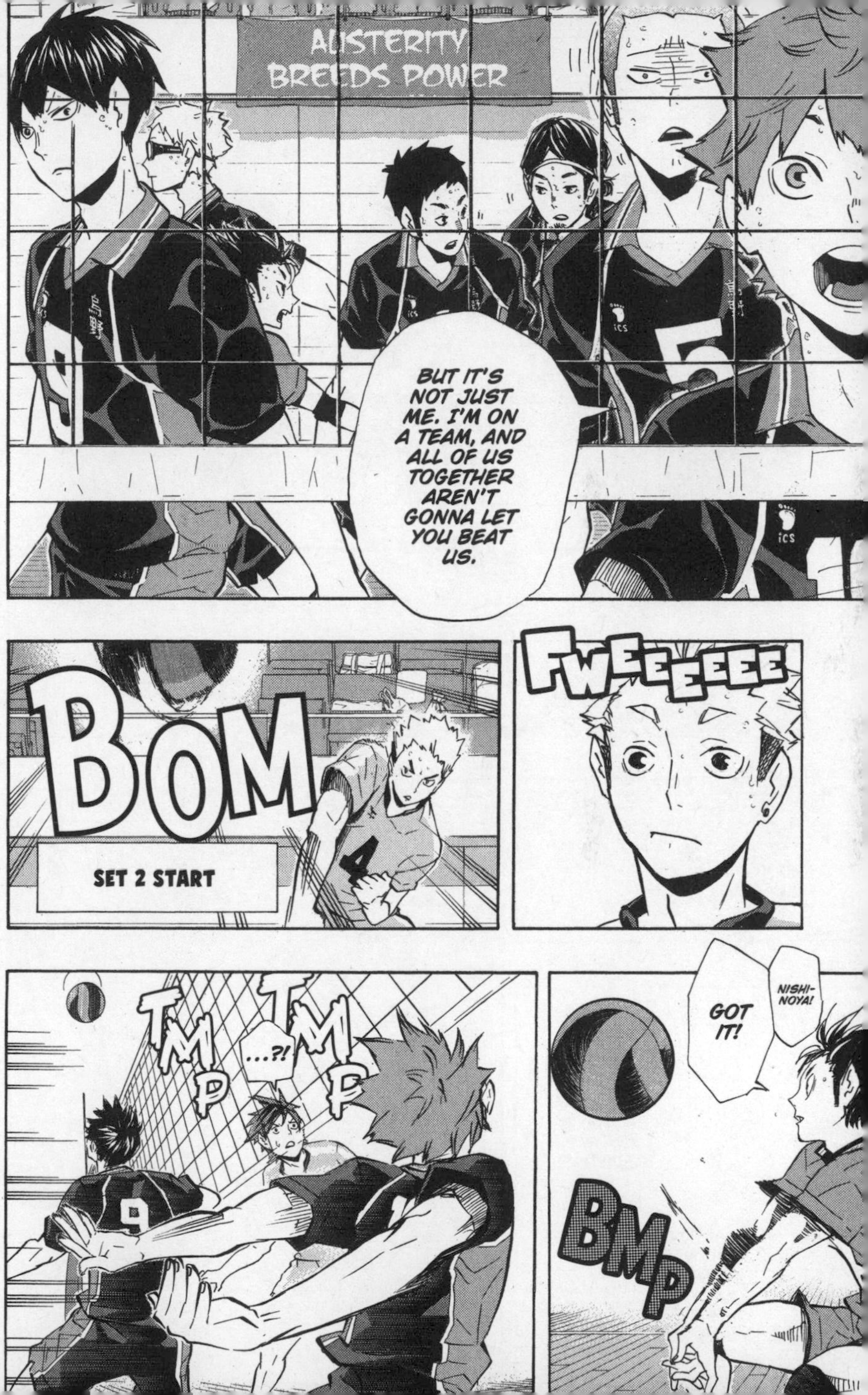
AUSTERITY BREEDS POWER
BUT IT'S NOT JUST ME. I'M ON A TEAM, AND ALL OF US TOGETHER AREN'T GONNA LET YOU BEAT US.
FWEEEEEEE
BOM
SET 2 START
NISHI-NOYA!
GOT IT!
BMP
TMP
...?!
TMP

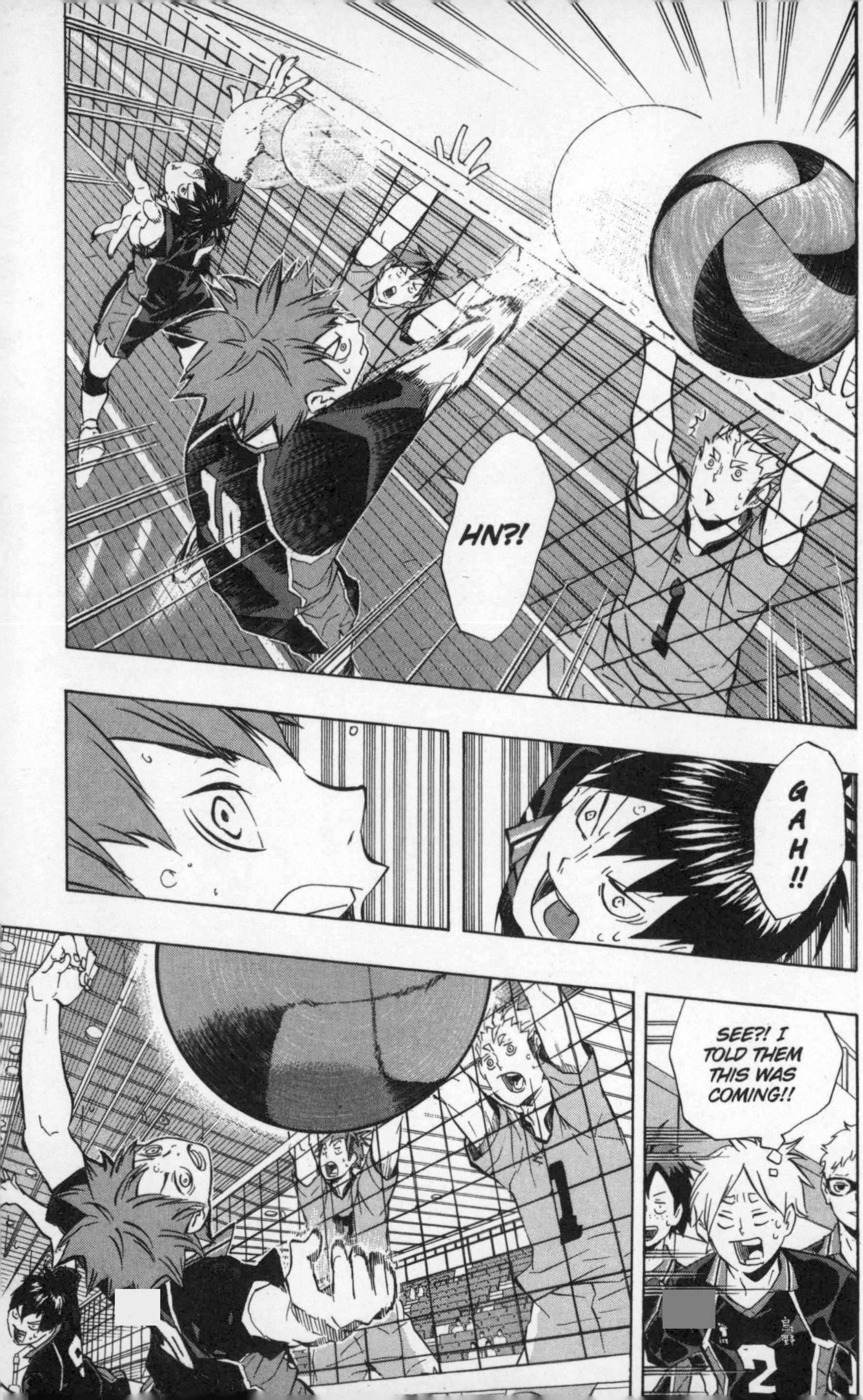
HN?!
GAH!!
SEE?! I TOLD THEM THIS WAS COMING!!

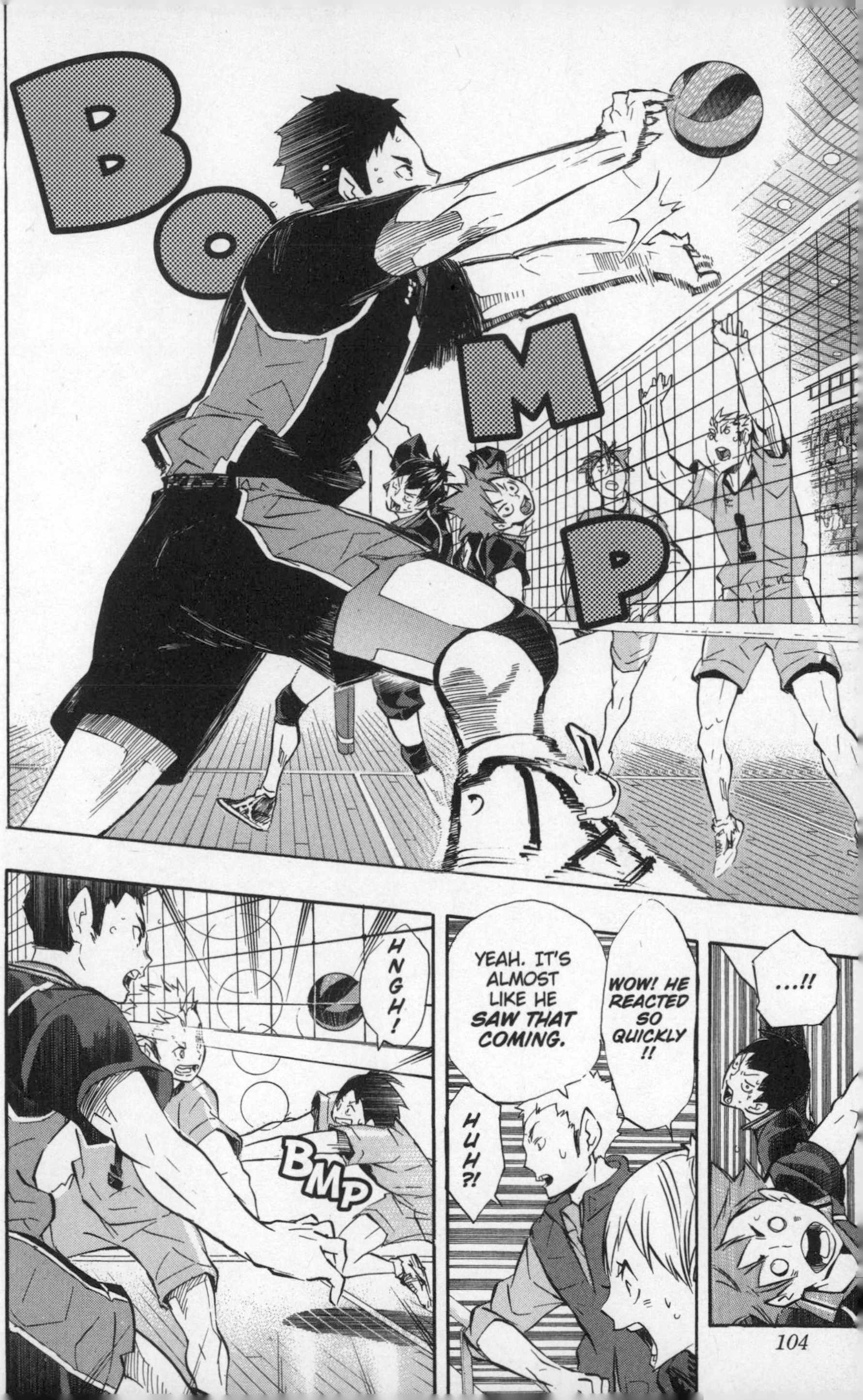
BOOMP
...!!
WOW! HE REACTED SO QUICKLY!!
YEAH. IT'S ALMOST LIKE HE SAW THAT COMING.
HUH?!
HNGH!
BMP

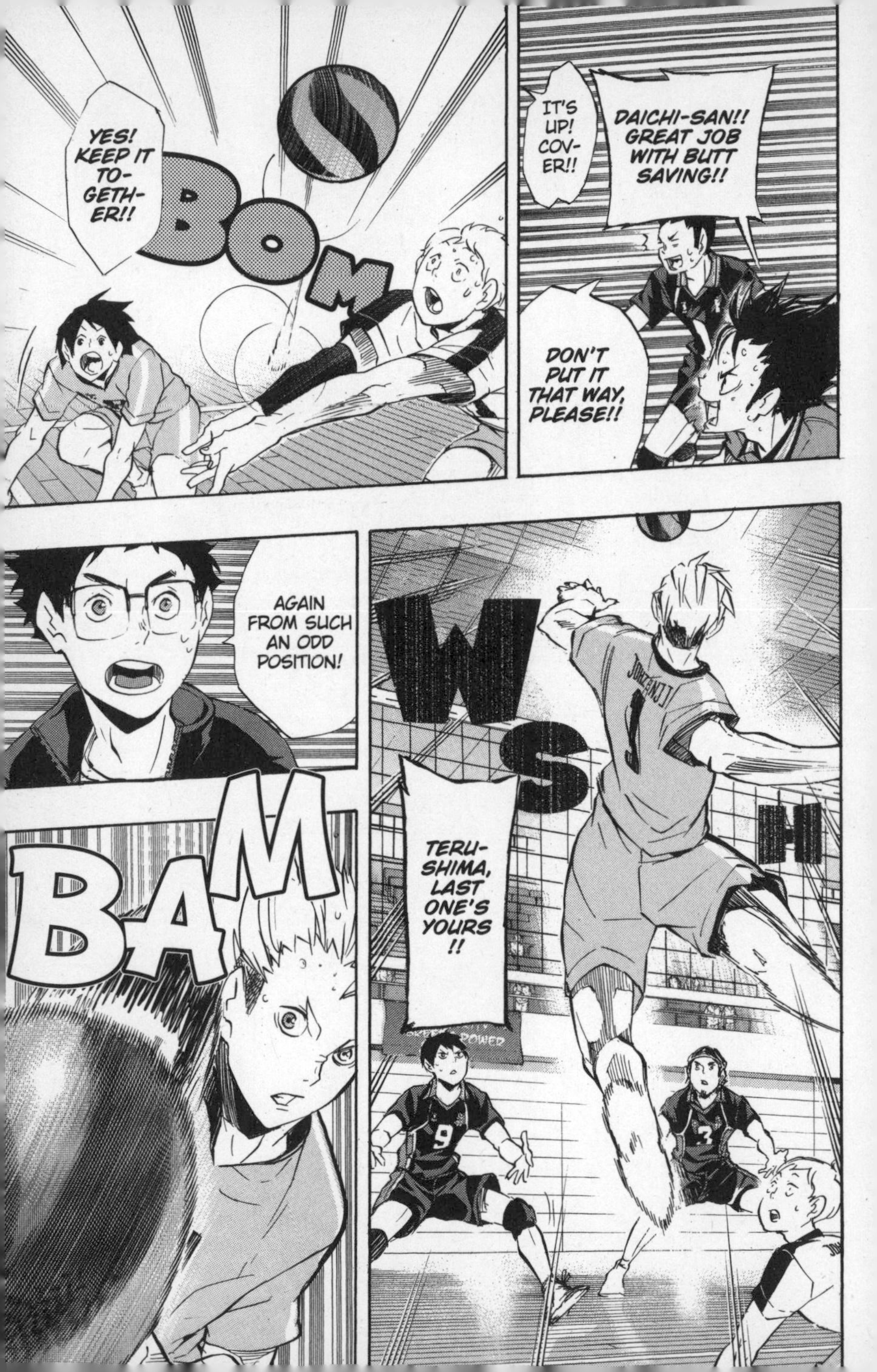
DAICHI-SAN!! GREAT JOB WITH BUTT SAVING!!
IT'S UP! COVER!!
DON'T PUT IT THAT WAY, PLEASE!!
BOM
YES! KEEP IT TO-GETH-ER!!
WSH
TERU-SHIMA, LAST ONE'S YOURS !!
AGAIN FROM SUCH AN ODD POSITION!
BAM

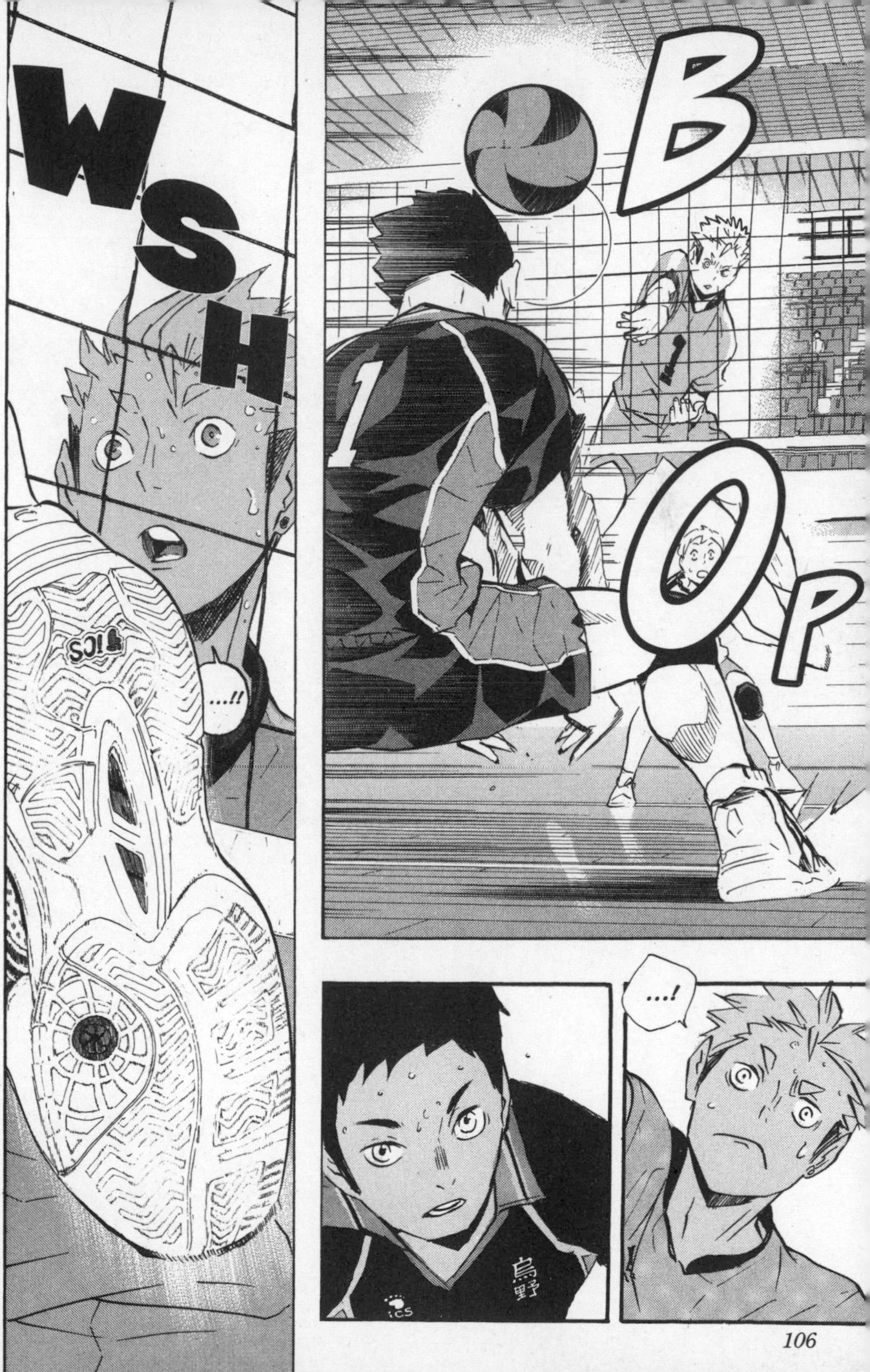
BOOP
...!
WSH
...!!

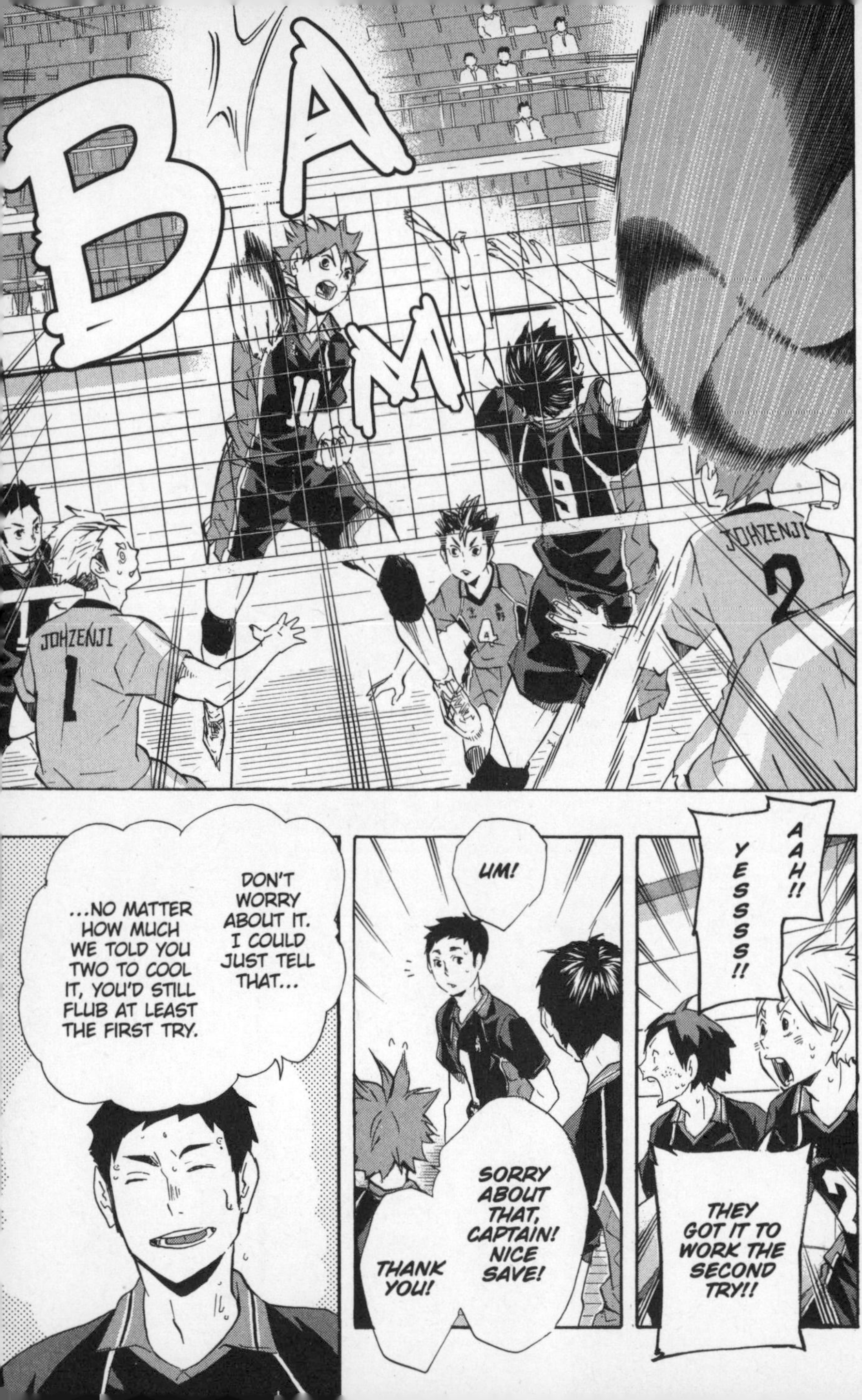
BAM
AAH!! YESSSS!!
THEY GOT IT TO WORK THE SECOND TRY!!
UM!
SORRY ABOUT THAT, CAPTAIN! NICE SAVE!
THANK YOU!
DON'T WORRY ABOUT IT. I COULD JUST TELL THAT...
...NO MATTER HOW MUCH WE TOLD YOU TWO TO COOL IT, YOU'D STILL FLUB AT LEAST THE FIRST TRY.

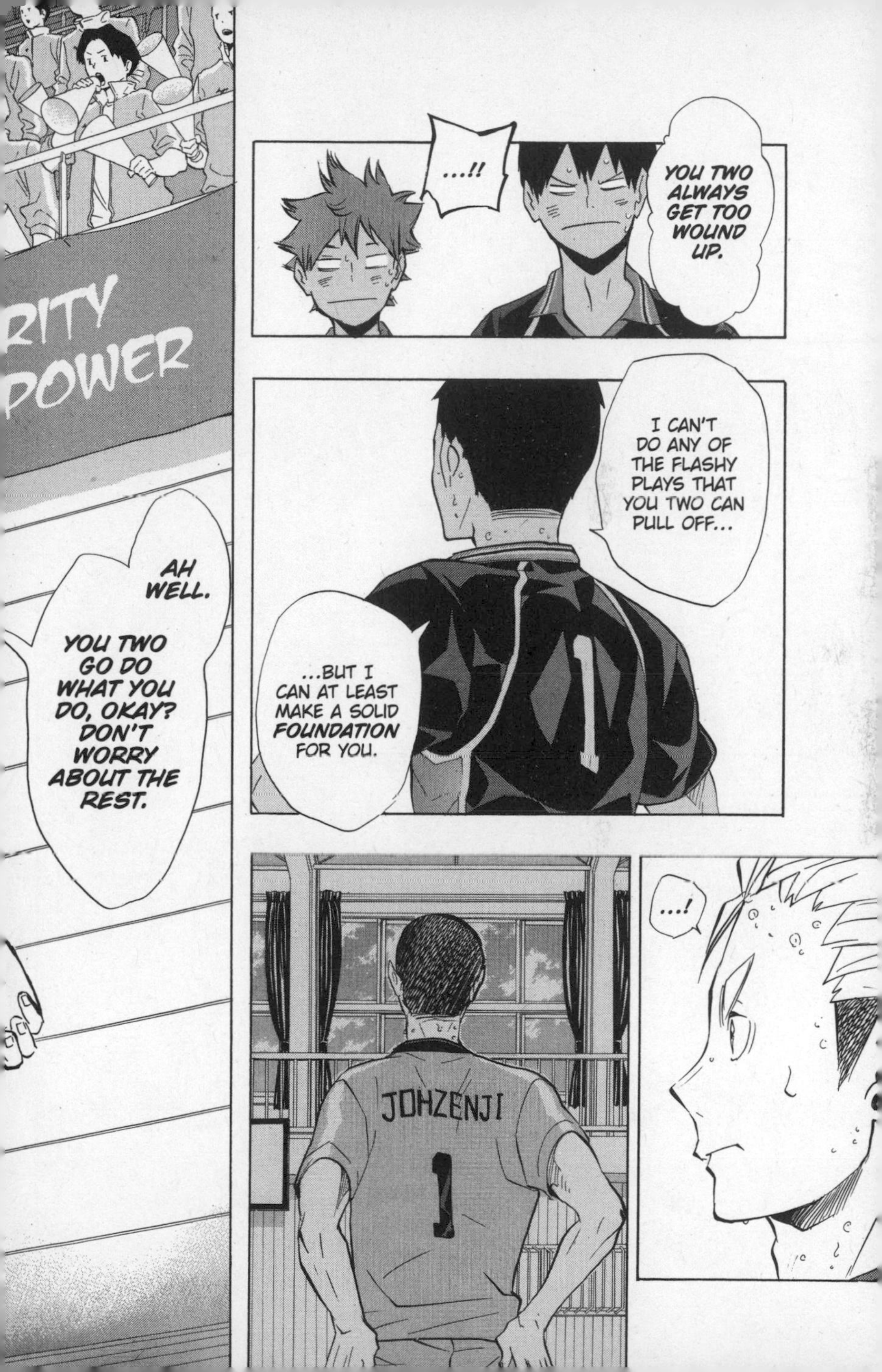
YOU TWO ALWAYS GET TOO WOUND UP.
...!!
I CAN'T DO ANY OF THE FLASHY PLAYS THAT YOU TWO CAN PULL OFF...
...BUT I CAN AT LEAST MAKE A SOLID FOUNDATION FOR YOU.
...!
JOHZENJI
1
RITY
POWER
AH WELL.
YOU TWO GO DO WHAT YOU DO, OKAY? DON'T WORRY ABOUT THE REST.

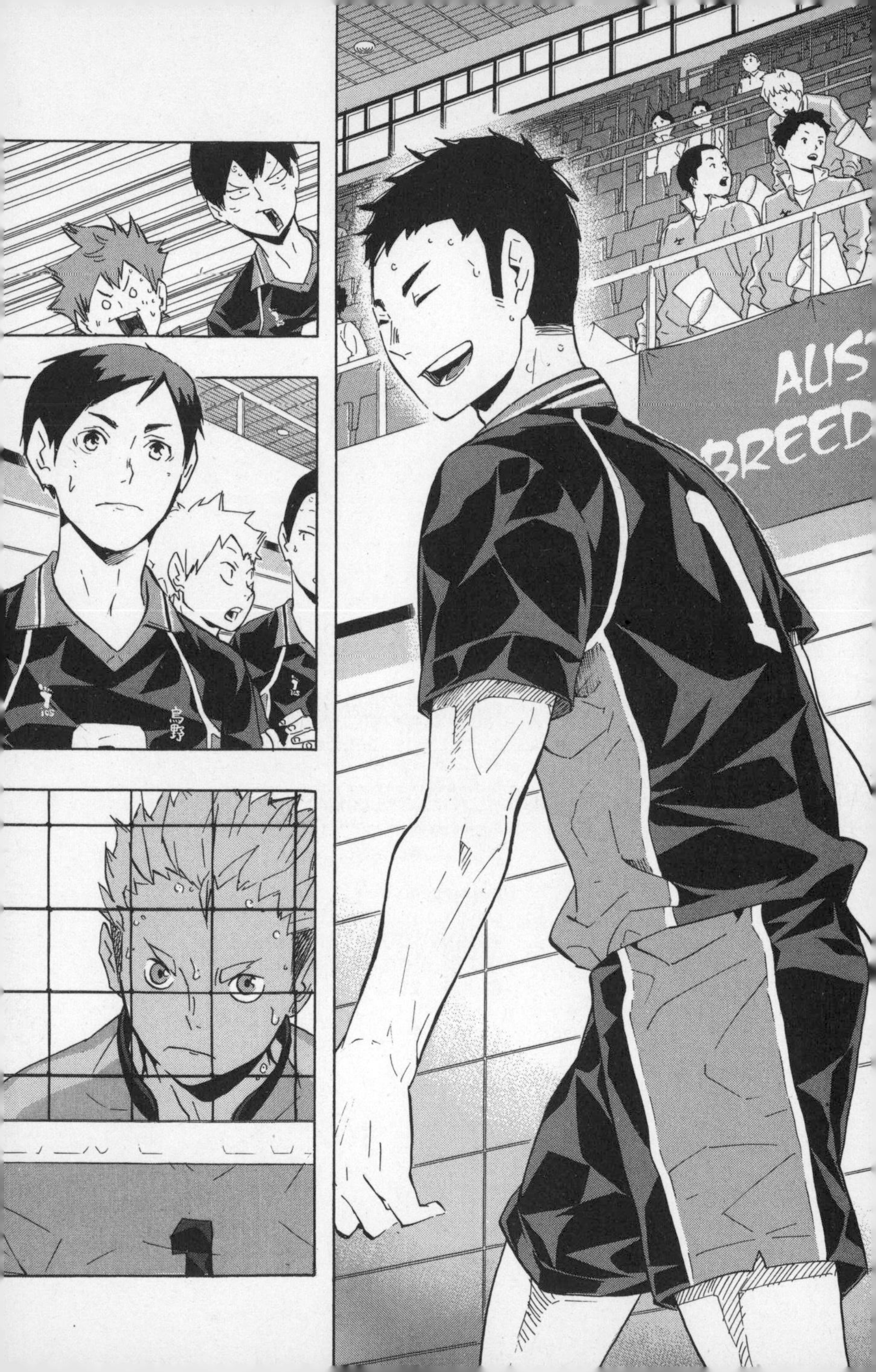
AUS
BREED
烏野

KAZUMA BOBATA

JOHZENJI HIGH SCHOOL
CLASS 2-1

POSITION:
MIDDLE BLOCKER

HEIGHT: 6'1"

WEIGHT: 158 LBS.
(AS OF APRIL, 2ND YEAR OF HIGH SCHOOL)

ABILITY PARAMETERS
(5-POINT SCALE)

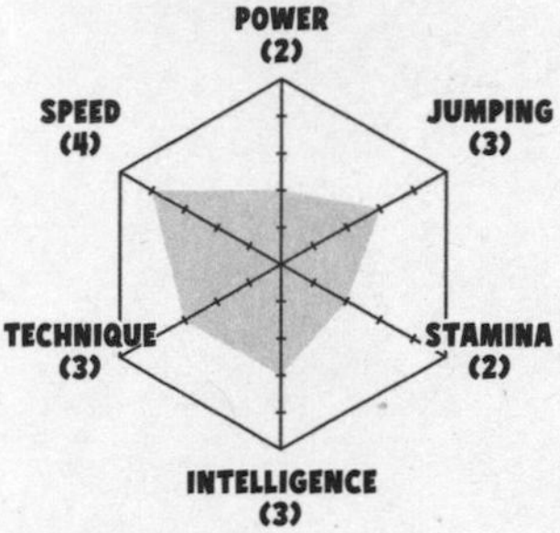
POWER (2)
JUMPING (3)
STAMINA (2)
INTELLIGENCE (3)
TECHNIQUE (3)
SPEED (4)

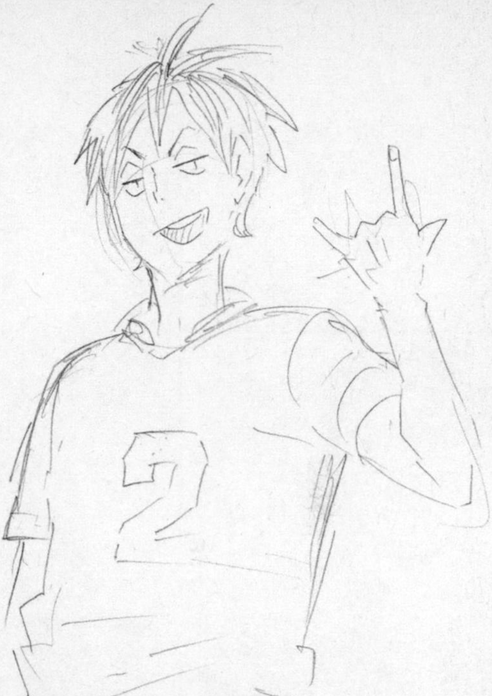

NOBUYOSHI IIZAKA

JOHZENJI HIGH SCHOOL
CLASS 2-4

POSITION:
MIDDLE BLOCKER

HEIGHT: 6'1"

WEIGHT: 169 LBS.
(AS OF APRIL, 2ND YEAR OF HIGH SCHOOL)

ABILITY PARAMETERS
(5-POINT SCALE)

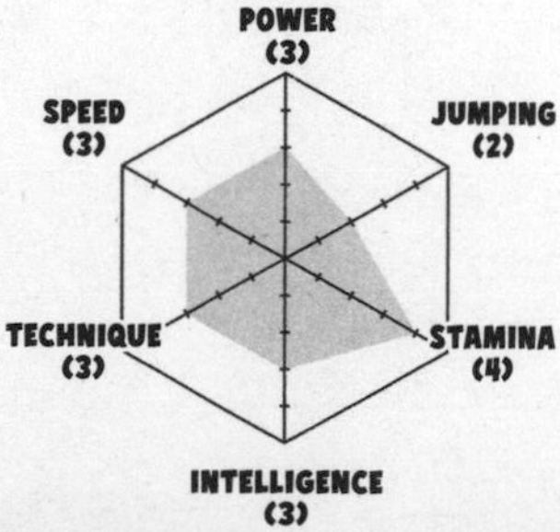
POWER (3)
JUMPING (2)
STAMINA (4)
INTELLIGENCE (3)
TECHNIQUE (3)
SPEED (3)

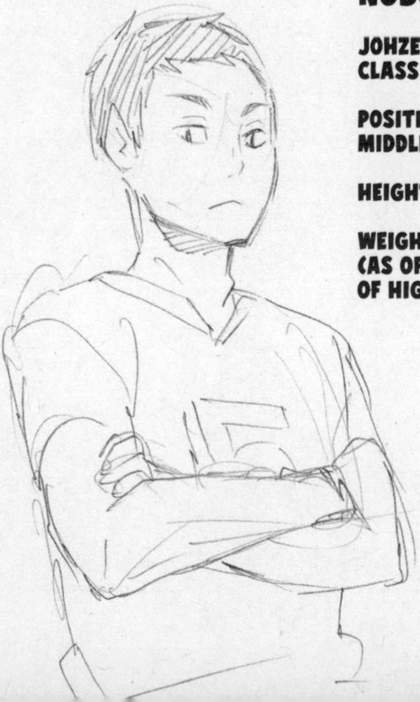

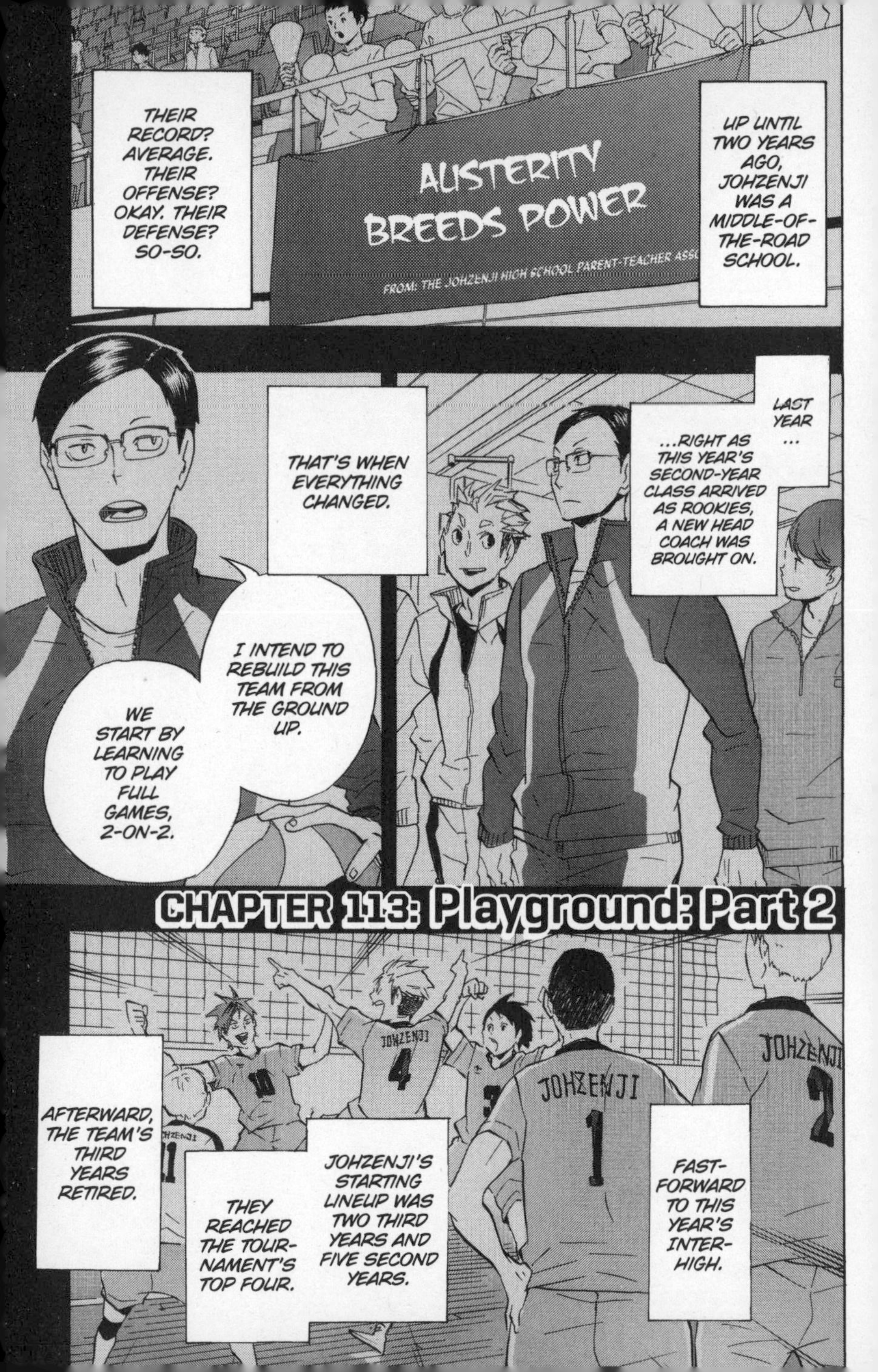
UP UNTIL TWO YEARS AGO, JOHZENJI WAS A MIDDLE-OF-THE-ROAD SCHOOL.
AUSTERITY BREEDS POWER
FROM: THE JOHZENJI HIGH SCHOOL PARENT-TEACHER
THEIR RECORD? AVERAGE. THEIR OFFENSE? OKAY. THEIR DEFENSE? SO-SO.
LAST YEAR...
...RIGHT AS THIS YEAR'S SECOND-YEAR CLASS ARRIVED AS ROOKIES, A NEW HEAD COACH WAS BROUGHT ON.
THAT'S WHEN EVERYTHING CHANGED.
I INTEND TO REBUILD THIS TEAM FROM THE GROUND UP.
WE START BY LEARNING TO PLAY FULL GAMES, 2-ON-2.
CHAPTER 113: Playground: Part 2
FAST-FORWARD TO THIS YEAR'S INTER-HIGH.
JOHZENJI'S STARTING LINEUP WAS TWO THIRD YEARS AND FIVE SECOND YEARS.
THEY REACHED THE TOURNAMENT'S TOP FOUR.
AFTERWARD, THE TEAM'S THIRD YEARS RETIRED.

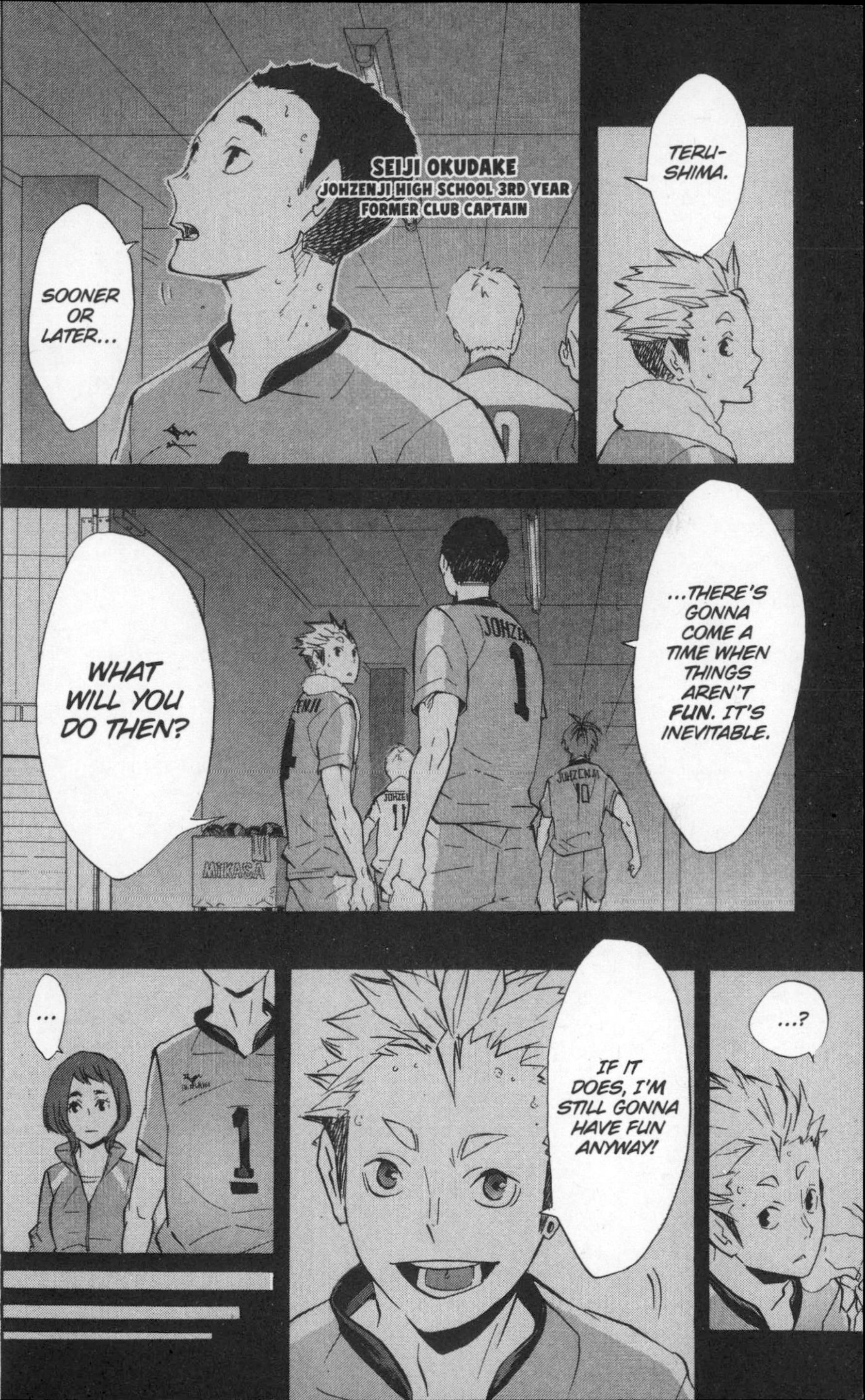
TERU-SHIMA.
SEIJI OKUDAKE
JOHZENJI HIGH SCHOOL 3RD YEAR
FORMER CLUB CAPTAIN
SOONER OR LATER...
...THERE'S GONNA COME A TIME WHEN THINGS AREN'T FUN. IT'S INEVITABLE.
WHAT WILL YOU DO THEN?
...?
IF IT DOES, I'M STILL GONNA HAVE FUN ANYWAY!
...

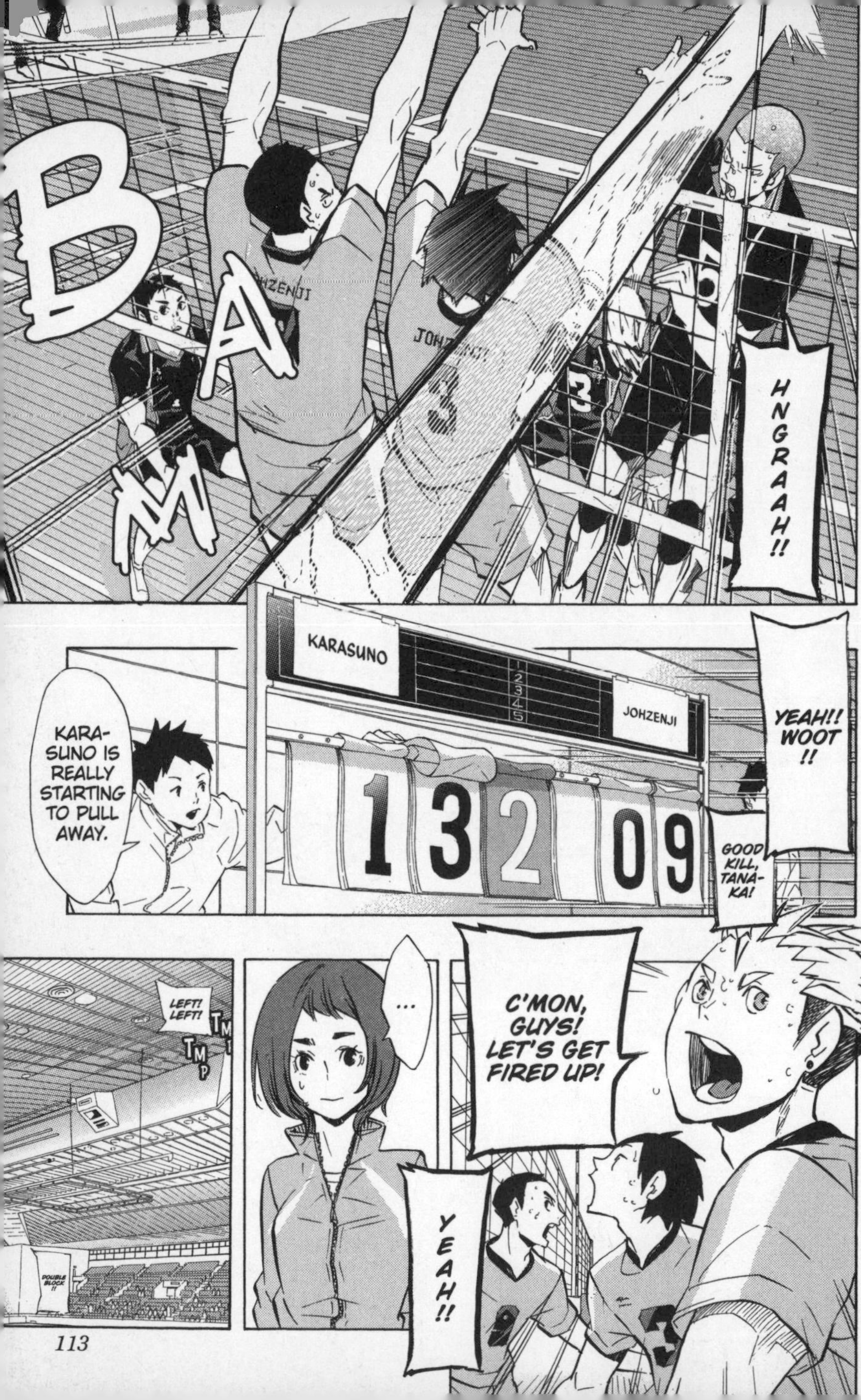
HNGRAAH!!
BAM
YEAH!! WOOT!!
GOOD KILL, TANAKA!
KARASUNO
JOHZENJI
1 2 3 4 5
13 2 09
KARA-SUNO IS REALLY STARTING TO PULL AWAY.
C'MON, GUYS! LET'S GET FIRED UP!
...
YEAH!!
LEFT! LEFT!
TMP TMP
DOUBLE BLOCK!!

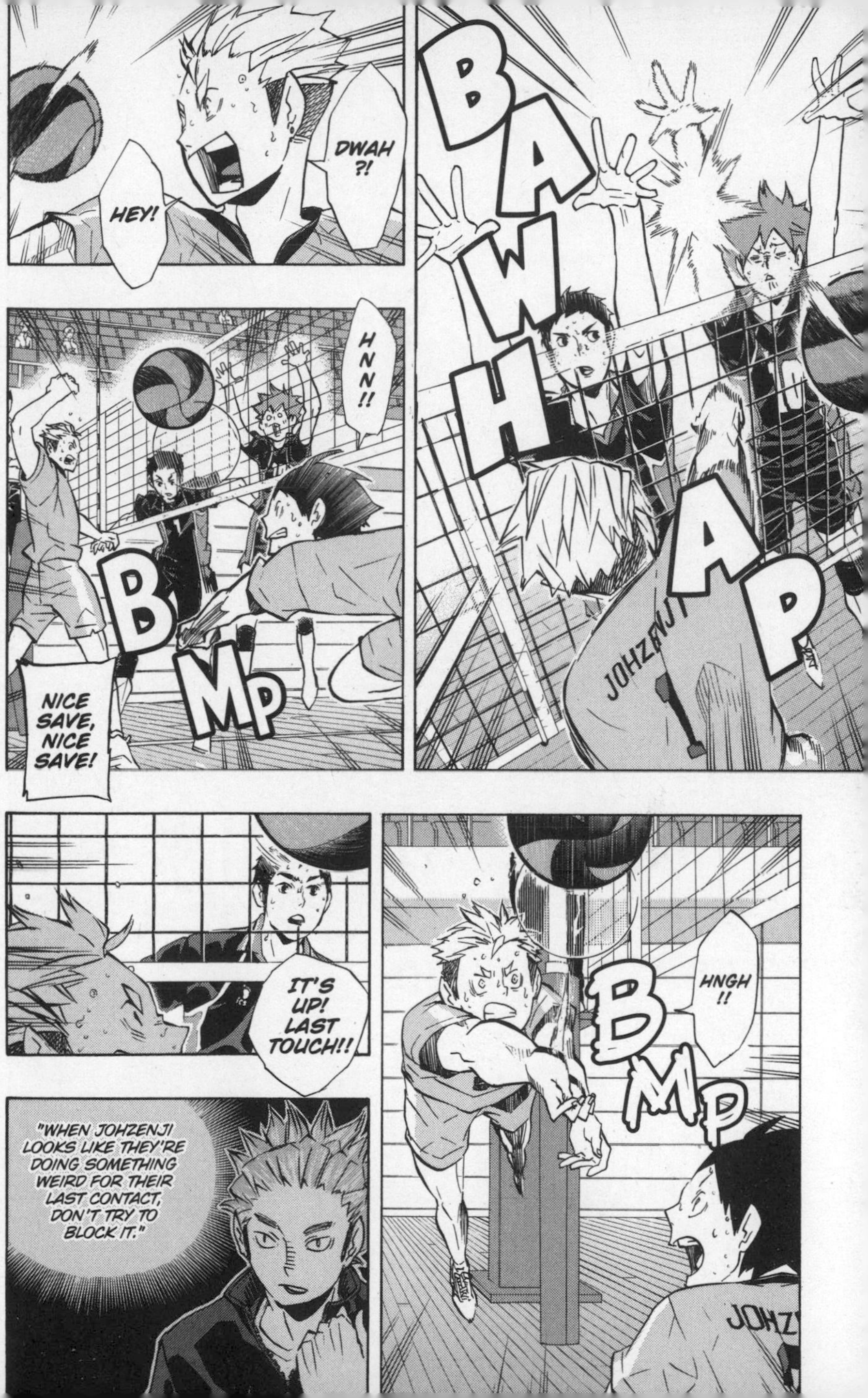
BAWHAP
DWAH ?!
HEY!
HNN!!
BMP
NICE SAVE, NICE SAVE!
HNGH !!
BMP
IT'S UP! LAST TOUCH!!
"WHEN JOHZENJI LOOKS LIKE THEY'RE DOING SOMETHING WEIRD FOR THEIR LAST CONTACT, DON'T TRY TO BLOCK IT."

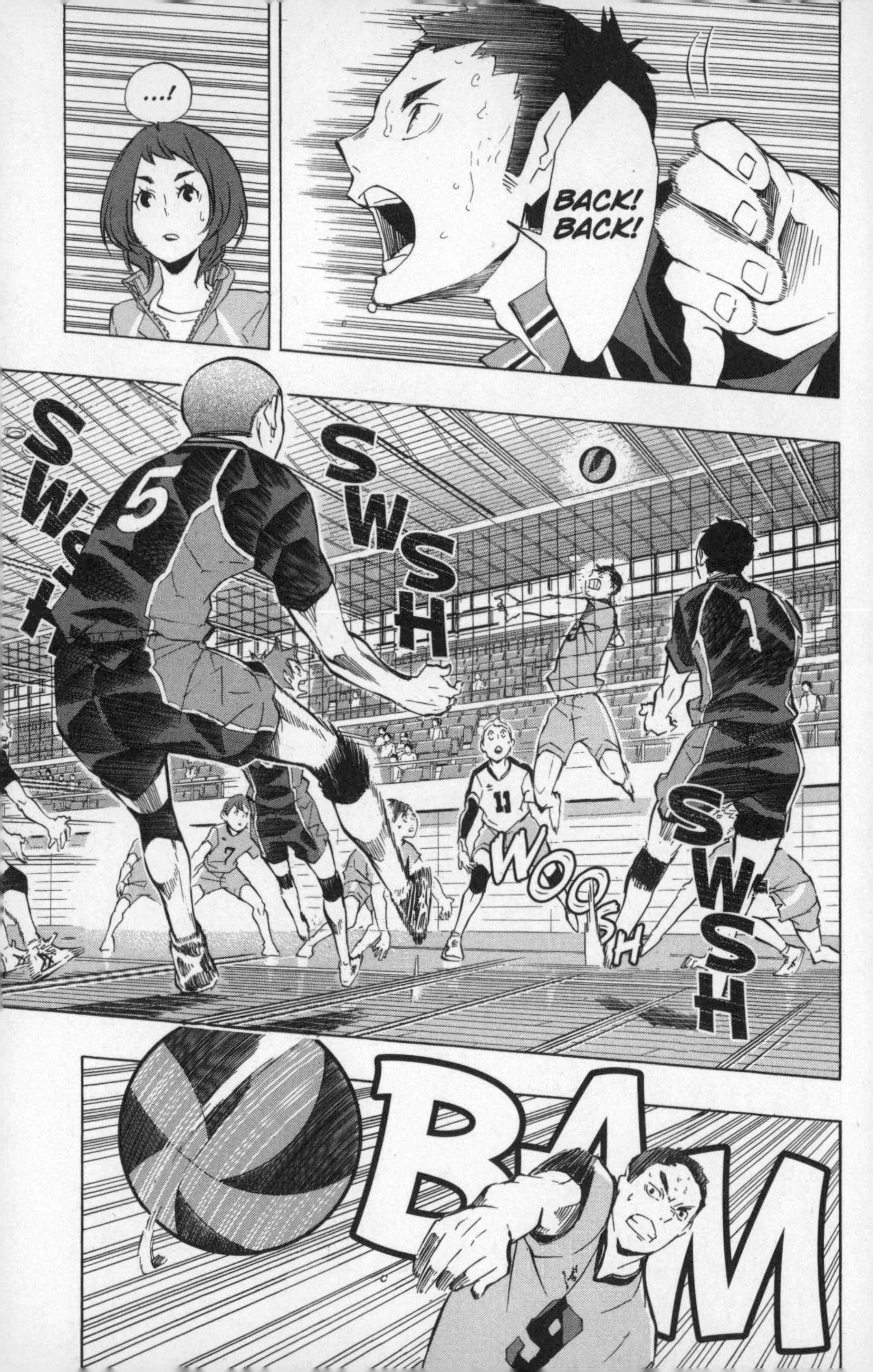
BACK! BACK!
...!
SWSH
SWSH
SWSH
WOOSH
BAM

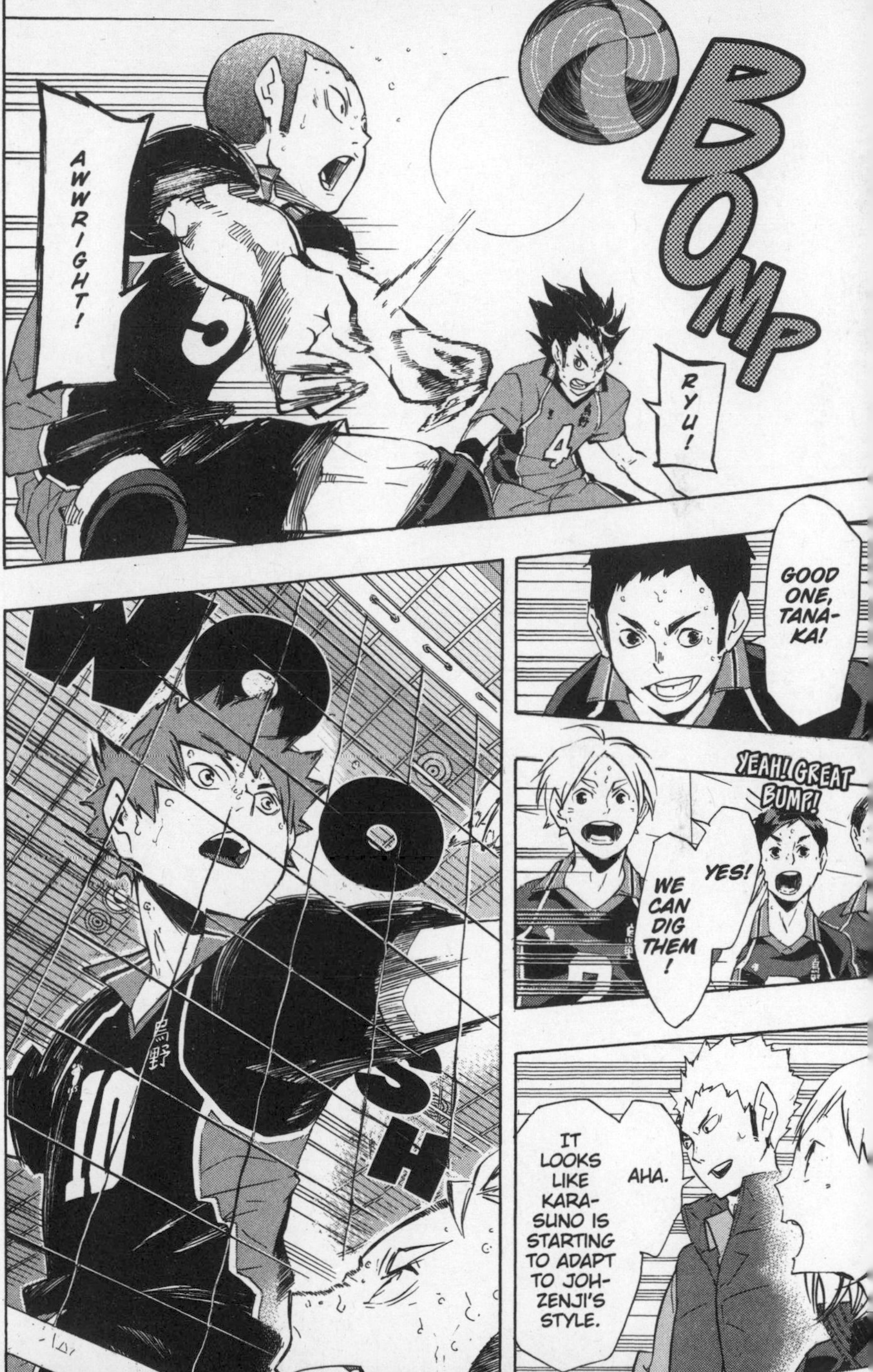
BOMP
RYU!
AWWRIGHT!
GOOD ONE, TANAKA!
YEAH! GREAT BUMP!
YES!
WE CAN DIG THEM!
AHA.
IT LOOKS LIKE KARASUNO IS STARTING TO ADAPT TO JOHZENJI'S STYLE.
WOOSH

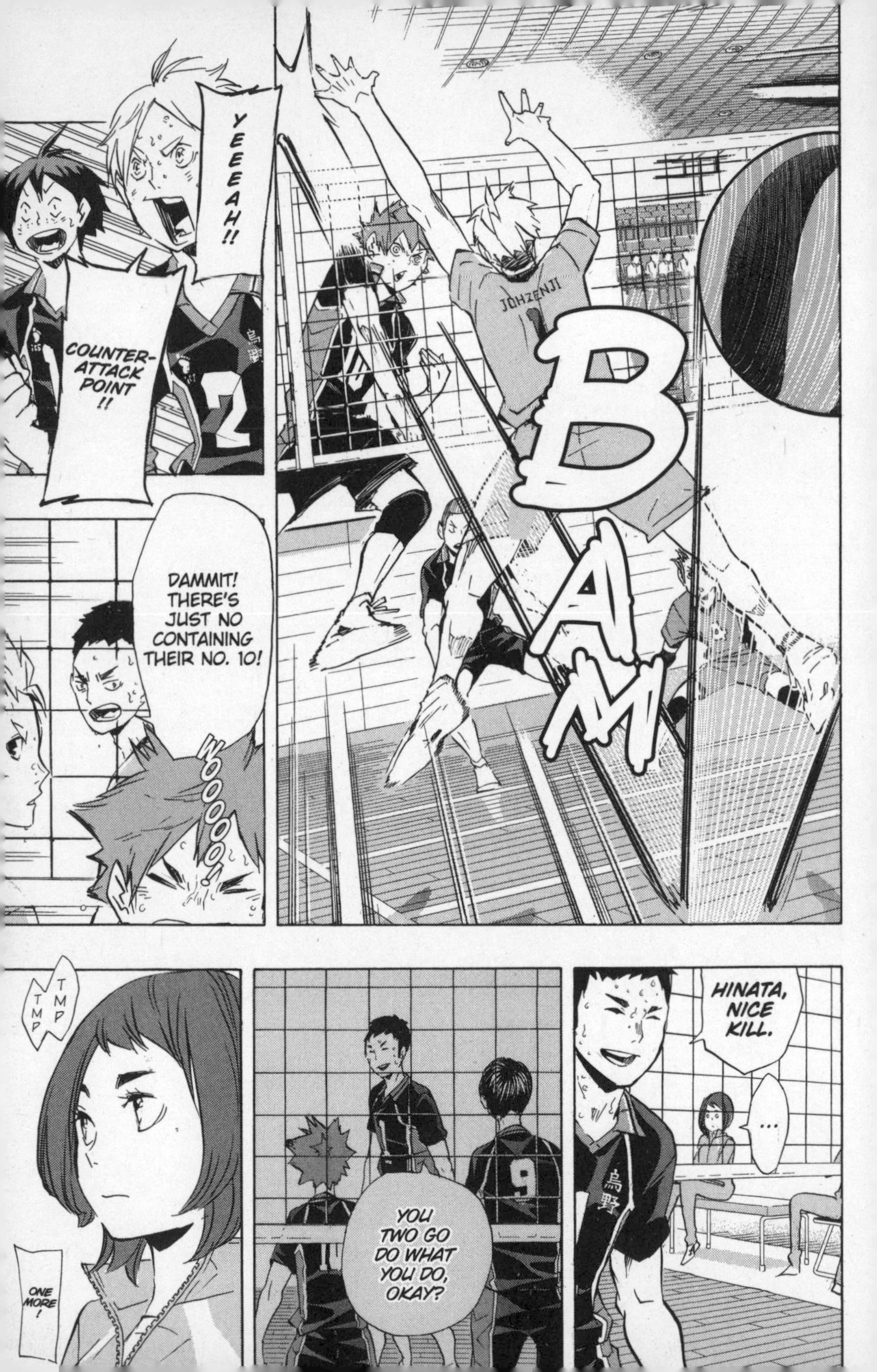
BAM
YEEEAH!!
COUNTER-ATTACK POINT!!
DAMMIT! THERE'S JUST NO CONTAINING THEIR NO. 10!
WOOOOOO!
HINATA, NICE KILL.
...
YOU TWO GO DO WHAT YOU DO, OKAY?
TMP TMP
ONE MORE!

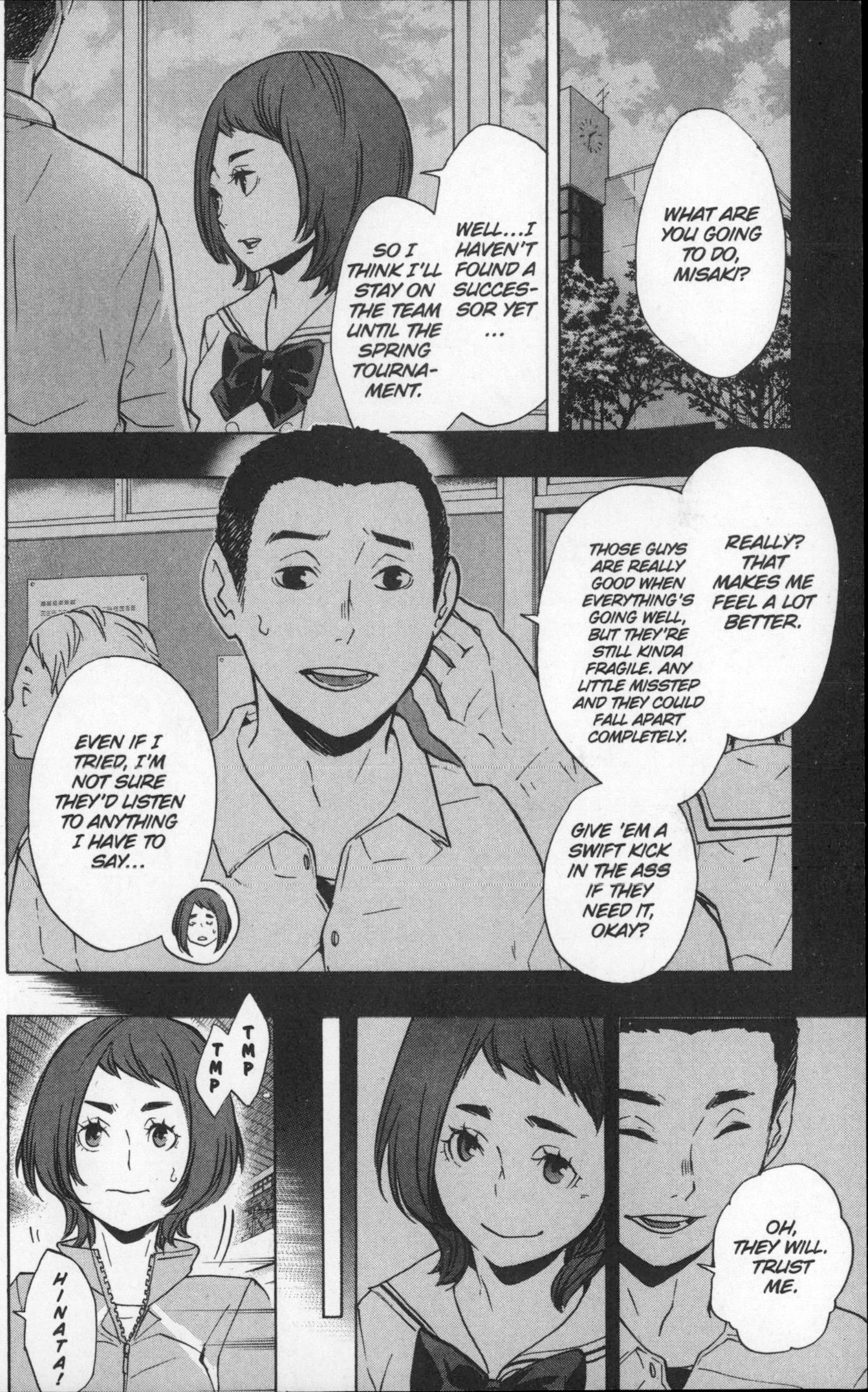
WHAT ARE YOU GOING TO DO, MISAKI?
WELL...I HAVEN'T FOUND A SUCCES-SOR YET...
SO I THINK I'LL STAY ON THE TEAM UNTIL THE SPRING TOURNA-MENT.
REALLY? THAT MAKES ME FEEL A LOT BETTER.
THOSE GUYS ARE REALLY GOOD WHEN EVERYTHING'S GOING WELL, BUT THEY'RE STILL KINDA FRAGILE. ANY LITTLE MISSTEP AND THEY COULD FALL APART COMPLETELY.
GIVE 'EM A SWIFT KICK IN THE ASS IF THEY NEED IT, OKAY?
EVEN IF I TRIED, I'M NOT SURE THEY'D LISTEN TO ANYTHING I HAVE TO SAY...
OH, THEY WILL. TRUST ME.
TMP TMP
HINATA!

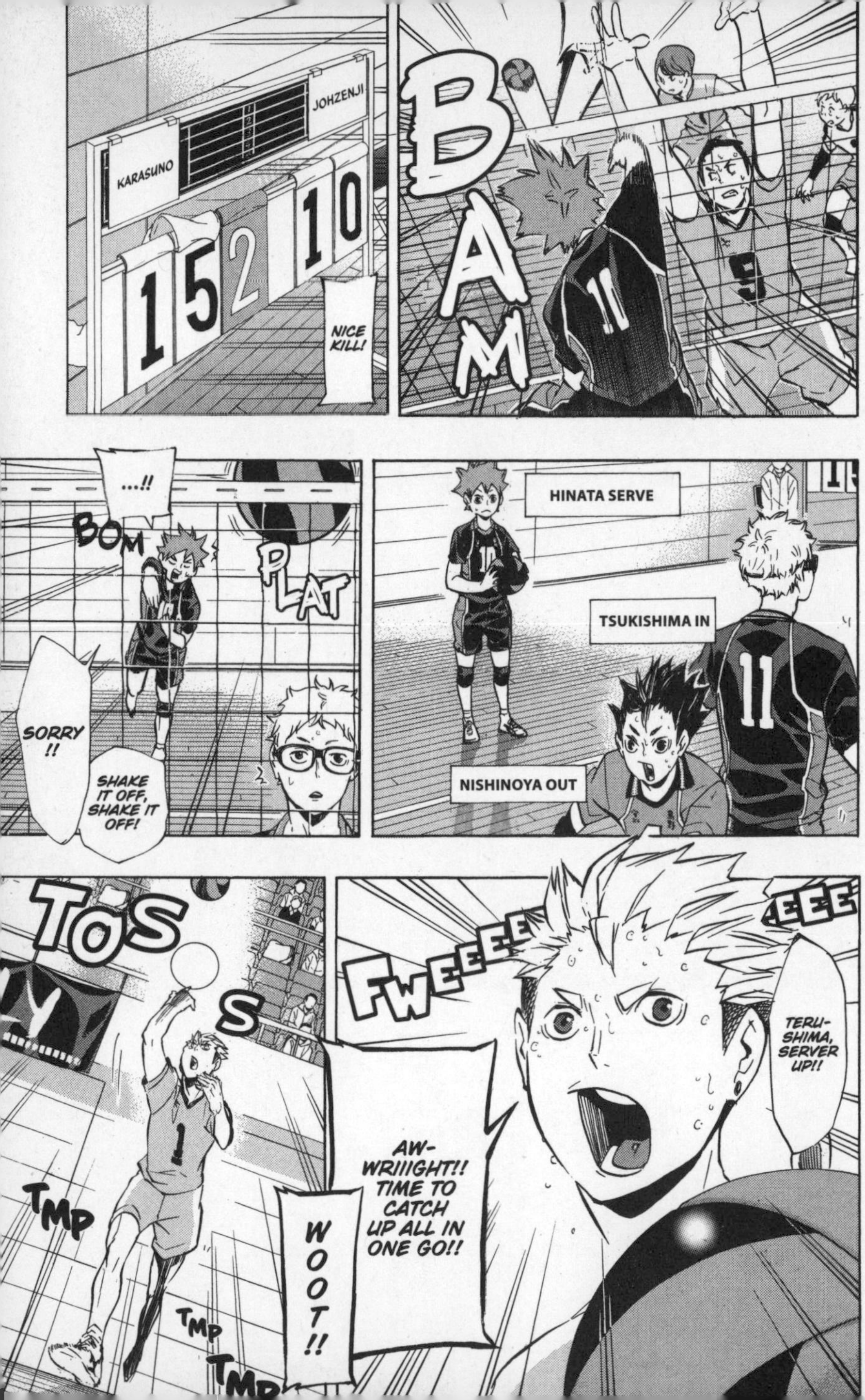
BAM
KARASUNO
JOHZENJI
15
2
10
NICE KILL!
HINATA SERVE
TSUKISHIMA IN
NISHINOYA OUT
...!!
BOM
PLAT
SORRY!!
SHAKE IT OFF, SHAKE IT OFF!
FWEEEE
EEE
TERU-SHIMA, SERVER UP!!
AW-WRIIIGHT!! TIME TO CATCH UP ALL IN ONE GO!!
WOOOT!!
TOS
S
TMP
TMP
TMP

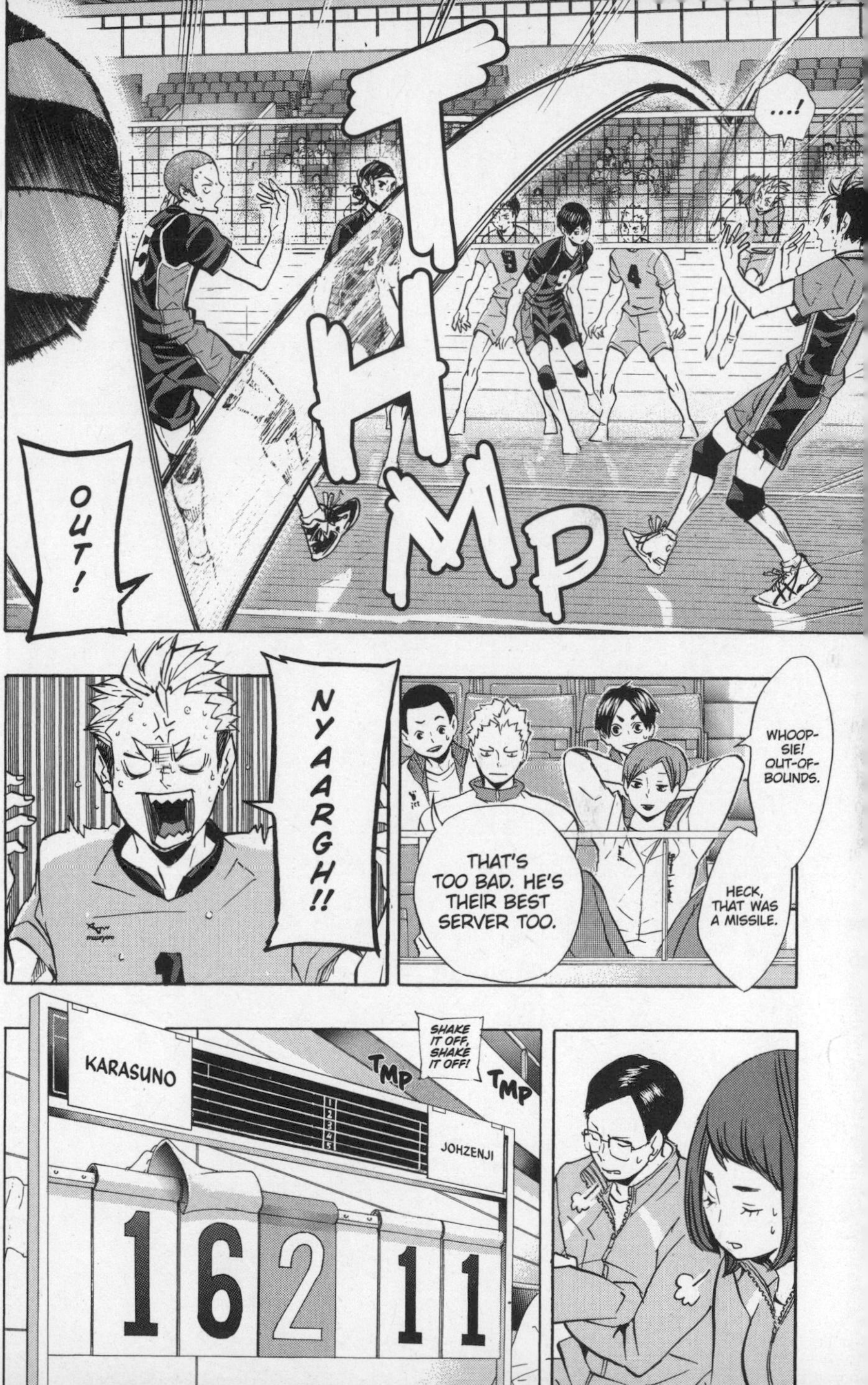
...!
THUMP
OUT!
WHOOP-SIE! OUT-OF-BOUNDS.
THAT'S TOO BAD. HE'S THEIR BEST SERVER TOO.
HECK, THAT WAS A MISSILE.
NYAARGH!!
TMP
SHAKE IT OFF, SHAKE IT OFF!
TMP
KARASUNO
JOHZENJI
1 2 3 4 5
16
2
11

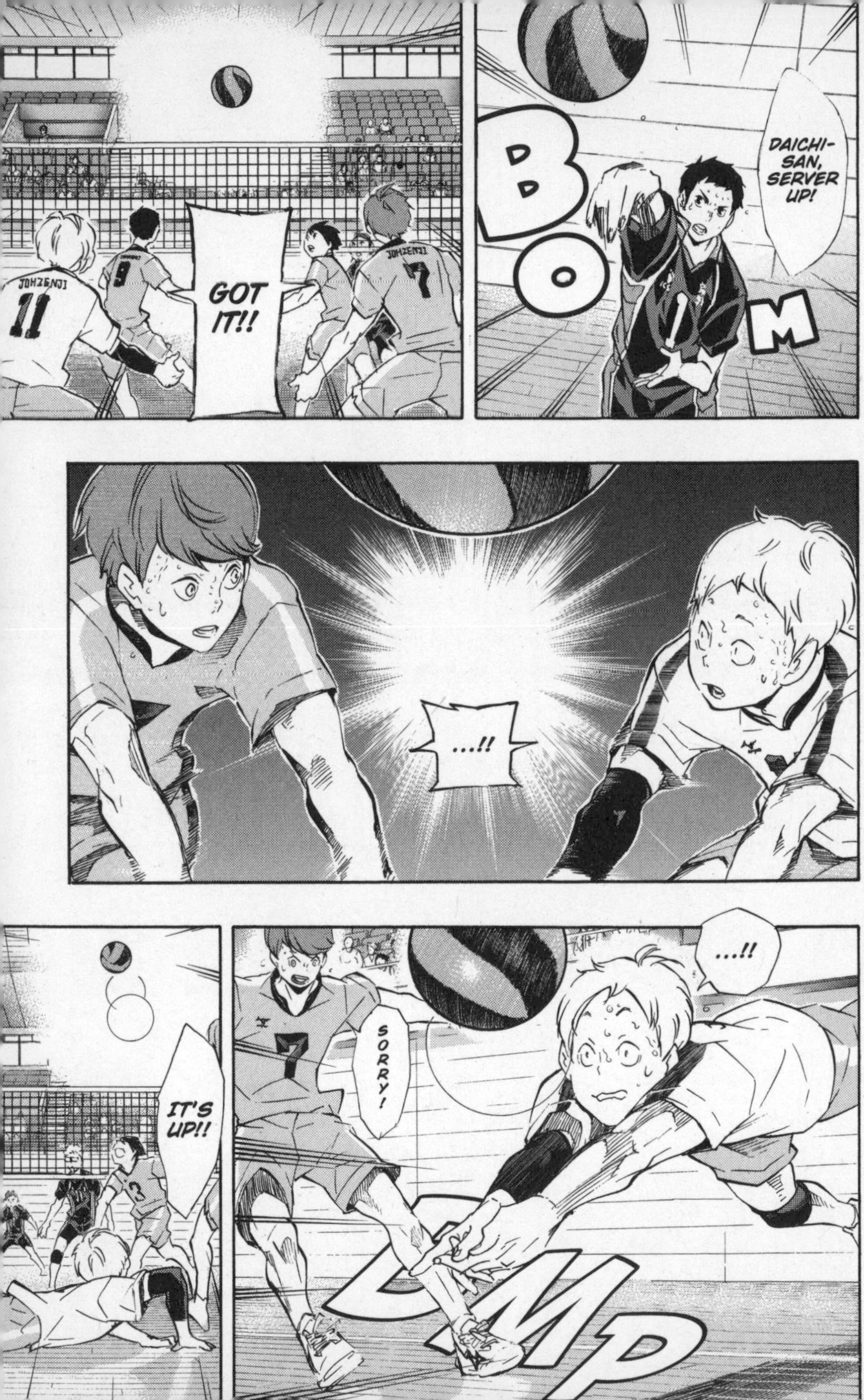
BOOM
DAICHI-SAN, SERVER UP!
GOT IT!!
...!!
...!!
SORRY!
IT'S UP!!

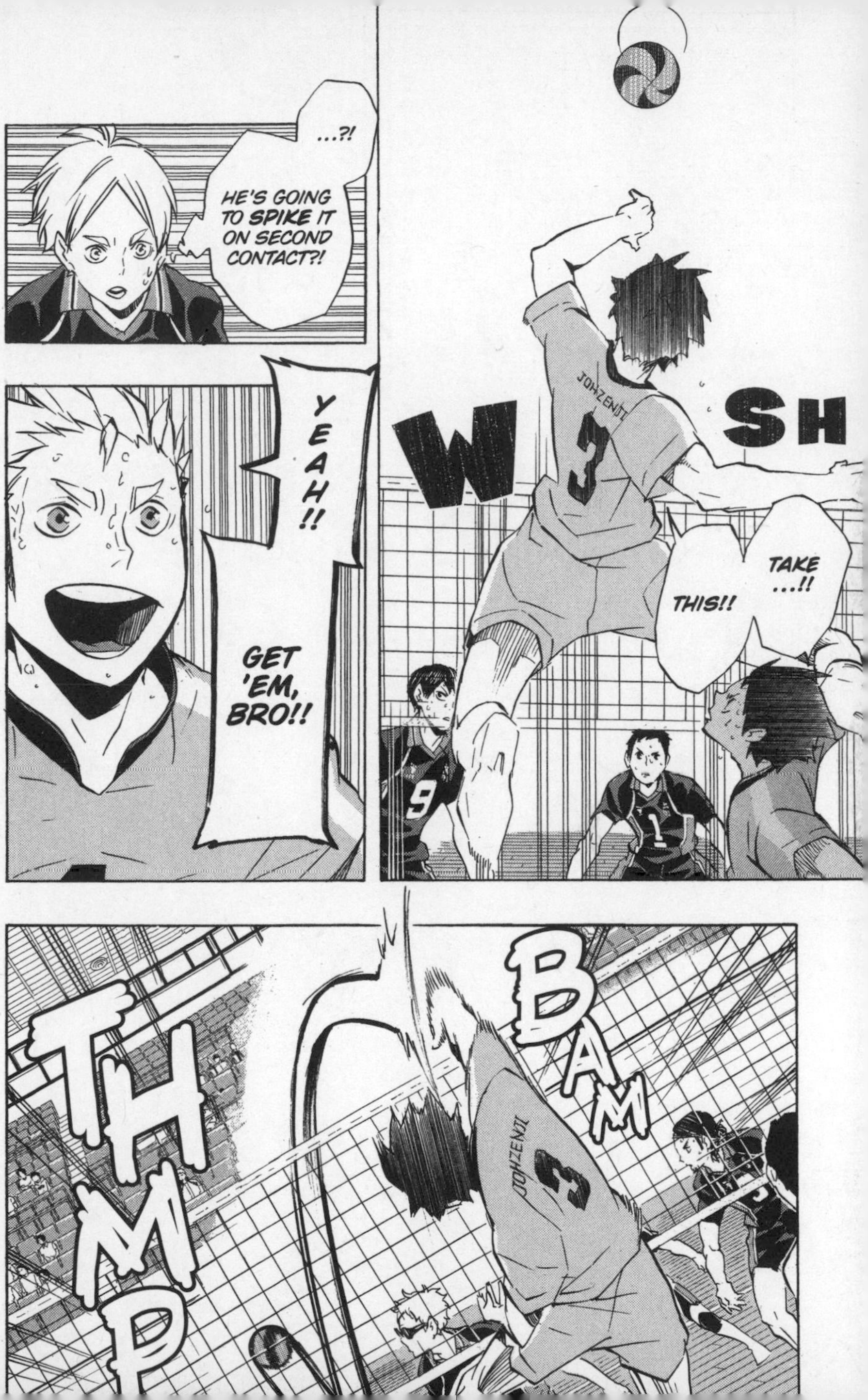
WSH
TAKE ...!!
THIS!!
...?!
HE'S GOING TO **SPIKE** IT ON SECOND CONTACT?!
YEAH!!
GET 'EM, BRO!!
BAM
THMP

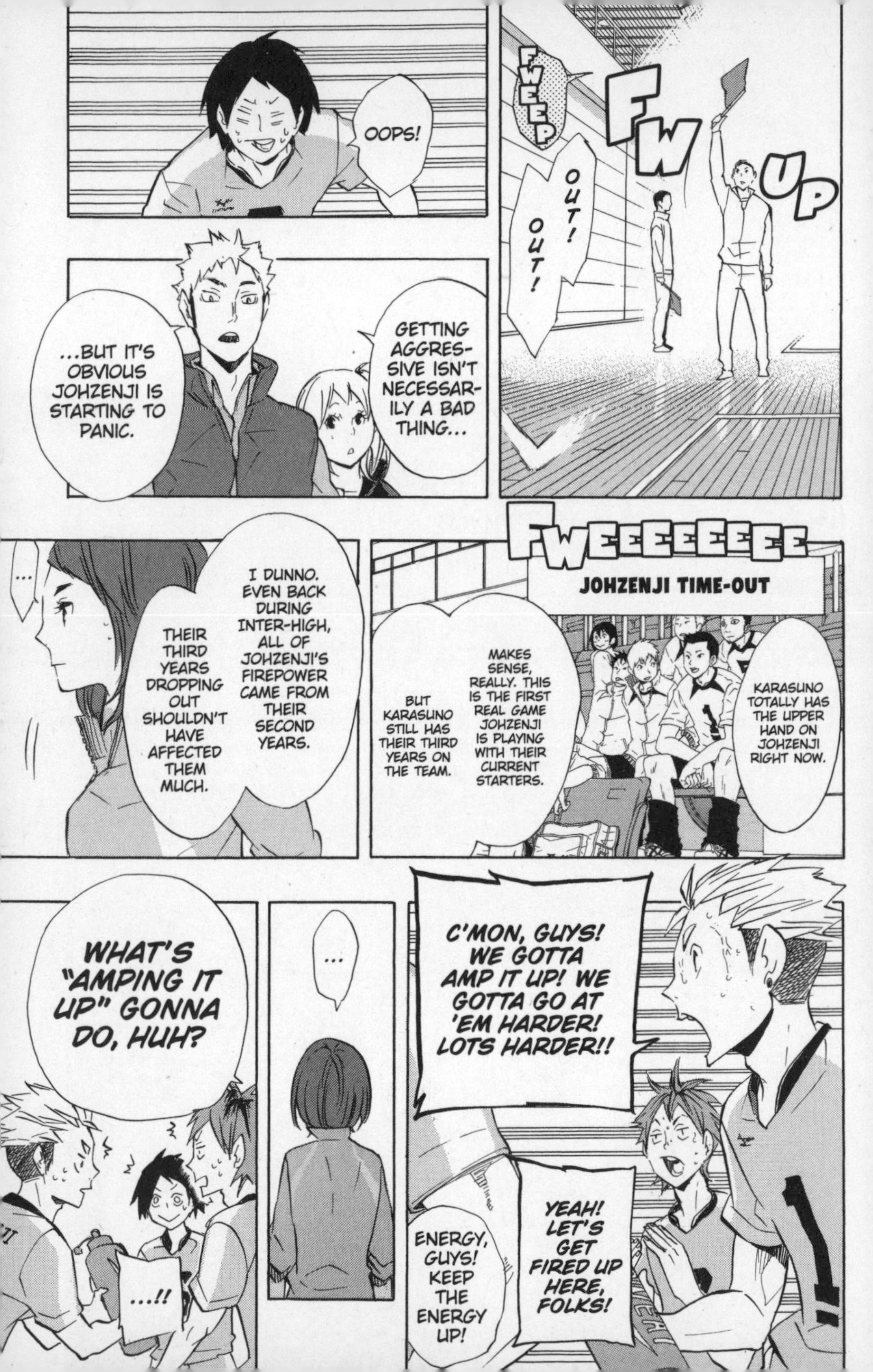
FW UP
FWEEP
OUT! OUT!
OOPS!
GETTING AGGRESSIVE ISN'T NECESSARILY A BAD THING...
...BUT IT'S OBVIOUS JOHZENJI IS STARTING TO PANIC.
FWEEEEEEEE
JOHZENJI TIME-OUT
KARASUNO TOTALLY HAS THE UPPER HAND ON JOHZENJI RIGHT NOW.
MAKES SENSE, REALLY. THIS IS THE FIRST REAL GAME JOHZENJI IS PLAYING WITH THEIR CURRENT STARTERS.
BUT KARASUNO STILL HAS THEIR THIRD YEARS ON THE TEAM.
I DUNNO. EVEN BACK DURING INTER-HIGH, ALL OF JOHZENJI'S FIREPOWER CAME FROM THEIR SECOND YEARS.
THEIR THIRD YEARS DROPPING OUT SHOULDN'T HAVE AFFECTED THEM MUCH.
...
C'MON, GUYS! WE GOTTA AMP IT UP! WE GOTTA GO AT 'EM HARDER! LOTS HARDER!!
YEAH! LET'S GET FIRED UP HERE, FOLKS!
ENERGY, GUYS! KEEP THE ENERGY UP!
...
WHAT'S "AMPING IT UP" GONNA DO, HUH?
...!!

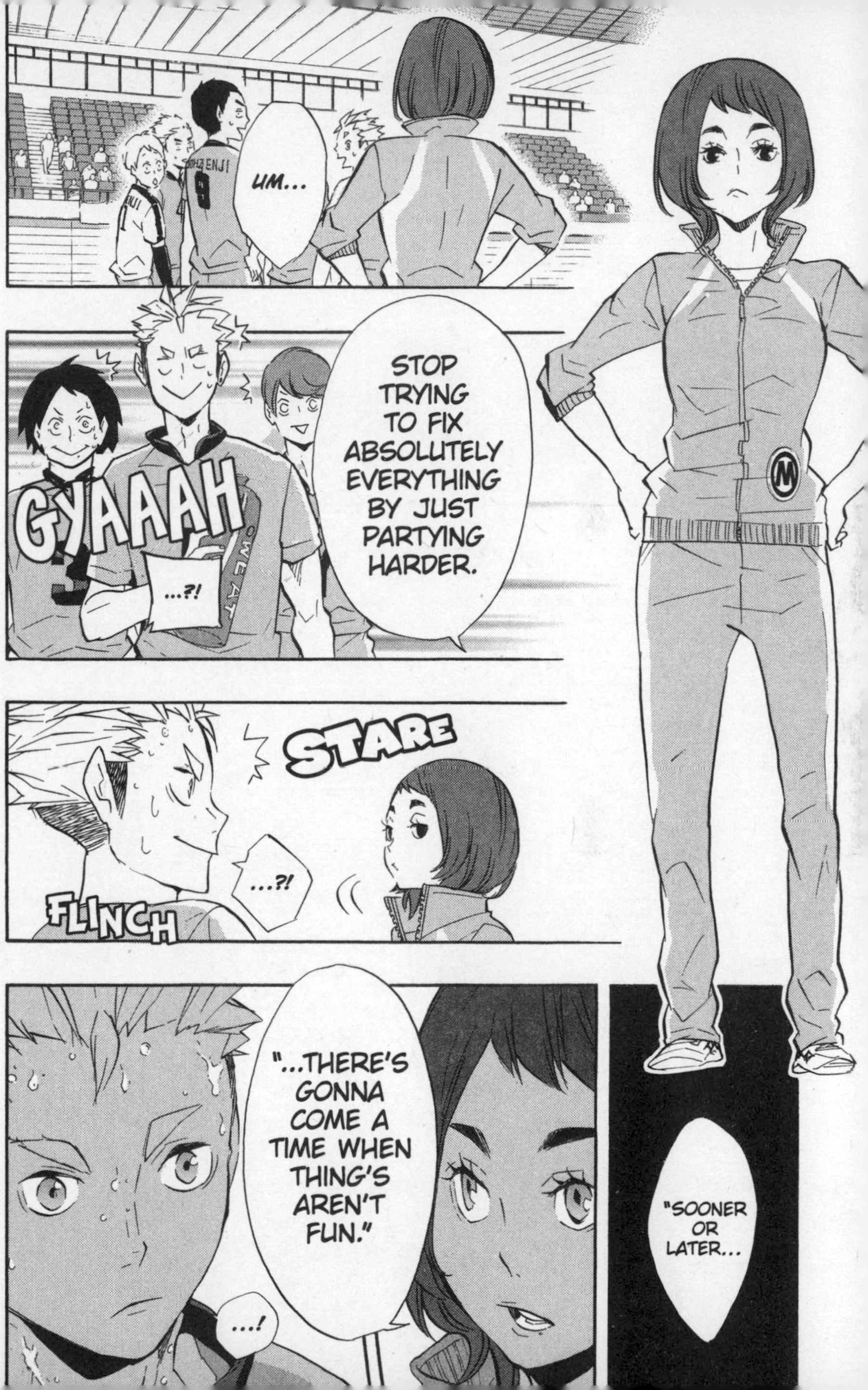
UM...
STOP TRYING TO FIX ABSOLUTELY EVERYTHING BY JUST PARTYING HARDER.
GYAAAH
...?!
STARE
...?!
FLINCH
"SOONER OR LATER...
"...THERE'S GONNA COME A TIME WHEN THING'S AREN'T FUN."
...!

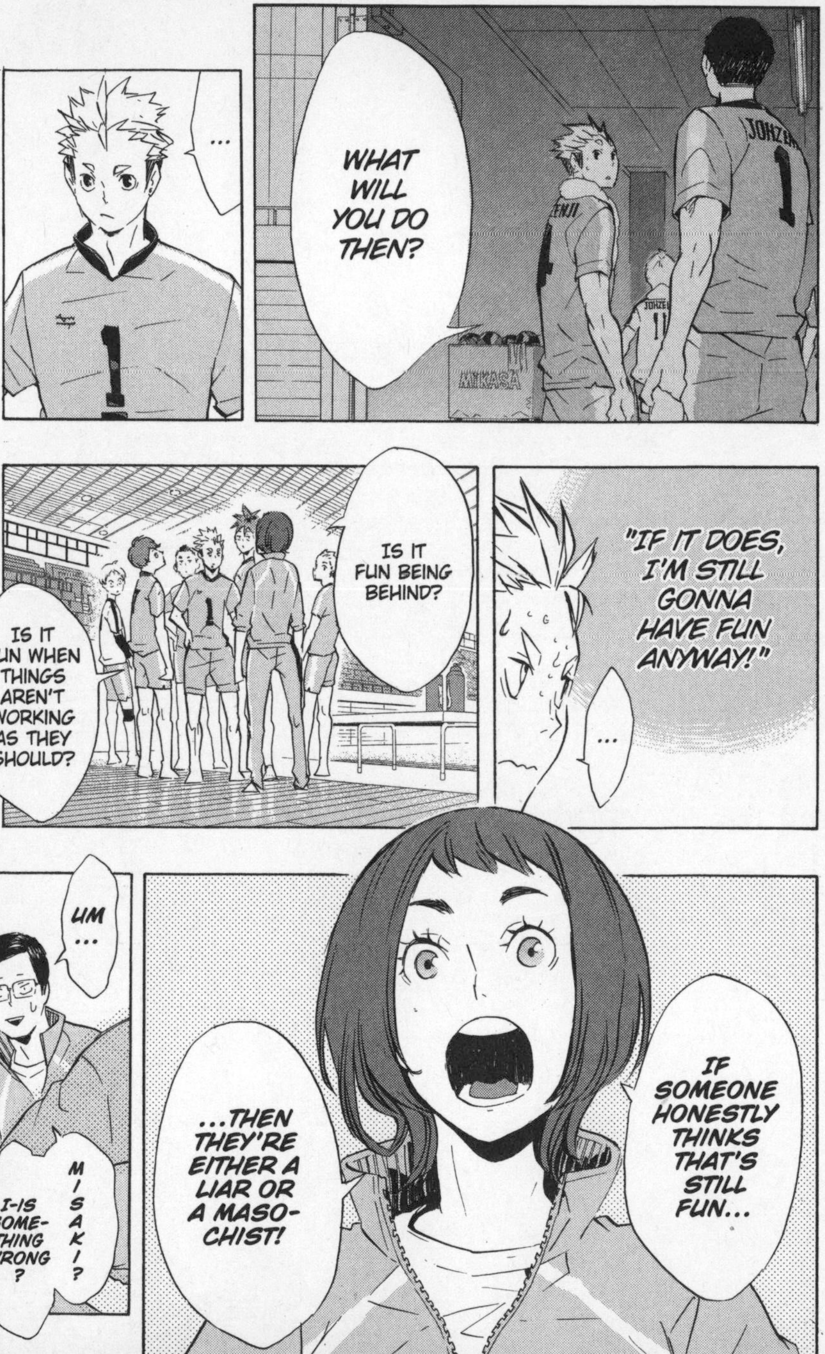
WHAT WILL YOU DO THEN?
...
"IF IT DOES, I'M STILL GONNA HAVE FUN ANYWAY!"
...
IS IT FUN BEING BEHIND?
IS IT FUN WHEN THINGS AREN'T WORKING AS THEY SHOULD?
IF SOMEONE HONESTLY THINKS THAT'S STILL FUN...
...THEN THEY'RE EITHER A LIAR OR A MASO-CHIST!
UM...
MISAKI?
I-IS SOME-THING WRONG?

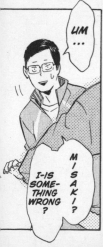

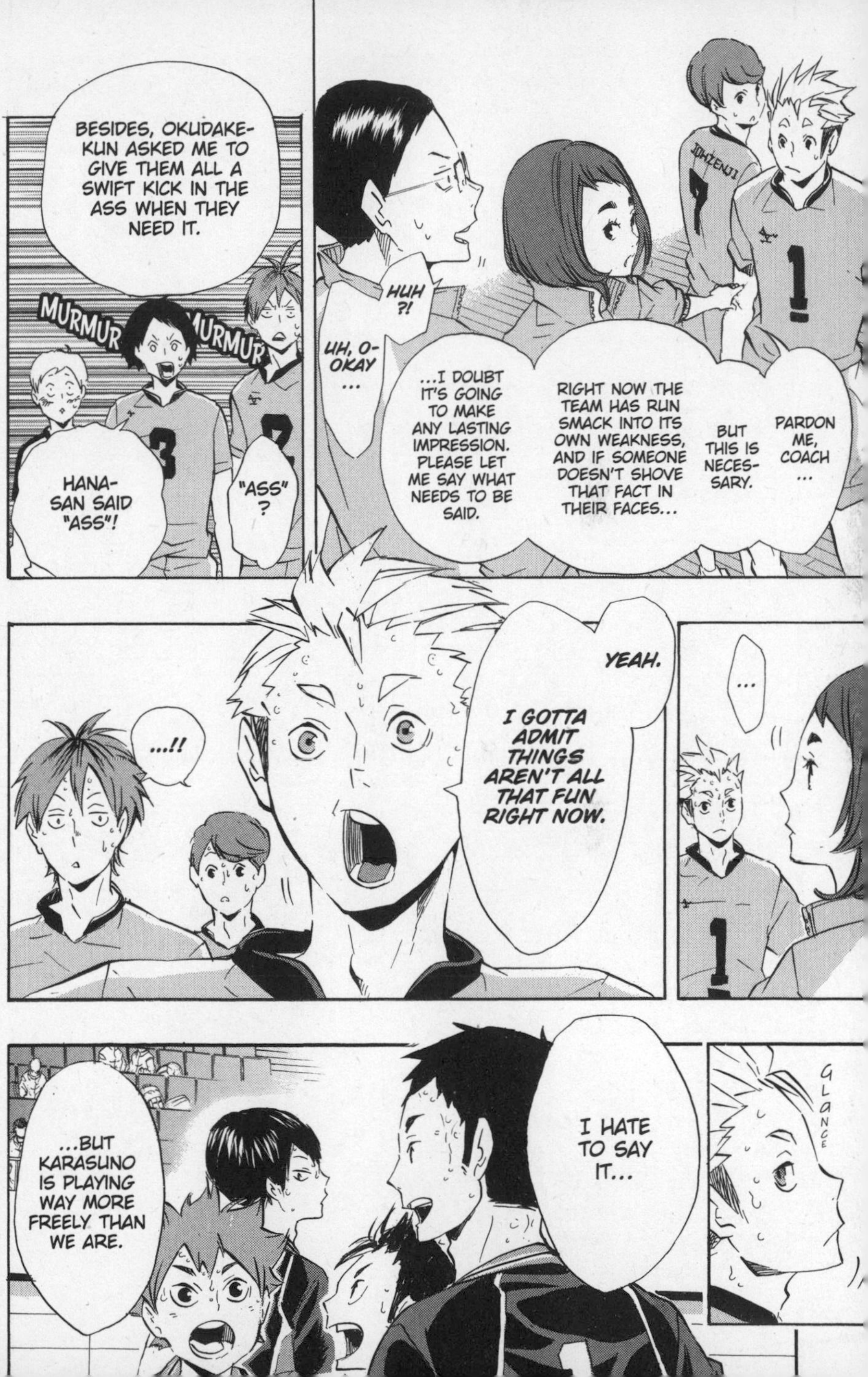
PARDON ME, COACH...
BUT THIS IS NECESSARY.
RIGHT NOW THE TEAM HAS RUN SMACK INTO ITS OWN WEAKNESS, AND IF SOMEONE DOESN'T SHOVE THAT FACT IN THEIR FACES...
...I DOUBT IT'S GOING TO MAKE ANY LASTING IMPRESSION. PLEASE LET ME SAY WHAT NEEDS TO BE SAID.
HUH ?!
UH, O-OKAY...
BESIDES, OKUDAKE-KUN ASKED ME TO GIVE THEM ALL A SWIFT KICK IN THE ASS WHEN THEY NEED IT.
MURMUR
MURMUR
"ASS"?
HANA-SAN SAID "ASS"!
...
YEAH.
I GOTTA ADMIT THINGS AREN'T ALL THAT FUN RIGHT NOW.
...!!
GLANCE
I HATE TO SAY IT...
...BUT KARASUNO IS PLAYING WAY MORE FREELY THAN WE ARE.

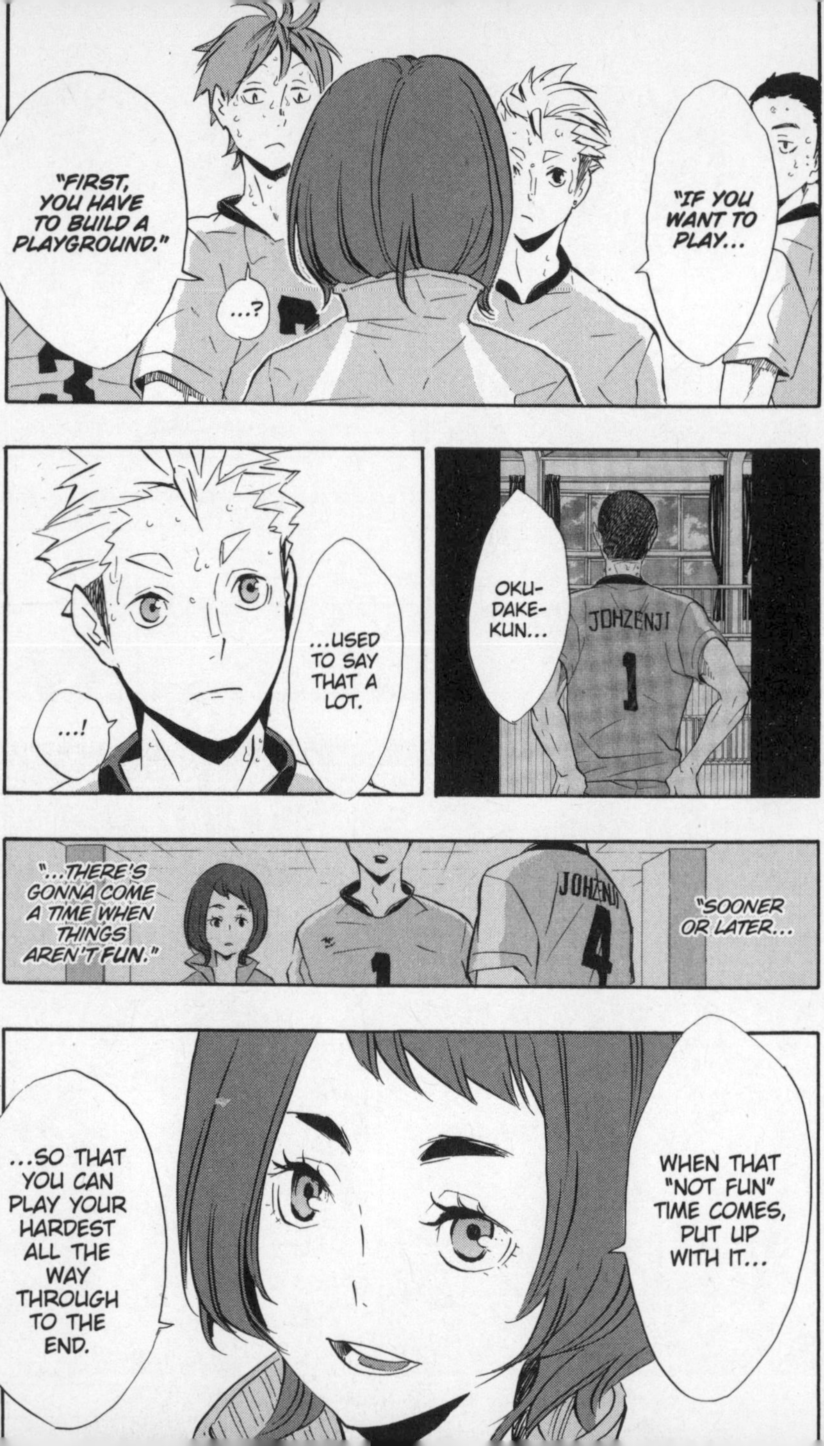
"IF YOU WANT TO PLAY...
"FIRST, YOU HAVE TO BUILD A PLAYGROUND."
...?
OKU-DAKE-KUN...
JOHZENJI 1
...USED TO SAY THAT A LOT.
...!
"SOONER OR LATER...
JOHZENJI 4
"...THERE'S GONNA COME A TIME WHEN THINGS AREN'T FUN."
WHEN THAT "NOT FUN" TIME COMES, PUT UP WITH IT...
...SO THAT YOU CAN PLAY YOUR HARDEST ALL THE WAY THROUGH TO THE END.

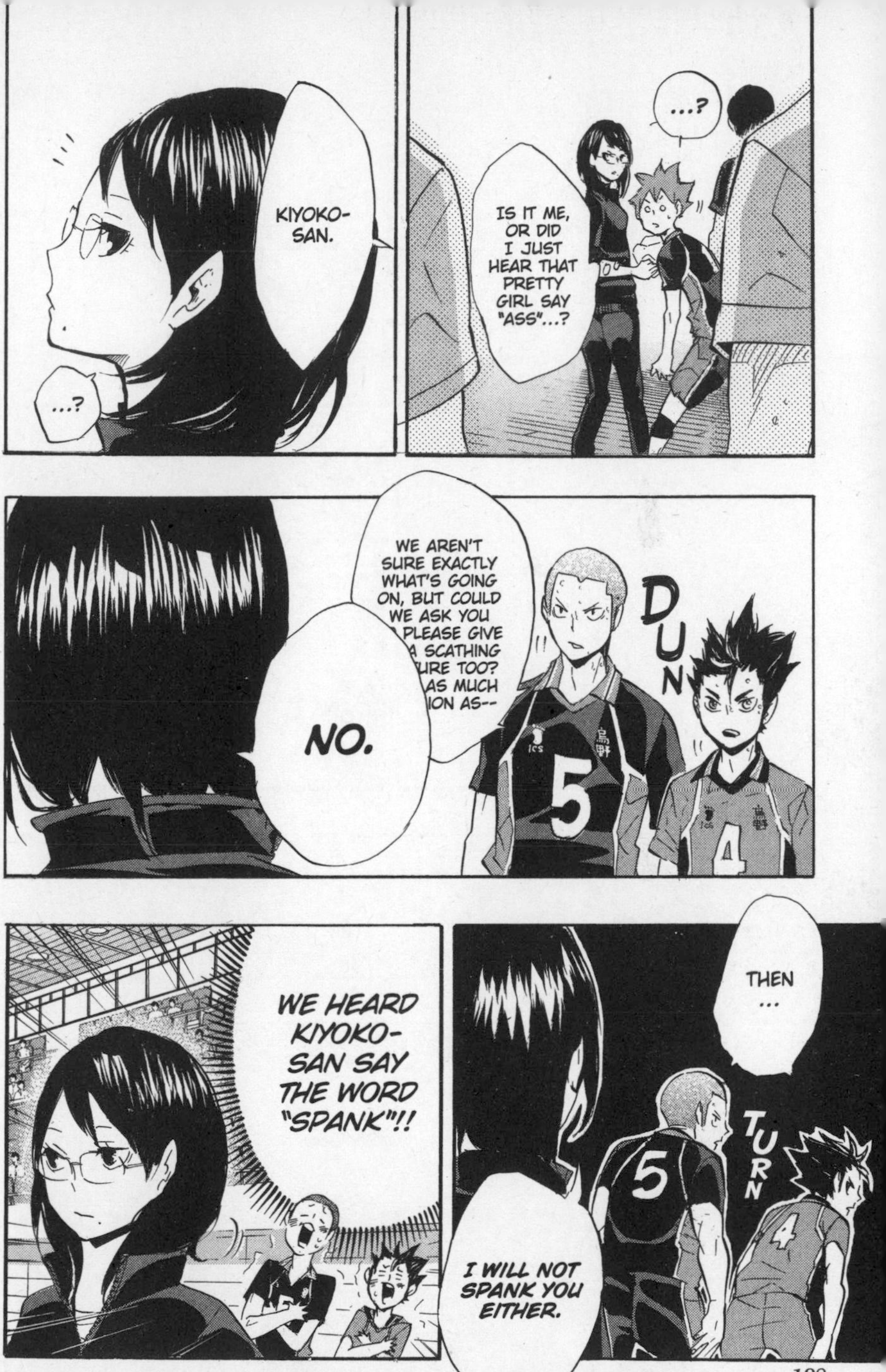
...?
IS IT ME, OR DID I JUST HEAR THAT PRETTY GIRL SAY "ASS"...?
KIYOKO-SAN.
...?
WE AREN'T SURE EXACTLY WHAT'S GOING ON, BUT COULD WE ASK YOU PLEASE GIVE A SCATHING TOO? AS MUCH AS--
DUN
NO.
THEN ...
TURN
I WILL NOT SPANK YOU EITHER.
WE HEARD KIYOKO-SAN SAY THE WORD "SPANK"!!

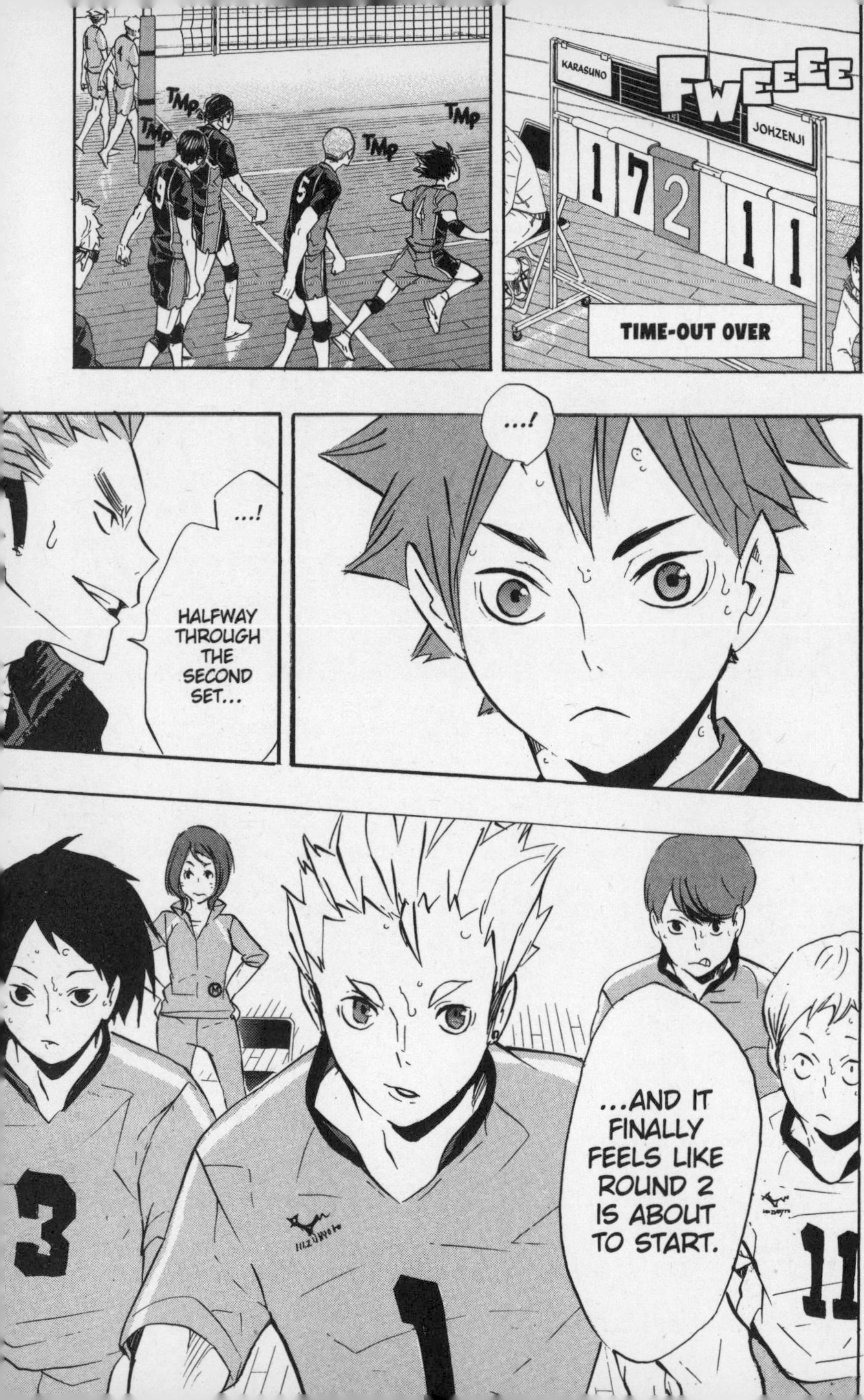
KARASUNO
FWEEEE
JOHZENJI
17
2
11
TIME-OUT OVER
TMP
TMP
TMP
TMP
...!
...!
HALFWAY THROUGH THE SECOND SET...
...AND IT FINALLY FEELS LIKE ROUND 2 IS ABOUT TO START.

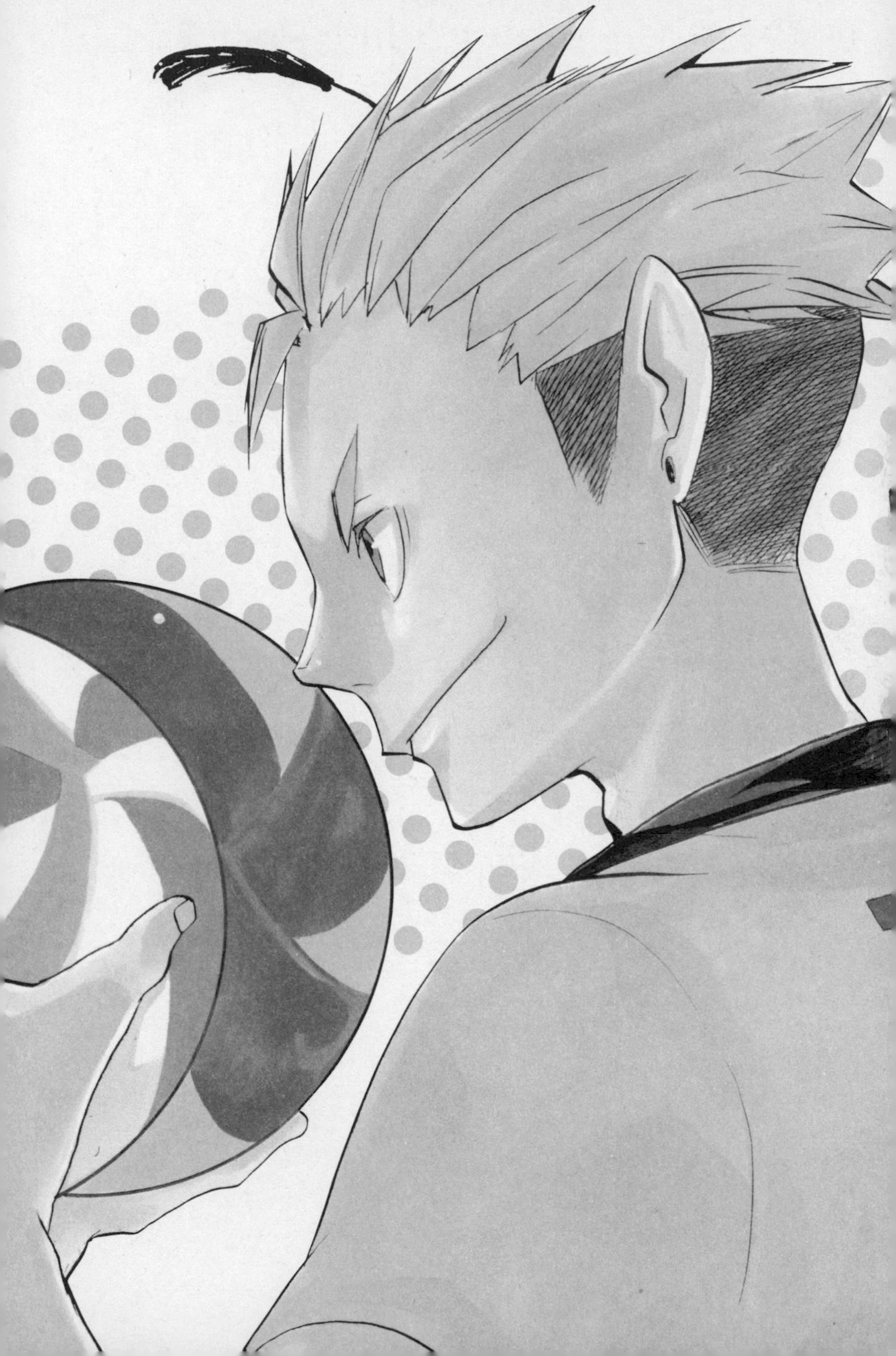

CHAPTER 114: Playground: Part 3

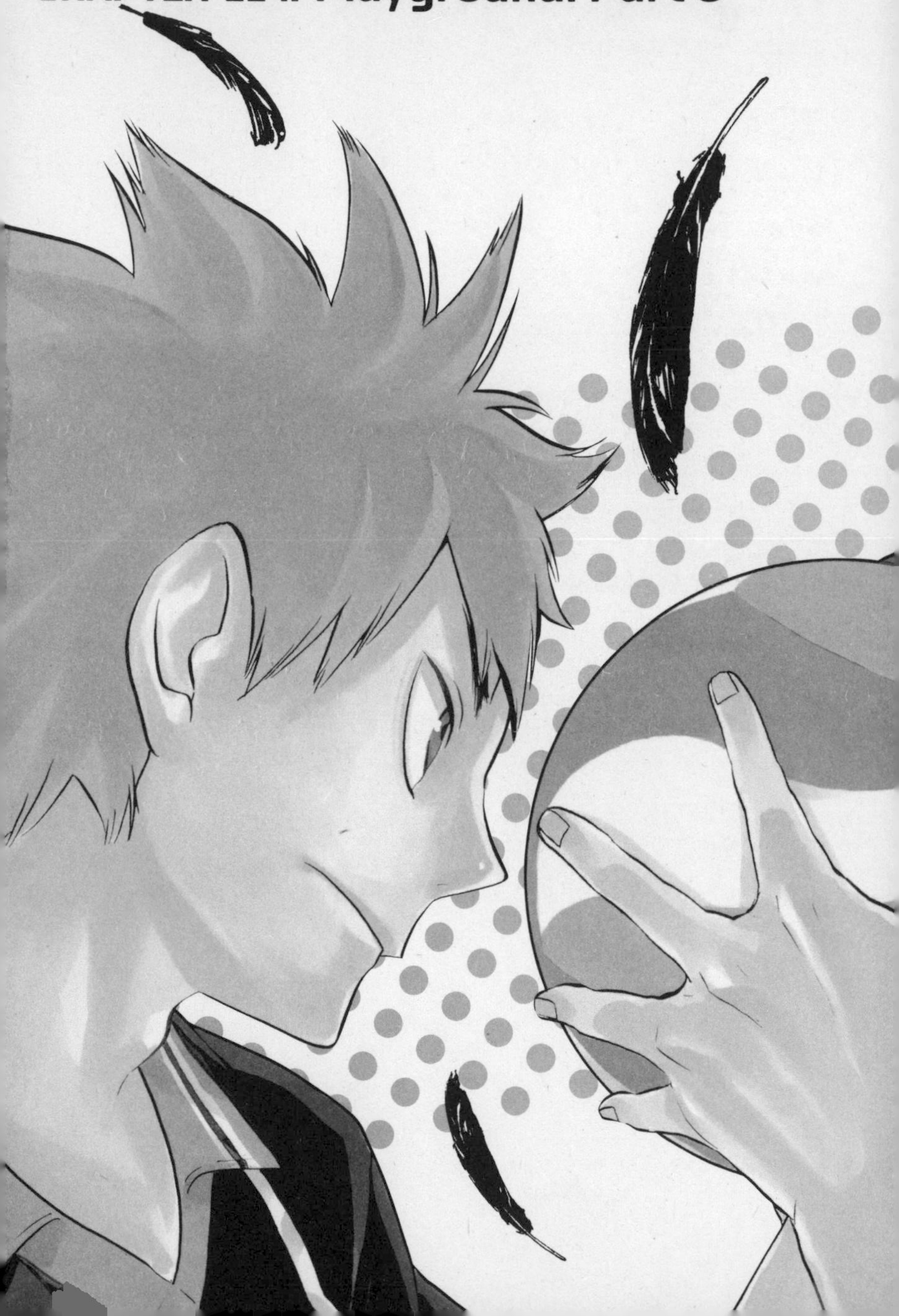

KATSUMICHI HIGASHIYAMA

JOHZENJI HIGH SCHOOL
CLASS 2-2

POSITION:
WING SPIKER

HEIGHT: 5'9"

WEIGHT: 145 LBS.
(AS OF APRIL, 2ND YEAR
OF HIGH SCHOOL)

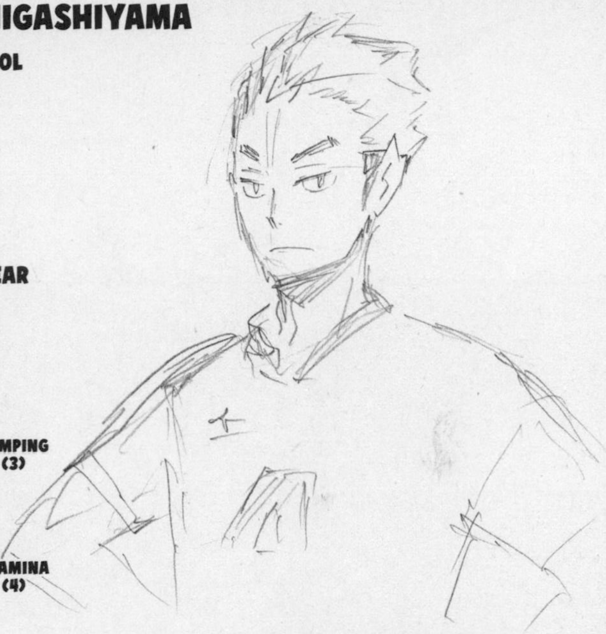

ABILITY PARAMETERS
(5-POINT SCALE)

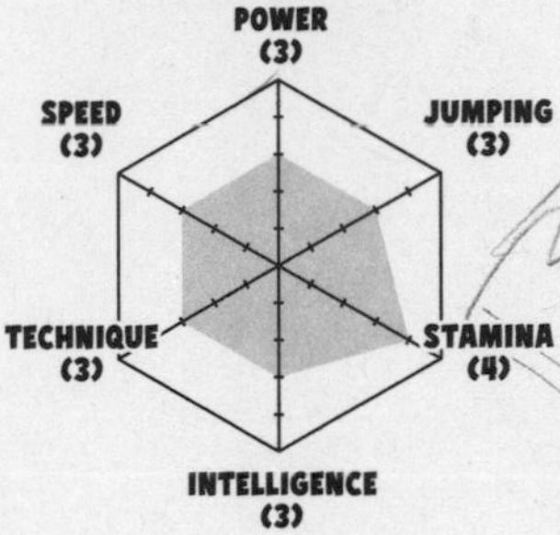
POWER
(3)
SPEED
(3)
JUMPING
(3)
TECHNIQUE
(3)
STAMINA
(4)
INTELLIGENCE
(3)

ARATA TSUCHIYU

JOHZENJI HIGH SCHOOL
CLASS 2-5

POSITION:
LIBERO

HEIGHT: 5'6"

WEIGHT: 129 LBS.
(AS OF APRIL, 2ND YEAR
OF HIGH SCHOOL)

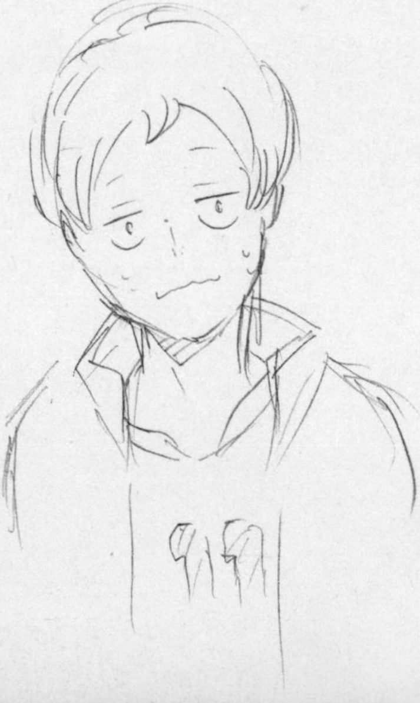

ABILITY PARAMETERS
(5-POINT SCALE)

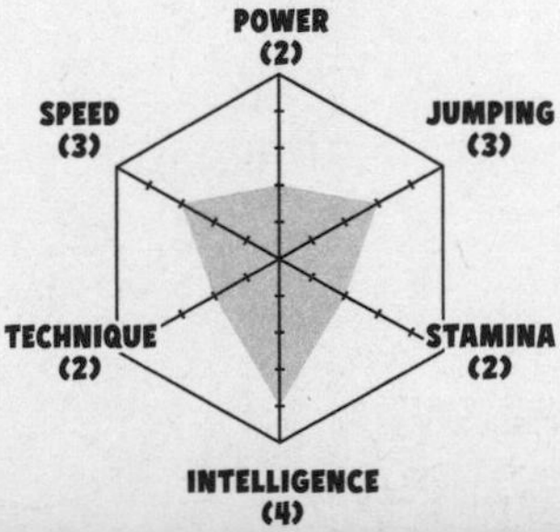
POWER
(2)
SPEED
(3)
JUMPING
(3)
TECHNIQUE
(2)
STAMINA
(2)
INTELLIGENCE
(4)

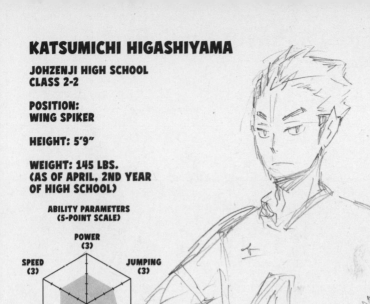

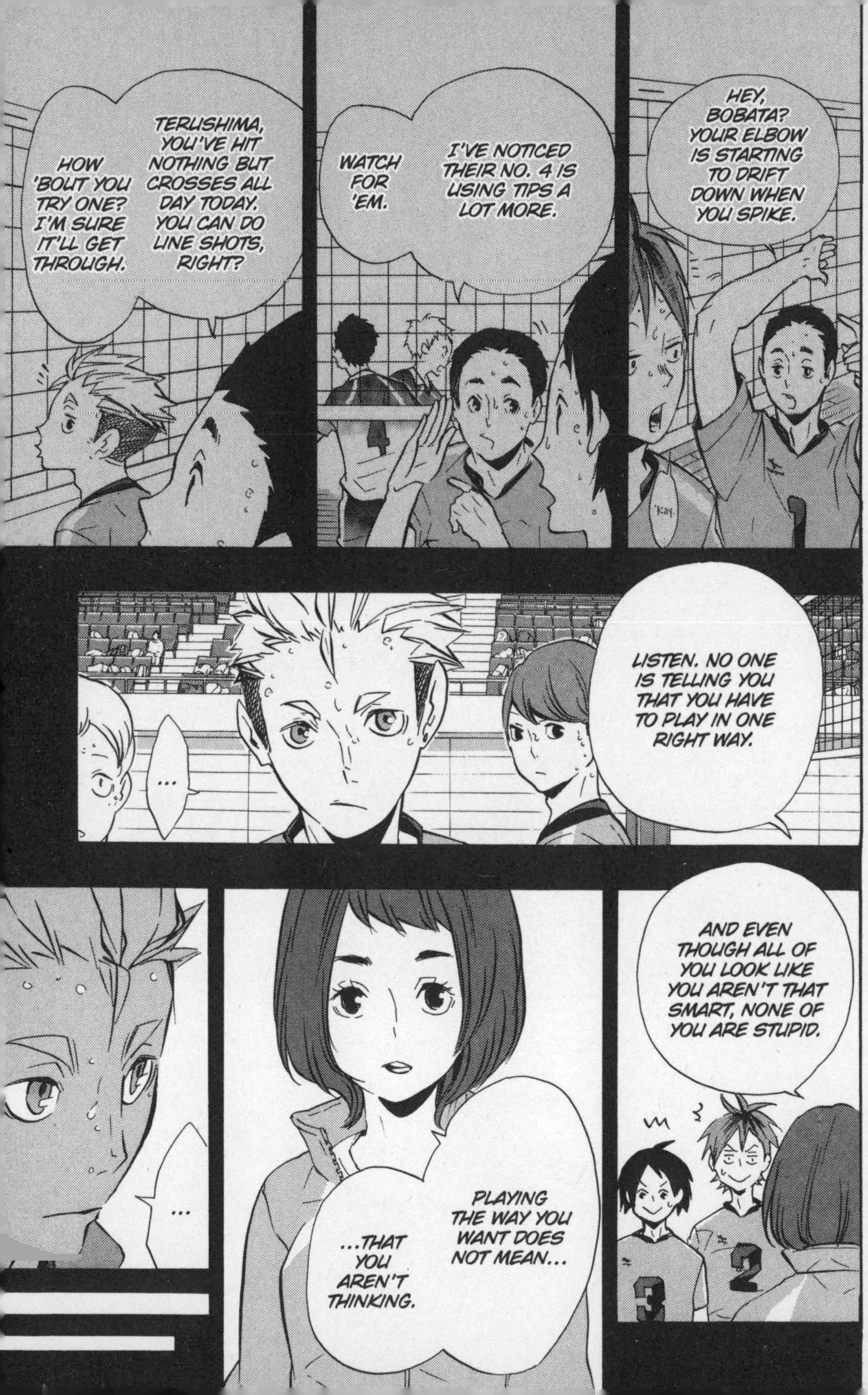
HEY, BOBATA? YOUR ELBOW IS STARTING TO DRIFT DOWN WHEN YOU SPIKE.
'kay.
I'VE NOTICED THEIR NO. 4 IS USING TIPS A LOT MORE.
WATCH FOR 'EM.
TERUSHIMA, YOU'VE HIT NOTHING BUT CROSSES ALL DAY TODAY. YOU CAN DO LINE SHOTS, RIGHT?
HOW 'BOUT YOU TRY ONE? I'M SURE IT'LL GET THROUGH.
LISTEN. NO ONE IS TELLING YOU THAT YOU HAVE TO PLAY IN ONE RIGHT WAY.
...
AND EVEN THOUGH ALL OF YOU LOOK LIKE YOU AREN'T THAT SMART, NONE OF YOU ARE STUPID.
PLAYING THE WAY YOU WANT DOES NOT MEAN...
...THAT YOU AREN'T THINKING.
...

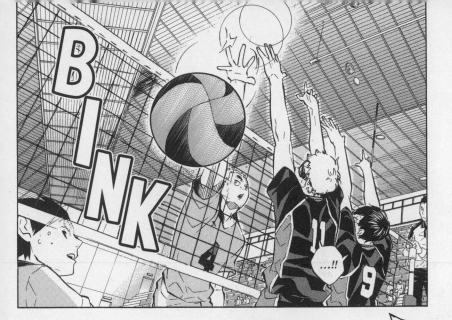

BINK

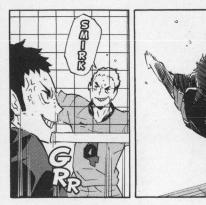

SMIRK

GRR

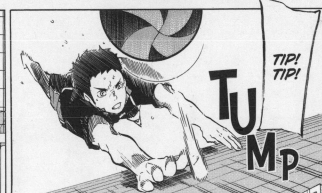

TIP! TIP!

TUMP

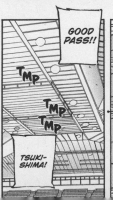

GOOD PASS!!

TMP

TMP
TMP

TSUKI-SHIMA!

*CURRENT ROTATION

AZUMANE | SAWAMURA | HINATA (NOYA)
TSUKISHIMA | KAGEYAMA **NET** | TANAKA
FUTAMATA | BOHATA | HIGASHIYAMA
TERUSHIMA | IIZAKA (TSUCHIYU) | NUMAJIRI

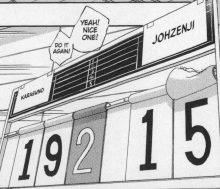

YEAH! NICE ONE!

DO IT AGAIN!

JOHZENJI

KARASUNO

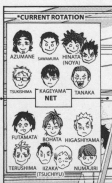

19 2 15

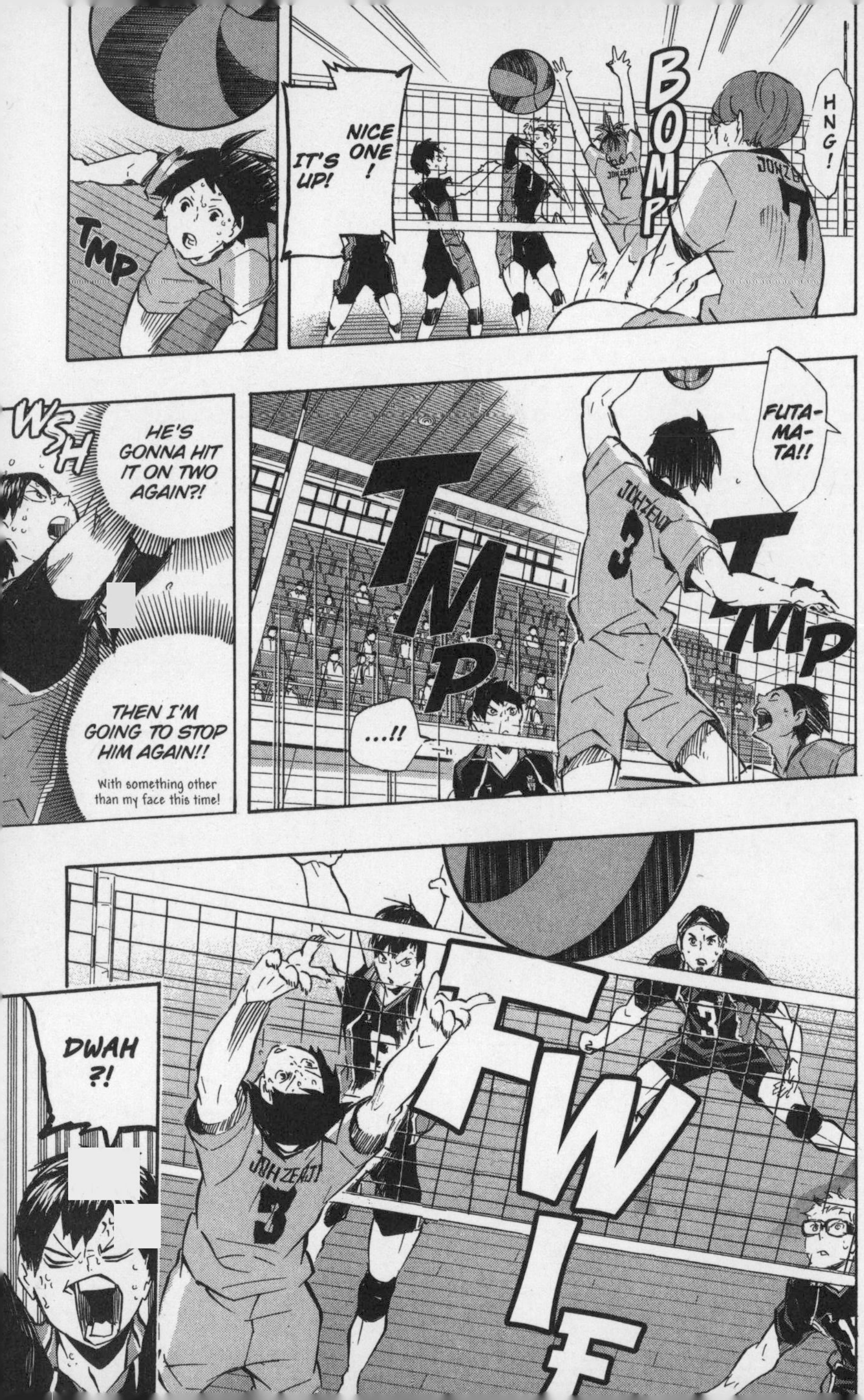
HNG!
BOMP
NICE ONE!
IT'S UP!
TMP
FUTA-MA-TA!!
TMP
TMP
...!!
WSH
HE'S GONNA HIT IT ON TWO AGAIN?!
THEN I'M GOING TO STOP HIM AGAIN!!
With something other than my face this time!
TWIF
DWAH ?!

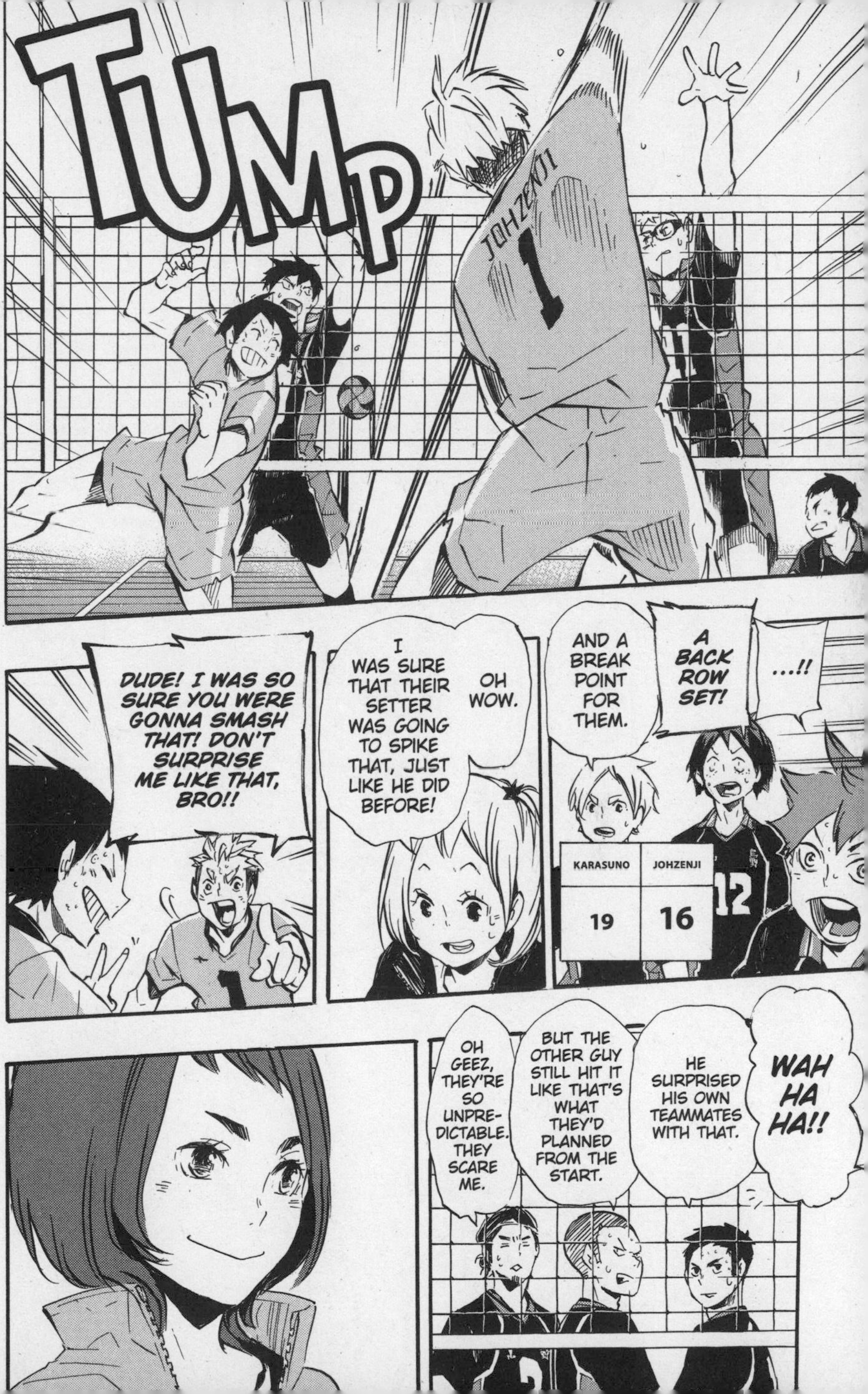
TUMP
JOHZENJI 1
...!!
A BACK ROW SET!
AND A BREAK POINT FOR THEM.
KARASUNO 19
JOHZENJI 16
OH WOW.
I WAS SURE THAT THEIR SETTER WAS GOING TO SPIKE THAT, JUST LIKE HE DID BEFORE!
DUDE! I WAS SO SURE YOU WERE GONNA SMASH THAT! DON'T SURPRISE ME LIKE THAT, BRO!!
WAH HA HA!!
HE SURPRISED HIS OWN TEAMMATES WITH THAT.
BUT THE OTHER GUY STILL HIT IT LIKE THAT'S WHAT THEY'D PLANNED FROM THE START.
OH GEEZ, THEY'RE SO UNPREDICTABLE. THEY SCARE ME.

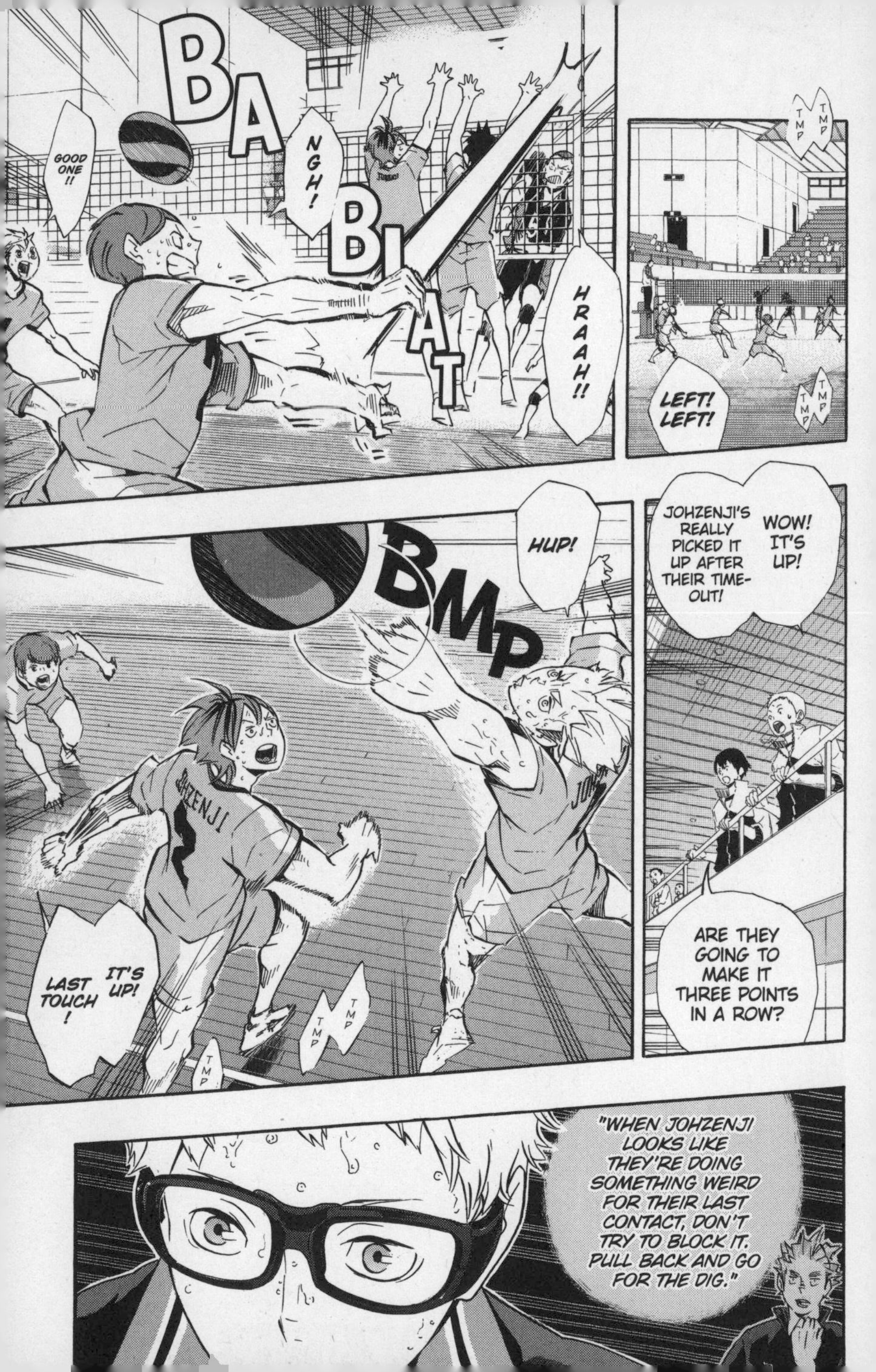
TMP TMP
LEFT! LEFT!
TMP TMP
HRAAAH!!
BABIAT
NGH!
GOOD ONE!!
WOW! IT'S UP!
JOHZENJI'S REALLY PICKED IT UP AFTER THEIR TIME-OUT!
ARE THEY GOING TO MAKE IT THREE POINTS IN A ROW?
HUP!
BMP
IT'S UP!
LAST TOUCH!
TMP TMP
TMP
"WHEN JOHZENJI LOOKS LIKE THEY'RE DOING SOMETHING WEIRD FOR THEIR LAST CONTACT, DON'T TRY TO BLOCK IT. PULL BACK AND GO FOR THE DIG."

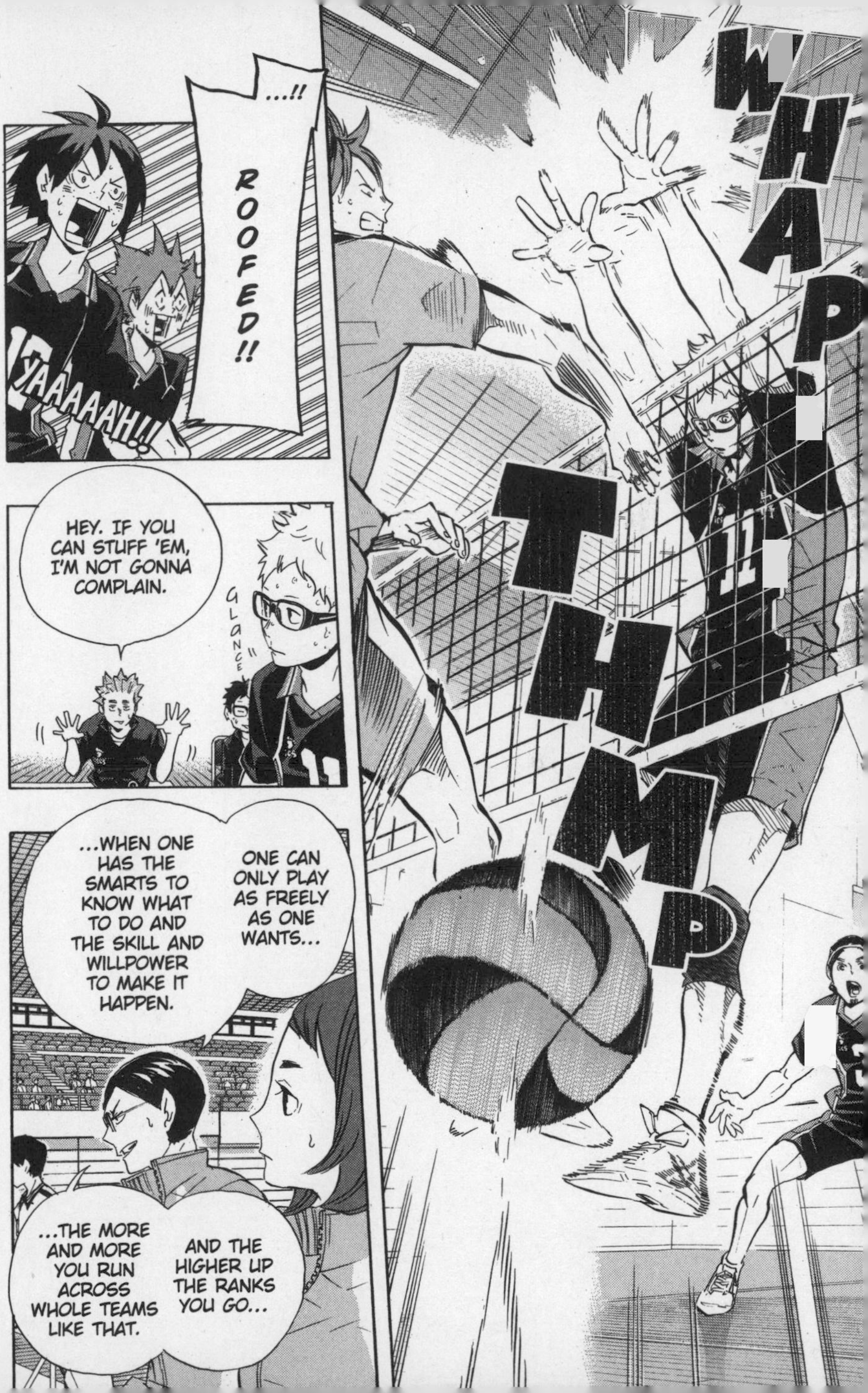
WHAP!
THUMP
...!!
ROOFED!!
YAAAAAH!!
HEY. IF YOU CAN STUFF 'EM, I'M NOT GONNA COMPLAIN.
GLANCE
ONE CAN ONLY PLAY AS FREELY AS ONE WANTS...
...WHEN ONE HAS THE SMARTS TO KNOW WHAT TO DO AND THE SKILL AND WILLPOWER TO MAKE IT HAPPEN.
AND THE HIGHER UP THE RANKS YOU GO...
...THE MORE AND MORE YOU RUN ACROSS WHOLE TEAMS LIKE THAT.

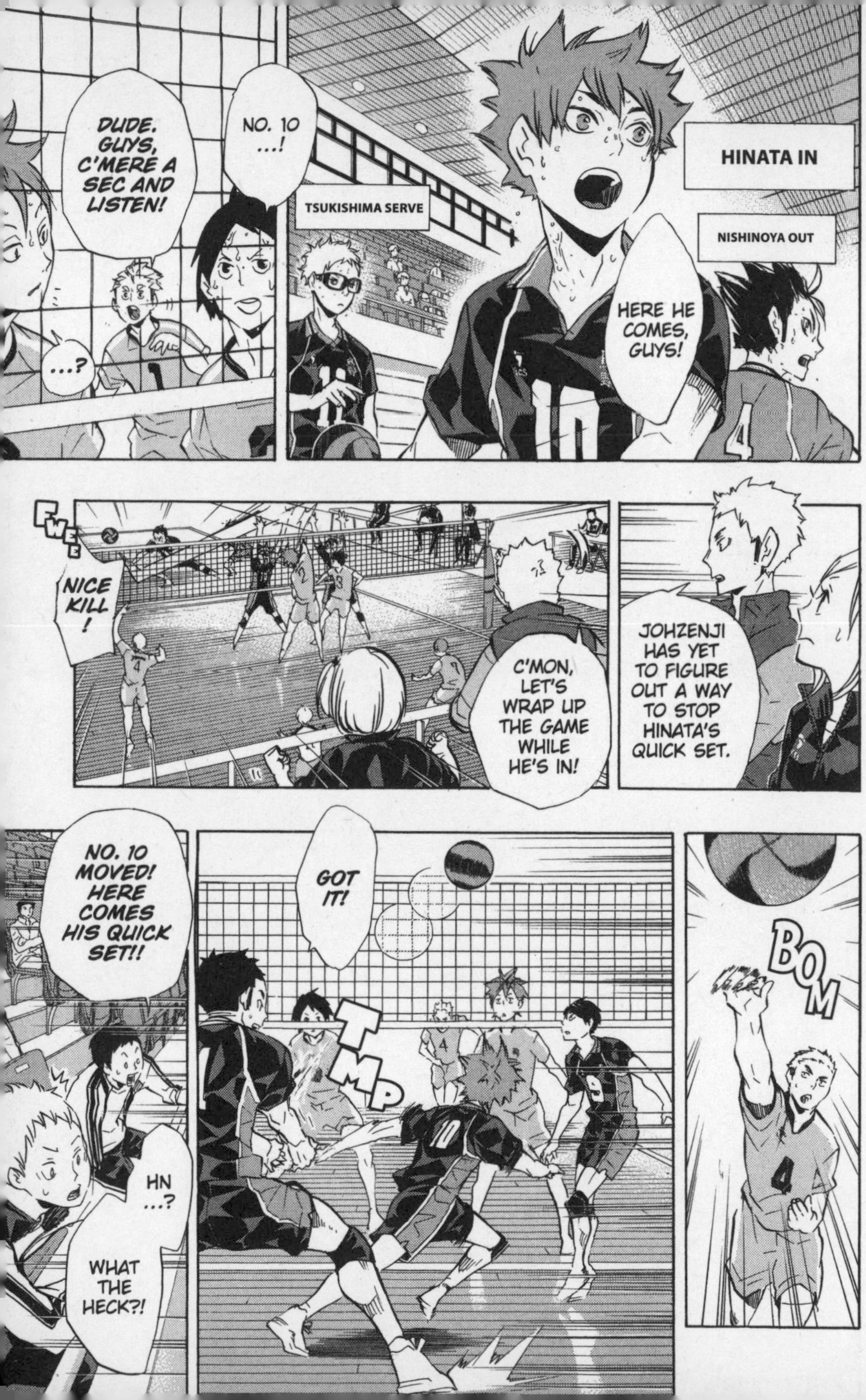

HINATA IN
NISHINOYA OUT
HERE HE COMES, GUYS!
TSUKISHIMA SERVE
NO. 10 ...!
DUDE. GUYS, C'MERE A SEC AND LISTEN!
...?
JOHZENJI HAS YET TO FIGURE OUT A WAY TO STOP HINATA'S QUICK SET.
C'MON, LET'S WRAP UP THE GAME WHILE HE'S IN!
FWEE
NICE KILL!
BOM
GOT IT!
TMP
NO. 10 MOVED! HERE COMES HIS QUICK SET!!
HN ...?
WHAT THE HECK?!

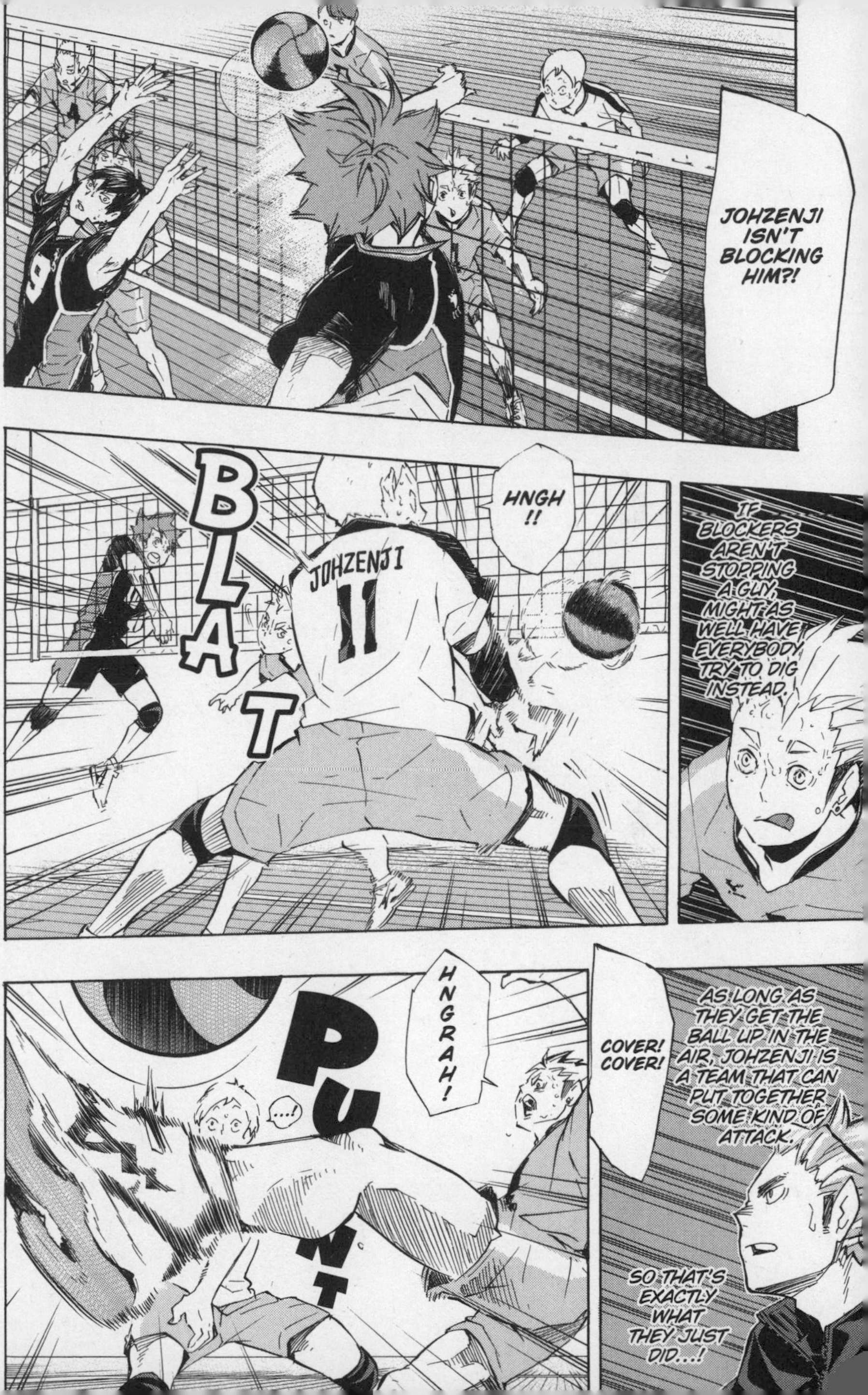
JOHZENJI ISN'T BLOCKING HIM?!
IF BLOCKERS AREN'T STOPPING A GUY, MIGHT AS WELL HAVE EVERYBODY TRY TO DIG INSTEAD.
HNGH !!
JOHZENJI 11
BLAT
AS LONG AS THEY GET THE BALL UP IN THE AIR, JOHZENJI IS A TEAM THAT CAN PUT TOGETHER SOME KIND OF ATTACK.
SO THAT'S EXACTLY WHAT THEY JUST DID...!
COVER! COVER!
HNGRAH!
...!
PUNT

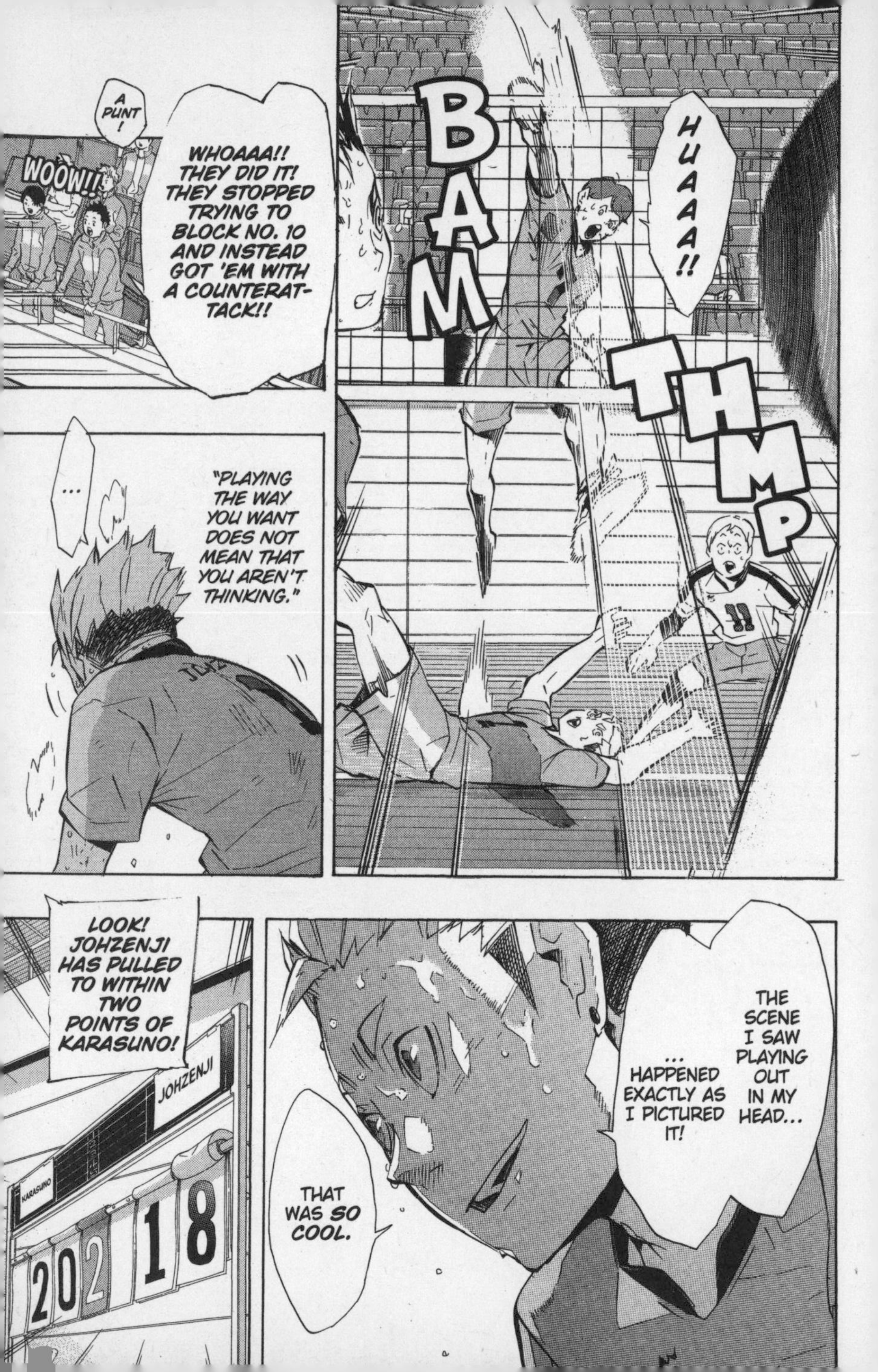
HUAAAA!!
BAM
THMP
WHOAAA!! THEY DID IT! THEY STOPPED TRYING TO BLOCK NO. 10 AND INSTEAD GOT 'EM WITH A COUNTERAT-TACK!!
A PUNT!
WOOW!!
...
"PLAYING THE WAY YOU WANT DOES NOT MEAN THAT YOU AREN'T THINKING."
THE SCENE I SAW PLAYING OUT IN MY HEAD...
... HAPPENED EXACTLY AS I PICTURED IT!
THAT WAS SO COOL.
LOOK! JOHZENJI HAS PULLED TO WITHIN TWO POINTS OF KARASUNO!
JOHZENJI
KARASUNO
20 18

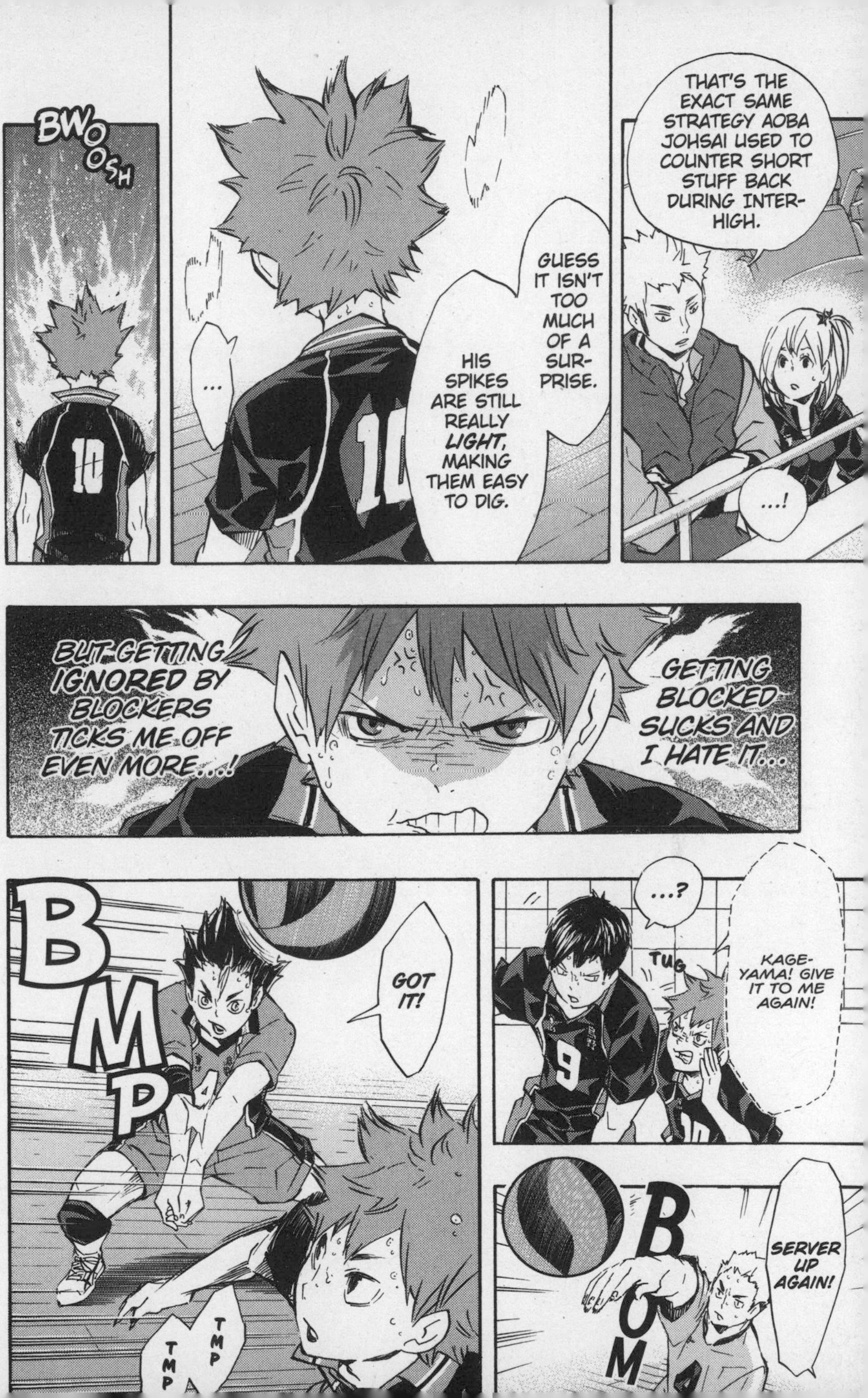
THAT'S THE EXACT SAME STRATEGY AOBA JOHSAI USED TO COUNTER SHORT STUFF BACK DURING INTER-HIGH.
...!
GUESS IT ISN'T TOO MUCH OF A SUR-PRISE.
HIS SPIKES ARE STILL REALLY *LIGHT*, MAKING THEM EASY TO DIG.
...
BWOOSH
GETTING BLOCKED SUCKS AND I HATE IT...
BUT GETTING IGNORED BY BLOCKERS TICKS ME OFF EVEN MORE...!
KAGE-YAMA! GIVE IT TO ME AGAIN!
...?
TUG
SERVER UP AGAIN!
BOOM
GOT IT!
BMP
TMP TMP

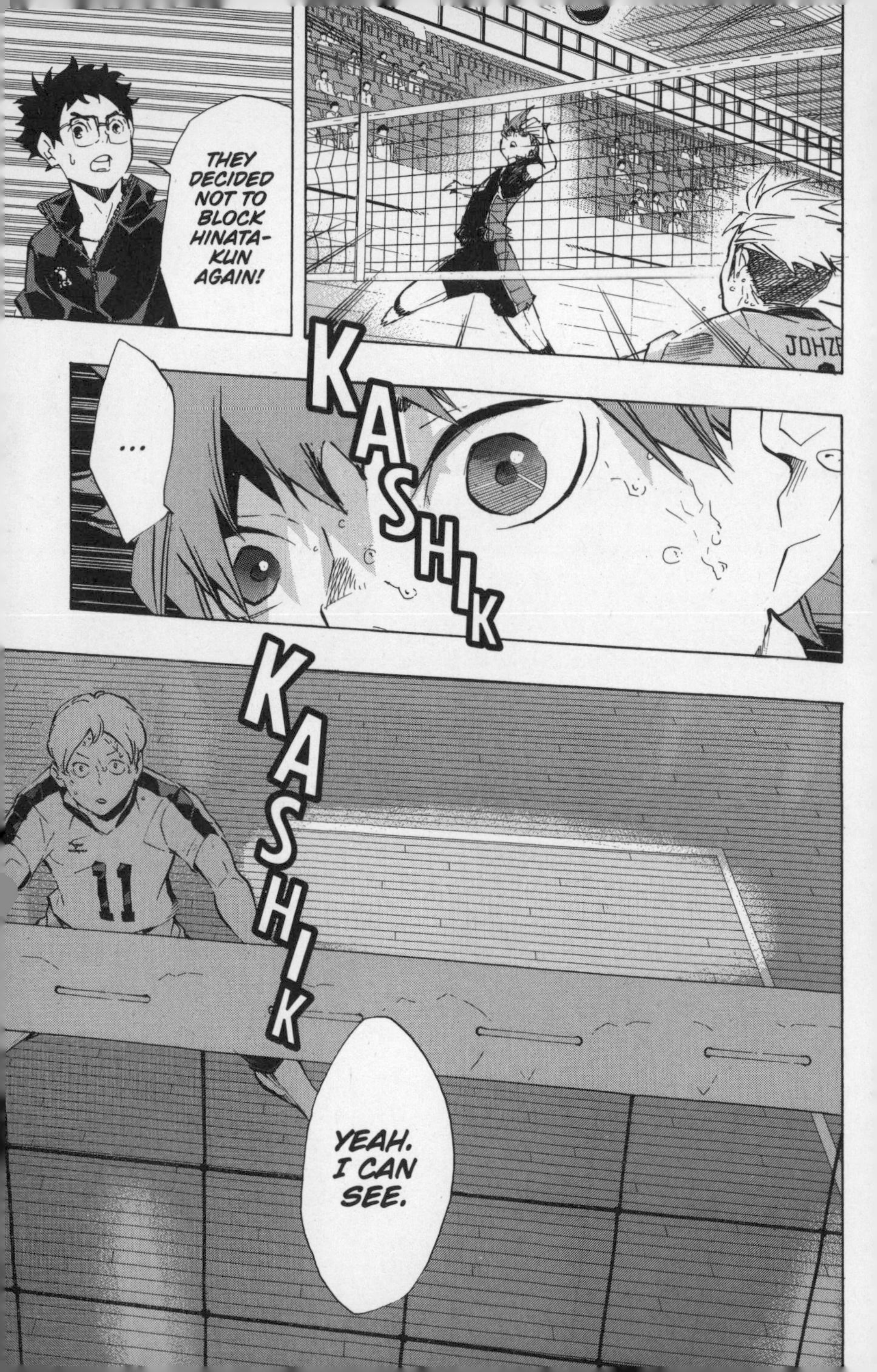
THEY DECIDED NOT TO BLOCK HINATA-KUN AGAIN!
JOHZE
KASHIK
...
KASHIK
YEAH. I CAN SEE.

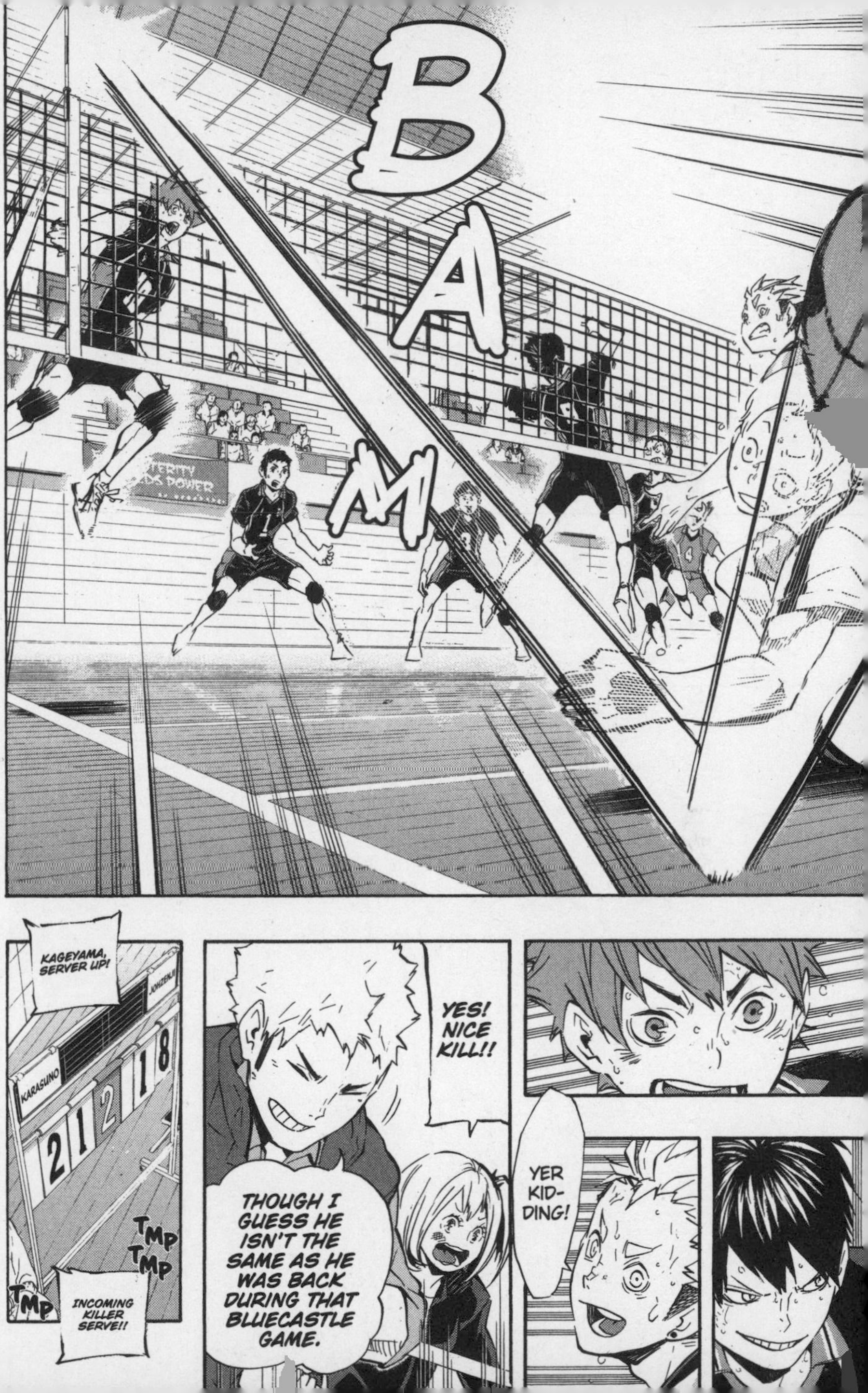
BAM
YER KID-DING!
YES! NICE KILL!!
THOUGH I GUESS HE ISN'T THE SAME AS HE WAS BACK DURING THAT BLUECASTLE GAME.
KAGEYAMA, SERVER UP!
JOHZENJI
KARASUNO
21
18
TMP
TMP
TMP
INCOMING KILLER SERVE!!

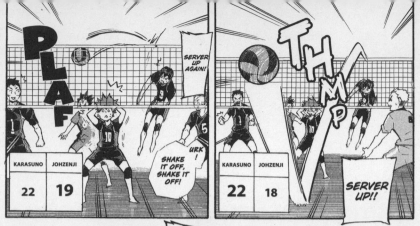

KARASUNO	JOHZENJI
22	19

KARASUNO	JOHZENJI
22	18

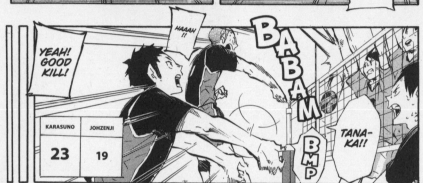

KARASUNO	JOHZENJI
23	19

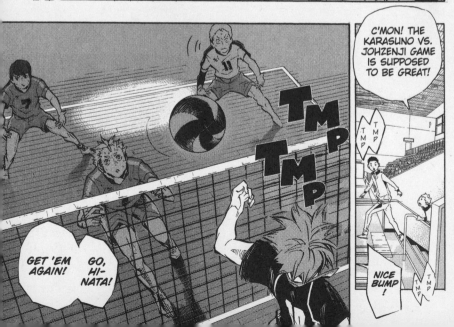

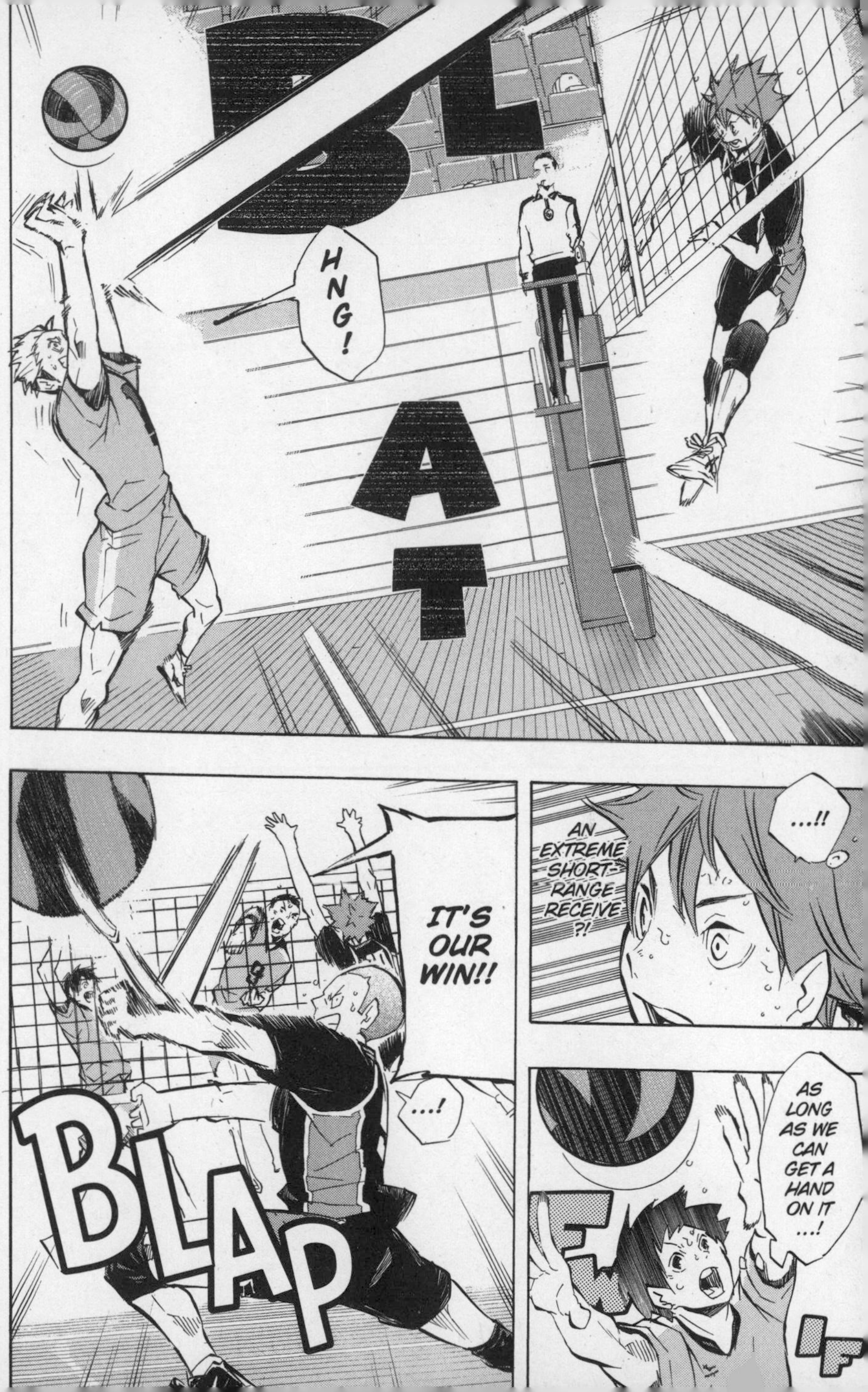
BLAT
HNG!
...!!
AN EXTREME SHORT-RANGE RECEIVE?!
AS LONG AS WE CAN GET A HAND ON IT ...!
IT'S OUR WIN!!
...!
BLAP

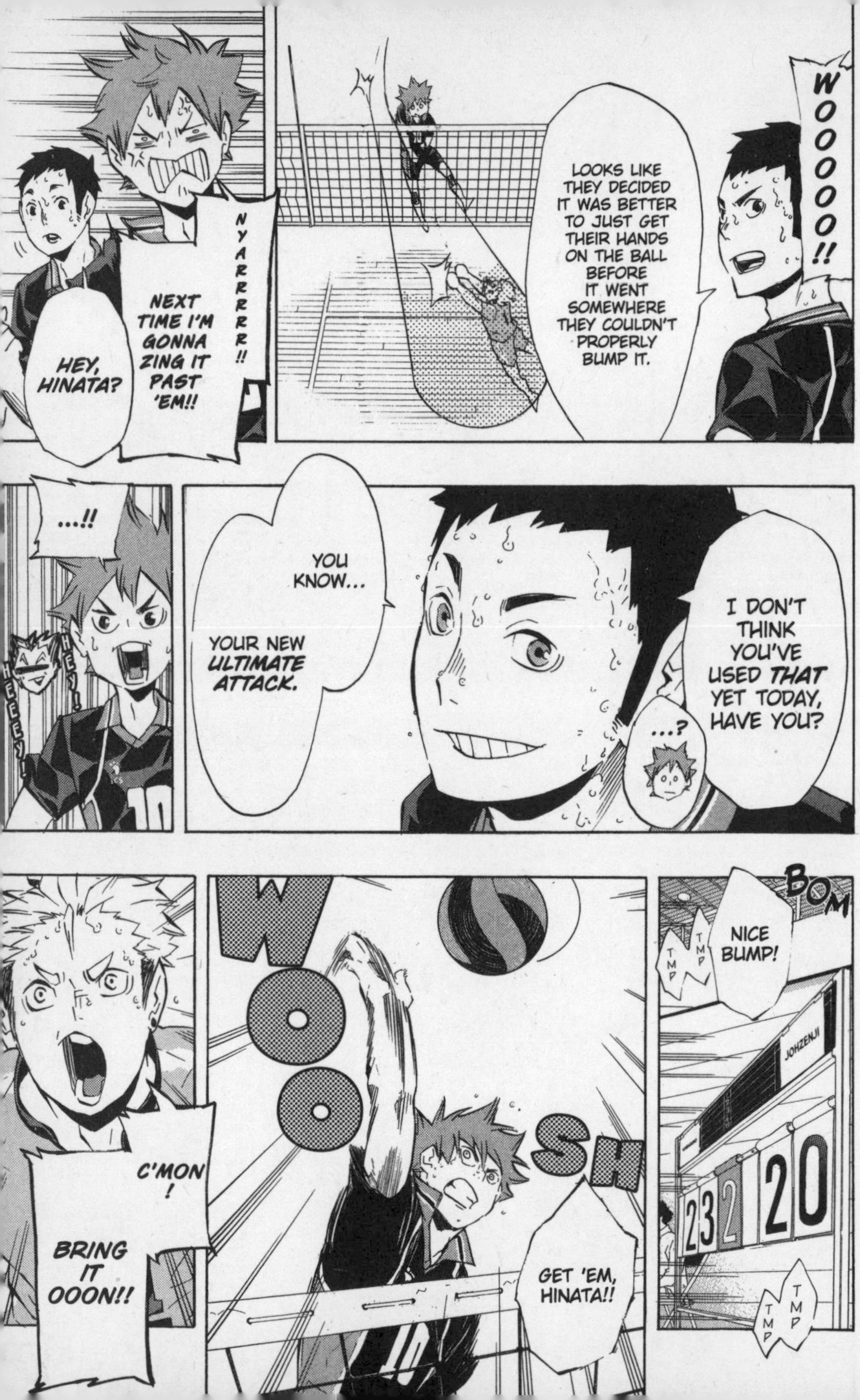
WOOOOOO!!
LOOKS LIKE THEY DECIDED IT WAS BETTER TO JUST GET THEIR HANDS ON THE BALL BEFORE IT WENT SOMEWHERE THEY COULDN'T PROPERLY BUMP IT.
NYARRRRR!!
NEXT TIME I'M GONNA ZING IT PAST 'EM!!
HEY, HINATA?
I DON'T THINK YOU'VE USED THAT YET TODAY, HAVE YOU?
...?
YOU KNOW...
YOUR NEW ULTIMATE ATTACK.
...!!
HEY!
HEEEY!
BOM
NICE BUMP!
TMP TMP
JOHZENJI
23
20
TMP TMP
WOOOSH
GET 'EM, HINATA!!
C'MON!
BRING IT OOON!!

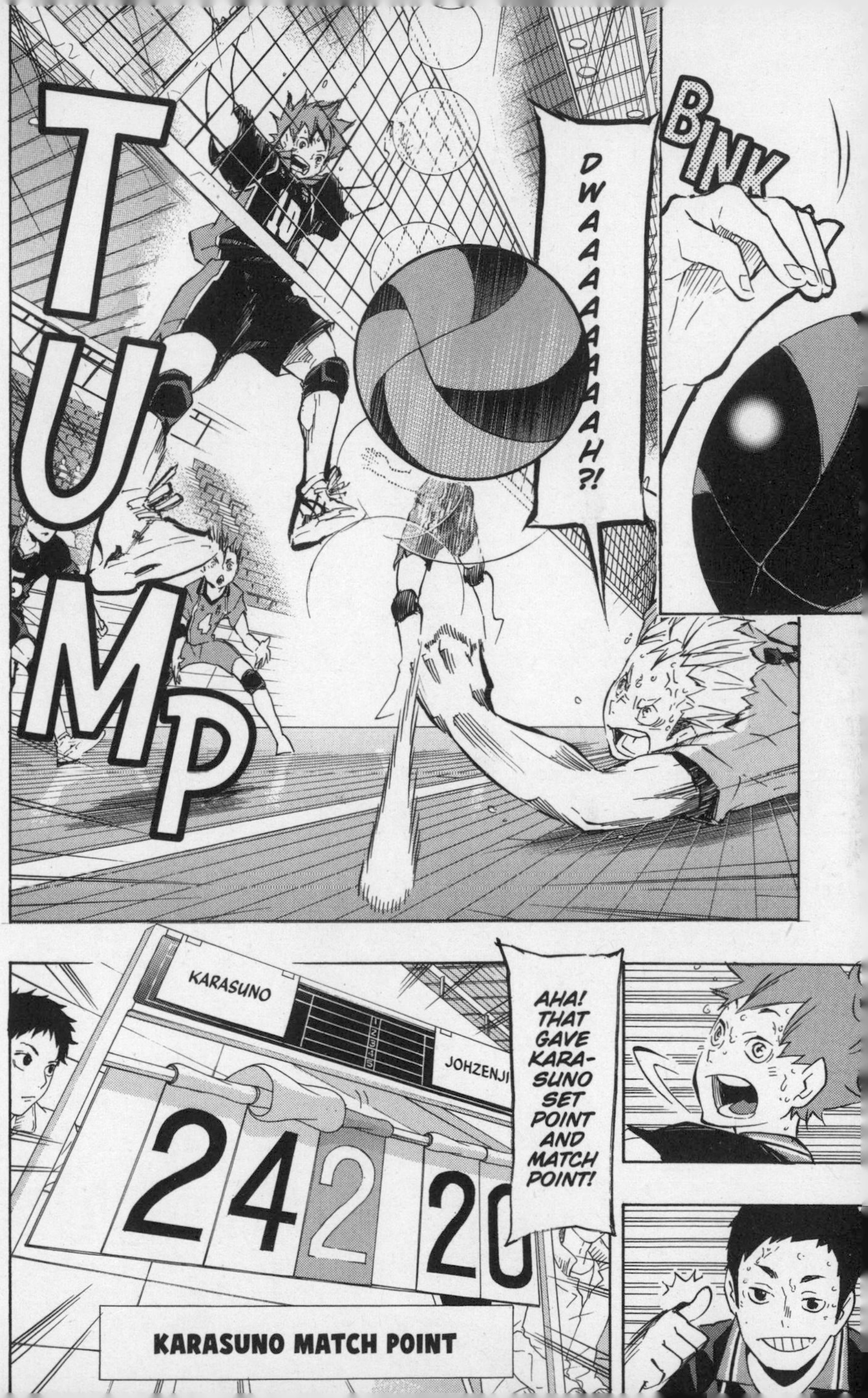
BINK
DWAAAAAAAAH?!
TUMP
AHA! THAT GAVE KARASUNO SET POINT AND MATCH POINT!
KARASUNO
JOHZENJI
24 2 20
KARASUNO MATCH POINT

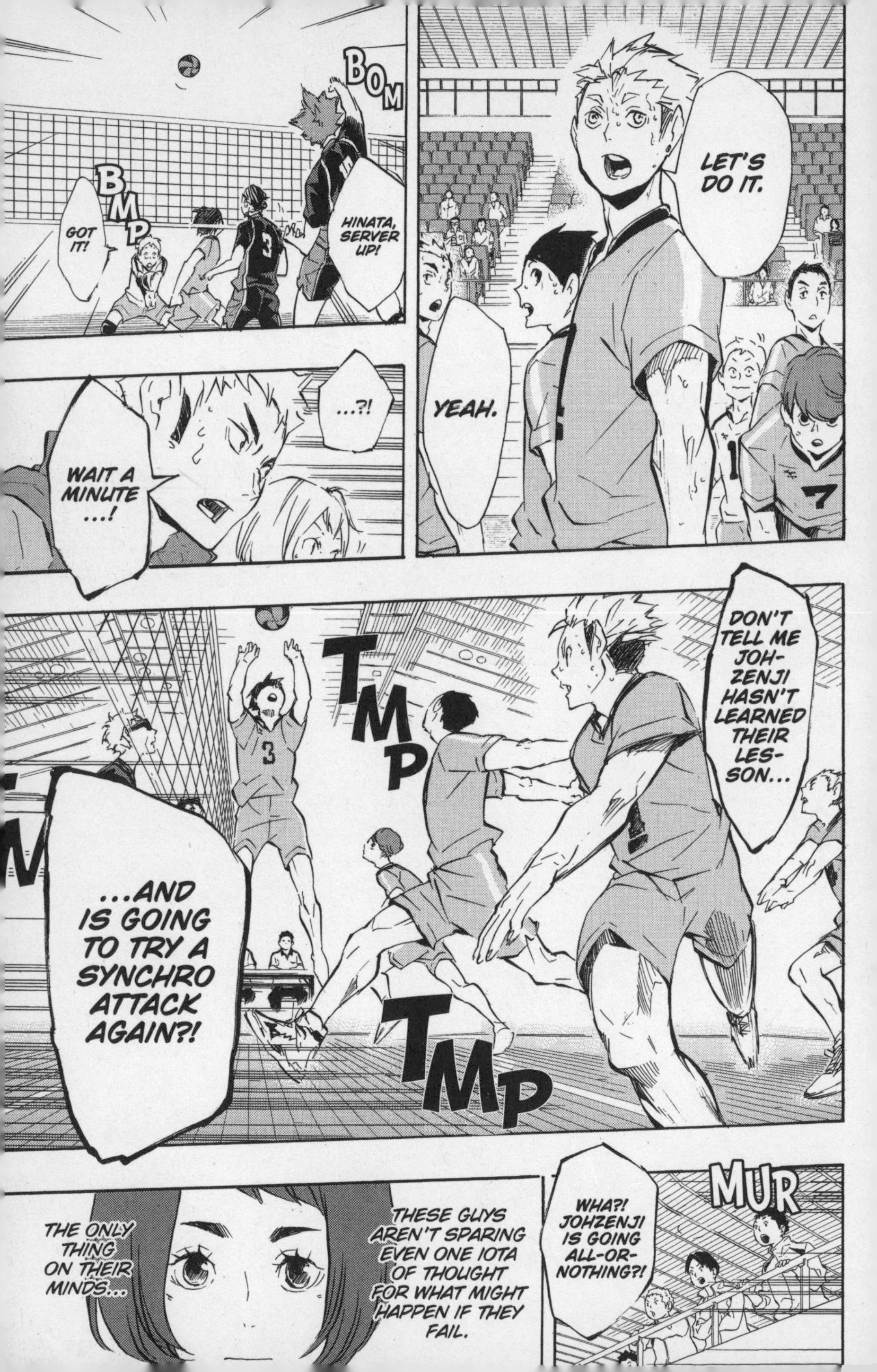
LET'S DO IT.
YEAH.
BOM
HINATA, SERVER UP!
BMP
GOT IT!
...?!
WAIT A MINUTE ...!
DON'T TELL ME JOHZENJI HASN'T LEARNED THEIR LESSON...
TMP
TMP
...AND IS GOING TO TRY A SYNCHRO ATTACK AGAIN?!
MUR
WHA?! JOHZENJI IS GOING ALL-OR-NOTHING?!
THESE GUYS AREN'T SPARING EVEN ONE IOTA OF THOUGHT FOR WHAT MIGHT HAPPEN IF THEY FAIL.
THE ONLY THING ON THEIR MINDS...

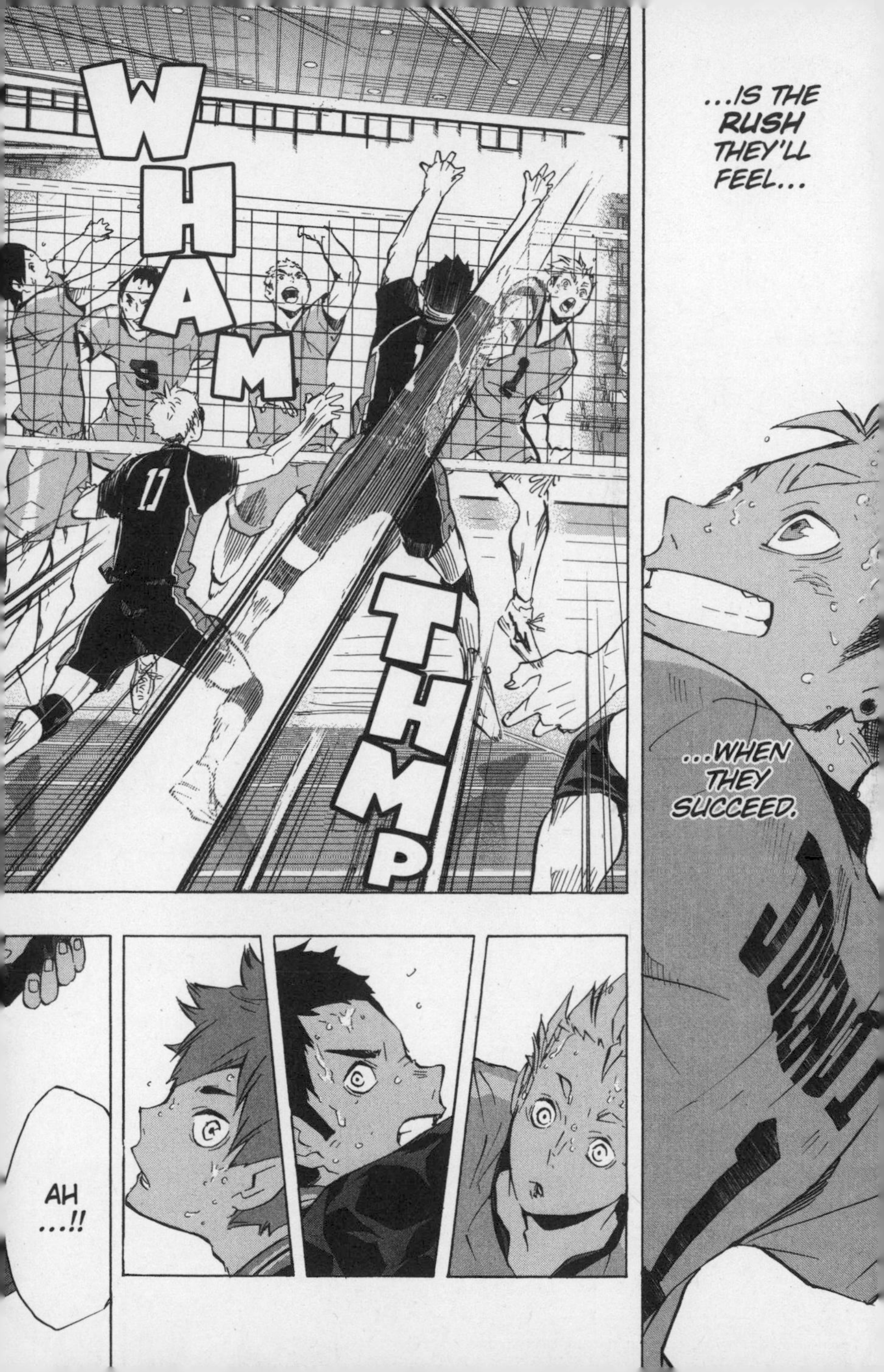
...IS THE RUSH THEY'LL FEEL...
...WHEN THEY SUCCEED.
WHAM
THMP
AH ...!!

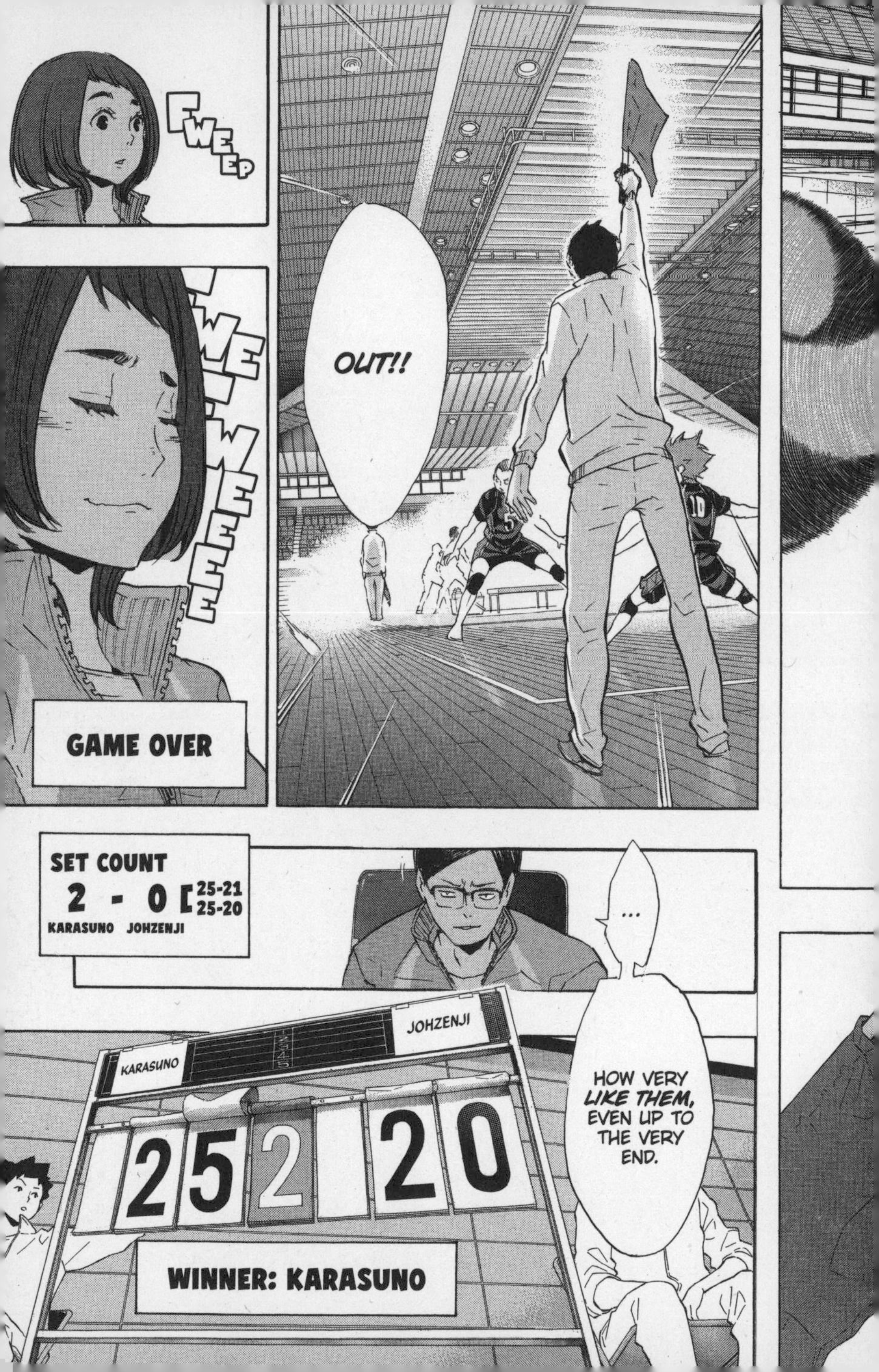

OUT!!
FWEEP
WEEEE
GAME OVER
...
SET COUNT
2 - 0 [25-21 25-20
KARASUNO JOHZENJI
HOW VERY *LIKE THEM,* EVEN UP TO THE VERY END.
JOHZENJI
KARASUNO
25 2 20
WINNER: KARASUNO

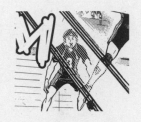

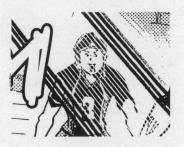

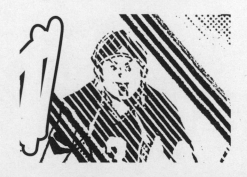

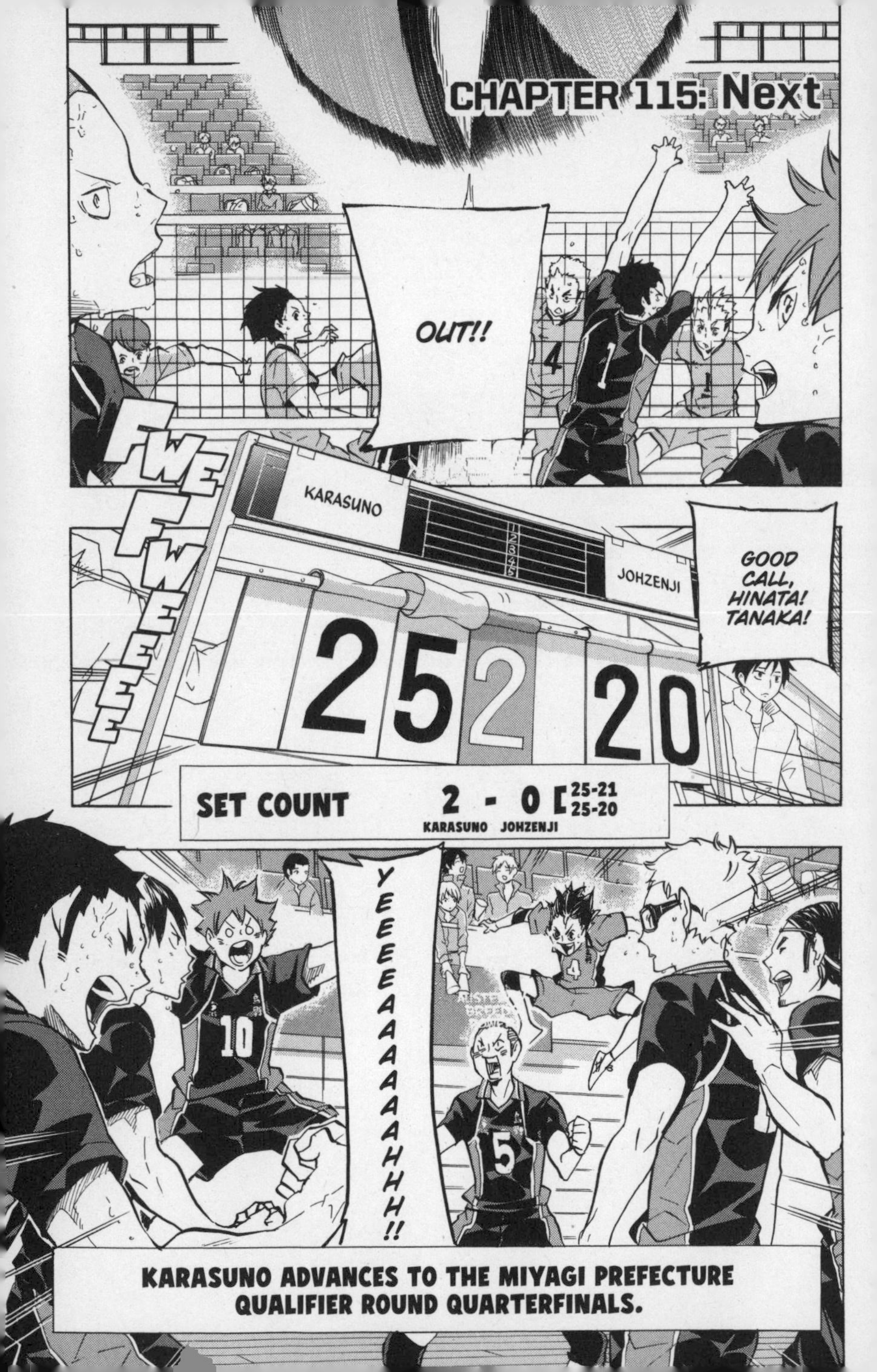

CHAPTER 115: Next
OUT!!
FWE FWEEEE
GOOD CALL, HINATA! TANAKA!
KARASUNO
JOHZENJI
25 2 20
SET COUNT 2 - 0 [25-21 25-20
KARASUNO JOHZENJI
YEEEEAAAAAHHH!!
KARASUNO ADVANCES TO THE MIYAGI PREFECTURE QUALIFIER ROUND QUARTERFINALS.

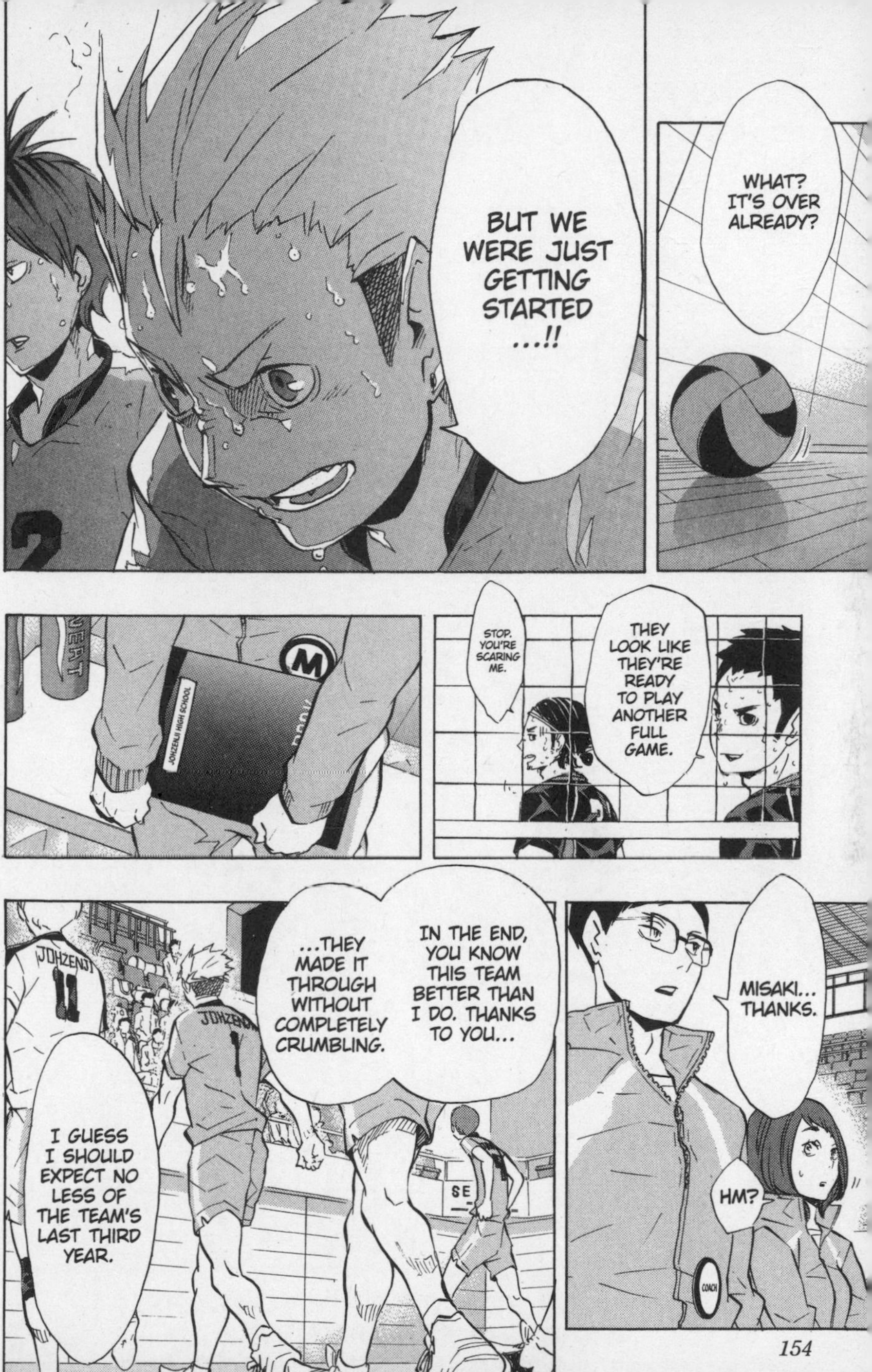
WHAT? IT'S OVER ALREADY?
BUT WE WERE JUST GETTING STARTED ...!!
THEY LOOK LIKE THEY'RE READY TO PLAY ANOTHER FULL GAME.
STOP. YOU'RE SCARING ME.
JOHZENJI HIGH SCHOOL
MISAKI... THANKS.
HM?
COACH
IN THE END, YOU KNOW THIS TEAM BETTER THAN I DO. THANKS TO YOU...
...THEY MADE IT THROUGH WITHOUT COMPLETELY CRUMBLING.
I GUESS I SHOULD EXPECT NO LESS OF THE TEAM'S LAST THIRD YEAR.

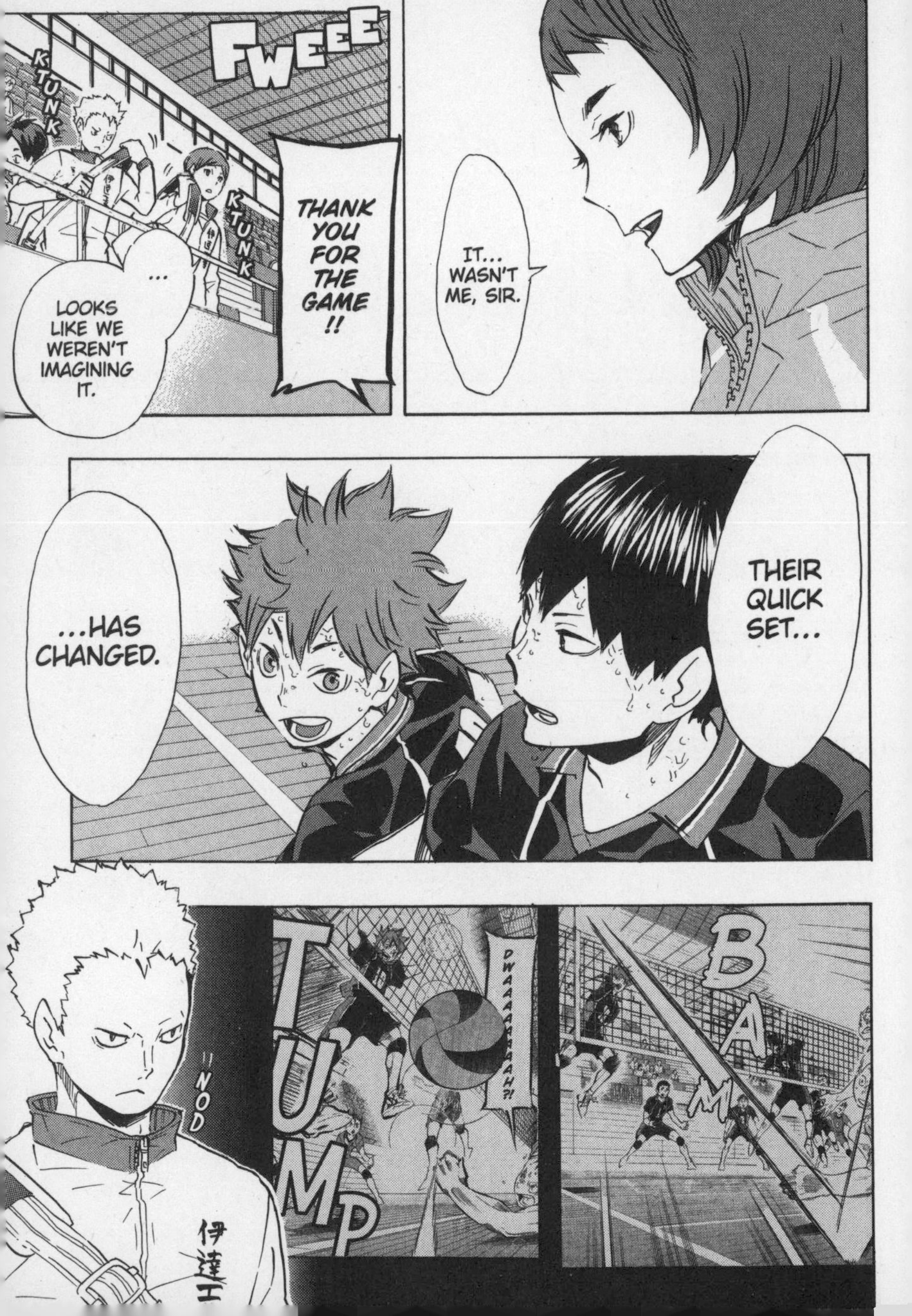
IT... WASN'T ME, SIR.
FWEEE
THANK YOU FOR THE GAME!!
KTUNK
KTUNK
...
LOOKS LIKE WE WEREN'T IMAGINING IT.
THEIR QUICK SET...
...HAS CHANGED.
BAM
TUMP
DWAAAAAAAH?!
NOD
伊達工

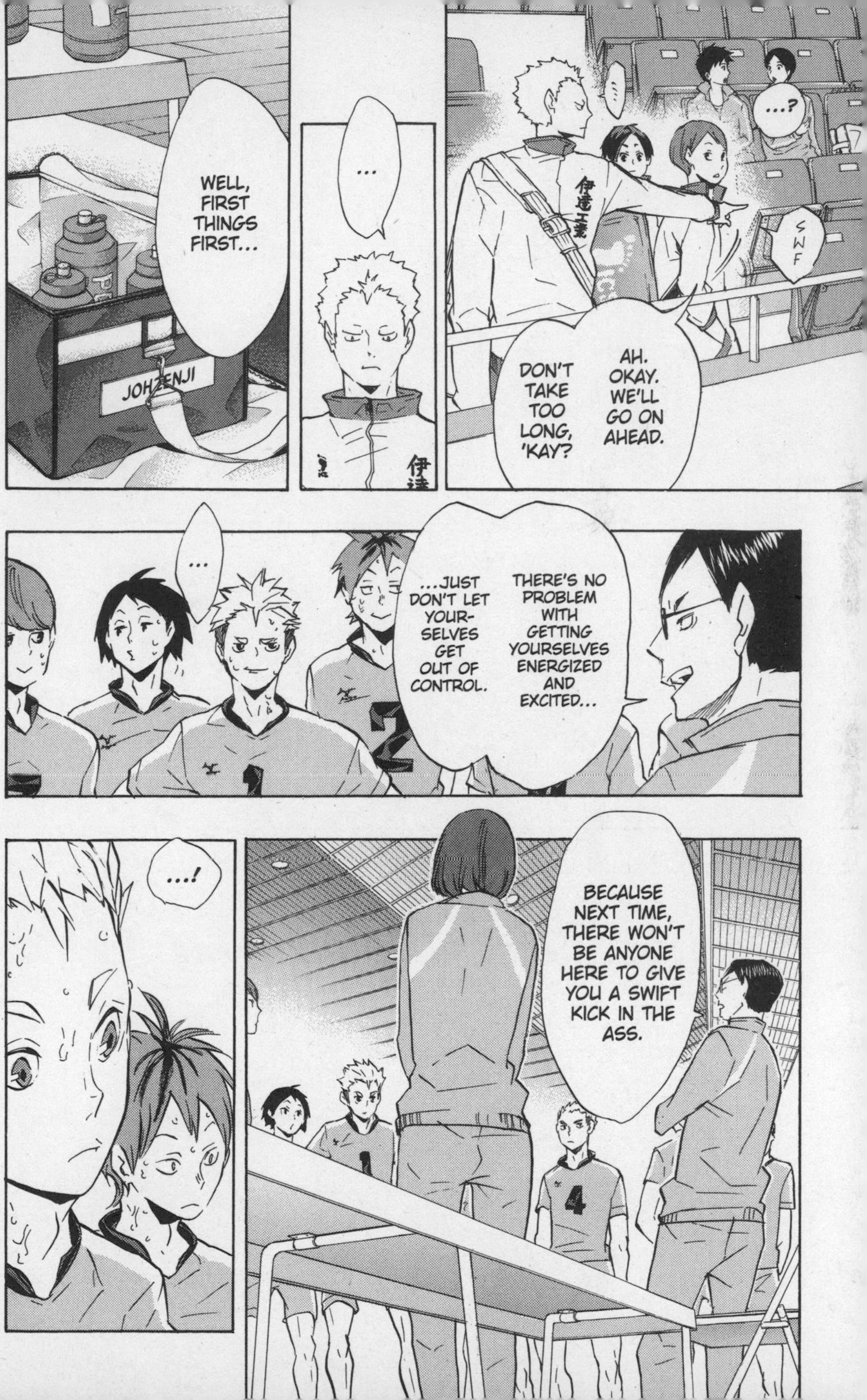
...
...?
SWF
AH. OKAY. WE'LL GO ON AHEAD.
DON'T TAKE TOO LONG, 'KAY?
...
WELL, FIRST THINGS FIRST...
THERE'S NO PROBLEM WITH GETTING YOURSELVES ENERGIZED AND EXCITED...
...JUST DON'T LET YOURSELVES GET OUT OF CONTROL.
...
BECAUSE NEXT TIME, THERE WON'T BE ANYONE HERE TO GIVE YOU A SWIFT KICK IN THE ASS.
...!

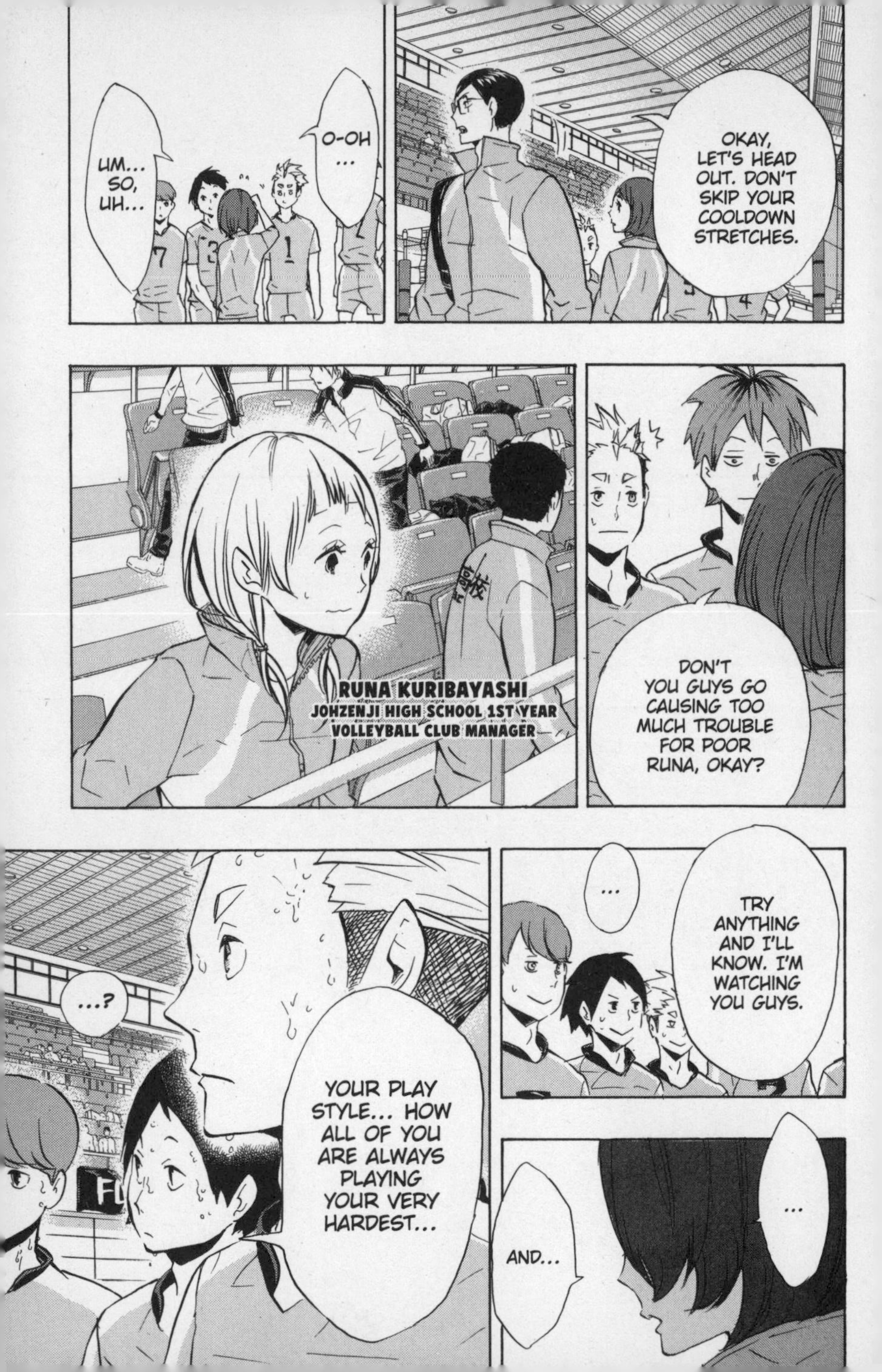
OKAY, LET'S HEAD OUT. DON'T SKIP YOUR COOLDOWN STRETCHES.
O-OH ...
UM... SO, UH...
DON'T YOU GUYS GO CAUSING TOO MUCH TROUBLE FOR POOR RUNA, OKAY?
RUNA KURIBAYASHI
JOHZENJI HIGH SCHOOL 1ST YEAR
VOLLEYBALL CLUB MANAGER
TRY ANYTHING AND I'LL KNOW. I'M WATCHING YOU GUYS.
...
...
AND...
...?
YOUR PLAY STYLE... HOW ALL OF YOU ARE ALWAYS PLAYING YOUR VERY HARDEST...

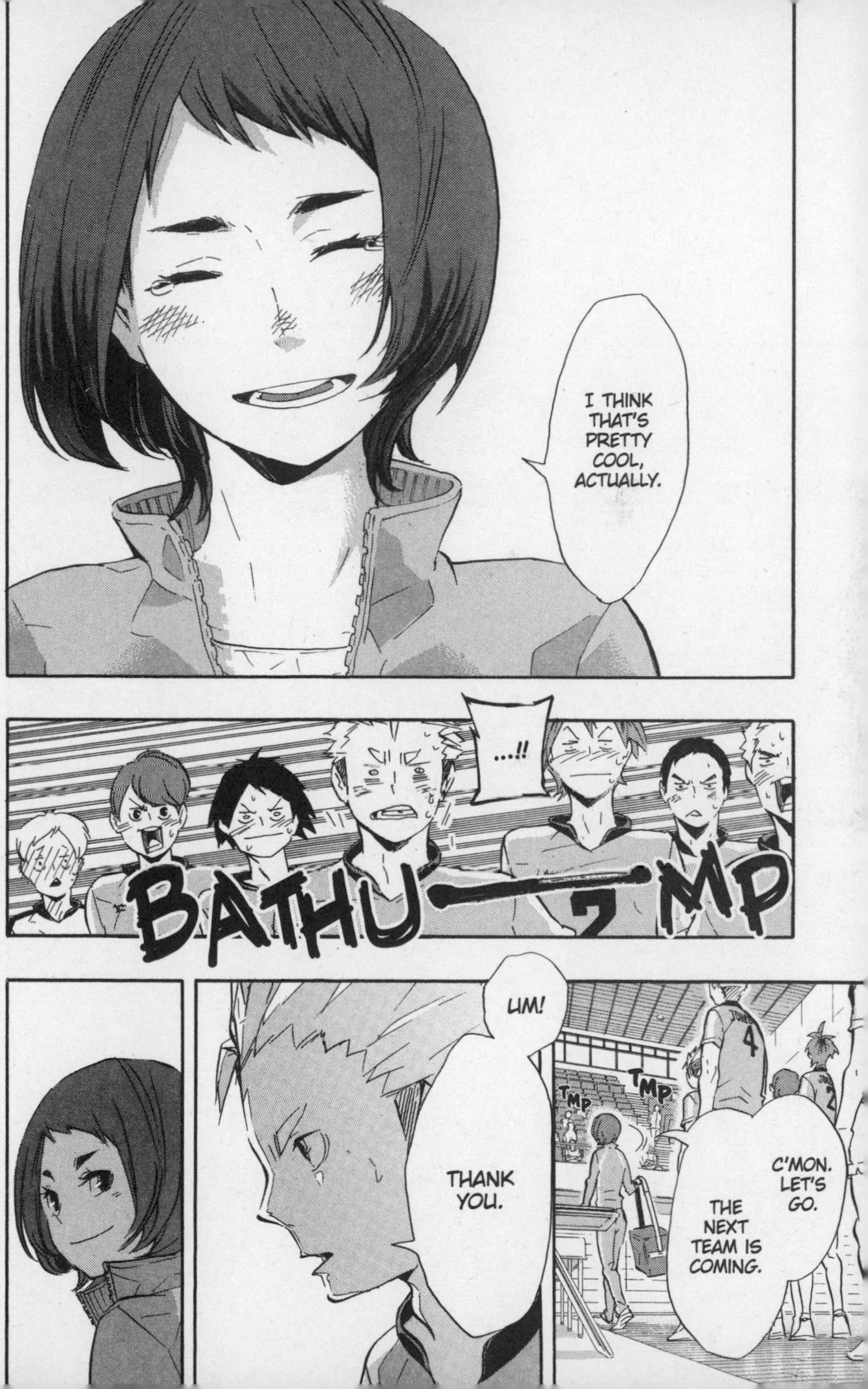
I THINK THAT'S PRETTY COOL, ACTUALLY.
...!!
BATHU—MP
C'MON. LET'S GO.
THE NEXT TEAM IS COMING.
TMP
TMP
UM!
THANK YOU.

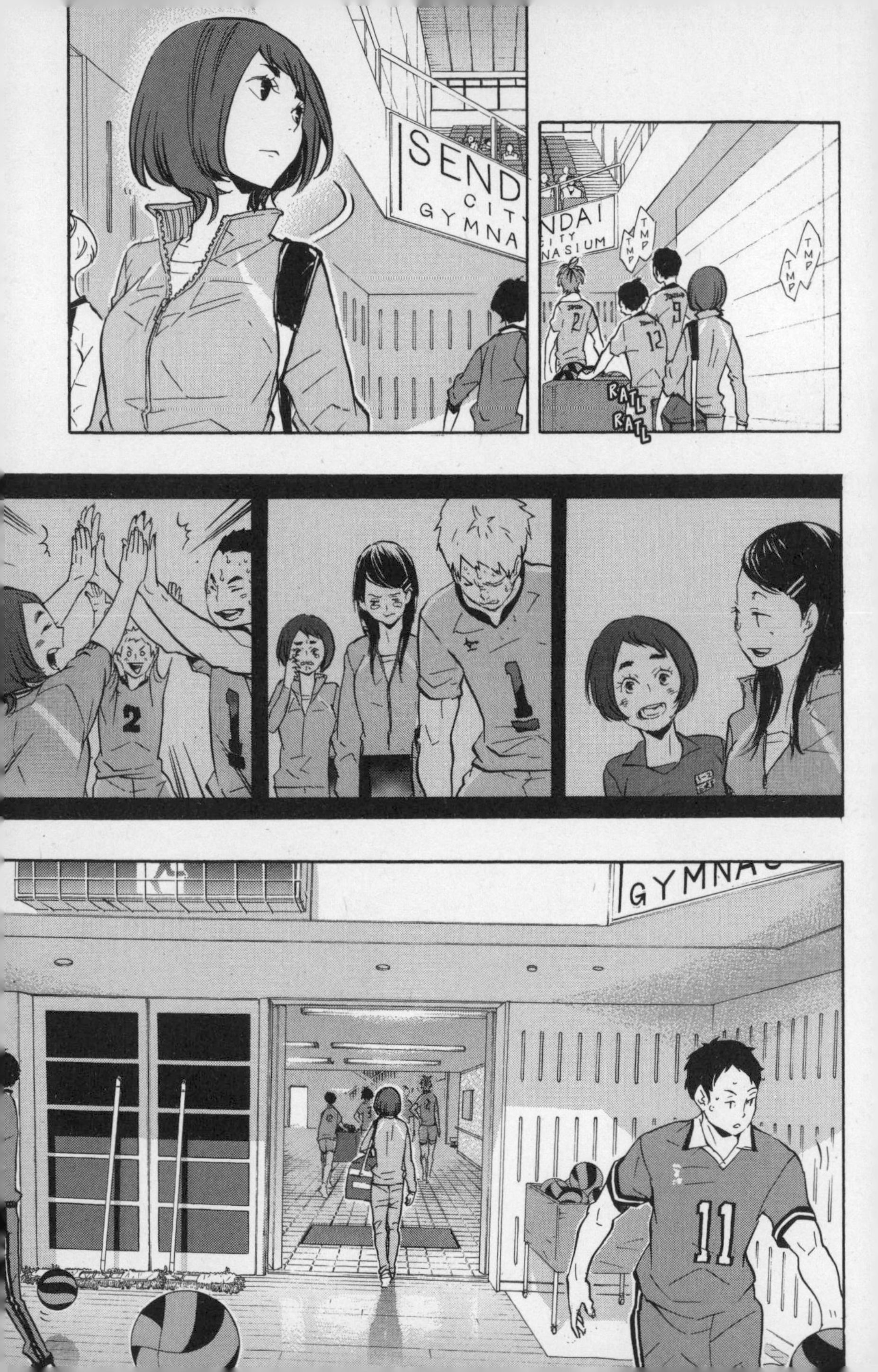

NDAI
CITY
NASIUM
TMP
TMP
TMP
TMP
RATL
RATL
SEND
CITY
GYMNA
GYMNA

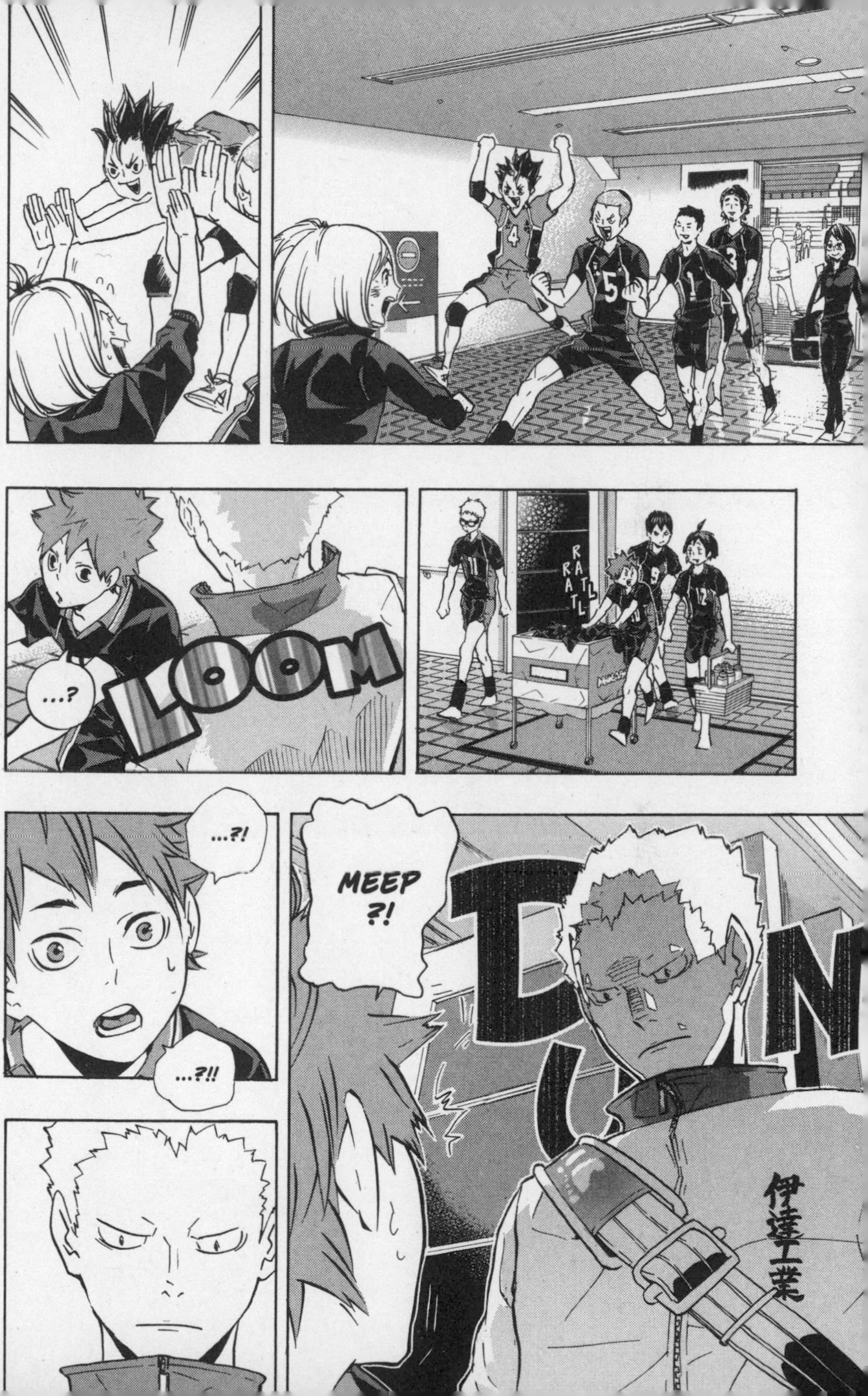
RATL
RATL
...?
LOOM
MEEP ?!
伊達工業
...?!
...?!!

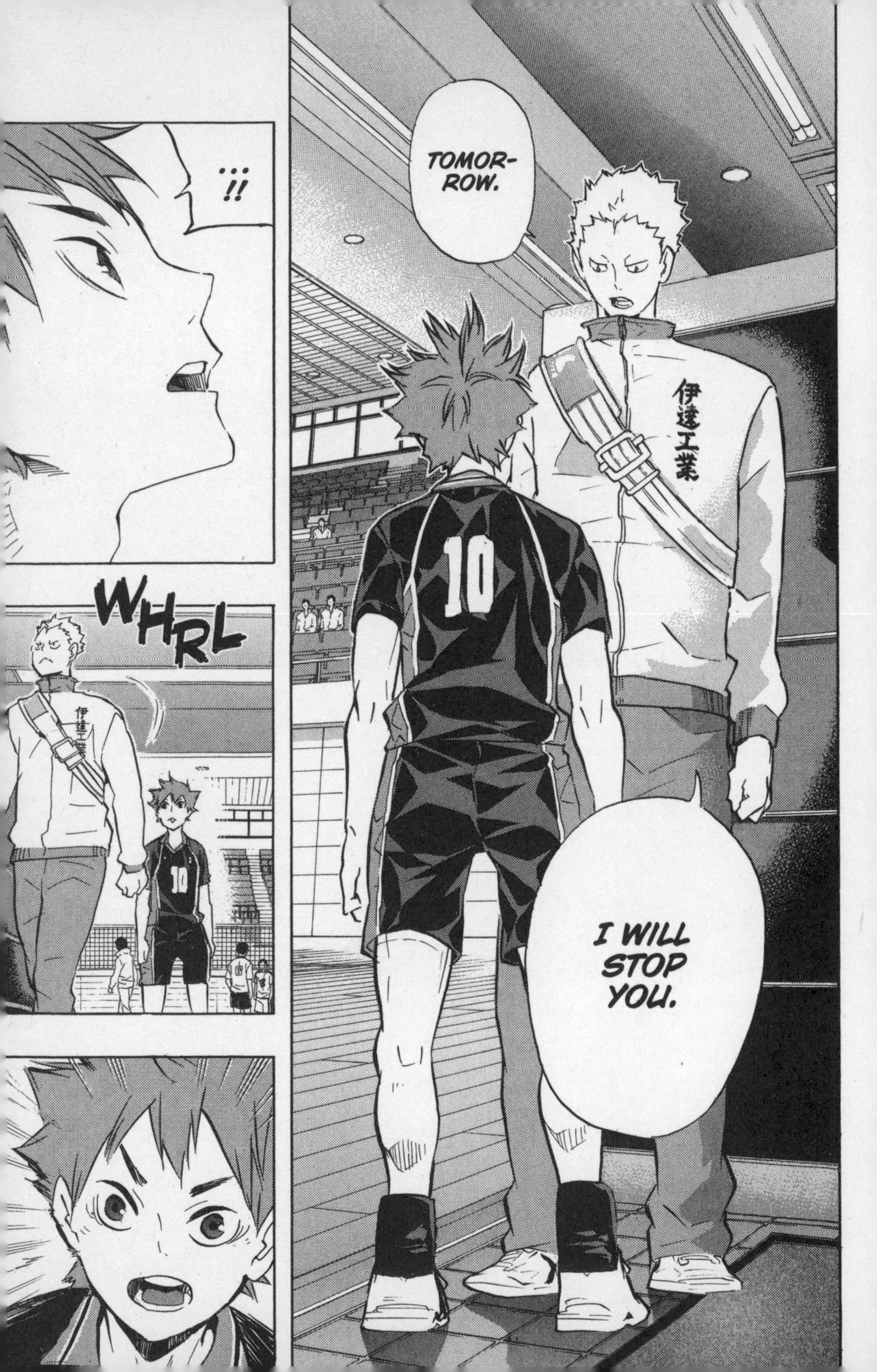
TOMOR-
ROW.
伊達工業
I WILL STOP YOU.
...!!
WHRL
伊達工業

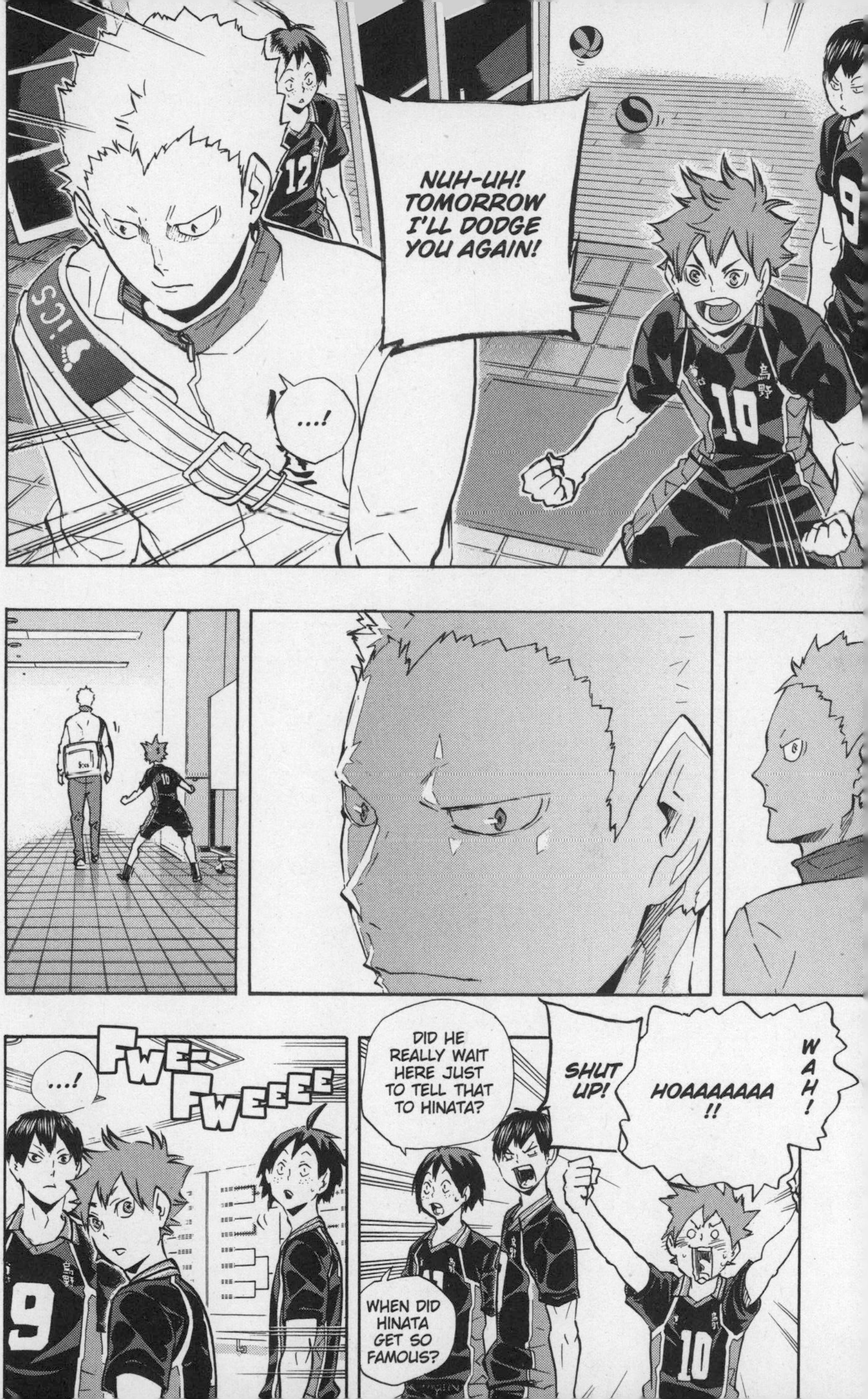
NUH-UH! TOMORROW I'LL DODGE YOU AGAIN!
...!
WAH!
HOAAAAAAA !!
SHUT UP!
DID HE REALLY WAIT HERE JUST TO TELL THAT TO HINATA?
WHEN DID HINATA GET SO FAMOUS?
FWE-FWEEEE
...!

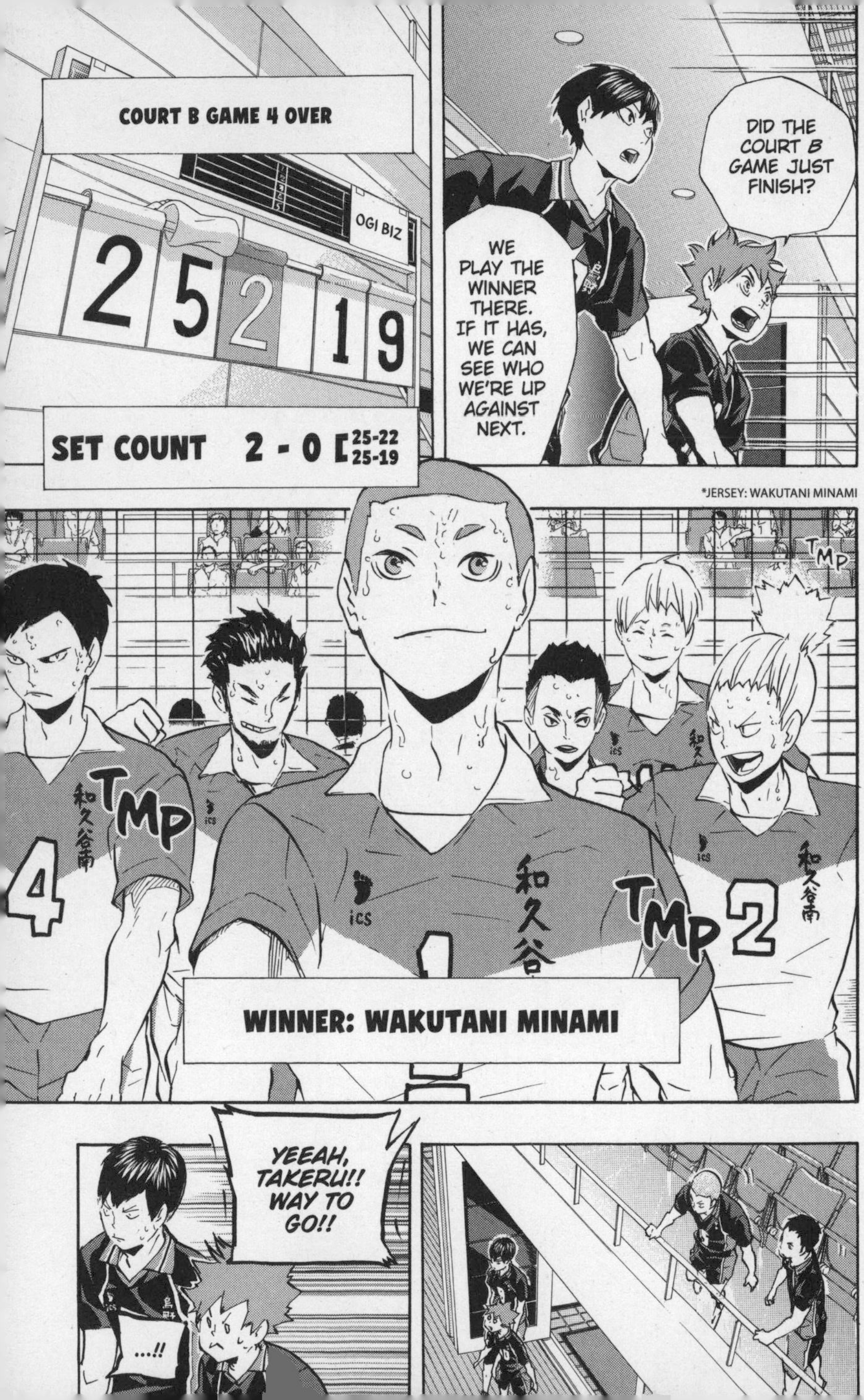
DID THE COURT B GAME JUST FINISH?
WE PLAY THE WINNER THERE. IF IT HAS, WE CAN SEE WHO WE'RE UP AGAINST NEXT.
COURT B GAME 4 OVER
OGI BIZ
25 2 19
SET COUNT 2 - 0 [25-22 25-19
*JERSEY: WAKUTANI MINAMI
TMP
TMP
TMP
WINNER: WAKUTANI MINAMI
YEEAH, TAKERU!! WAY TO GO!!
...!!

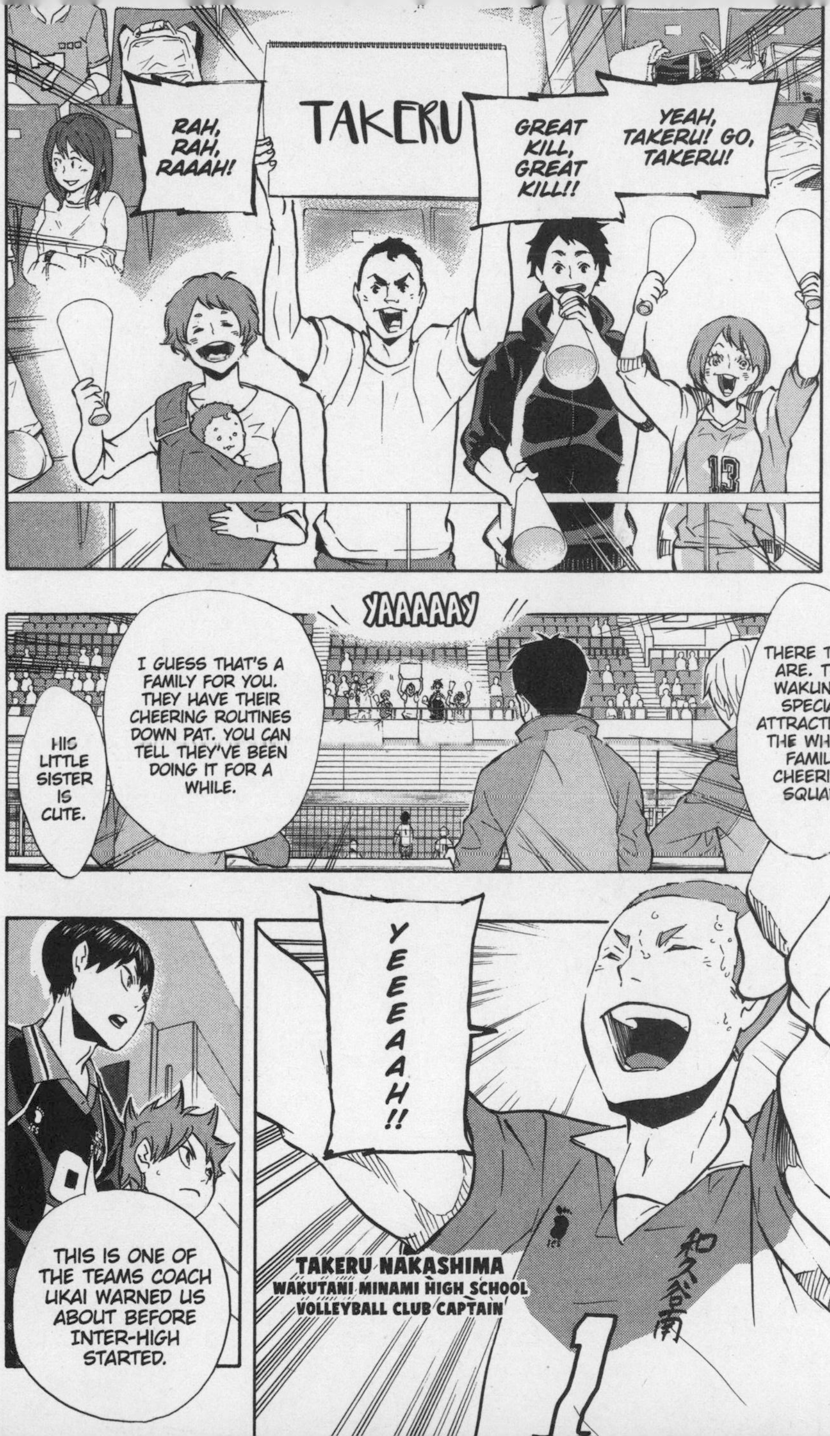
YEAH, TAKERU! GO, TAKERU!
GREAT KILL, GREAT KILL!!
TAKERU
RAH, RAH, RAAAH!
YAAAAAY
THERE THEY ARE. THE WAKUNAN SPECIAL ATTRACTION-- THE WHOLE FAMILY CHEERING SQUAD.
I GUESS THAT'S A FAMILY FOR YOU. THEY HAVE THEIR CHEERING ROUTINES DOWN PAT. YOU CAN TELL THEY'VE BEEN DOING IT FOR A WHILE.
HIS LITTLE SISTER IS CUTE.
YEEEAAAH!!
TAKERU NAKASHIMA
WAKUTANI MINAMI HIGH SCHOOL
VOLLEYBALL CLUB CAPTAIN
THIS IS ONE OF THE TEAMS COACH UKAI WARNED US ABOUT BEFORE INTER-HIGH STARTED.

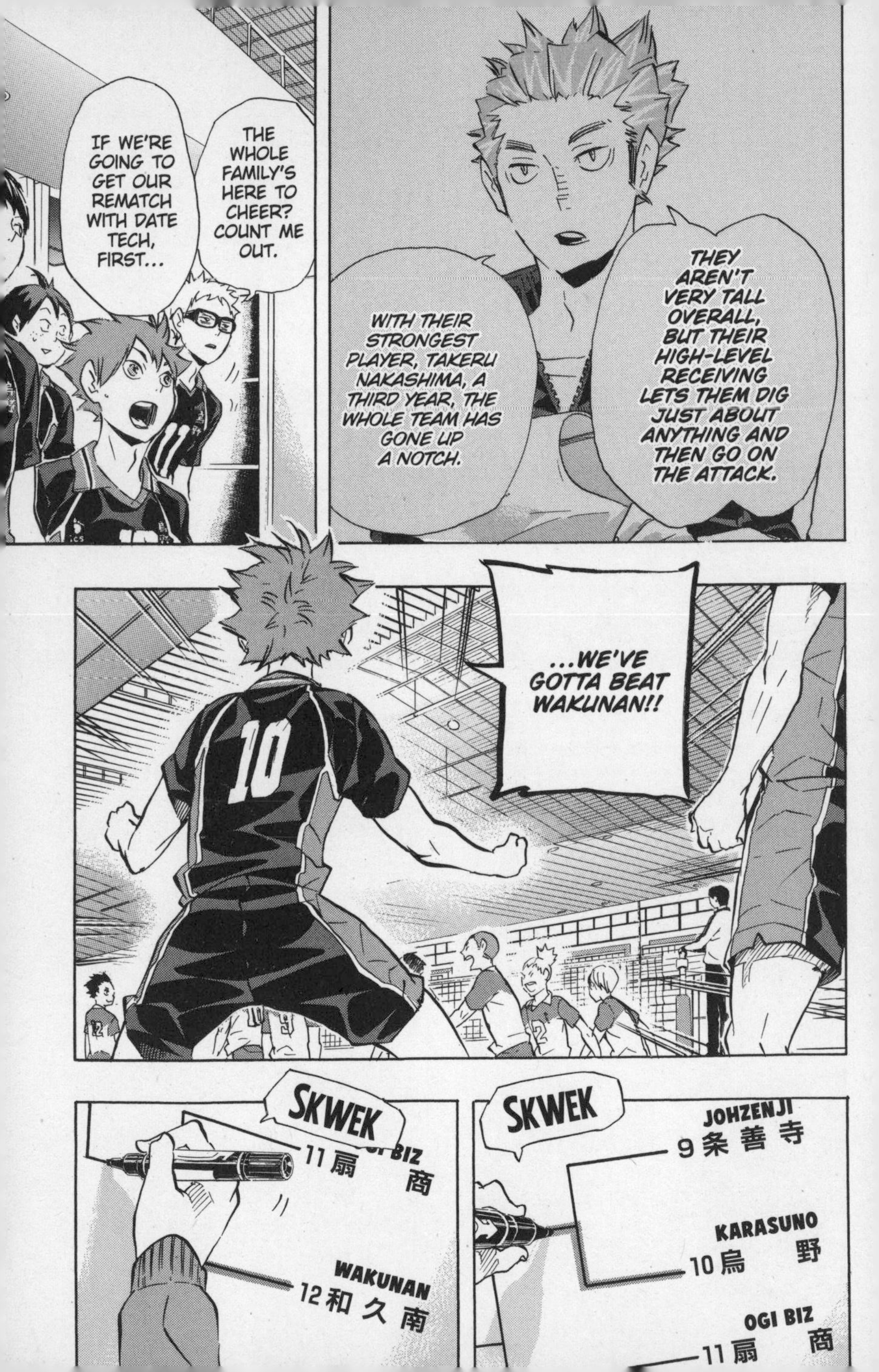
THEY AREN'T VERY TALL OVERALL, BUT THEIR HIGH-LEVEL RECEIVING LETS THEM DIG JUST ABOUT ANYTHING AND THEN GO ON THE ATTACK.
WITH THEIR STRONGEST PLAYER, TAKERU NAKASHIMA, A THIRD YEAR, THE WHOLE TEAM HAS GONE UP A NOTCH.
THE WHOLE FAMILY'S HERE TO CHEER? COUNT ME OUT.
IF WE'RE GOING TO GET OUR REMATCH WITH DATE TECH, FIRST...
...WE'VE GOTTA BEAT WAKUNAN!!
SKWEK
JOHZENJI
9 条善寺
KARASUNO
10 烏野
OGI BIZ
11 扇商
SKWEK
11 扇商
WAKUNAN
12 和久南

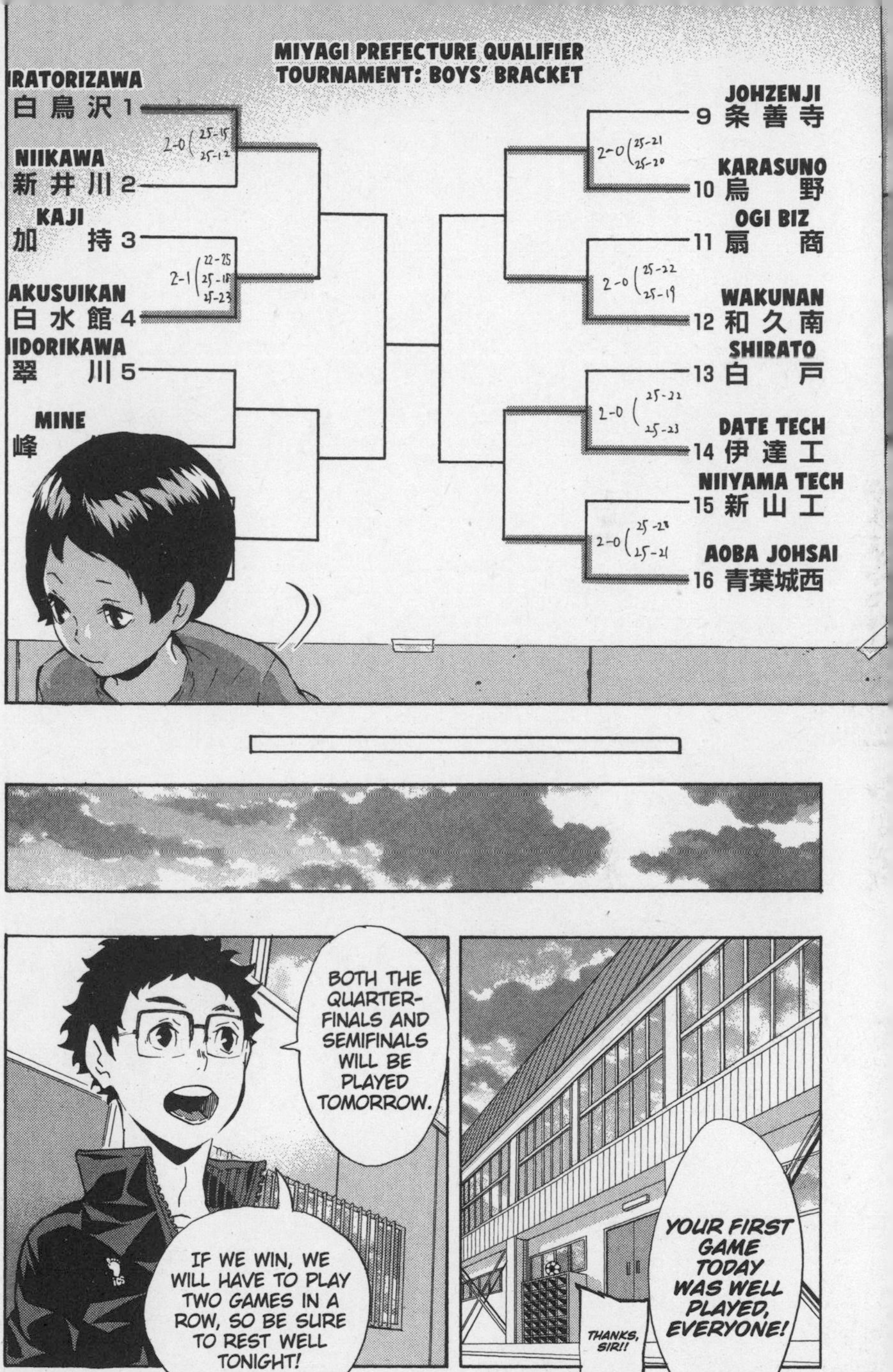
MIYAGI PREFECTURE QUALIFIER TOURNAMENT: BOYS' BRACKET
IRATORIZAWA 白鳥沢 1
NIIKAWA 新井川 2
2-0 (25-15 25-12
KAJI 加持 3
AKUSUIKAN 白水館 4
2-1 (22-25 25-18 25-23
IDORIKAWA 翠川 5
MINE 峰
JOHZENJI 9 条善寺
KARASUNO 10 烏野
2-0 (25-21 25-20
OGI BIZ 11 扇商
WAKUNAN 12 和久南
2-0 (25-22 25-19
SHIRATO 13 白戸
DATE TECH 14 伊達工
2-0 (25-22 25-23
NIIYAMA TECH 15 新山工
AOBA JOHSAI 16 青葉城西
2-0 (25-28 25-21
YOUR FIRST GAME TODAY WAS WELL PLAYED, EVERYONE!
THANKS, SIR!!
BOTH THE QUARTERFINALS AND SEMIFINALS WILL BE PLAYED TOMORROW.
IF WE WIN, WE WILL HAVE TO PLAY TWO GAMES IN A ROW, SO BE SURE TO REST WELL TONIGHT!

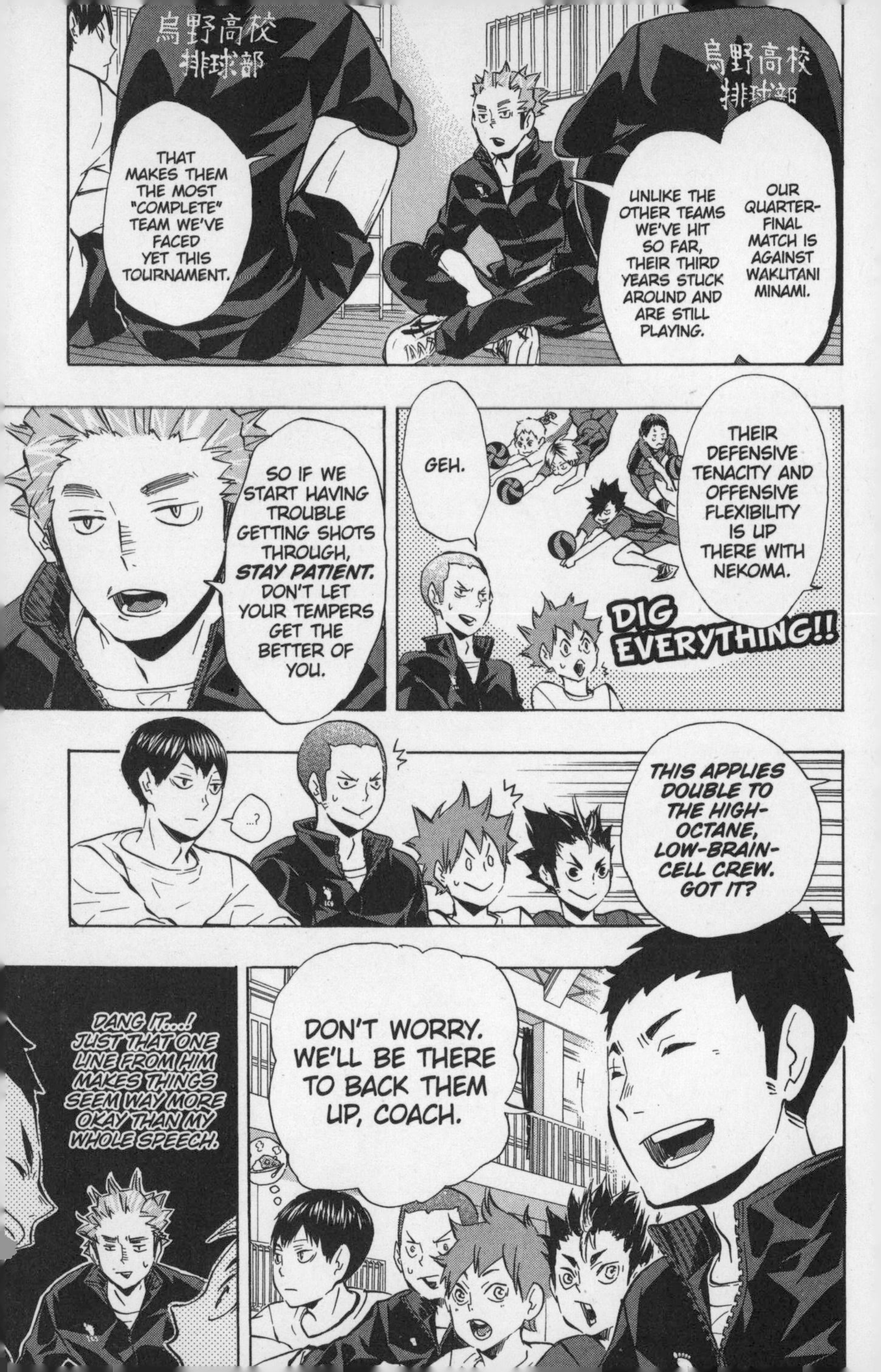
烏野高校 排球部
OUR QUARTER-FINAL MATCH IS AGAINST WAKUTANI MINAMI.
UNLIKE THE OTHER TEAMS WE'VE HIT SO FAR, THEIR THIRD YEARS STUCK AROUND AND ARE STILL PLAYING.
烏野高校 排球部
THAT MAKES THEM THE MOST "COMPLETE" TEAM WE'VE FACED YET THIS TOURNAMENT.
THEIR DEFENSIVE TENACITY AND OFFENSIVE FLEXIBILITY IS UP THERE WITH NEKOMA.
GEH.
DIG EVERYTHING!!
SO IF WE START HAVING TROUBLE GETTING SHOTS THROUGH, STAY PATIENT. DON'T LET YOUR TEMPERS GET THE BETTER OF YOU.
THIS APPLIES DOUBLE TO THE HIGH-OCTANE, LOW-BRAIN-CELL CREW. GOT IT?
...?
DON'T WORRY. WE'LL BE THERE TO BACK THEM UP, COACH.
DANG IT...! JUST THAT ONE LINE FROM HIM MAKES THINGS SEEM WAY MORE OKAY THAN MY WHOLE SPEECH.

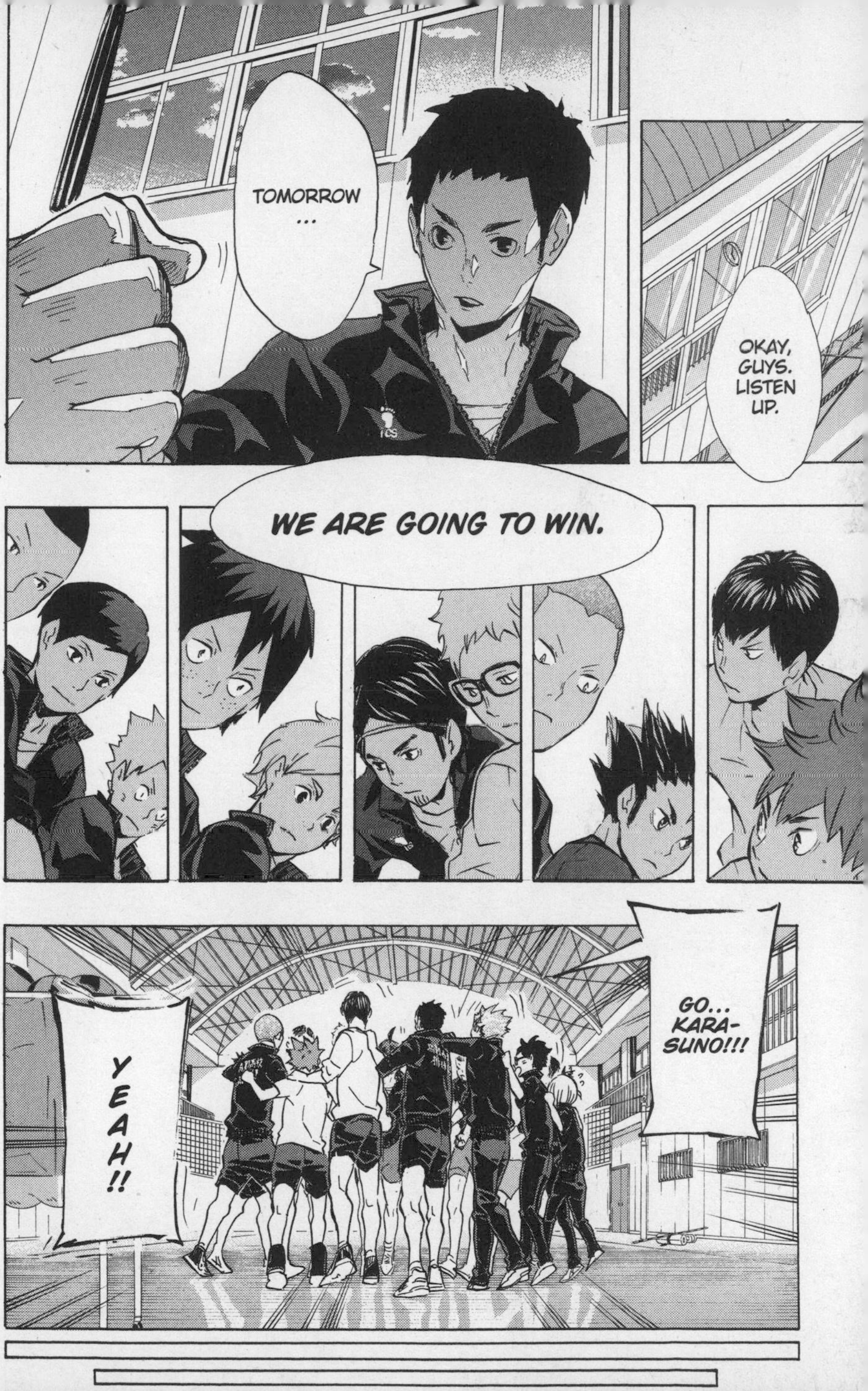
OKAY, GUYS. LISTEN UP.
TOMORROW ...
WE ARE GOING TO WIN.
GO... KARA-SUNO!!!
YEAH!!

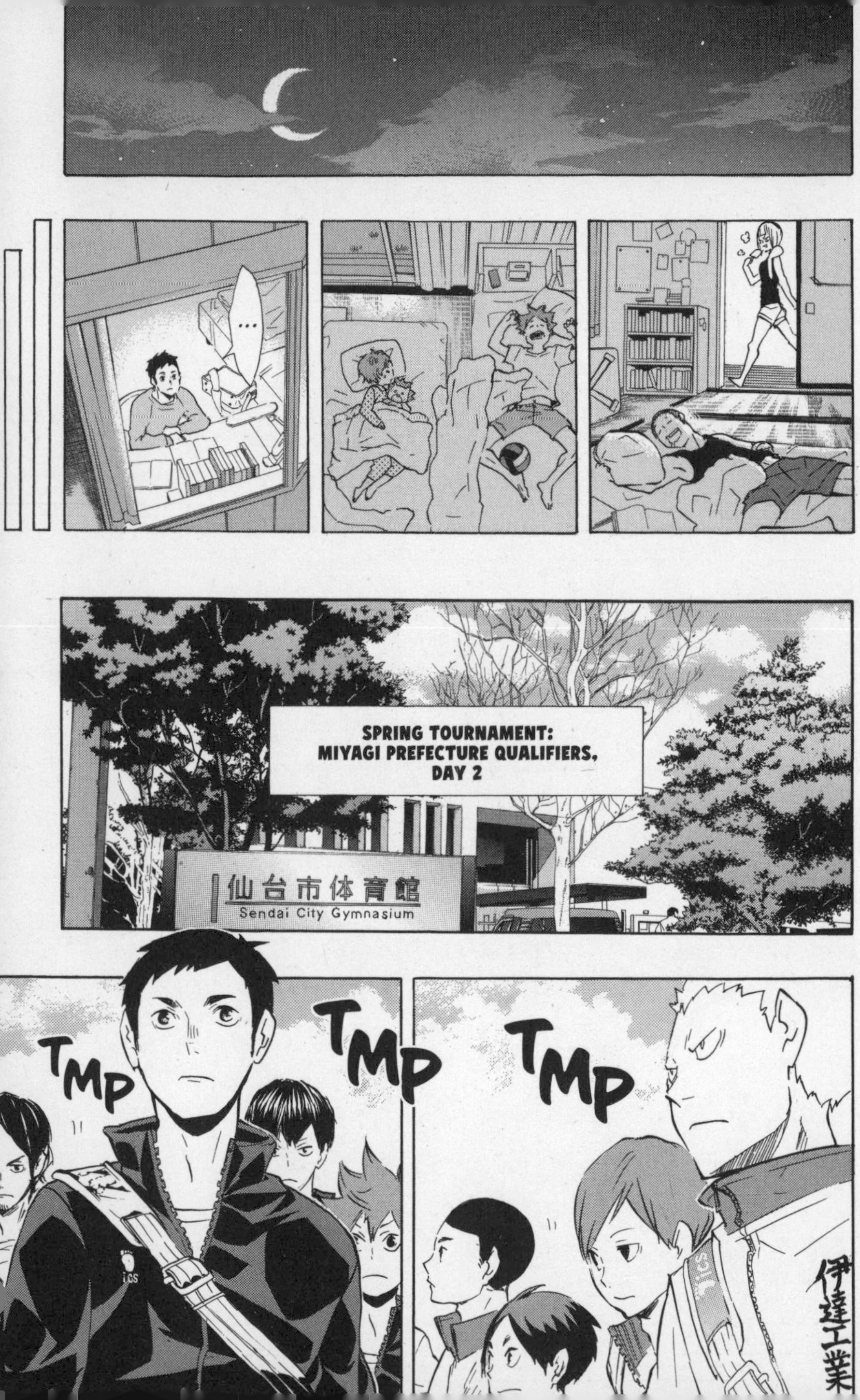
...
SPRING TOURNAMENT:
MIYAGI PREFECTURE QUALIFIERS,
DAY 2
仙台市体育館
Sendai City Gymnasium
TMP
伊達工業
TMP
TMP

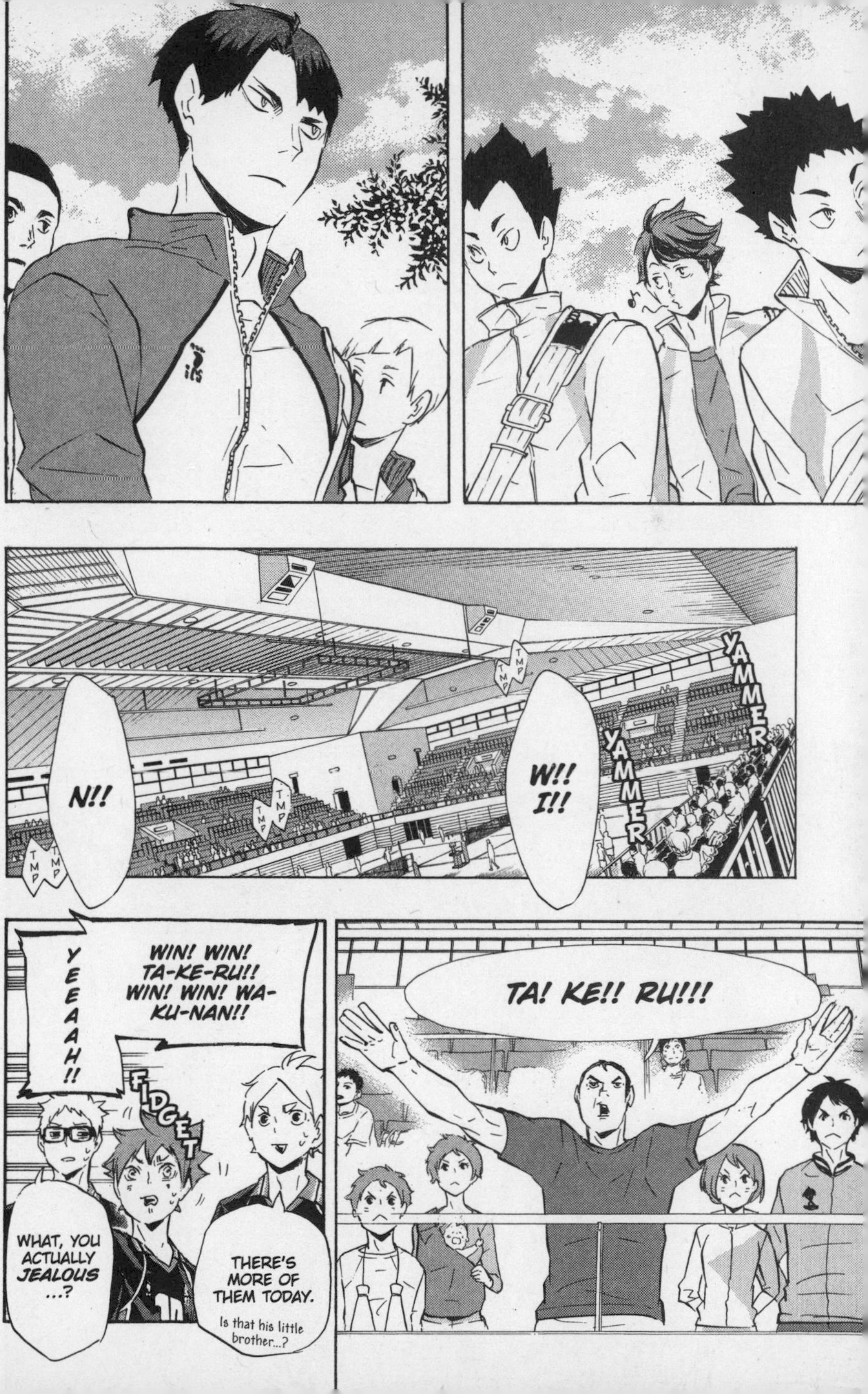
YAMMER
YAMMER
W!! I!!
TMP TMP
N!!
TMP TMP
TMP TMP
TA! KE!! RU!!!
WIN! WIN! TA-KE-RU!! WIN! WIN! WA-KU-NAN!!
YEEAAAH!!
FIDGET
THERE'S MORE OF THEM TODAY.
Is that his little brother...?
WHAT, YOU ACTUALLY JEALOUS ...?

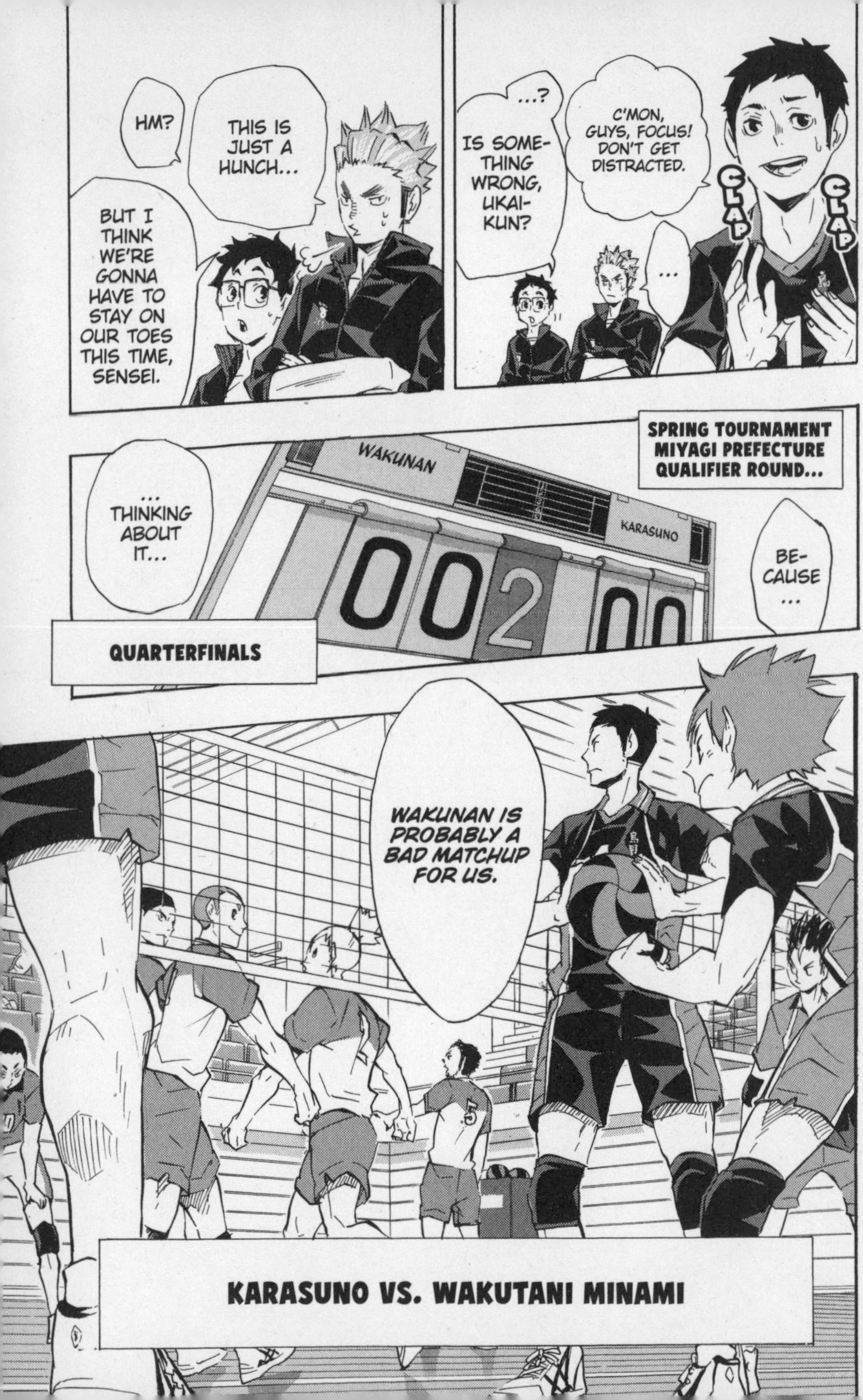
C'MON, GUYS, FOCUS! DON'T GET DISTRACTED.
CLAP CLAP
...
...?
IS SOME-THING WRONG, UKAI-KUN?
THIS IS JUST A HUNCH...
HM?
BUT I THINK WE'RE GONNA HAVE TO STAY ON OUR TOES THIS TIME, SENSEI.
SPRING TOURNAMENT MIYAGI PREFECTURE QUALIFIER ROUND...
BE-CAUSE...
WAKUNAN
KARASUNO
... THINKING ABOUT IT...
QUARTERFINALS
WAKUNAN IS PROBABLY A BAD MATCHUP FOR US.
KARASUNO VS. WAKUTANI MINAMI

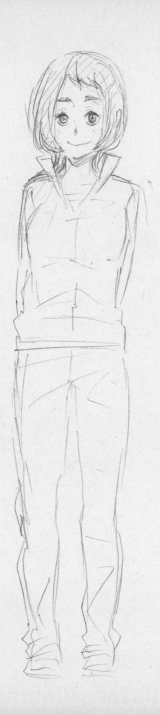

HANA MISAKI

**JOHZENJI HIGH SCHOOL
CLASS 3-6**

VOLLEYBALL CLUB MANAGER

HEIGHT: 5'4"

**WEIGHT: 109 LBS.
(AS OF APRIL, 3RD YEAR
OF HIGH SCHOOL)**

BIRTHDAY: MAY 30

**FAVORITE FOOD:
MINIATURE *CASTELLA* CAKES**

**CURRENT WORRY:
FRIENDS KEEP TELLING HER
SHE SHOULD LET HER BANGS
GROW OUT.**

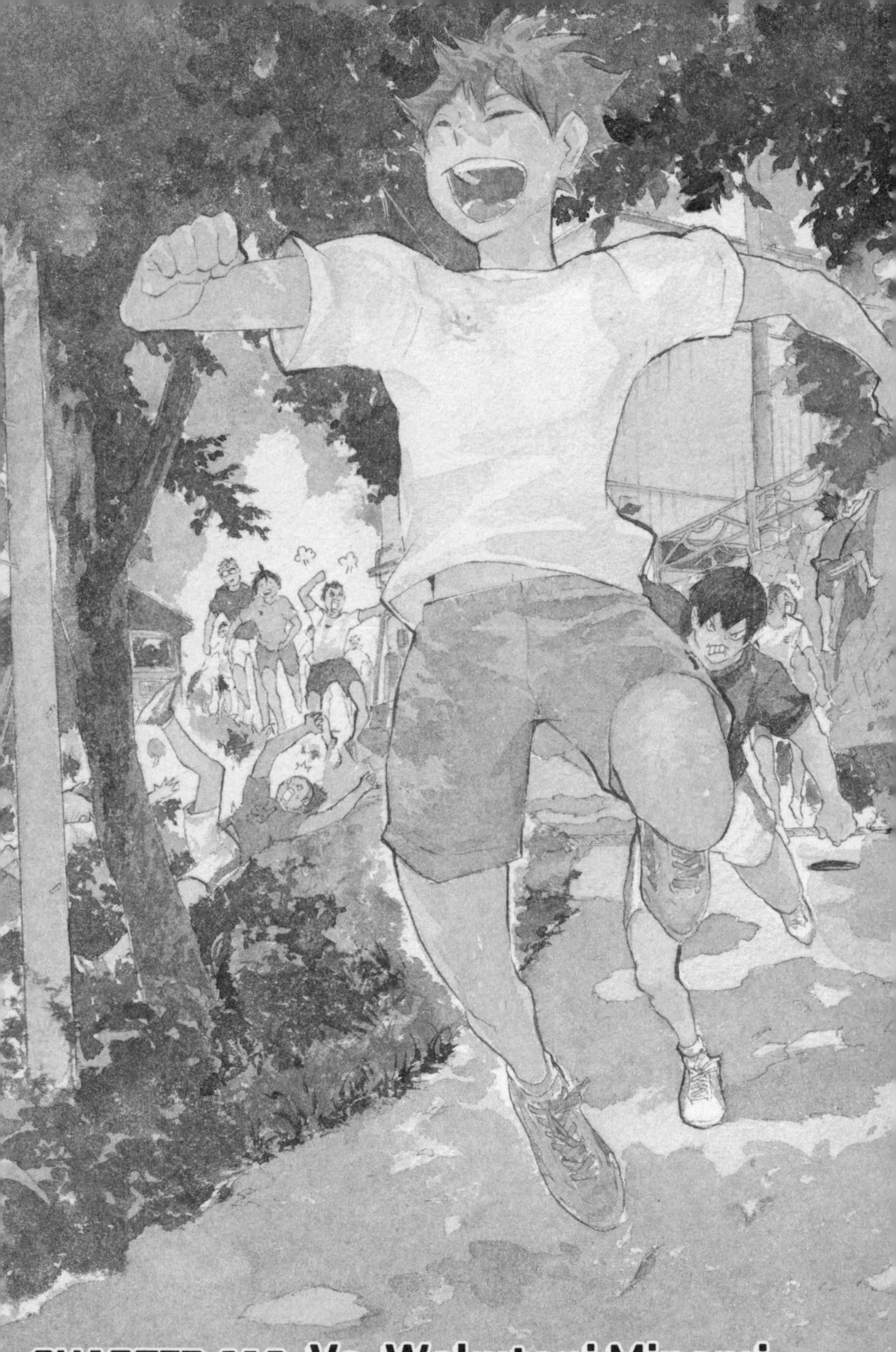

CHAPTER 116: Vs. Wakutani Minami

HAIKYU!!

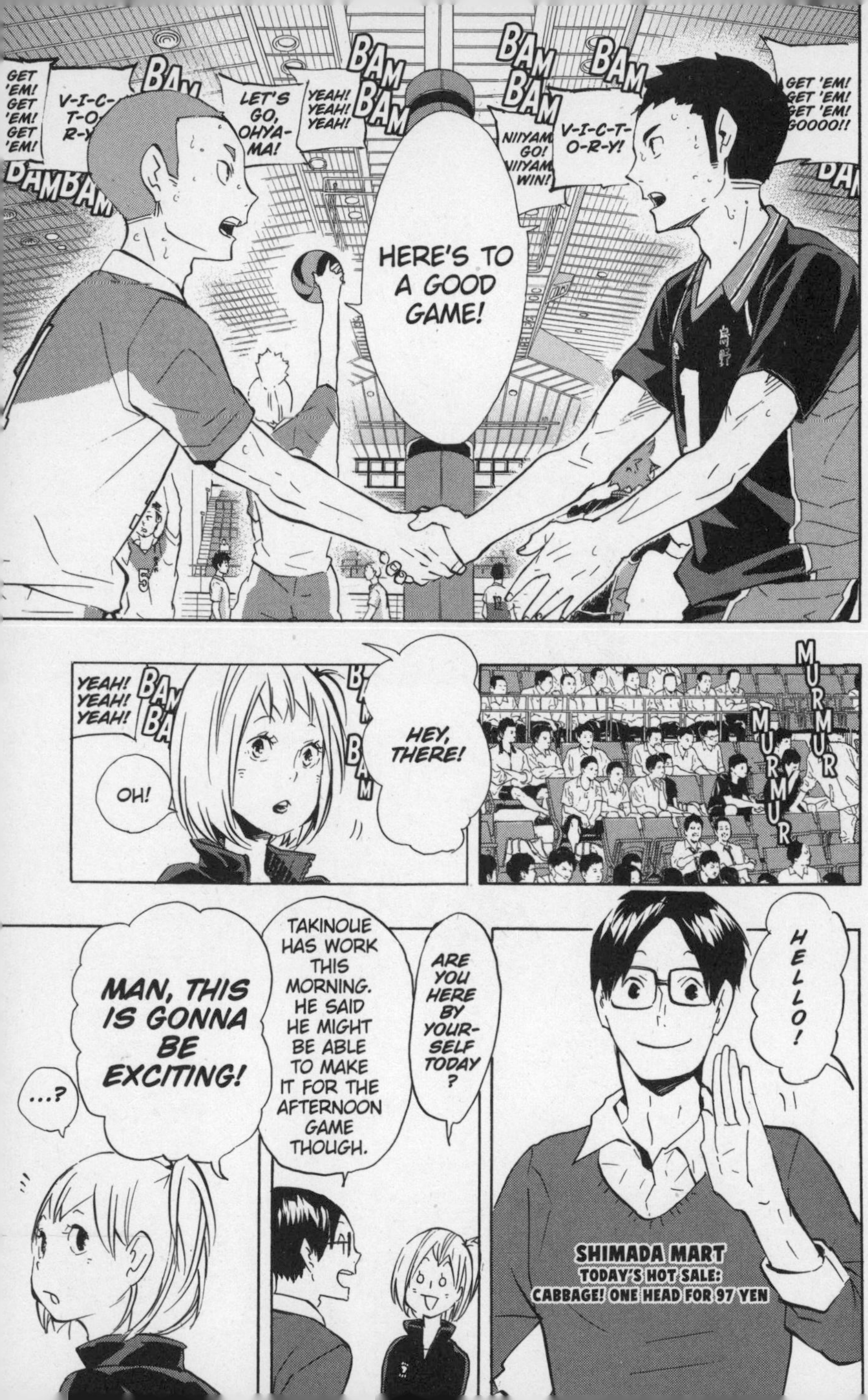
GET 'EM! GET 'EM! GET 'EM! GOOOO!!
BAM BAM
BAM BAM
V-I-C-T-O-R-Y!
NIIYAM GO! NIIYAM WIN!
YEAH! YEAH! YEAH!
BAM BAM
LET'S GO, OHYAMA!
V-I-C- T-O- R-Y
GET 'EM! GET 'EM! GET 'EM!
BAMBAM
HERE'S TO A GOOD GAME!
MURMUR
MURMUR
MURMUR
HEY, THERE!
OH!
YEAH! YEAH! YEAH!
HELLO!
SHIMADA MART
TODAY'S HOT SALE:
CABBAGE! ONE HEAD FOR 97 YEN
ARE YOU HERE BY YOURSELF TODAY?
TAKINOUE HAS WORK THIS MORNING. HE SAID HE MIGHT BE ABLE TO MAKE IT FOR THE AFTERNOON GAME THOUGH.
MAN, THIS IS GONNA BE EXCITING!
...?
!!

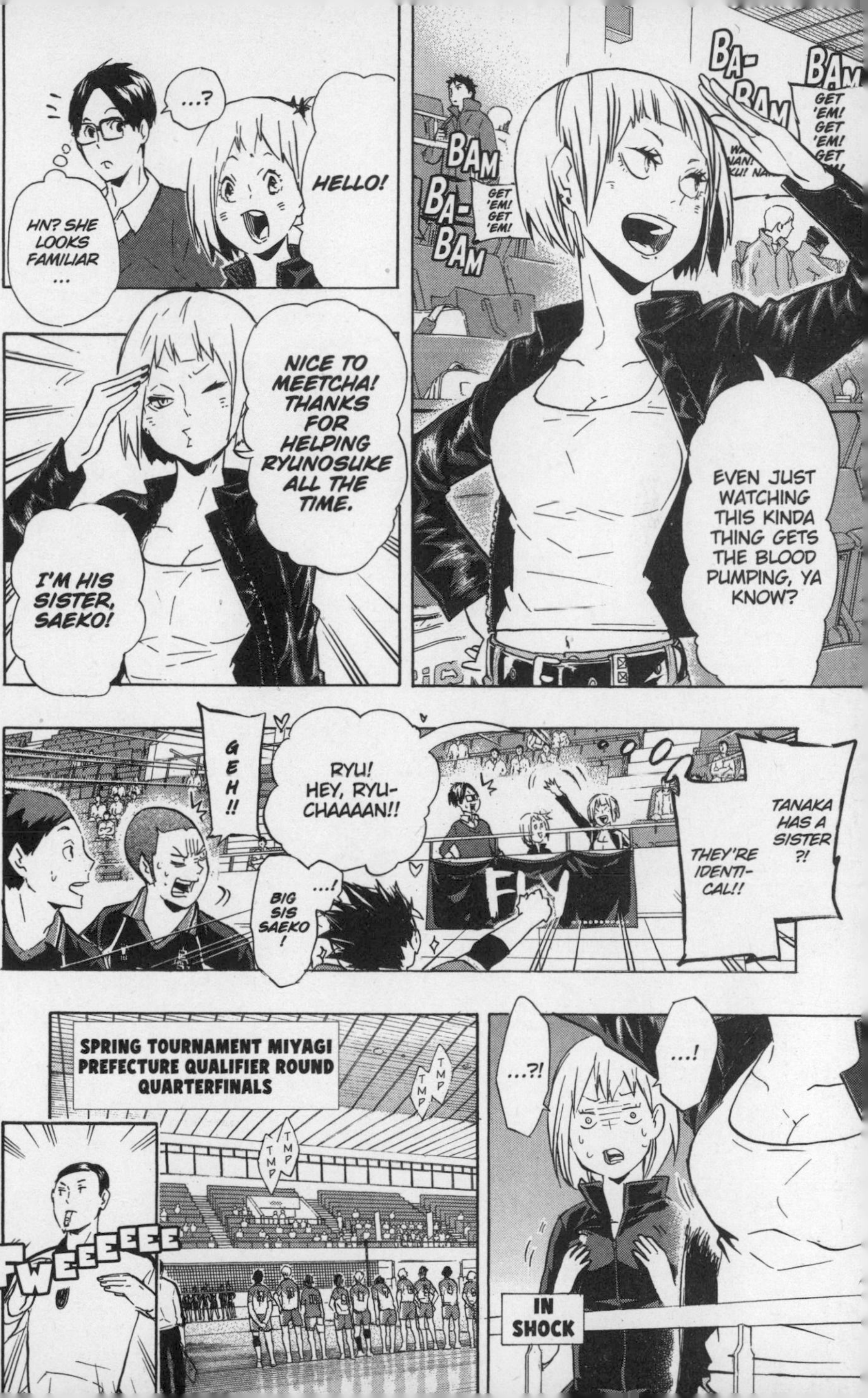

BA-BAM
BAM
GET 'EM! GET 'EM! GET
BAM
BA-BAM
GET 'EM! GET 'EM!
EVEN JUST WATCHING THIS KINDA THING GETS THE BLOOD PUMPING, YA KNOW?
HELLO!
...?
HN? SHE LOOKS FAMILIAR ...
NICE TO MEETCHA! THANKS FOR HELPING RYUNOSUKE ALL THE TIME.
I'M HIS SISTER, SAEKO!
TANAKA HAS A SISTER ?!
THEY'RE IDENTICAL!!
RYU! HEY, RYU-CHAAAAN!!
GEH!!
...!
BIG SIS SAEKO!
...!
...?!
IN SHOCK
SPRING TOURNAMENT MIYAGI PREFECTURE QUALIFIER ROUND QUARTERFINALS
TMP TMP
TMP TMP
FWEEEEEE

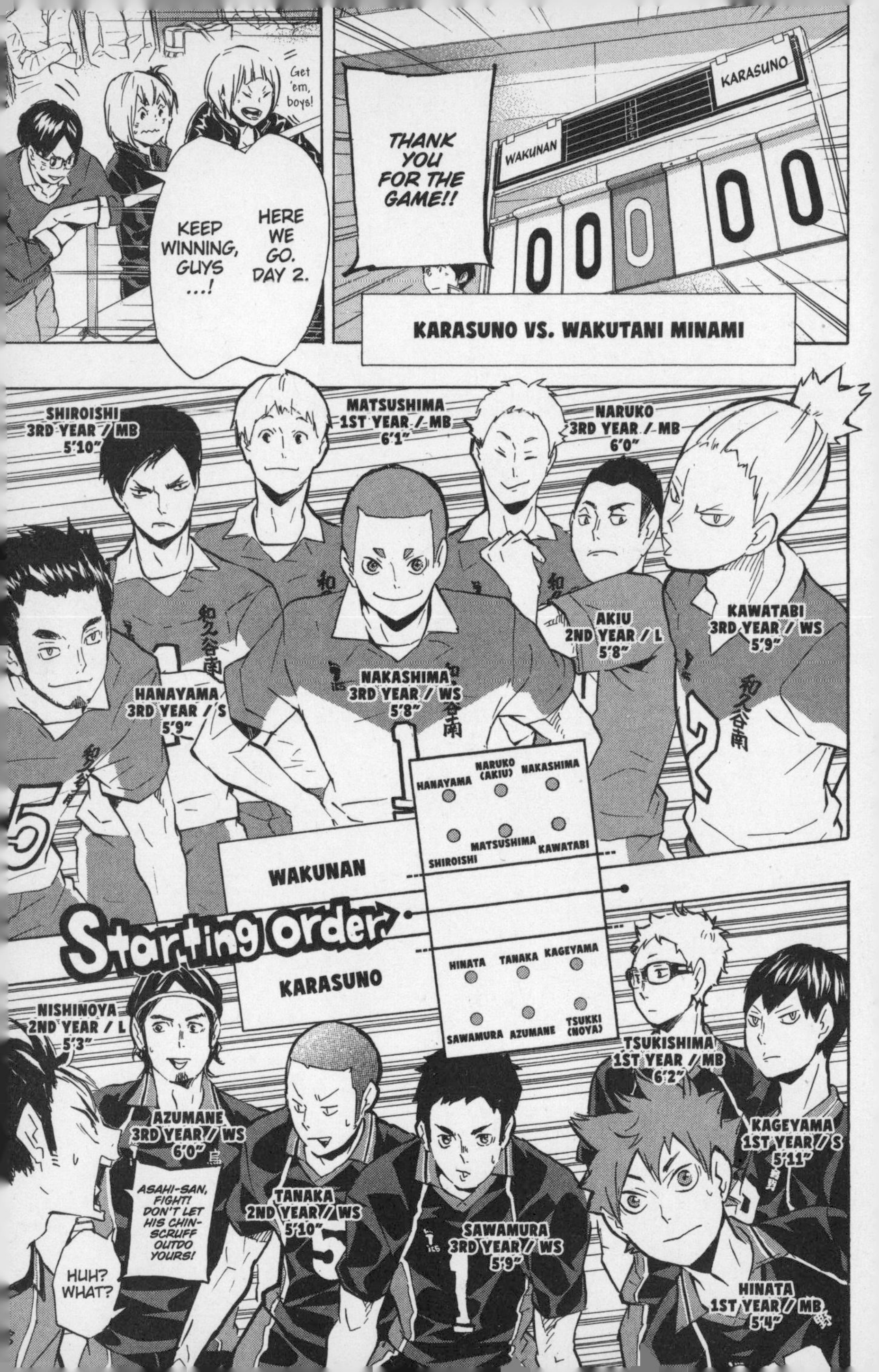
KARASUNO
WAKUNAN
THANK YOU FOR THE GAME!!
KARASUNO VS. WAKUTANI MINAMI
Get 'em, boys!
HERE WE GO. DAY 2.
KEEP WINNING, GUYS ...!
NARUKO 3RD YEAR / MB 6'0"
MATSUSHIMA 1ST YEAR / MB 6'1"
SHIROISHI 3RD YEAR / MB 5'10"
KAWATABI 3RD YEAR / WS 5'9"
AKIU 2ND YEAR / L 5'8"
NAKASHIMA 3RD YEAR / WS 5'8"
HANAYAMA 3RD YEAR / S 5'9"
WAKUNAN
HANAYAMA
NARUKO (AKIU)
NAKASHIMA
SHIROISHI
MATSUSHIMA
KAWATABI
Starting order
KARASUNO
HINATA
TANAKA
KAGEYAMA
SAWAMURA
AZUMANE
TSUKKI (NOYA)
TSUKISHIMA 1ST YEAR / MB 6'2"
NISHINOYA 2ND YEAR / L 5'3"
KAGEYAMA 1ST YEAR / S 5'11"
AZUMANE 3RD YEAR / WS 6'0"
ASAHI-SAN, FIGHT! DON'T LET HIS CHIN-SCRUFF OUTDO YOURS!
TANAKA 2ND YEAR / WS 5'10"
SAWAMURA 3RD YEAR / WS 5'9"
HUH? WHAT?
HINATA 1ST YEAR / MB 5'4"

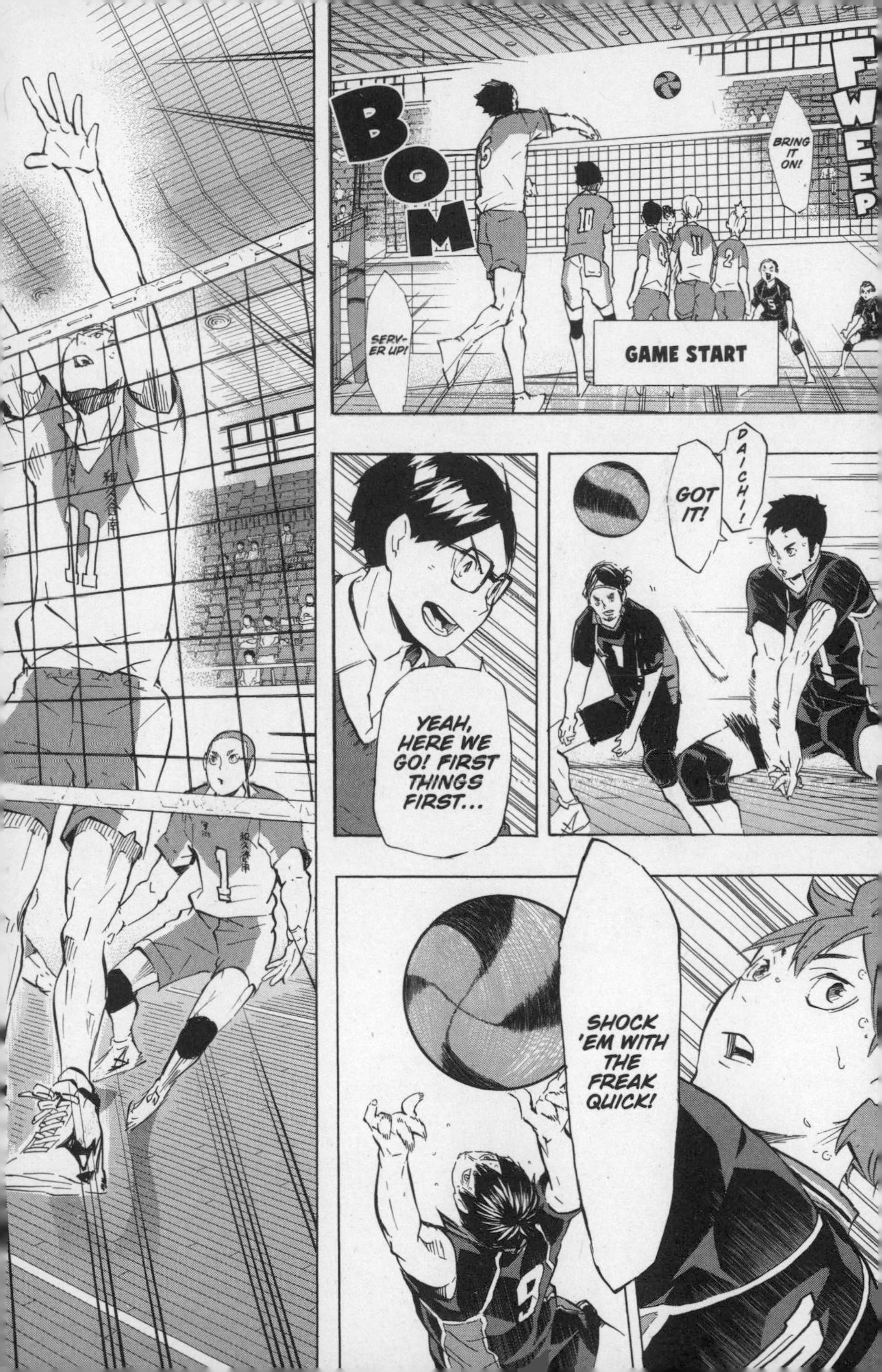
FWEEP
BRING IT ON!
BOM
GAME START
SERV-ER UP!
DAICHI!
GOT IT!
YEAH, HERE WE GO! FIRST THINGS FIRST...
SHOCK 'EM WITH THE FREAK QUICK!

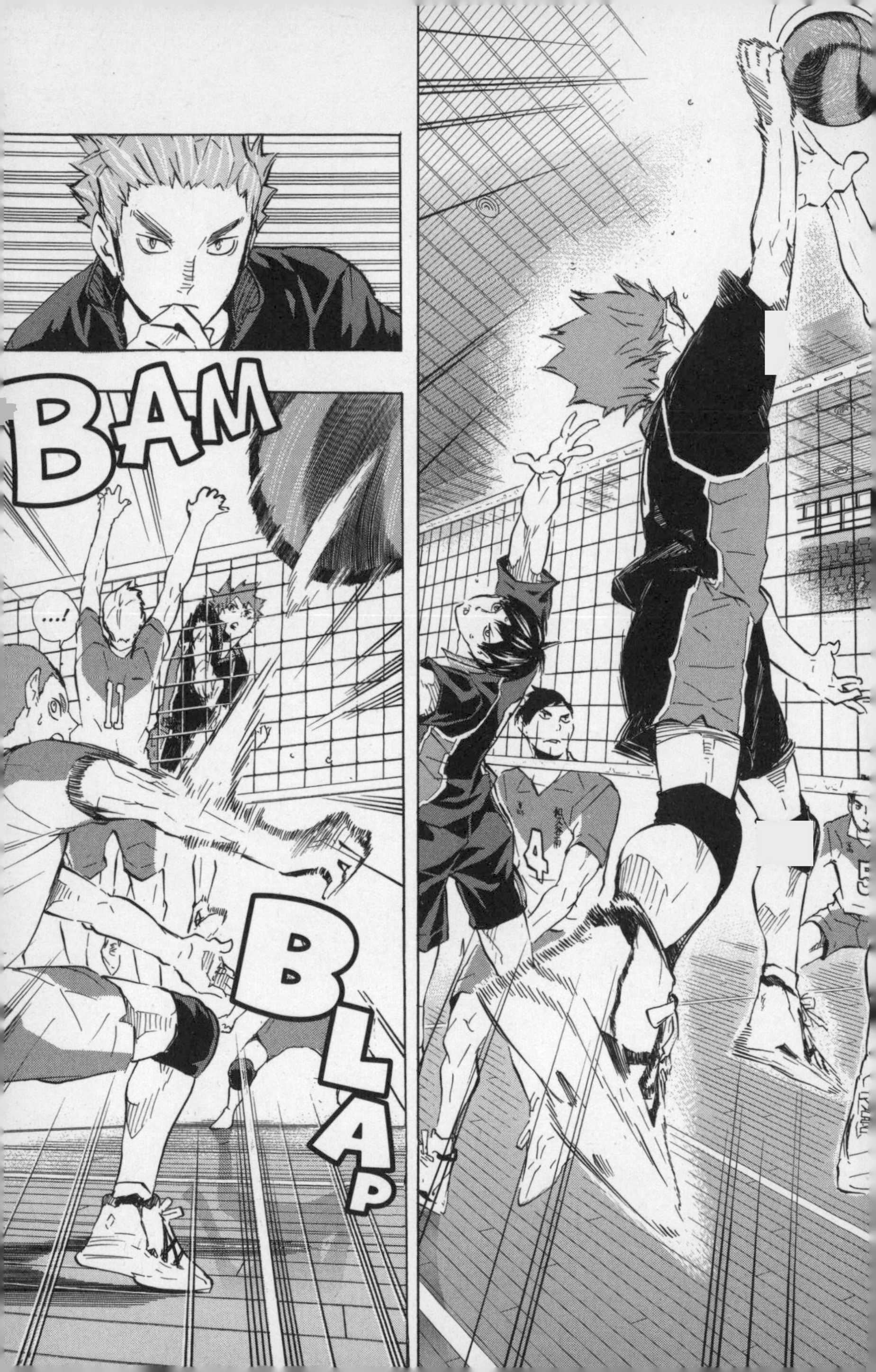
BAM
...!
BLAP

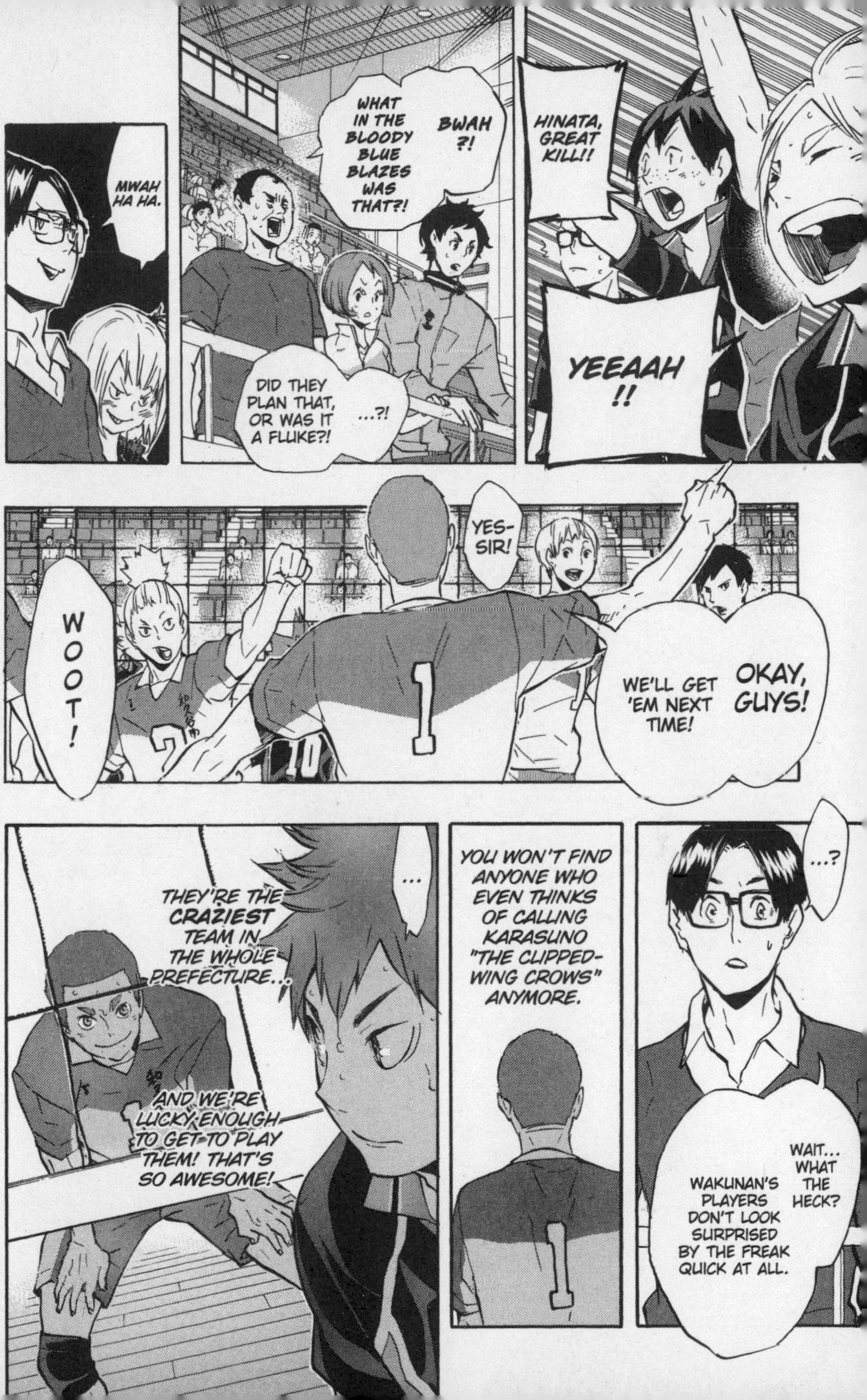
HINATA, GREAT KILL!!
YEEAAH!!
BWAH ?!
WHAT IN THE BLOODY BLUE BLAZES WAS THAT?!
...?!
DID THEY PLAN THAT, OR WAS IT A FLUKE?!
MWAH HA HA.
OKAY, GUYS!
WE'LL GET 'EM NEXT TIME!
YES-SIR!
WOOT!
...?
WAIT... WHAT THE HECK?
WAKUNAN'S PLAYERS DON'T LOOK SURPRISED BY THE FREAK QUICK AT ALL.
YOU WON'T FIND ANYONE WHO EVEN THINKS OF CALLING KARASUNO "THE CLIPPED-WING CROWS" ANYMORE.
...
THEY'RE THE CRAZIEST TEAM IN THE WHOLE PREFECTURE...
AND WE'RE LUCKY ENOUGH TO GET TO PLAY THEM! THAT'S SO AWESOME!

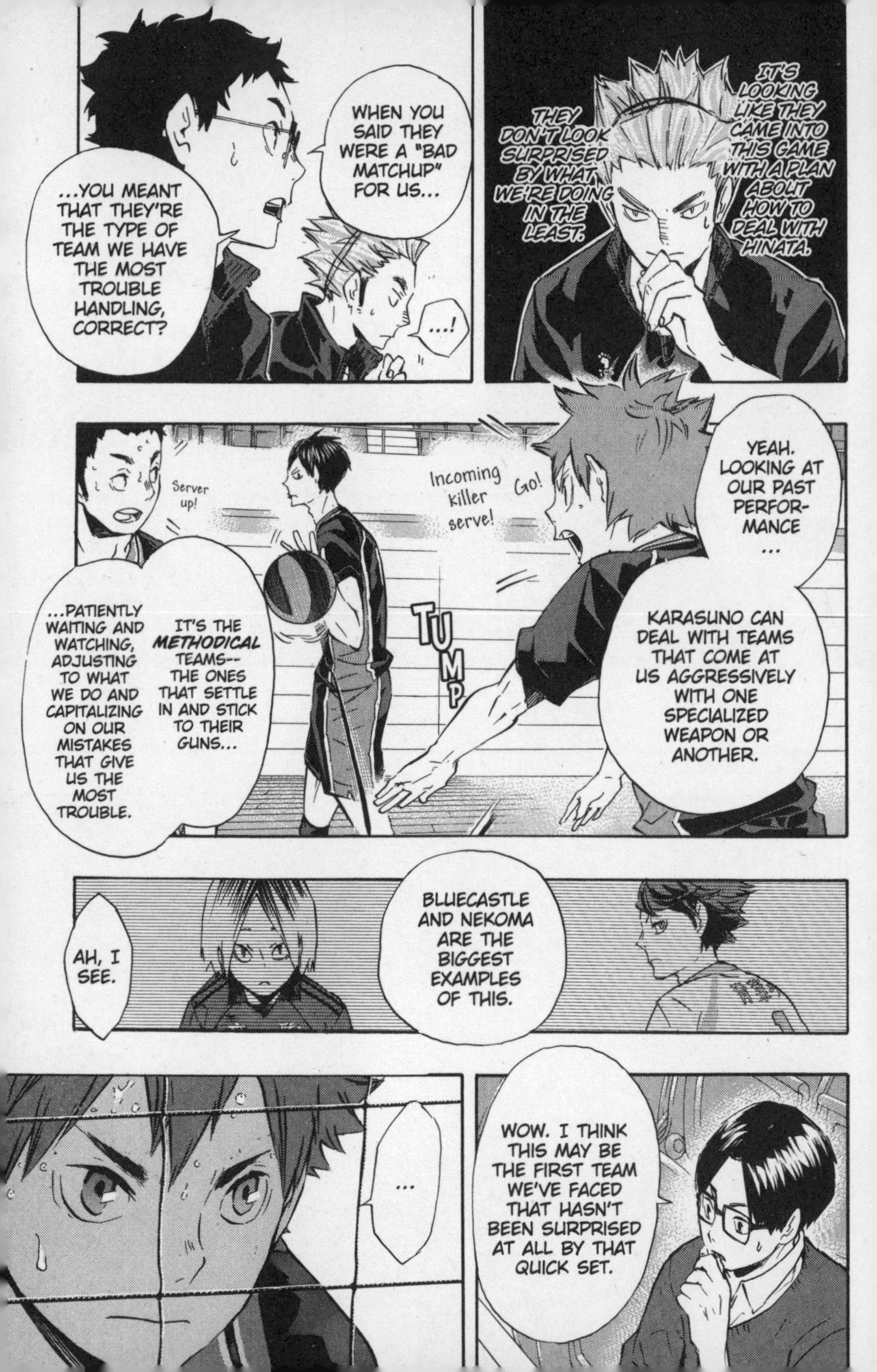
IT'S LOOKING LIKE THEY CAME INTO THIS GAME WITH A PLAN ABOUT HOW TO DEAL WITH HINATA.
THEY DON'T LOOK SURPRISED BY WHAT WE'RE DOING IN THE LEAST.
WHEN YOU SAID THEY WERE A "BAD MATCHUP" FOR US...
...YOU MEANT THAT THEY'RE THE TYPE OF TEAM WE HAVE THE MOST TROUBLE HANDLING, CORRECT?
...!
YEAH. LOOKING AT OUR PAST PERFORMANCE...
Go!
Incoming killer serve!
KARASUNO CAN DEAL WITH TEAMS THAT COME AT US AGGRESSIVELY WITH ONE SPECIALIZED WEAPON OR ANOTHER.
TUMP
Server up!
IT'S THE *METHODICAL* TEAMS-- THE ONES THAT SETTLE IN AND STICK TO THEIR GUNS...
...PATIENTLY WAITING AND WATCHING, ADJUSTING TO WHAT WE DO AND CAPITALIZING ON OUR MISTAKES THAT GIVE US THE MOST TROUBLE.
BLUECASTLE AND NEKOMA ARE THE BIGGEST EXAMPLES OF THIS.
AH, I SEE.
WOW. I THINK THIS MAY BE THE FIRST TEAM WE'VE FACED THAT HASN'T BEEN SURPRISED AT ALL BY THAT QUICK SET.
...

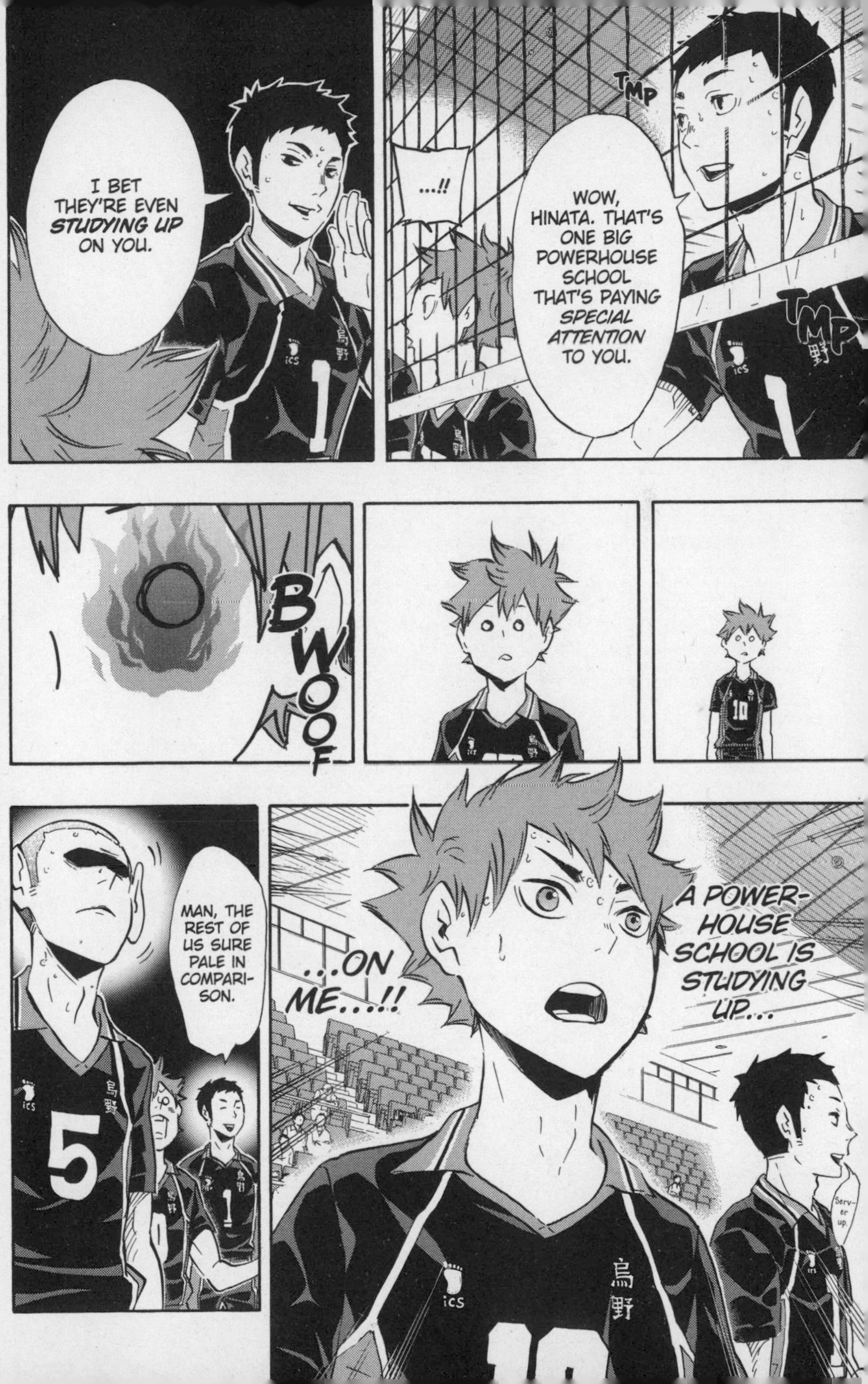
TMP
...!!
WOW, HINATA. THAT'S ONE BIG POWERHOUSE SCHOOL THAT'S PAYING SPECIAL ATTENTION TO YOU.
TMP
I BET THEY'RE EVEN STUDYING UP ON YOU.
BWOOF
A POWER-HOUSE SCHOOL IS STUDYING UP...
...ON ME...!!
Serv-er up.
MAN, THE REST OF US SURE PALE IN COMPARI-SON.

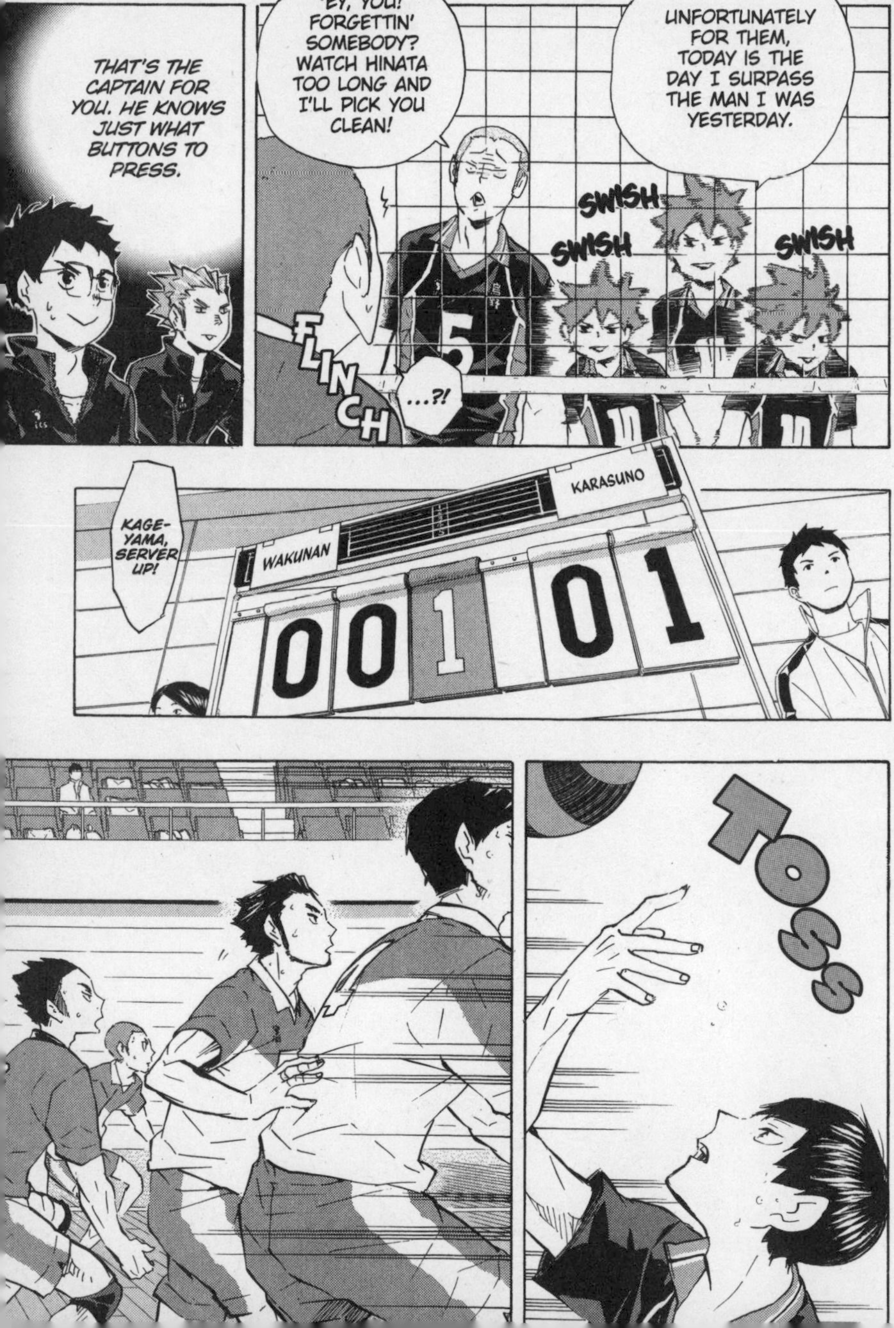
UNFORTUNATELY FOR THEM, TODAY IS THE DAY I SURPASS THE MAN I WAS YESTERDAY.
'EY, YOU! FORGETTIN' SOMEBODY? WATCH HINATA TOO LONG AND I'LL PICK YOU CLEAN!
SWISH
SWISH
SWISH
FLINCH
...?!
THAT'S THE CAPTAIN FOR YOU. HE KNOWS JUST WHAT BUTTONS TO PRESS.
KARASUNO
KAGE-YAMA, SERVER UP!
WAKUNAN
0 0 1 0 1
TOSS

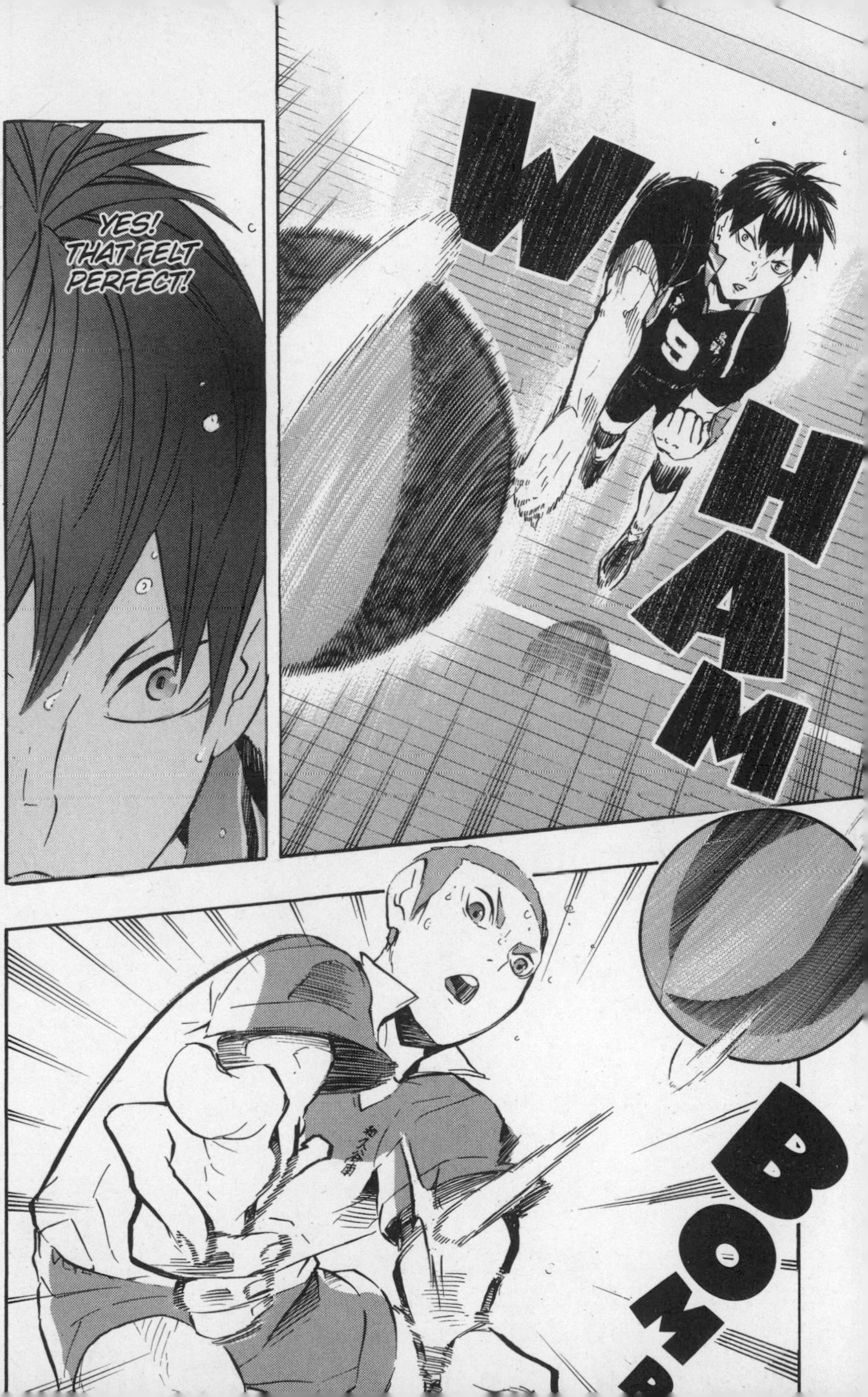
WHAM
YES! THAT FELT PERFECT!
BOM

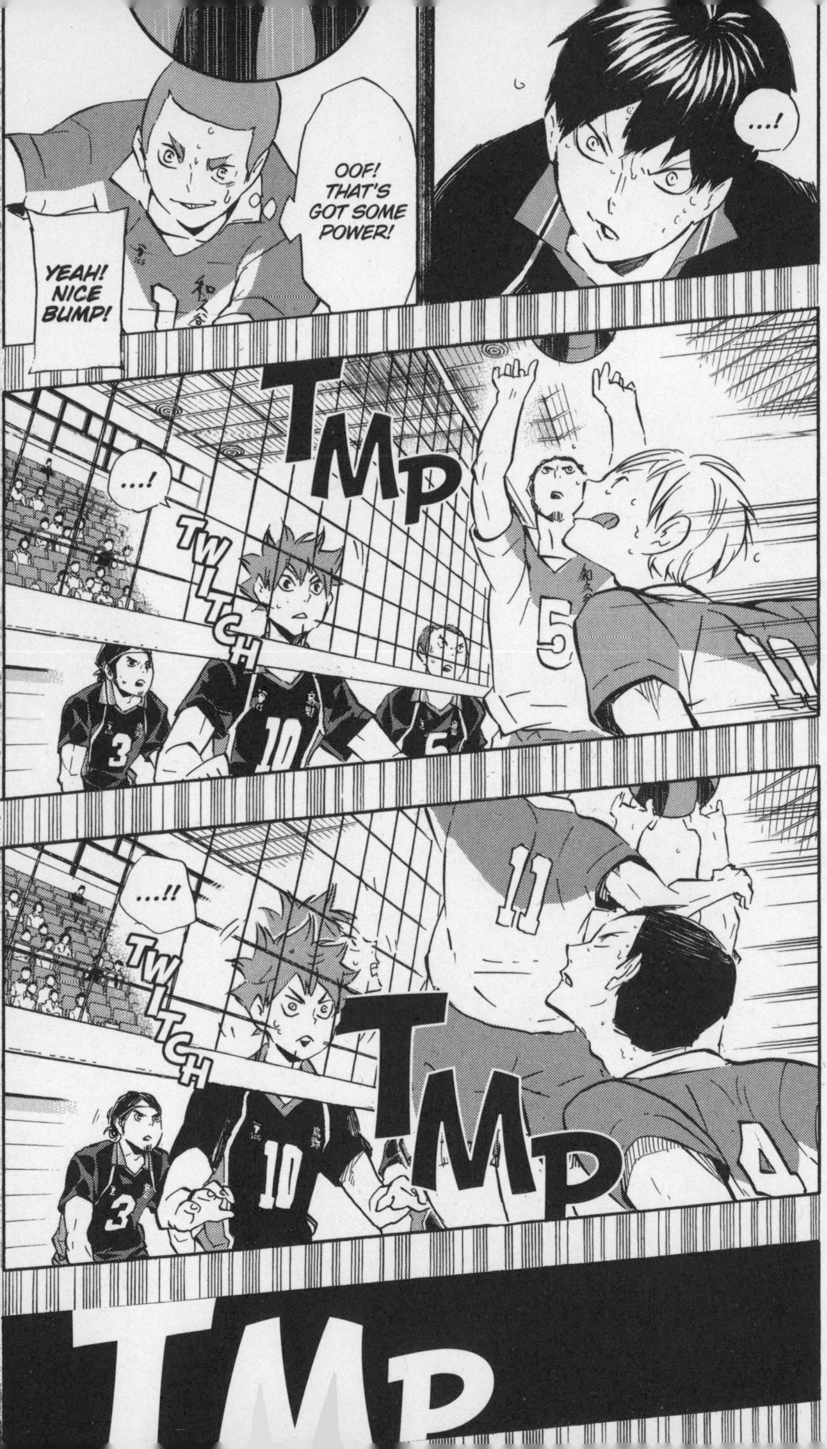
...!
OOF! THAT'S GOT SOME POWER!
YEAH! NICE BUMP!
TMP
...!
TWITCH
...!!
TWITCH
TMP
TMP

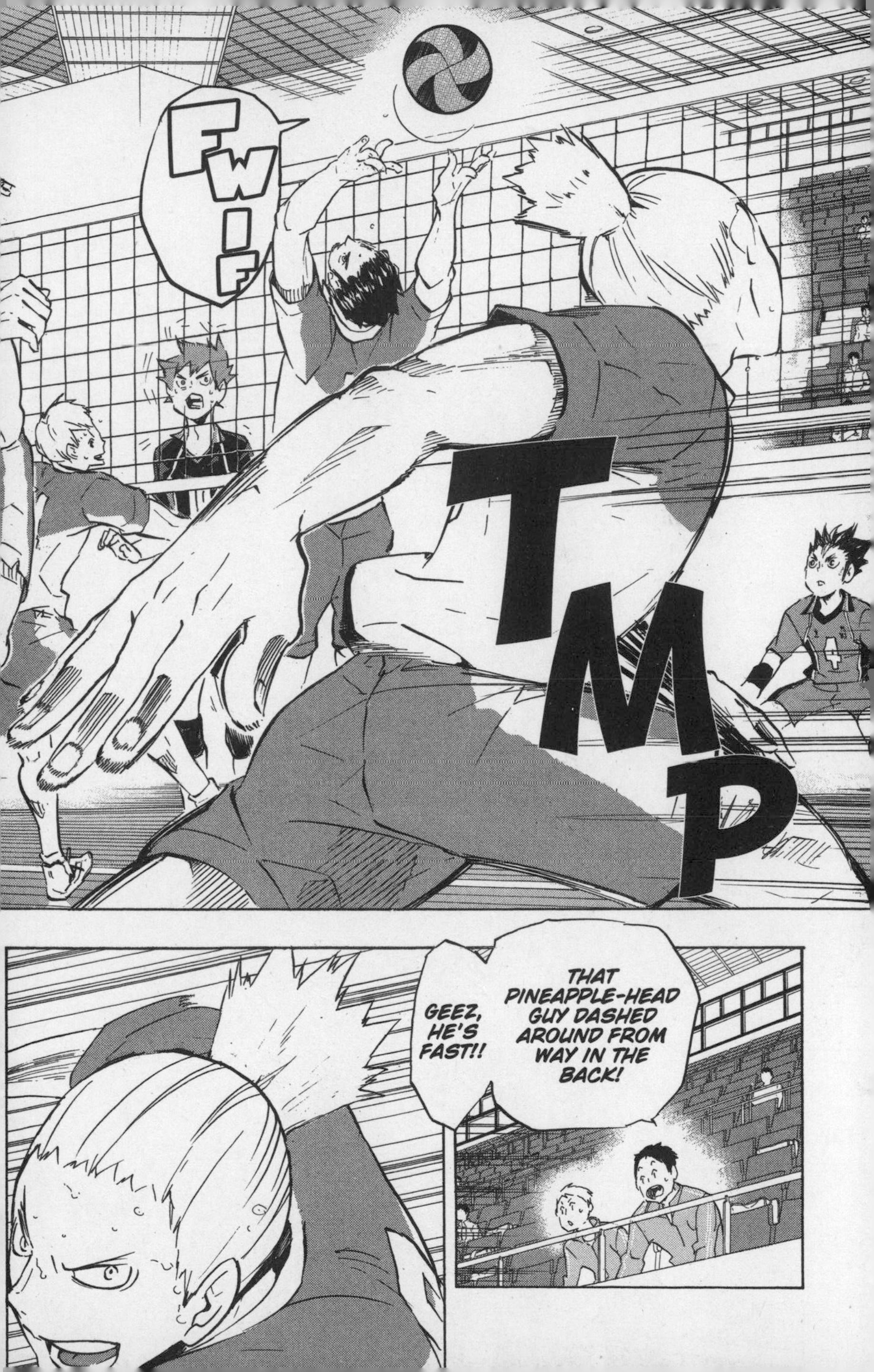
FWIF
TMP
THAT PINEAPPLE-HEAD GUY DASHED AROUND FROM WAY IN THE BACK!
GEEZ, HE'S FAST!!

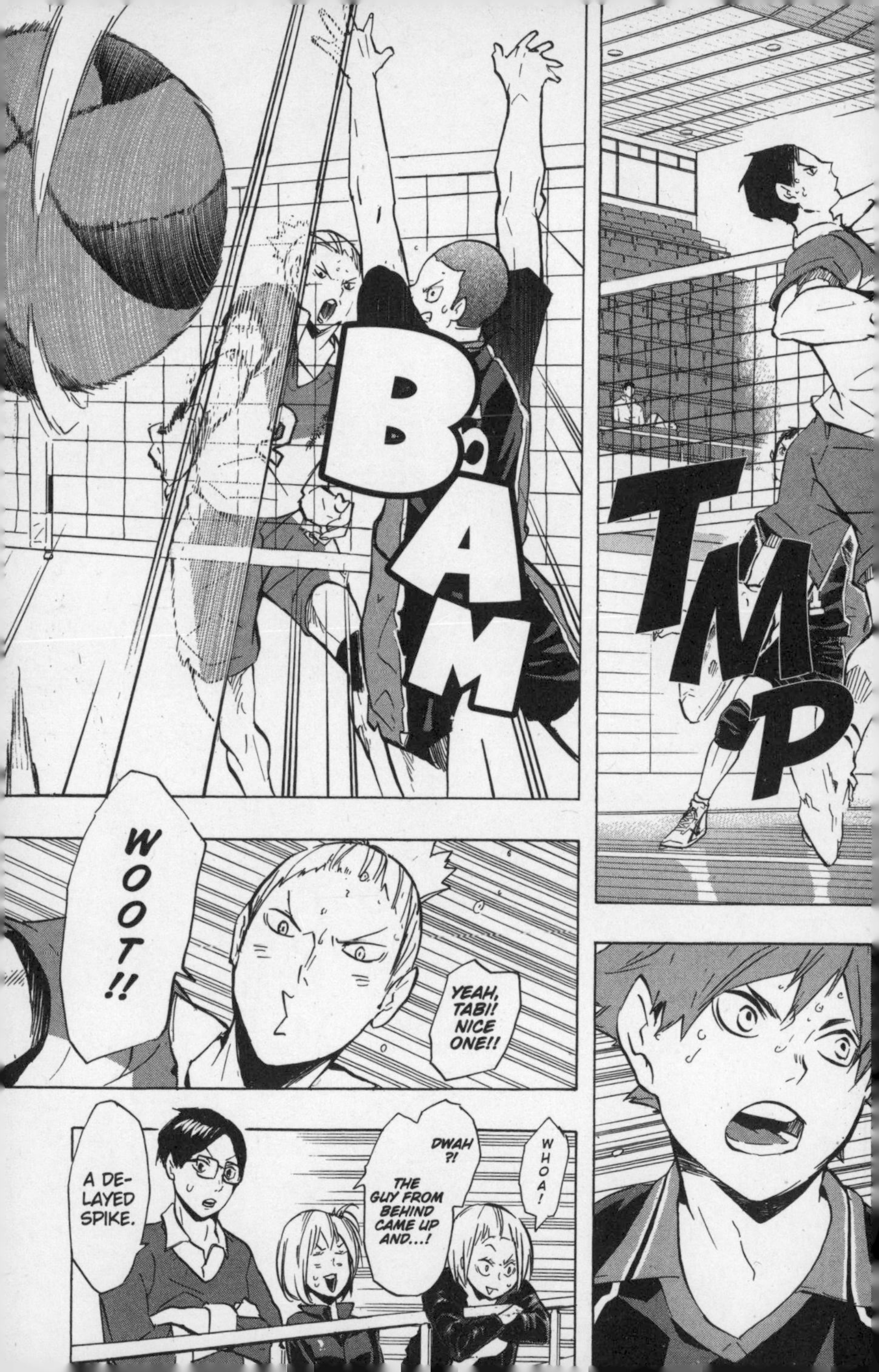
TMP
BAM
YEAH, TABI! NICE ONE!!
WOOT!!
WHOA!
DWAH?!
THE GUY FROM BEHIND CAME UP AND...!
A DE-LAYED SPIKE.

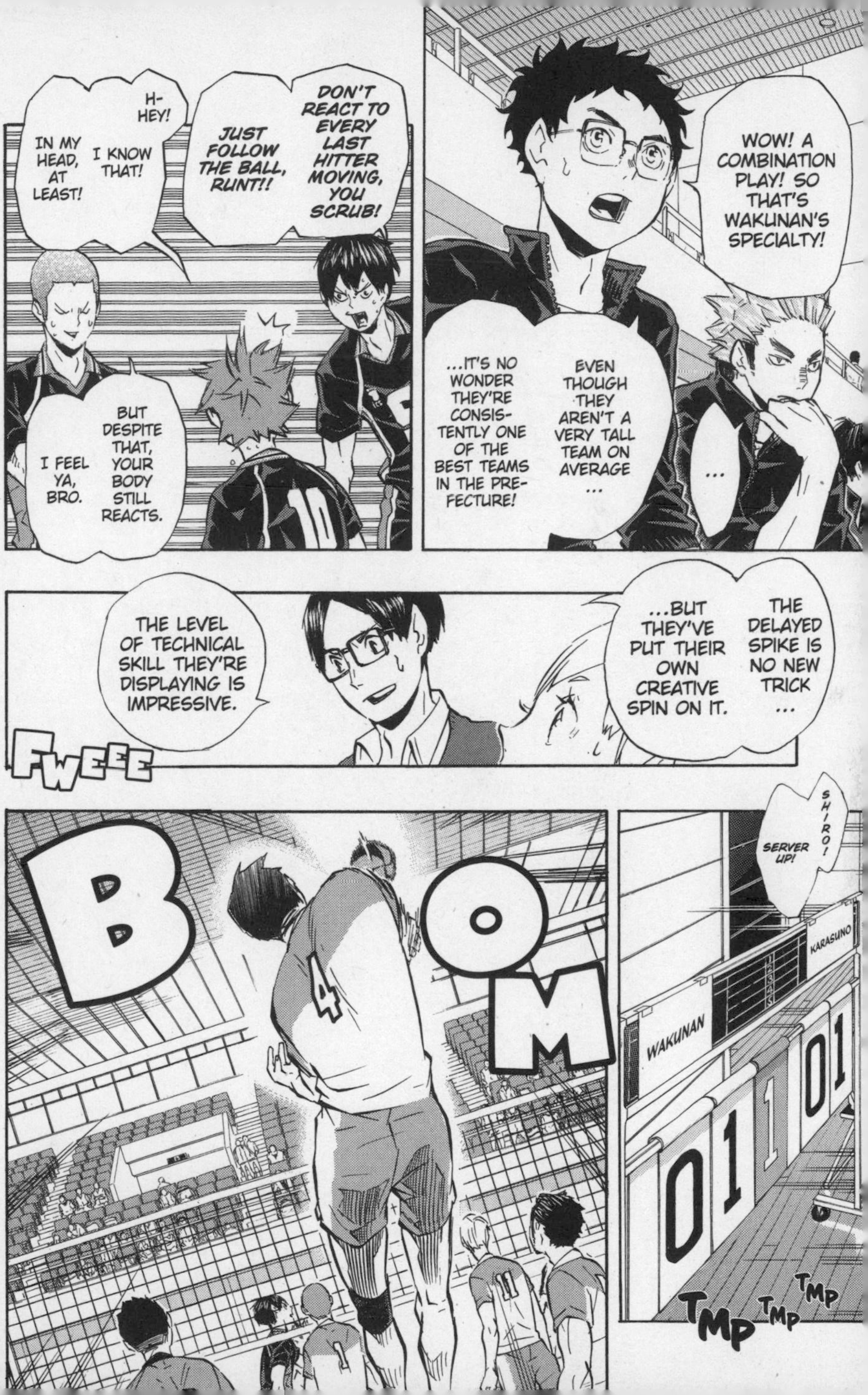
WOW! A COMBINATION PLAY! SO THAT'S WAKUNAN'S SPECIALTY!
...
EVEN THOUGH THEY AREN'T A VERY TALL TEAM ON AVERAGE...
...IT'S NO WONDER THEY'RE CONSIS-TENTLY ONE OF THE BEST TEAMS IN THE PRE-FECTURE!
DON'T REACT TO EVERY LAST HITTER MOVING, YOU SCRUB!
JUST FOLLOW THE BALL, RUNT!!
H-HEY!
I KNOW THAT!
IN MY HEAD, AT LEAST!
BUT DESPITE THAT, YOUR BODY STILL REACTS.
I FEEL YA, BRO.
THE DELAYED SPIKE IS NO NEW TRICK...
...BUT THEY'VE PUT THEIR OWN CREATIVE SPIN ON IT.
THE LEVEL OF TECHNICAL SKILL THEY'RE DISPLAYING IS IMPRESSIVE.
FWEEE
SHIRO!
SERVER UP!
KARASUNO
WAKUNAN
TMP TMP TMP
BOOM

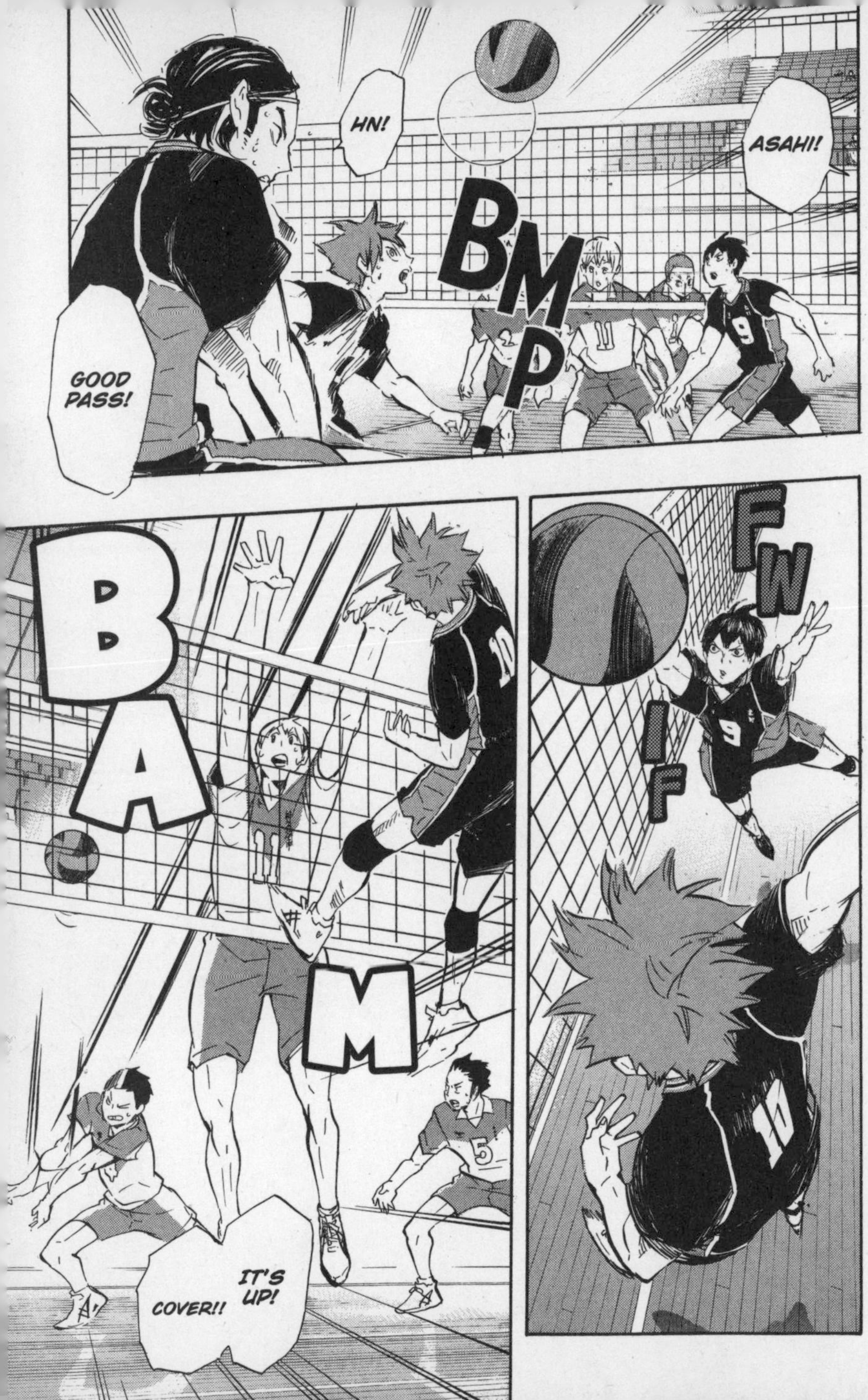
ASAHI!
HN!
BMP
GOOD PASS!
FWIF
BAM
IT'S UP!
COVER!!

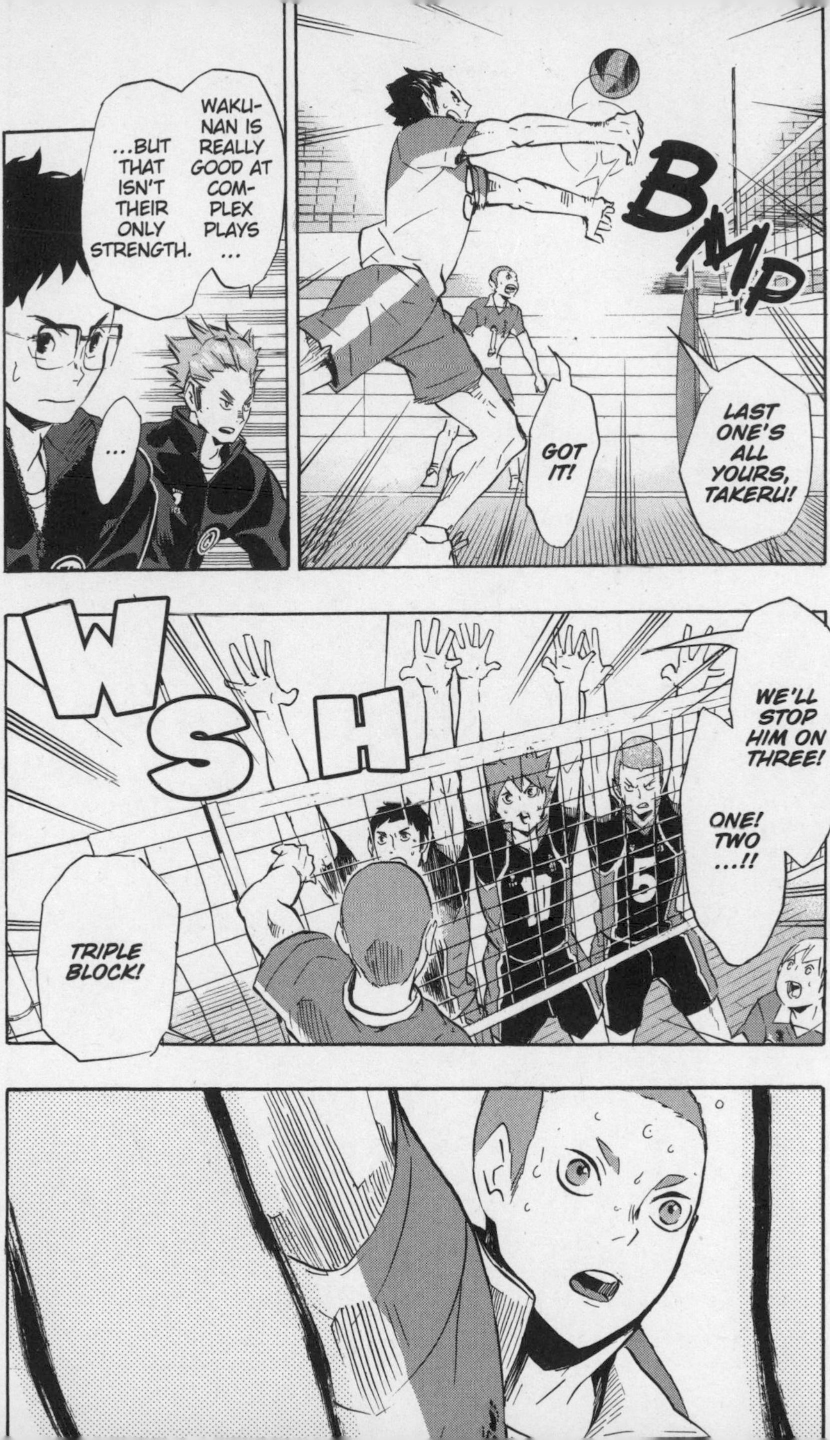
BMP
LAST ONE'S ALL YOURS, TAKERU!
GOT IT!
WAKUNAN IS REALLY GOOD AT COMPLEX PLAYS...
...BUT THAT ISN'T THEIR ONLY STRENGTH.
...
WSH
WE'LL STOP HIM ON THREE!
ONE! TWO...!!
TRIPLE BLOCK!

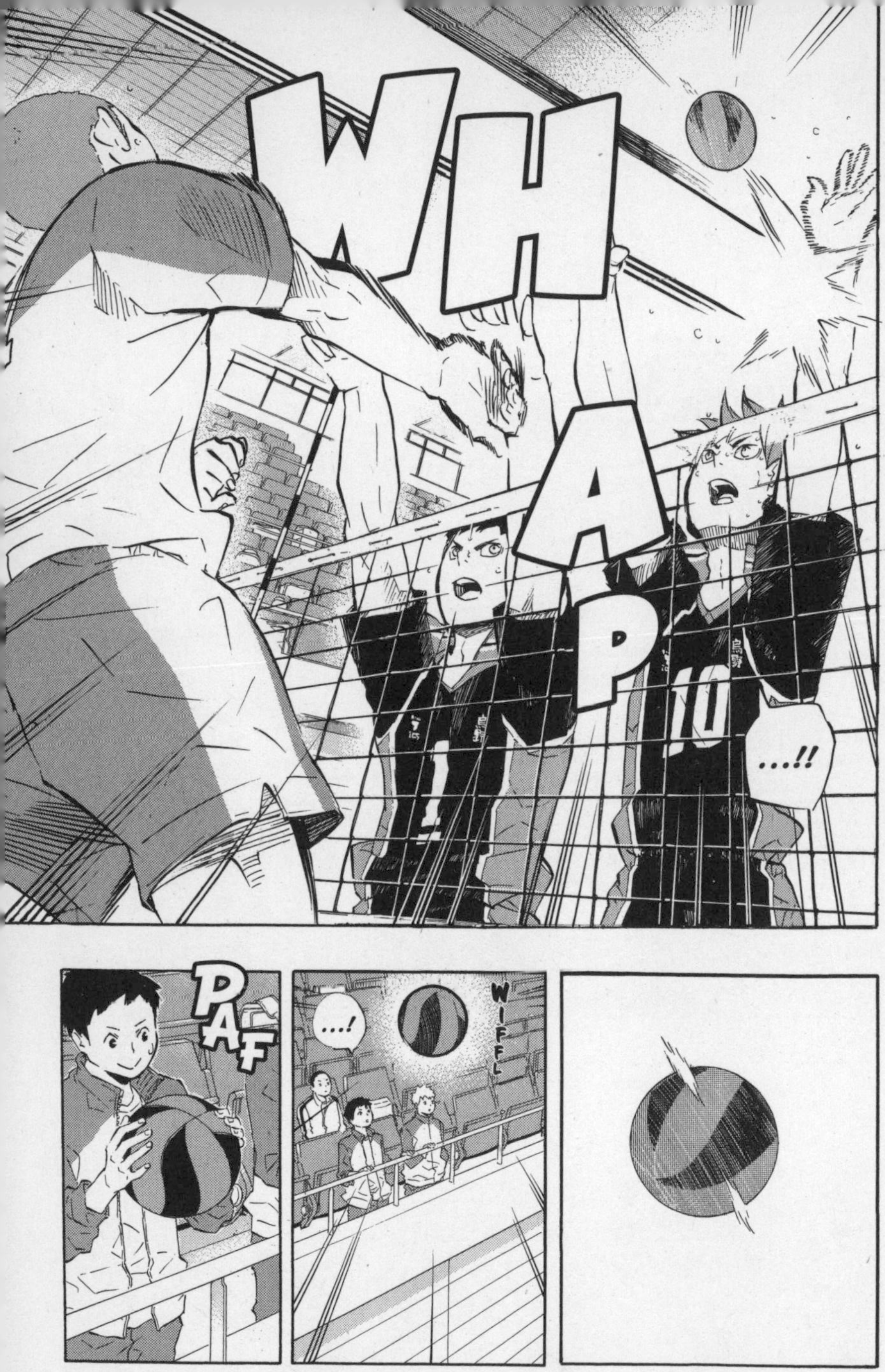
WHAP
...!!
WIFFL
...!
PAF

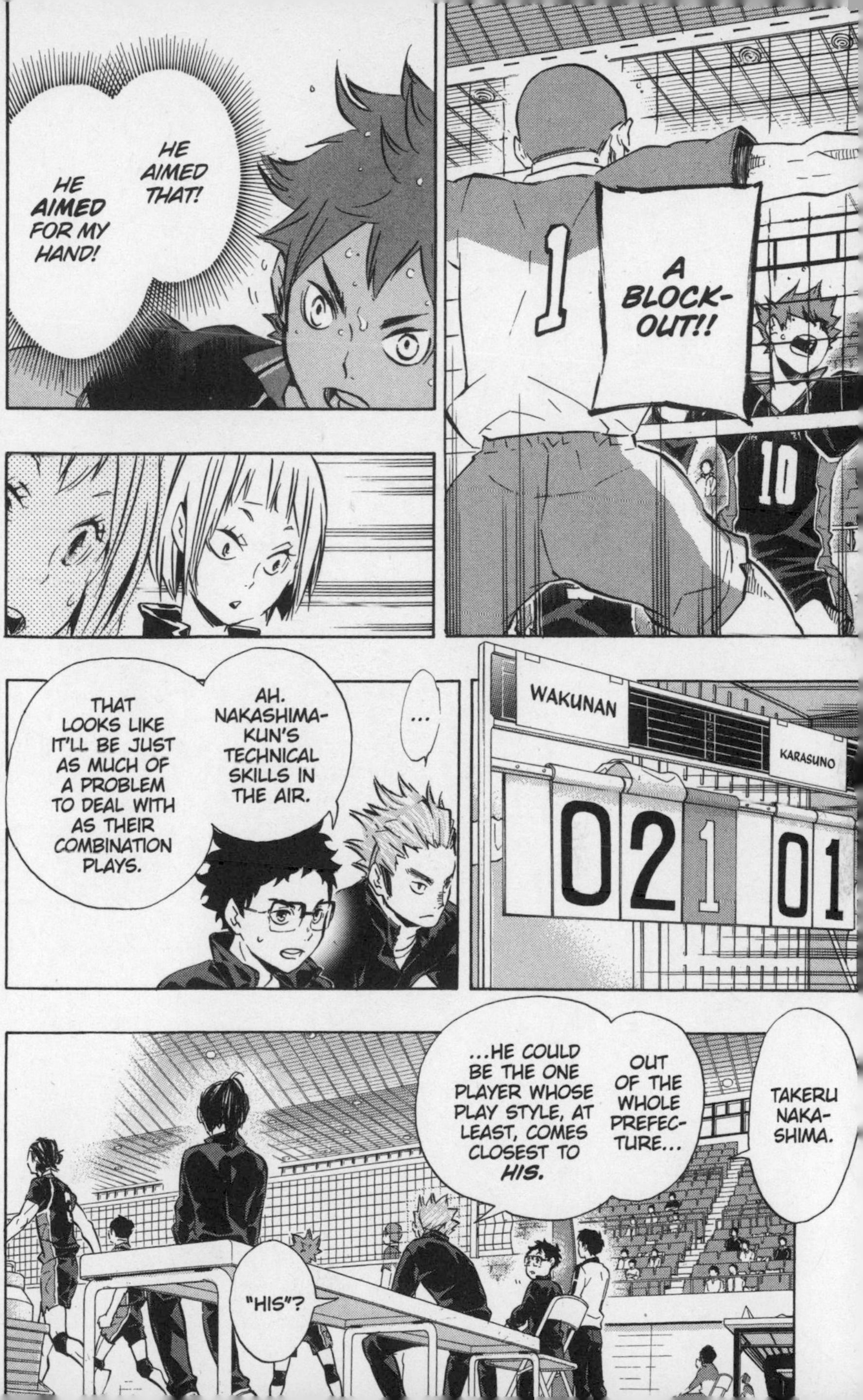
A BLOCK-OUT!!
HE AIMED THAT!
HE AIMED FOR MY HAND!
WAKUNAN
KARASUNO
02 1 01
...
AH. NAKASHIMA-KUN'S TECHNICAL SKILLS IN THE AIR.
THAT LOOKS LIKE IT'LL BE JUST AS MUCH OF A PROBLEM TO DEAL WITH AS THEIR COMBINATION PLAYS.
TAKERU NAKA-SHIMA.
OUT OF THE WHOLE PREFEC-TURE...
...HE COULD BE THE ONE PLAYER WHOSE PLAY STYLE, AT LEAST, COMES CLOSEST TO HIS.
"HIS"?

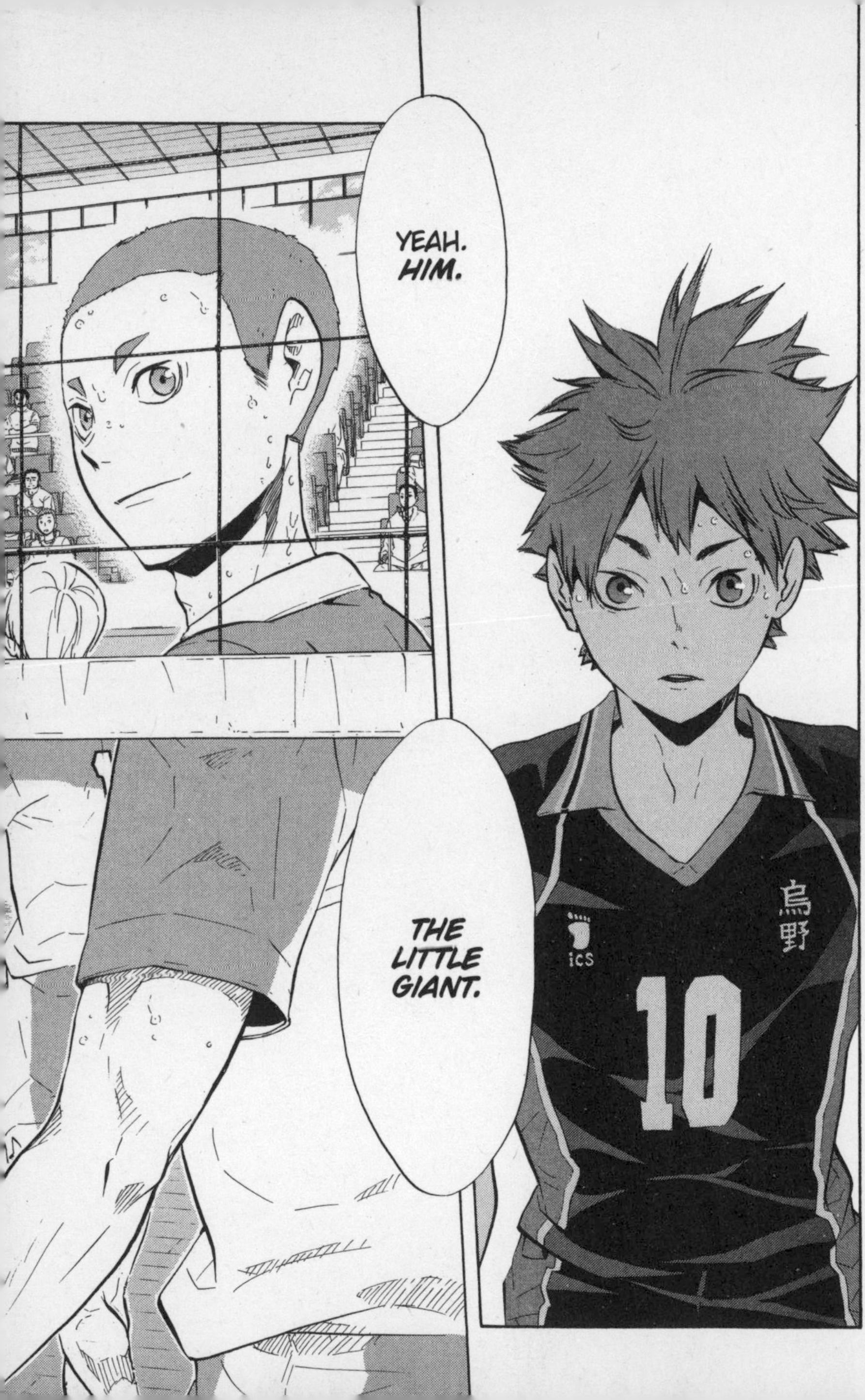
YEAH. HIM.
THE LITTLE GIANT.

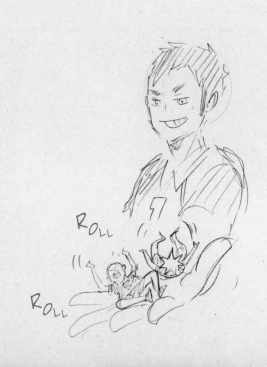

ROLL

ROLL

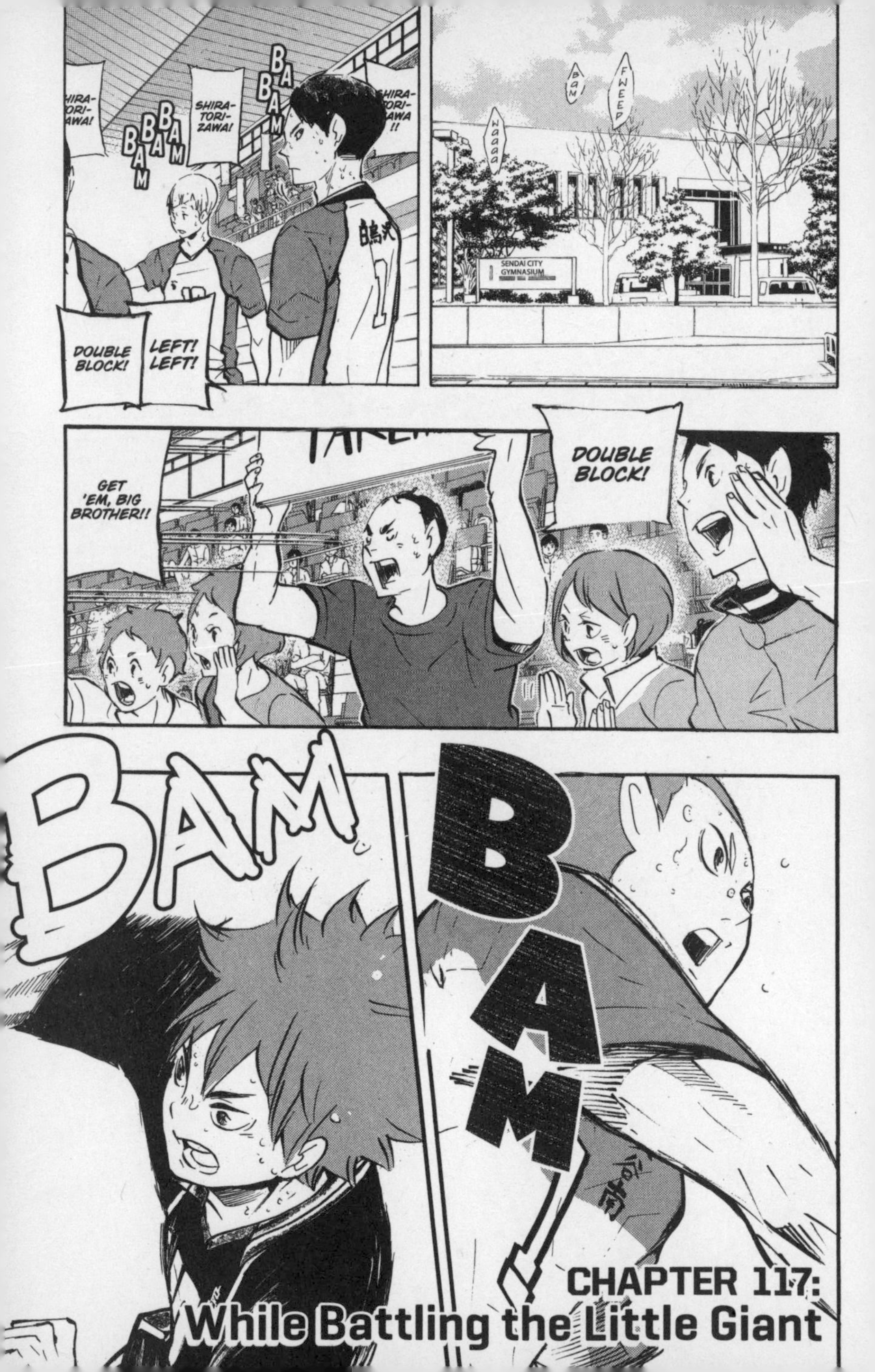
FWEEP
BAM
Waaaa
SENDAI CITY GYMNASIUM
SHIRA-TORI-ZAWA!!
BA BAM
SHIRA-TORI-ZAWA!
BAM BAM BAM
SHIRA-TORI-ZAWA!
LEFT! LEFT!
DOUBLE BLOCK!
DOUBLE BLOCK!
GET 'EM, BIG BROTHER!!
BAM
BAM
CHAPTER 117:
While Battling the Little Giant

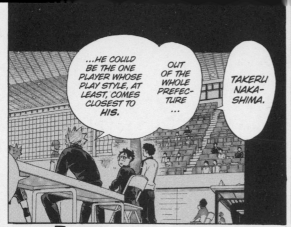

...HE COULD BE THE ONE PLAYER WHOSE PLAY STYLE, AT LEAST, COMES CLOSEST TO HIS.

OUT OF THE WHOLE PREFEC-TURE...

TAKERU NAKA-SHIMA.

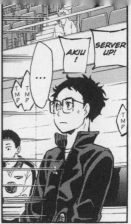

AKIU!

...

SERVER UP!

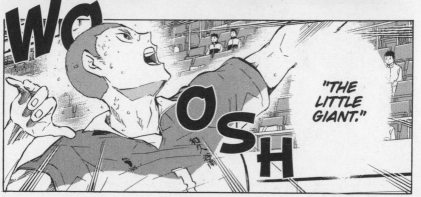

WOOSH

"THE LITTLE GIANT."

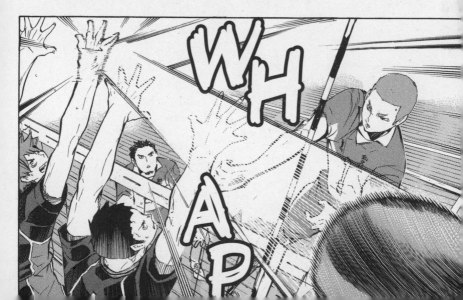

WH

AP

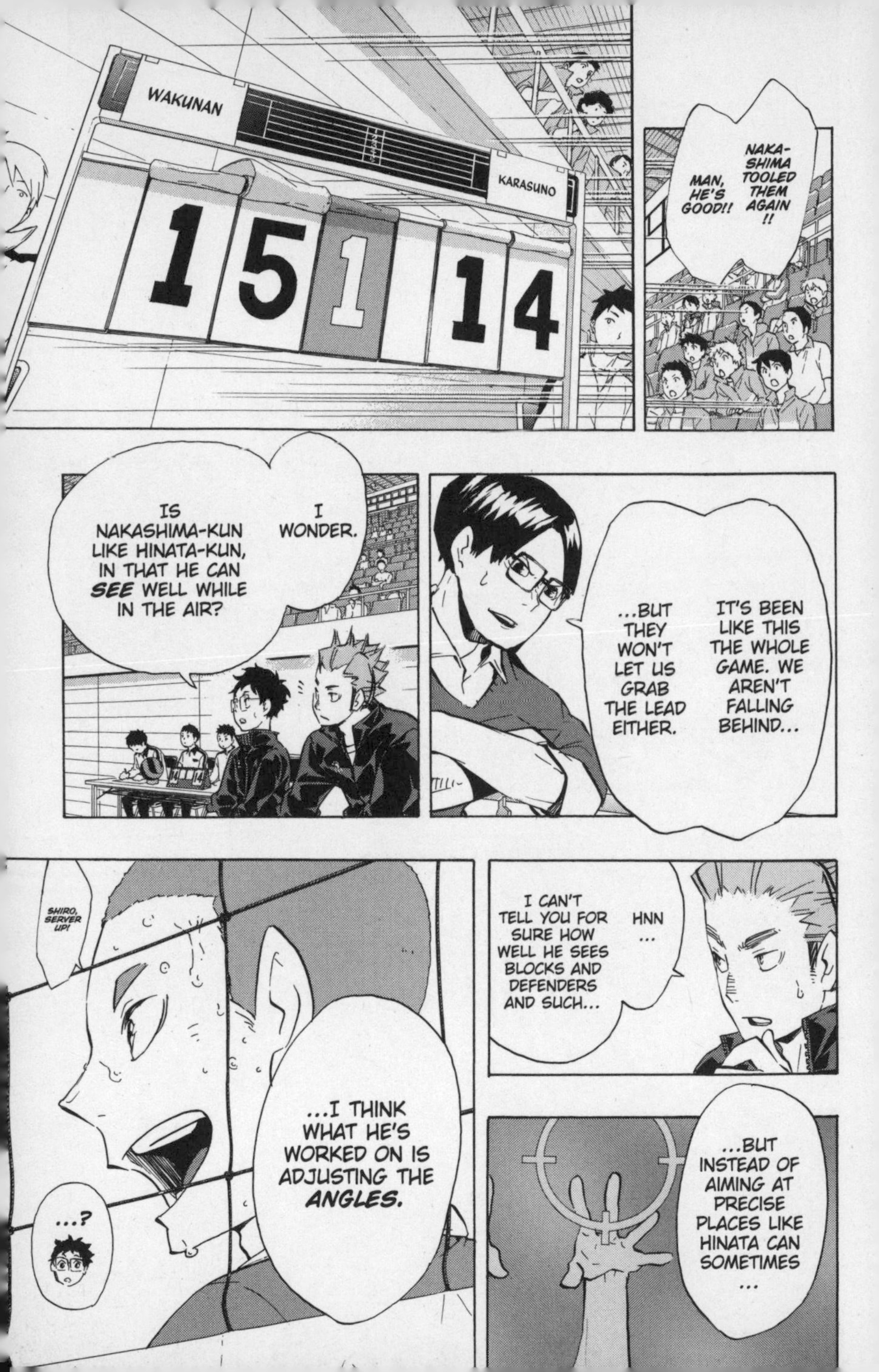
NAKA-SHIMA TOOLED THEM AGAIN!!
MAN, HE'S GOOD!!
WAKUNAN
KARASUNO
15 1 14
IT'S BEEN LIKE THIS THE WHOLE GAME. WE AREN'T FALLING BEHIND...
...BUT THEY WON'T LET US GRAB THE LEAD EITHER.
I WONDER.
IS NAKASHIMA-KUN LIKE HINATA-KUN, IN THAT HE CAN *SEE* WELL WHILE IN THE AIR?
HNN...
I CAN'T TELL YOU FOR SURE HOW WELL HE SEES BLOCKS AND DEFENDERS AND SUCH...
...BUT INSTEAD OF AIMING AT PRECISE PLACES LIKE HINATA CAN SOMETIMES...
SHIRO, SERVER UP!
...I THINK WHAT HE'S WORKED ON IS ADJUSTING THE *ANGLES.*
...?

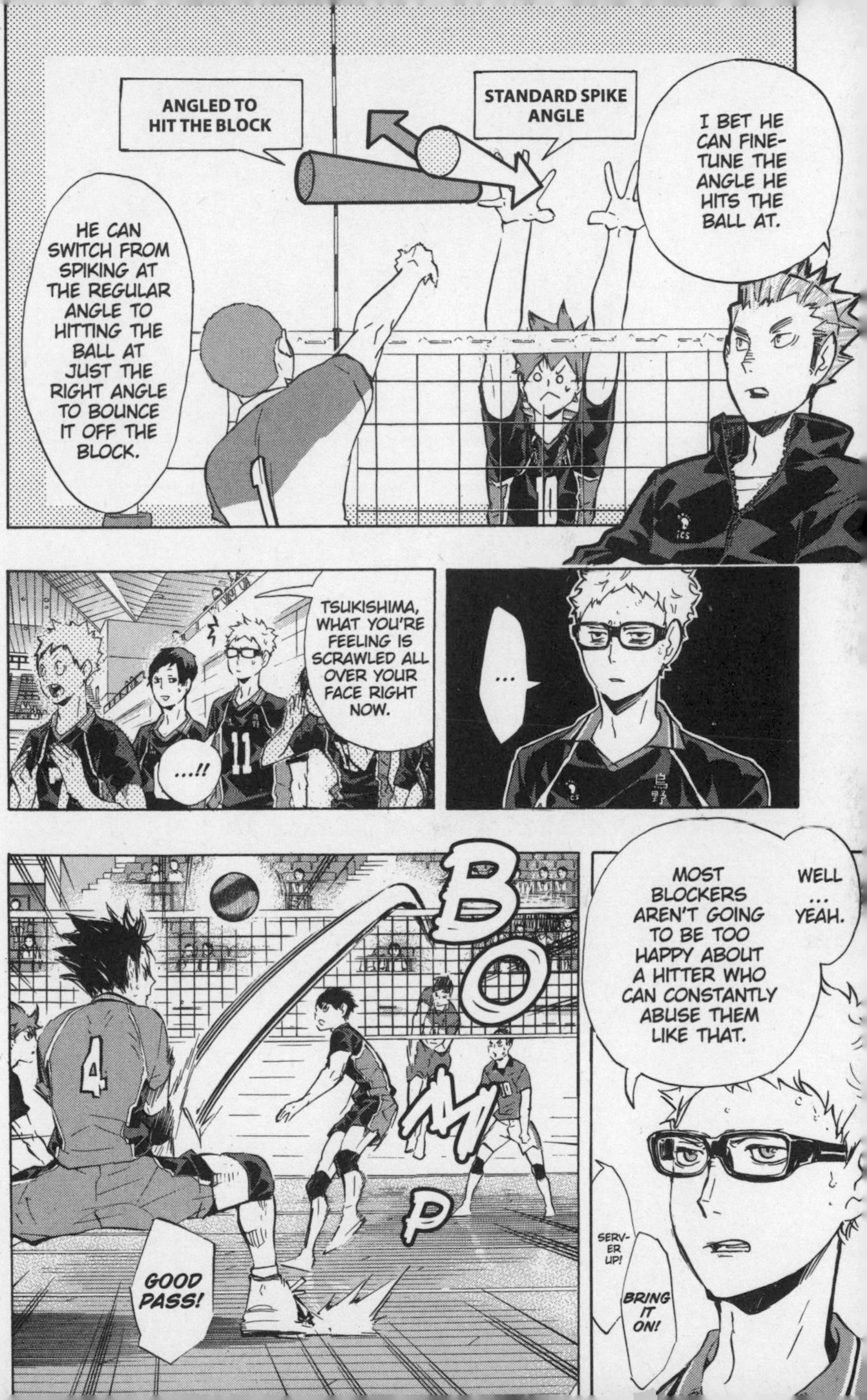
I BET HE CAN FINE-TUNE THE ANGLE HE HITS THE BALL AT.
STANDARD SPIKE ANGLE
ANGLED TO HIT THE BLOCK
HE CAN SWITCH FROM SPIKING AT THE REGULAR ANGLE TO HITTING THE BALL AT JUST THE RIGHT ANGLE TO BOUNCE IT OFF THE BLOCK.
...
TSUKISHIMA, WHAT YOU'RE FEELING IS SCRAWLED ALL OVER YOUR FACE RIGHT NOW.
...!!
WELL ... YEAH.
MOST BLOCKERS AREN'T GOING TO BE TOO HAPPY ABOUT A HITTER WHO CAN CONSTANTLY ABUSE THEM LIKE THAT.
SERV-ER UP!
BRING IT ON!
BOOMP
GOOD PASS!

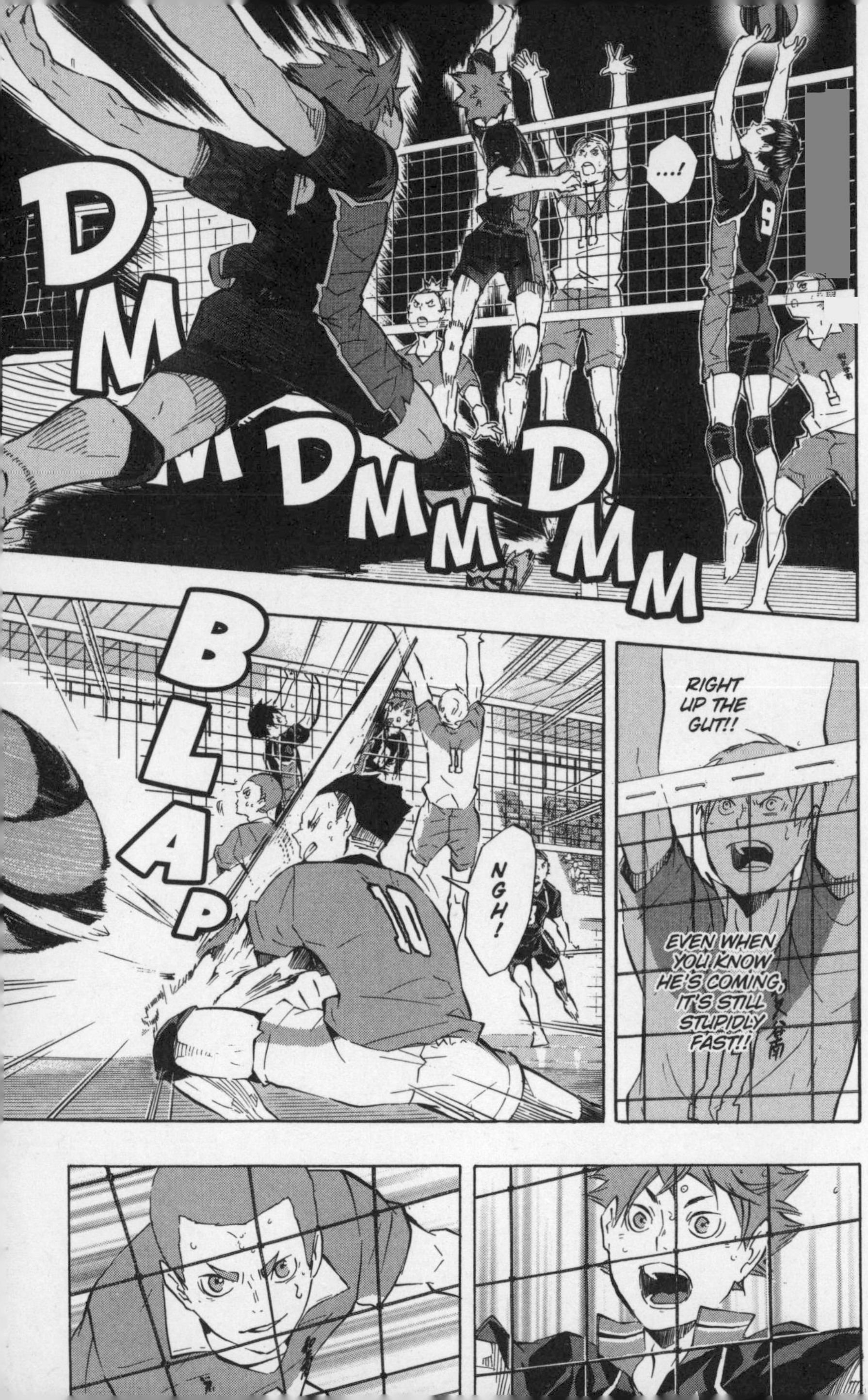
...!
DMM DMM DMM
RIGHT UP THE GUT!!
EVEN WHEN YOU KNOW HE'S COMING, IT'S STILL STUPIDLY FAST!!
BLAP
NGH!

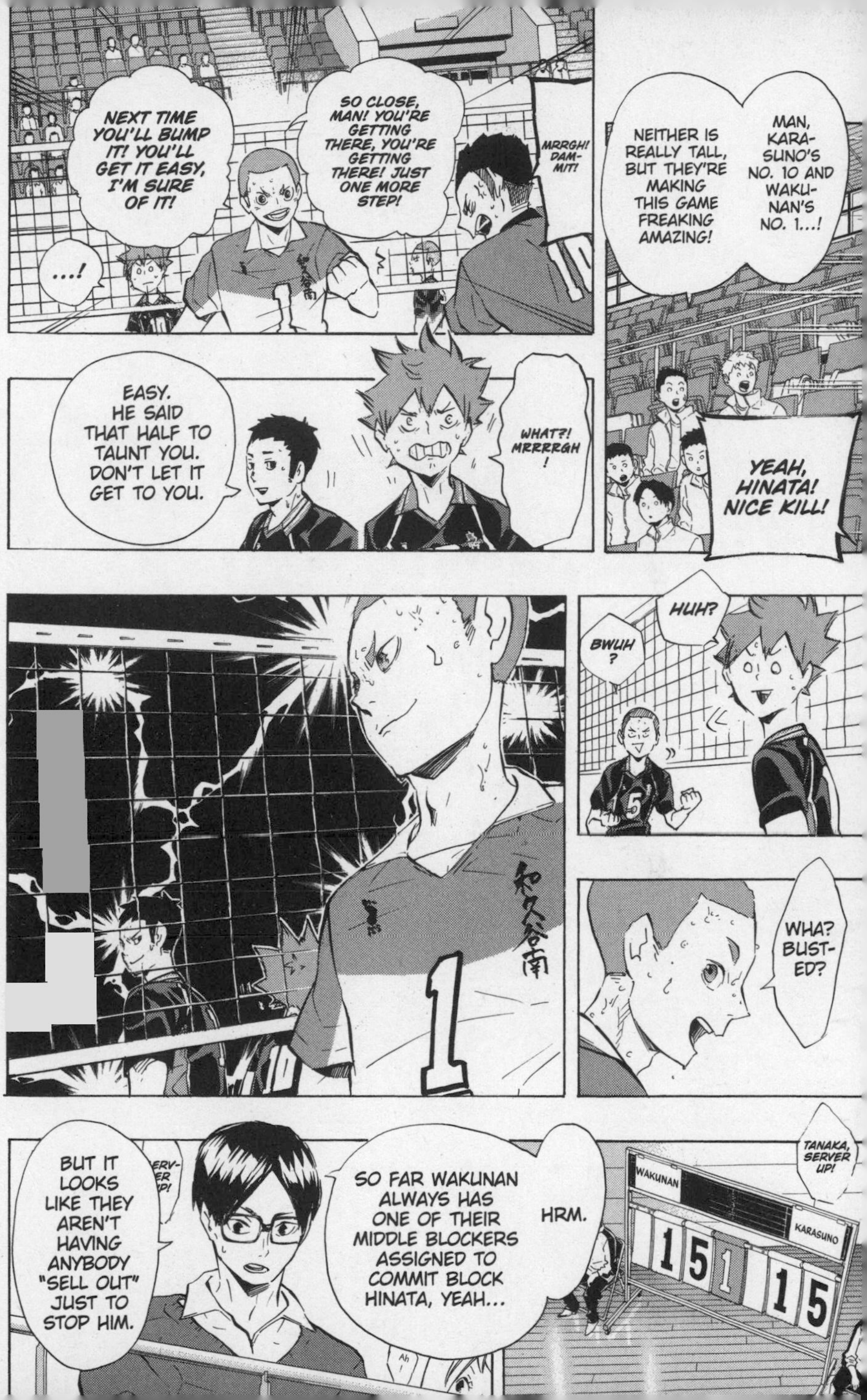
MAN, KARASUNO'S NO. 10 AND WAKUNAN'S NO. 1...!
NEITHER IS REALLY TALL, BUT THEY'RE MAKING THIS GAME FREAKING AMAZING!
YEAH, HINATA! NICE KILL!
MRRGH! DAMMIT!
SO CLOSE, MAN! YOU'RE GETTING THERE, YOU'RE GETTING THERE! JUST ONE MORE STEP!
NEXT TIME YOU'LL BUMP IT! YOU'LL GET IT EASY, I'M SURE OF IT!
...!
WHAT?! MRRRRGH!
EASY. HE SAID THAT HALF TO TAUNT YOU. DON'T LET IT GET TO YOU.
HUH?
BWUH?
WHA? BUSTED?
TANAKA, SERVER UP!
WAKUNAN
KARASUNO
15
15
HRM.
SO FAR WAKUNAN ALWAYS HAS ONE OF THEIR MIDDLE BLOCKERS ASSIGNED TO COMMIT BLOCK HINATA, YEAH...
BUT IT LOOKS LIKE THEY AREN'T HAVING ANYBODY "SELL OUT" JUST TO STOP HIM.
Ah

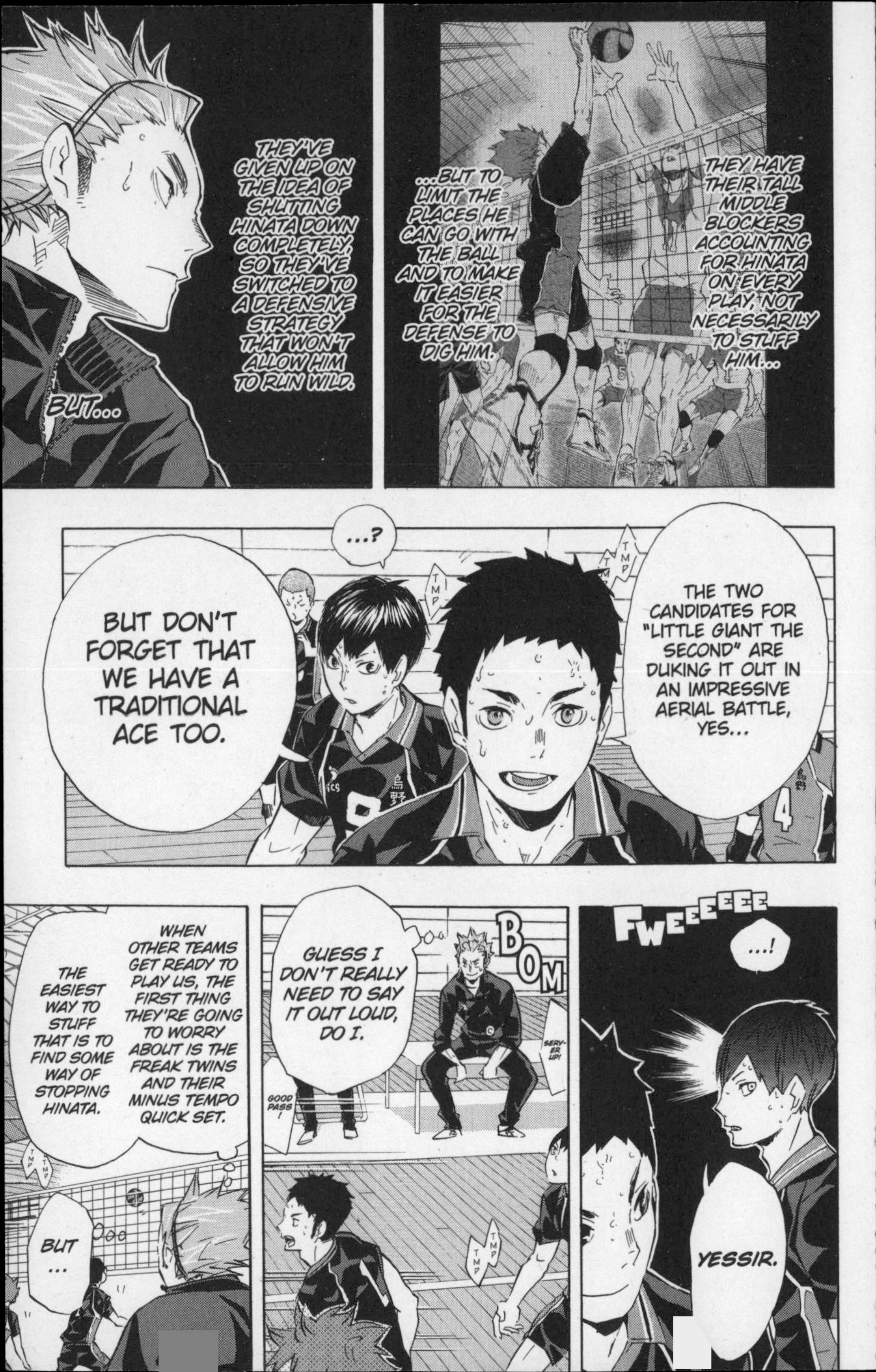
THEY HAVE THEIR TALL MIDDLE BLOCKERS ACCOUNTING FOR HINATA ON EVERY PLAY, NOT NECESSARILY TO STUFF HIM...
...BUT TO LIMIT THE PLACES HE CAN GO WITH THE BALL AND TO MAKE IT EASIER FOR THE DEFENSE TO DIG HIM.
THEY'VE GIVEN UP ON THE IDEA OF SHUTTING HINATA DOWN COMPLETELY, SO THEY'VE SWITCHED TO A DEFENSIVE STRATEGY THAT WON'T ALLOW HIM TO RUN WILD.
BUT...
THE TWO CANDIDATES FOR "LITTLE GIANT THE SECOND" ARE DUKING IT OUT IN AN IMPRESSIVE AERIAL BATTLE, YES...
TMP TMP
TMP
...?
BUT DON'T FORGET THAT WE HAVE A TRADITIONAL ACE TOO.
FWEEEEEE
...!
YESSIR.
BOM
GUESS I DON'T REALLY NEED TO SAY IT OUT LOUD, DO I.
SERV-ER UP!
GOOD PASS!
TMP TMP
WHEN OTHER TEAMS GET READY TO PLAY US, THE FIRST THING THEY'RE GOING TO WORRY ABOUT IS THE FREAK TWINS AND THEIR MINUS TEMPO QUICK SET.
THE EASIEST WAY TO STUFF THAT IS TO FIND SOME WAY OF STOPPING HINATA.
TMP TMP
BUT ...

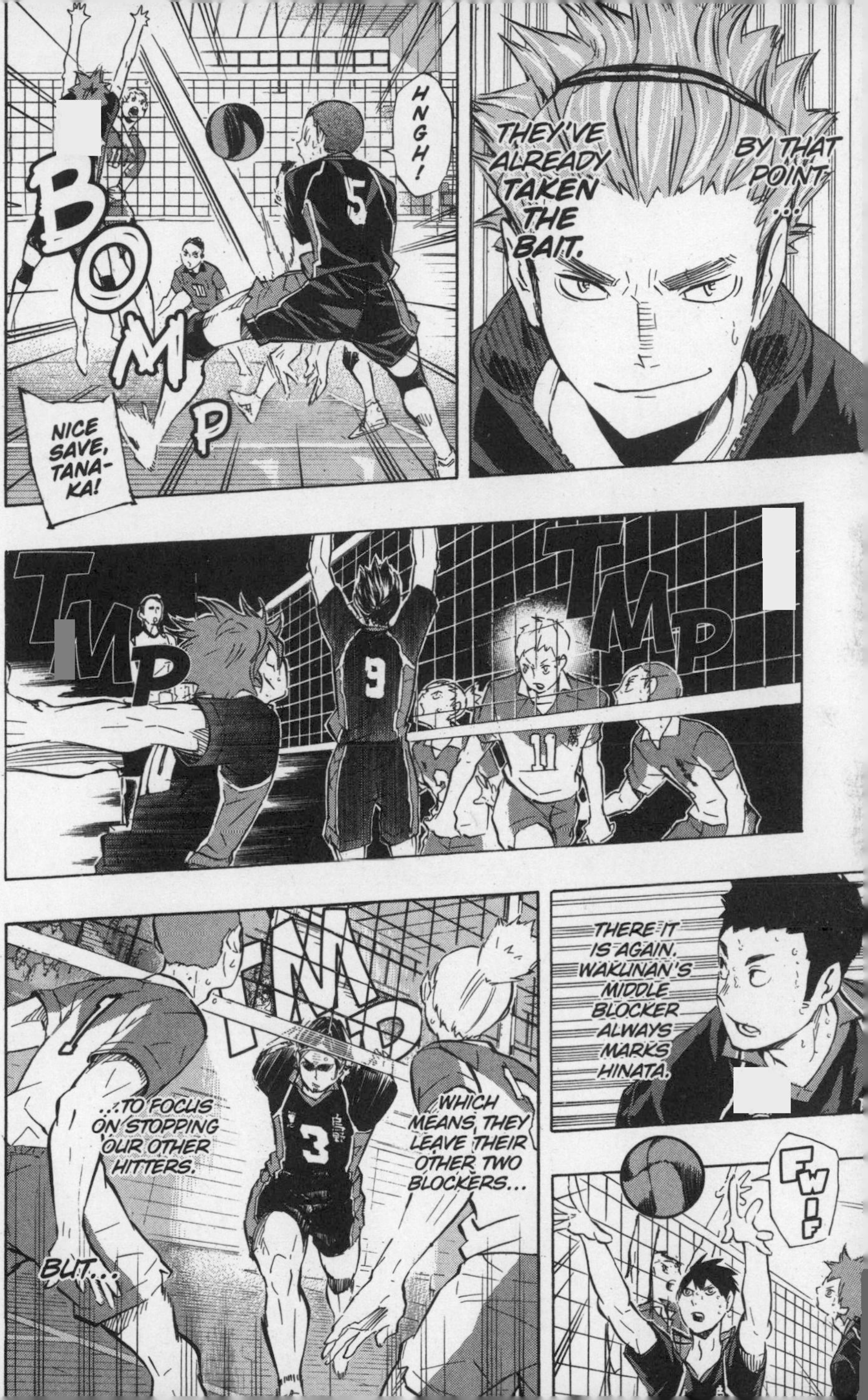
BY THAT POINT...
THEY'VE ALREADY TAKEN THE BAIT.
HNGH!
BOMP
NICE SAVE, TANAKA!
TMP
TMP
THERE IT IS AGAIN. WAKUNAN'S MIDDLE BLOCKER ALWAYS MARKS HINATA.
FWIF
WHICH MEANS, THEY LEAVE THEIR OTHER TWO BLOCKERS...
...TO FOCUS ON STOPPING OUR OTHER HITTERS.
BUT...

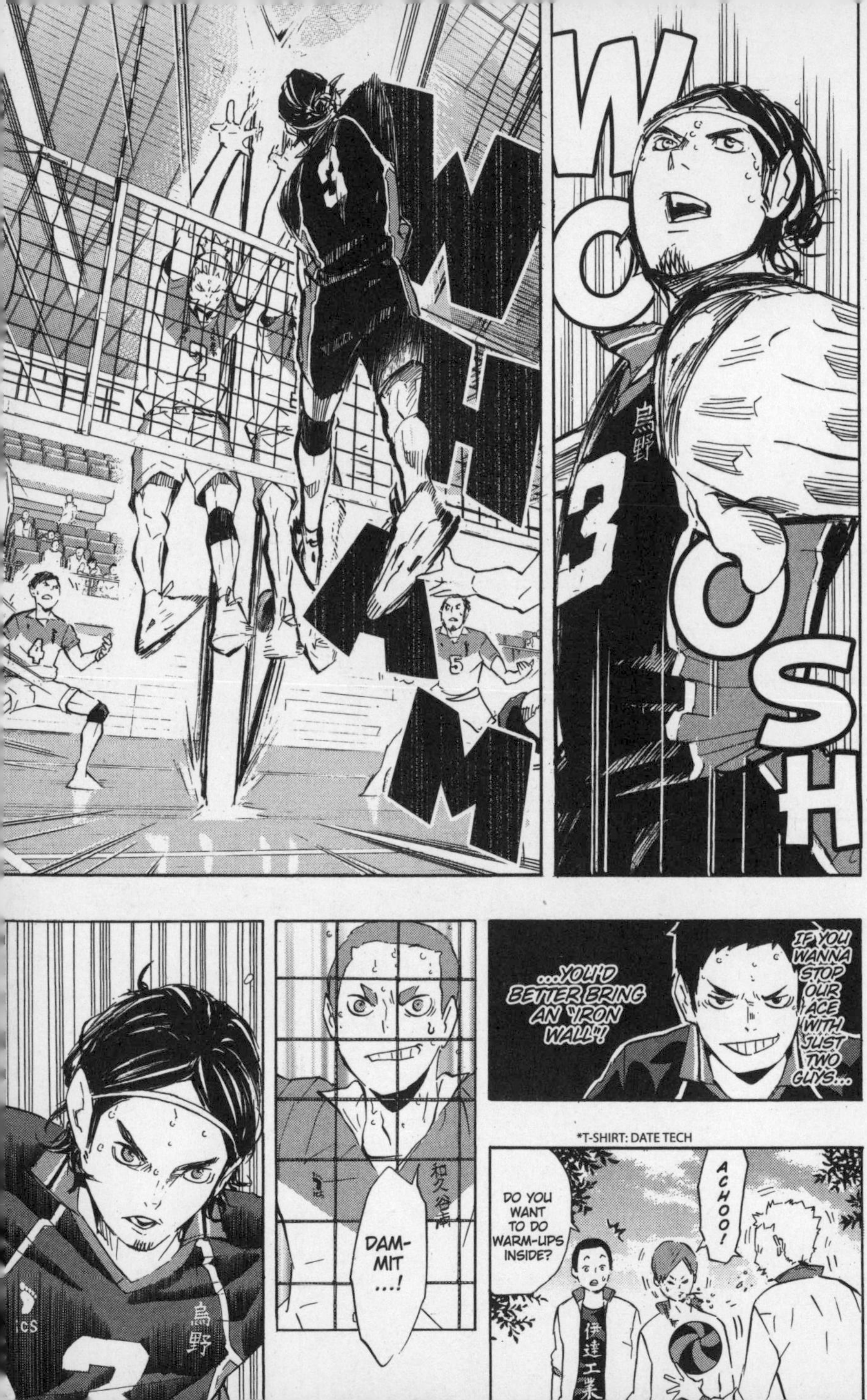
WOOSH
WHAM
IF YOU WANNA STOP OUR ACE WITH JUST TWO GUYS...
...YOU'D BETTER BRING AN "IRON WALL"!
ACHOO!
DO YOU WANT TO DO WARM-UPS INSIDE?
*T-SHIRT: DATE TECH
DAM-MIT ...!

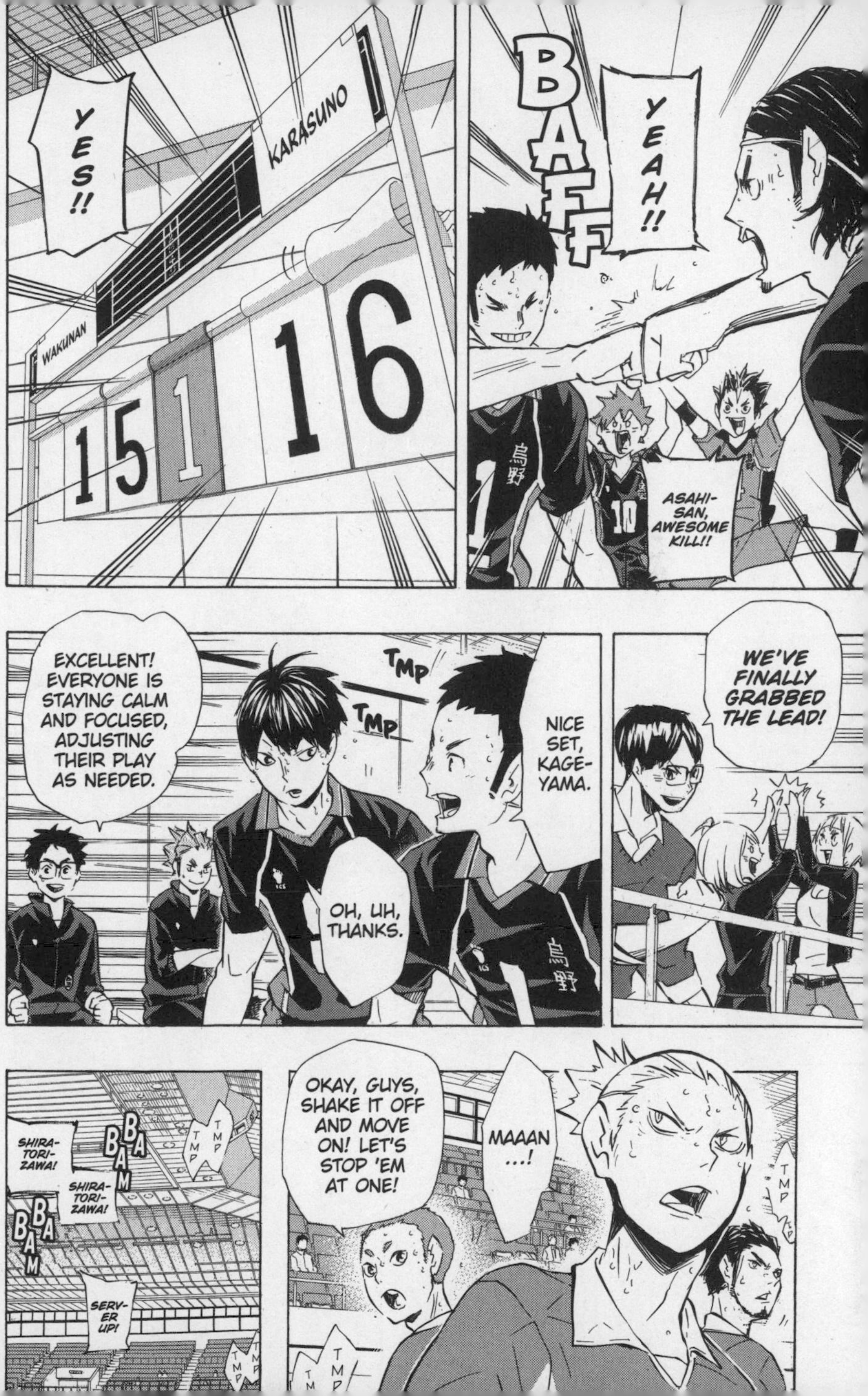
BAFF
YEAH!!
ASAHI-SAN, AWESOME KILL!!
YES!!
KARASUNO
WAKUNAN
15 1 16
WE'VE FINALLY GRABBED THE LEAD!
TMP
NICE SET, KAGE-YAMA.
TMP
EXCELLENT! EVERYONE IS STAYING CALM AND FOCUSED, ADJUSTING THEIR PLAY AS NEEDED.
OH, UH, THANKS.
TMP
MAAAN ...!
OKAY, GUYS, SHAKE IT OFF AND MOVE ON! LET'S STOP 'EM AT ONE!
TMP
TMP TMP
BABAM
SHIRA-TORI-ZAWA!
SHIRA-TORI-ZAWA!
BABAM
SERV-ER UP!
TMP TMP

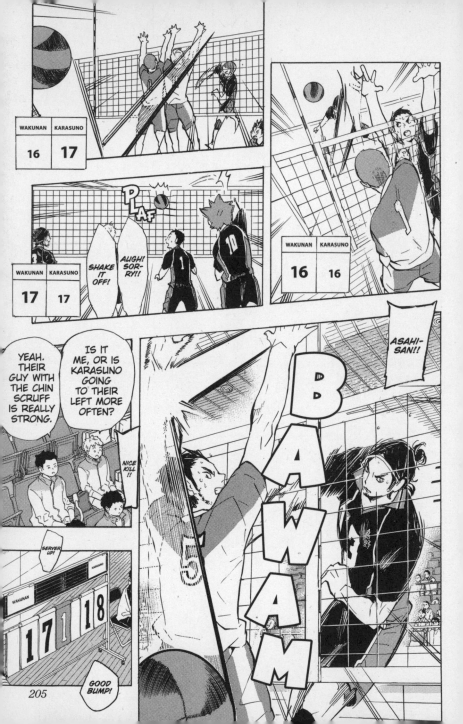

WAKUNAN	KARASUNO
16	17

WAKUNAN	KARASUNO
17	17

PLAF

SHAKE IT OFF!

AUGH! SORRY!!

WAKUNAN	KARASUNO
16	16

YEAH. THEIR GUY WITH THE CHIN SCRUFF IS REALLY STRONG.

IS IT ME, OR IS KARASUNO GOING TO THEIR LEFT MORE OFTEN?

ASAHI-SAN!!

NICE KILL!!

BAWAM

SERVER UP!

WAKUNAN 17 1 18 KARASUNO

GOOD BUMP!

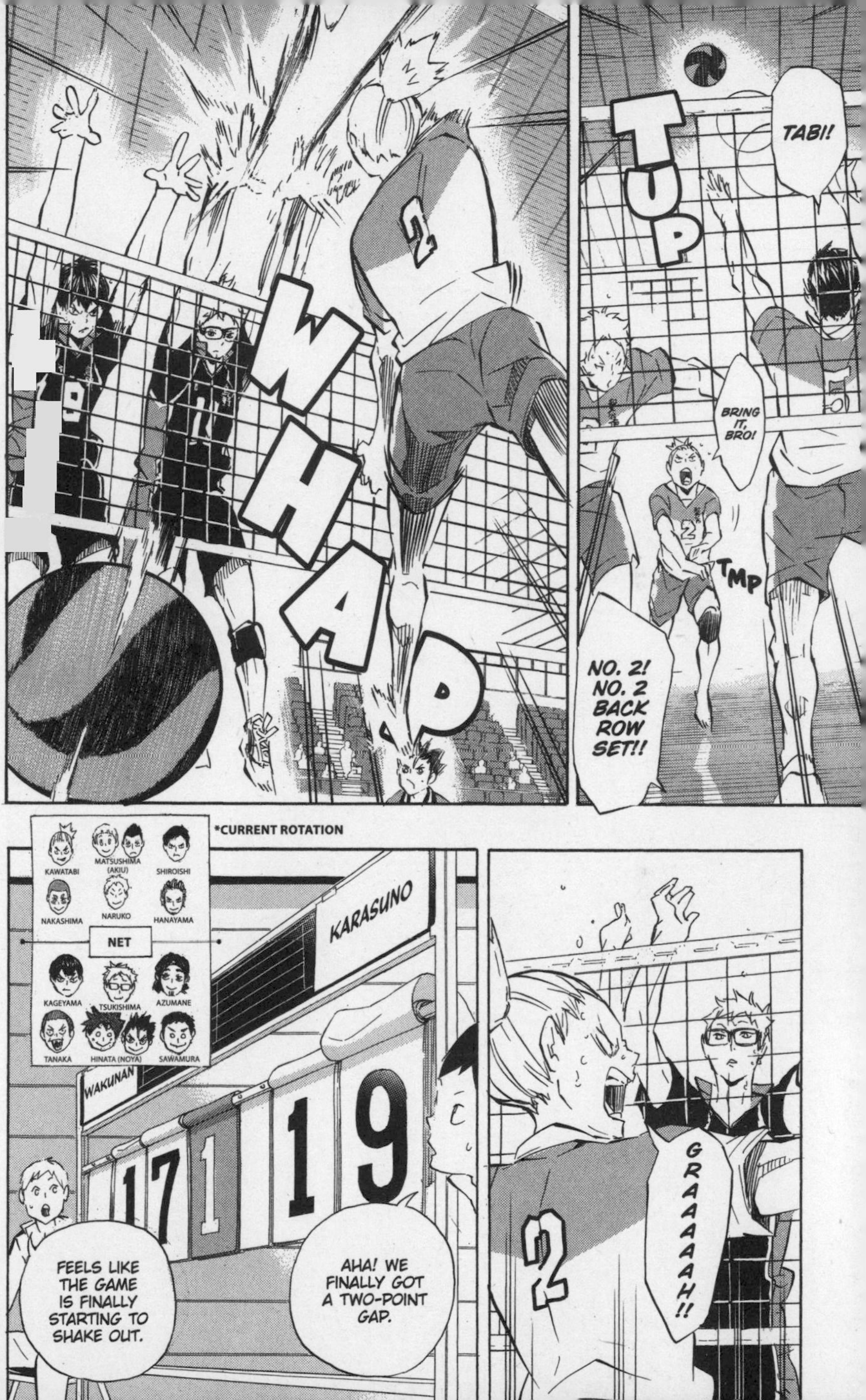
TABI!
TUP
BRING IT, BRO!
TMP
NO. 2! NO. 2 BACK ROW SET!!
WHAP
GRAAAAAH!!
*CURRENT ROTATION
KAWATABI
MATSUSHIMA (AKIU)
SHIROISHI
NAKASHIMA
NARUKO
HANAYAMA
NET
KAGEYAMA
TSUKISHIMA
AZUMANE
TANAKA
HINATA (NOYA)
SAWAMURA
KARASUNO
WAKUNAN
17
19
AHA! WE FINALLY GOT A TWO-POINT GAP.
FEELS LIKE THE GAME IS FINALLY STARTING TO SHAKE OUT.

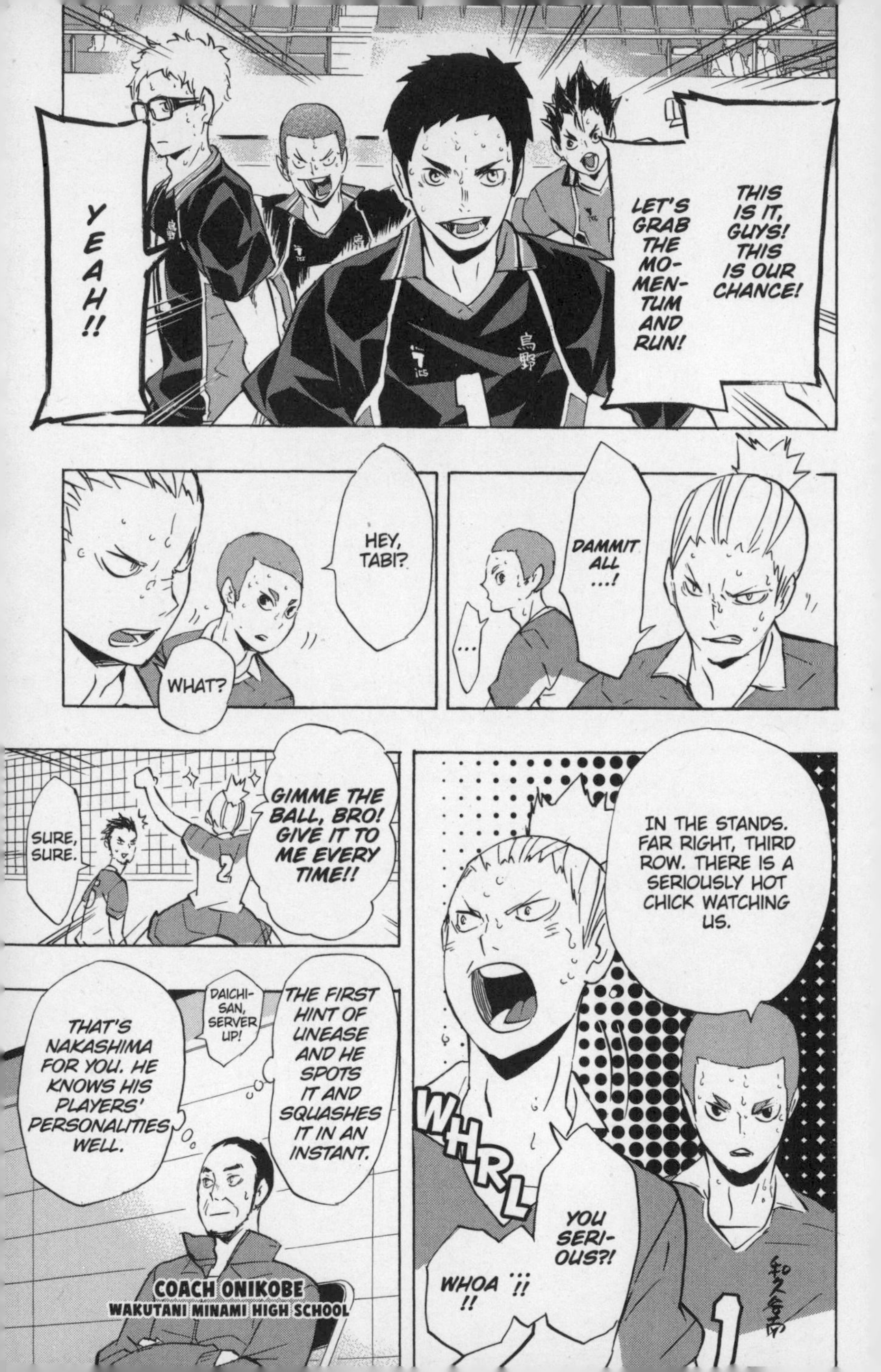
THIS IS IT, GUYS! THIS IS OUR CHANCE!
LET'S GRAB THE MOMENTUM AND RUN!
YEAH!!
DAMMIT ALL ...!
...
HEY, TABI?
WHAT?
IN THE STANDS. FAR RIGHT, THIRD ROW. THERE IS A SERIOUSLY HOT CHICK WATCHING US.
WHRL
YOU SERIOUS?!
...!!
WHOA !!
GIMME THE BALL, BRO! GIVE IT TO ME EVERY TIME!!
SURE, SURE.
THE FIRST HINT OF UNEASE AND HE SPOTS IT AND SQUASHES IT IN AN INSTANT.
DAICHI-SAN, SERVER UP!
THAT'S NAKASHIMA FOR YOU. HE KNOWS HIS PLAYERS' PERSONALITIES WELL.
COACH ONIKOBE
WAKUTANI MINAMI HIGH SCHOOL

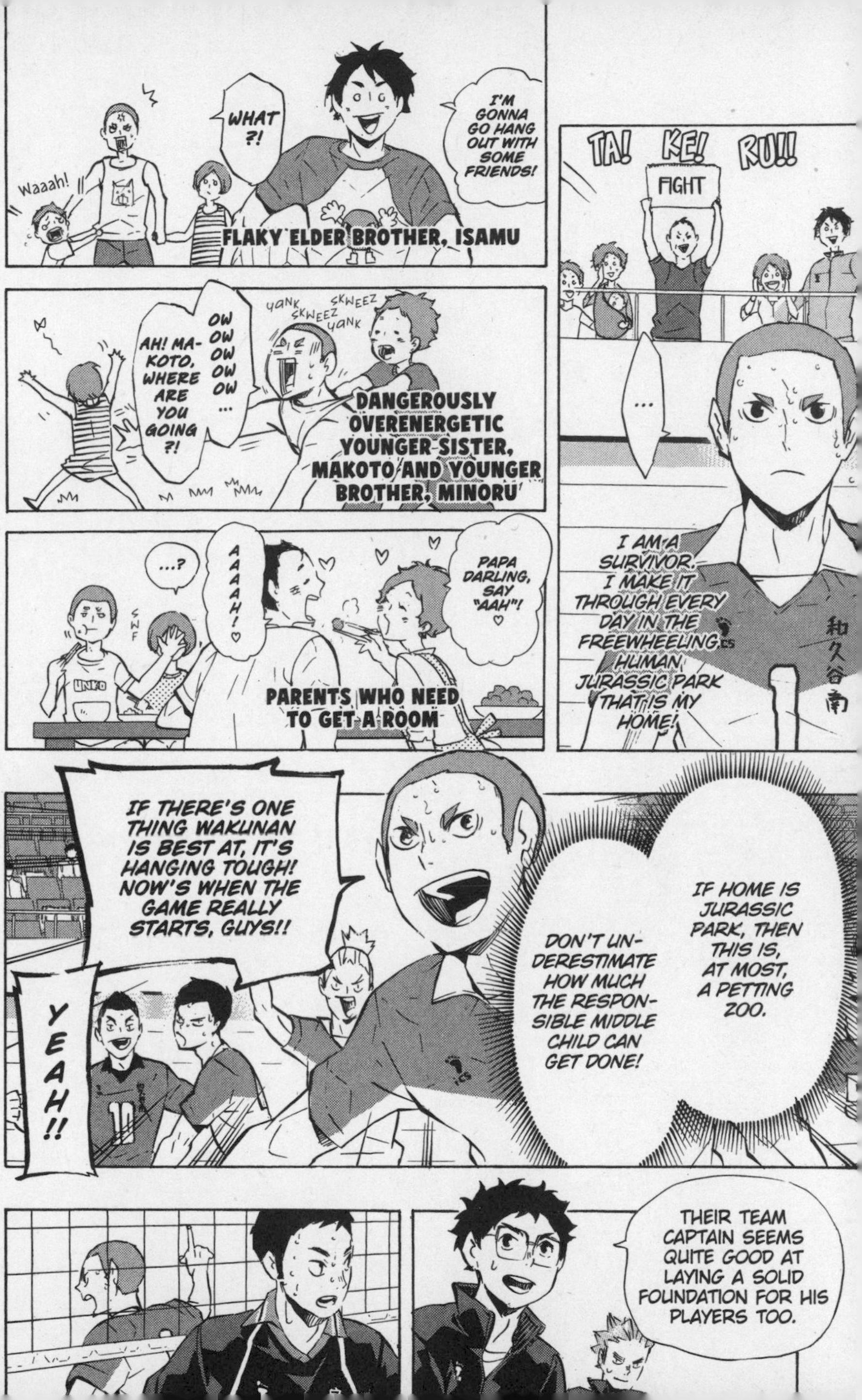
TA! KE! RU!!
FIGHT
...
I AM A SURVIVOR. I MAKE IT THROUGH EVERY DAY IN THE FREEWHEELING HUMAN JURASSIC PARK THAT IS MY HOME!
和久谷南
I'M GONNA GO HANG OUT WITH SOME FRIENDS!
WHAT ?!
Waaah!
FLAKY ELDER BROTHER, ISAMU
YANK SKWEEZ SKWEEZ YANK
OW OW OW OW OW ...
AH! MAKOTO, WHERE ARE YOU GOING ?!
DANGEROUSLY OVERENERGETIC YOUNGER SISTER, MAKOTO AND YOUNGER BROTHER, MINORU
PAPA DARLING, SAY "AAH"!
AAAAH!
...?
SNF
UNKO
PARENTS WHO NEED TO GET A ROOM
IF HOME IS JURASSIC PARK, THEN THIS IS, AT MOST, A PETTING ZOO.
DON'T UNDERESTIMATE HOW MUCH THE RESPONSIBLE MIDDLE CHILD CAN GET DONE!
IF THERE'S ONE THING WAKUNAN IS BEST AT, IT'S HANGING TOUGH! NOW'S WHEN THE GAME REALLY STARTS, GUYS!!
YEAH!!
THEIR TEAM CAPTAIN SEEMS QUITE GOOD AT LAYING A SOLID FOUNDATION FOR HIS PLAYERS TOO.

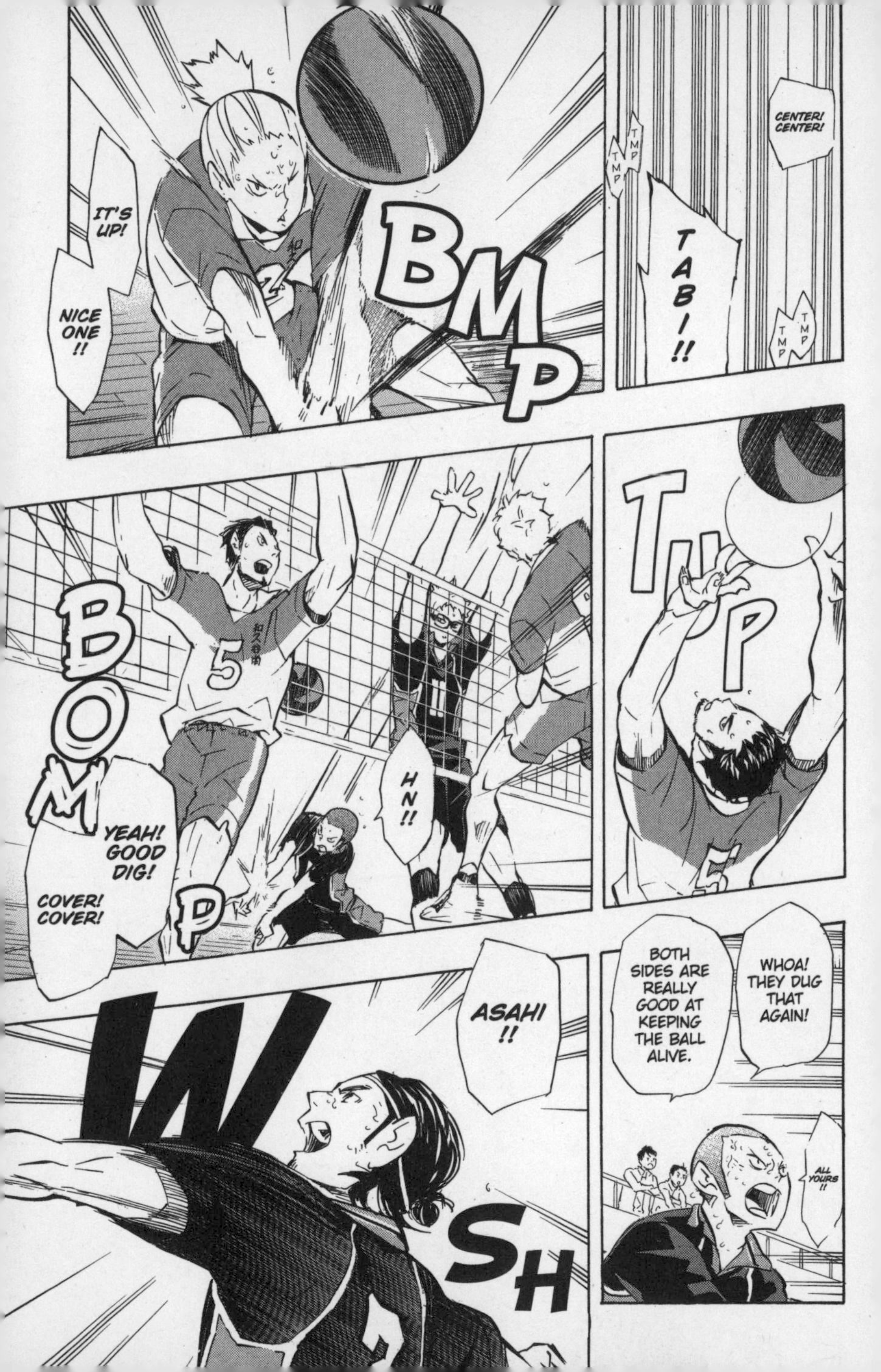
CENTER! CENTER!
TMP TMP
TABI!!
TMP TMP
BMP
IT'S UP!
NICE ONE!!
THP
BOMP
HN!!
YEAH! GOOD DIG!
COVER! COVER!
WHOA! THEY DUG THAT AGAIN!
BOTH SIDES ARE REALLY GOOD AT KEEPING THE BALL ALIVE.
ALL YOURS!!
ASAHI!!
WSH

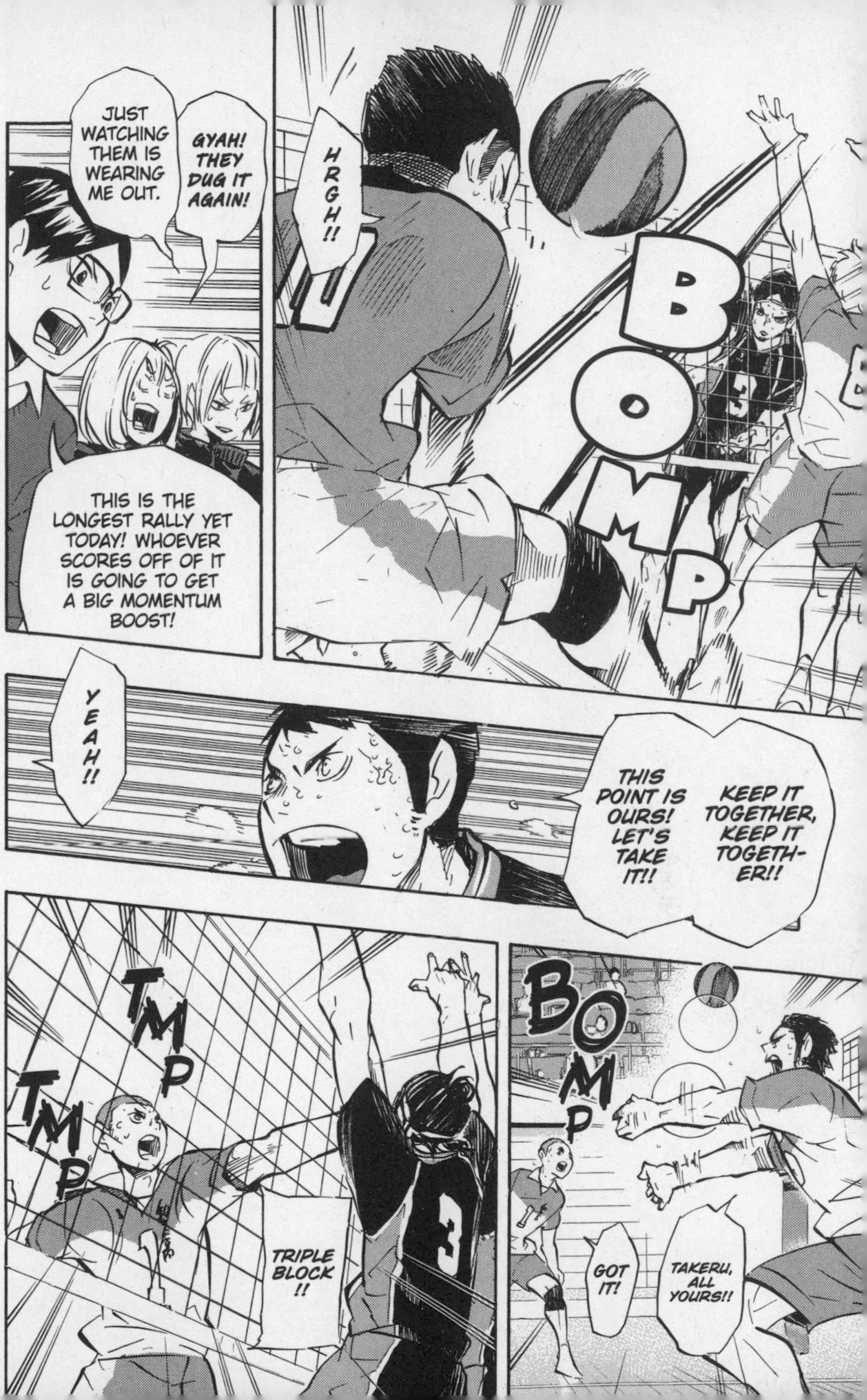
HRGH!!
BOMP
GYAH! THEY DUG IT AGAIN!
JUST WATCHING THEM IS WEARING ME OUT.
THIS IS THE LONGEST RALLY YET TODAY! WHOEVER SCORES OFF OF IT IS GOING TO GET A BIG MOMENTUM BOOST!
KEEP IT TOGETHER, KEEP IT TOGETH-ER!!
THIS POINT IS OURS! LET'S TAKE IT!!
YEAH!!
BOMP
TAKERU, ALL YOURS!!
GOT IT!
TMP
TMP
TRIPLE BLOCK!!

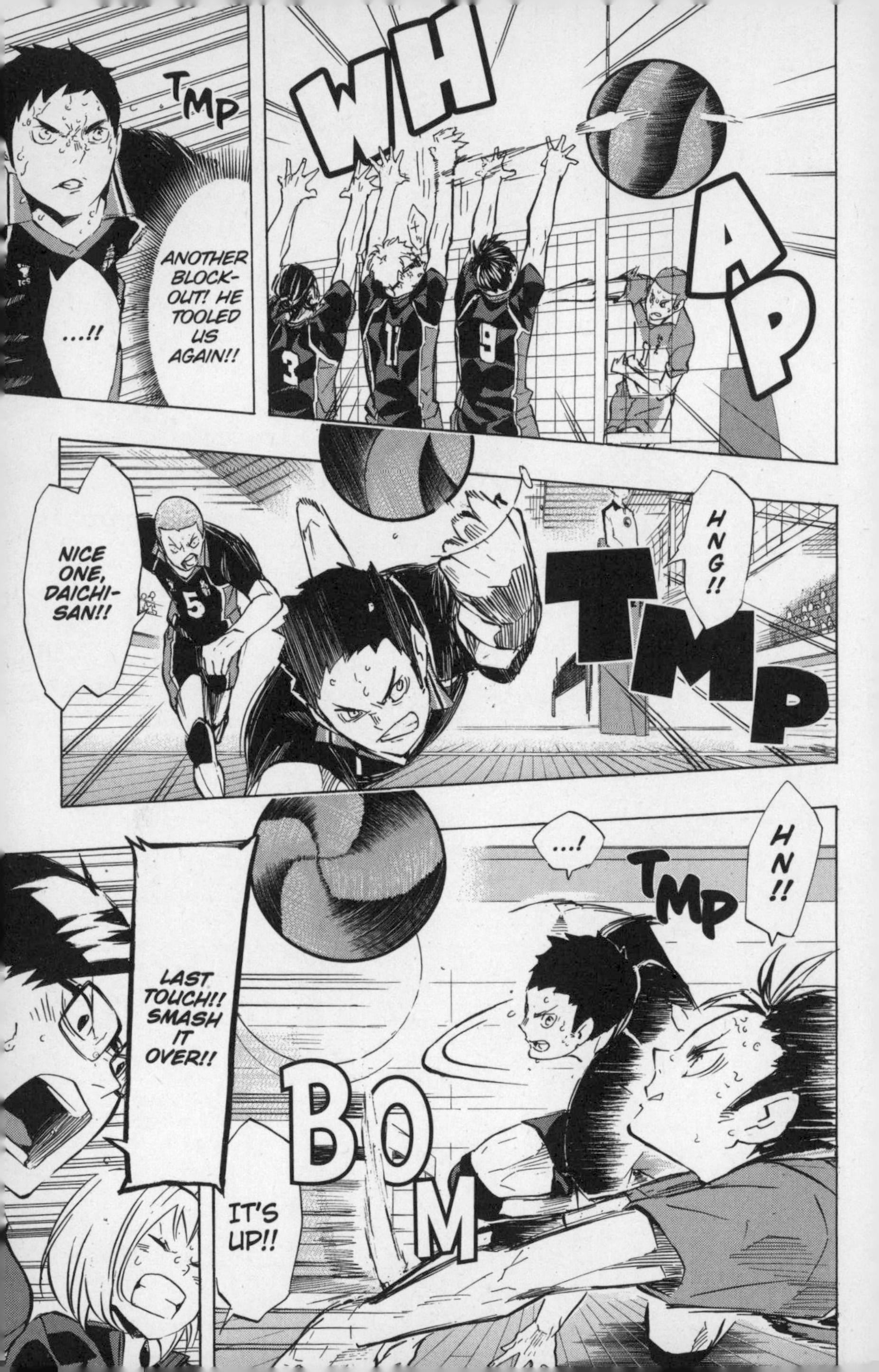
WHAP
TMP
ANOTHER BLOCK-OUT! HE TOOLED US AGAIN!!
...!!
HNG!!
TMP
NICE ONE, DAICHI-SAN!!
HN!!
TMP
...!
LAST TOUCH!! SMASH IT OVER!!
BOOM
IT'S UP!!

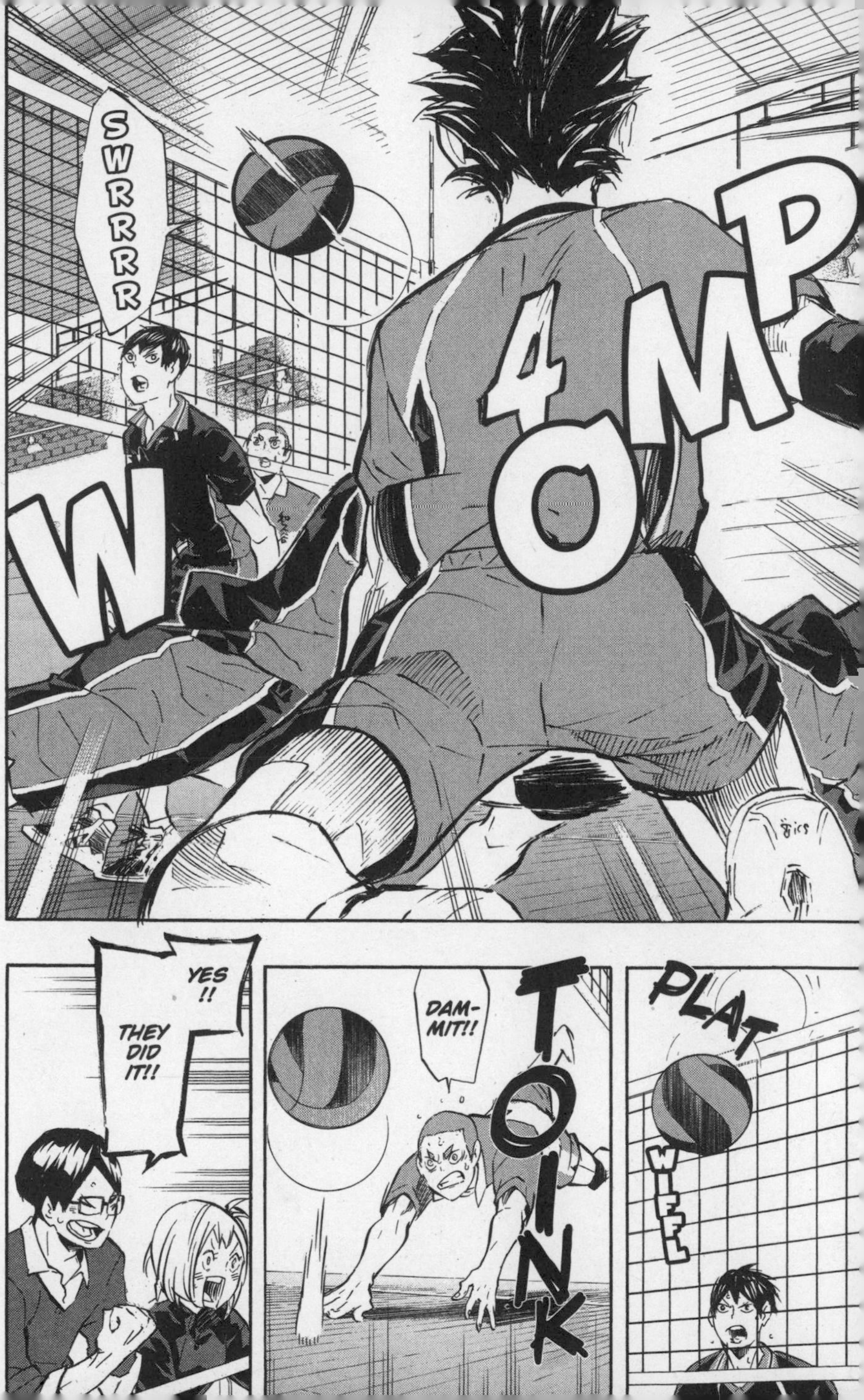
WOMP
SWRRRR
PLAT
WIFFL
TOINK
DAM-MIT!!
YES!! THEY DID IT!!

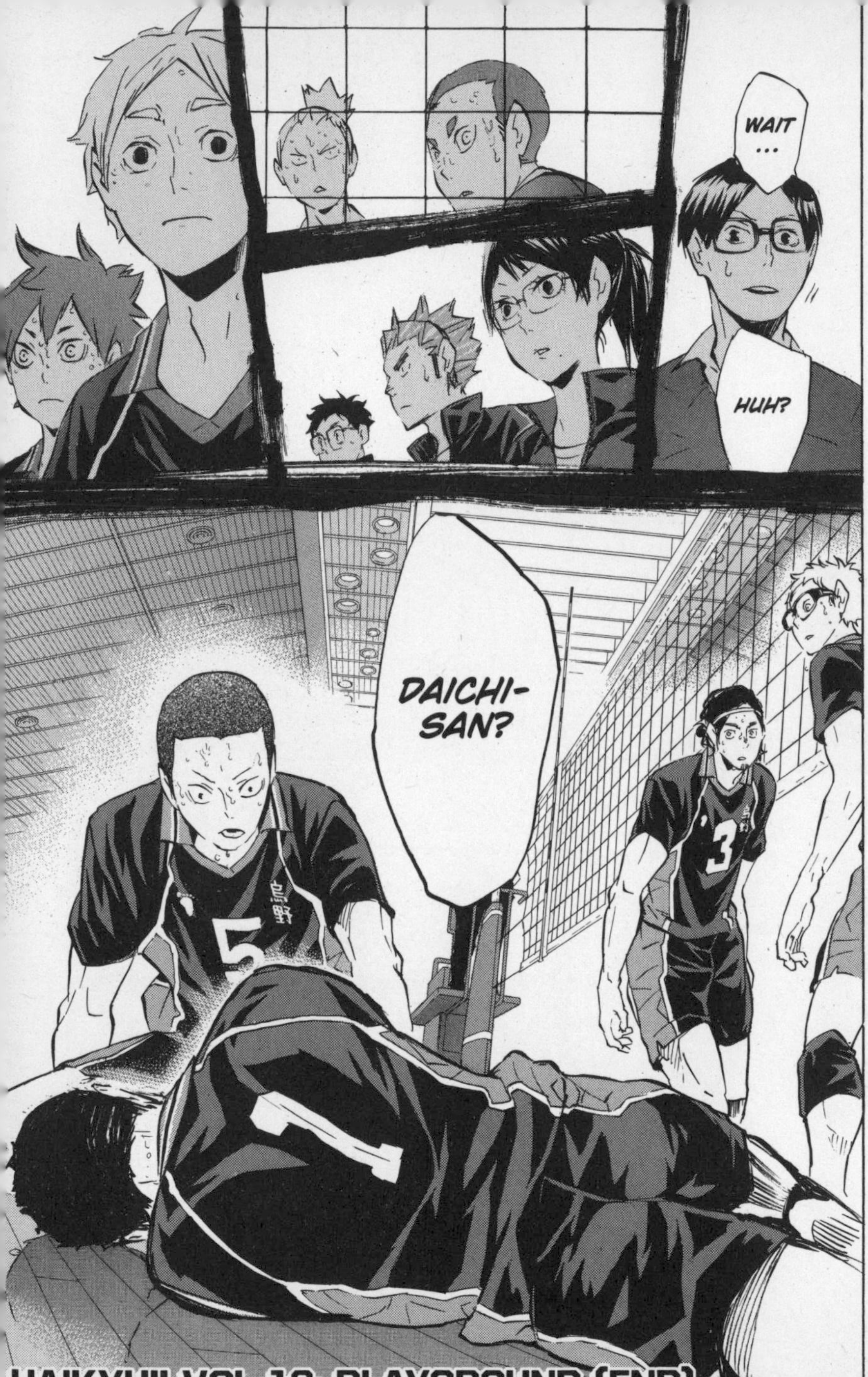
WAIT ...
HUH?
DAICHI-SAN?

HAIKYU!! VOL 13: PLAYGROUND (END)

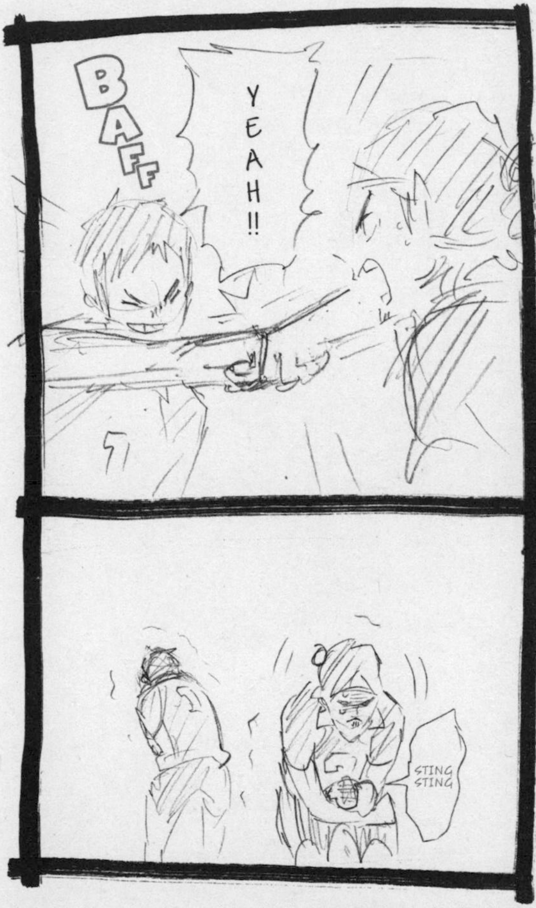
YEAH!!
BAFF
STING STING

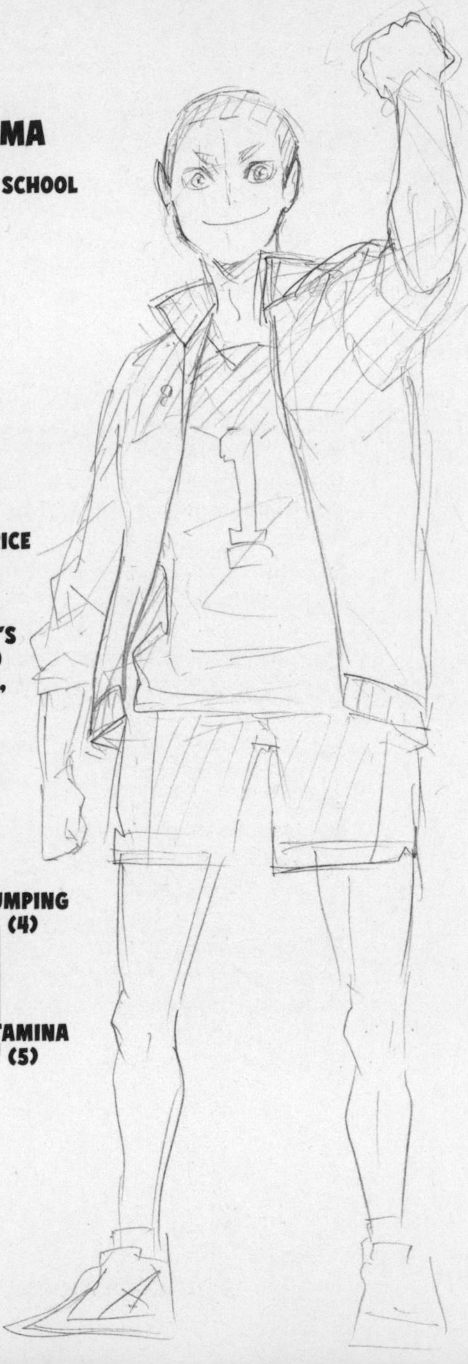

TAKERU NAKASHIMA

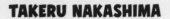

WAKUTANI MINAMI HIGH SCHOOL
CLASS 3-1

POSITION:
WING SPIKER

HEIGHT: 5'8"

WEIGHT: 145 LBS.
(AS OF APRIL, 3RD YEAR OF HIGH SCHOOL)

BIRTHDAY: AUGUST 20

FAVORITE FOOD:
***ZUNDA* MOCHI SOYBEAN RICE CAKES**

CURRENT WORRY:
IT FEELS LIKE HIS FATHER'S HAIRLINE IS STARTING TO RECEDE, LITTLE BY LITTLE, EVERY DAY.

ABILITY PARAMETERS
(5-POINT SCALE)

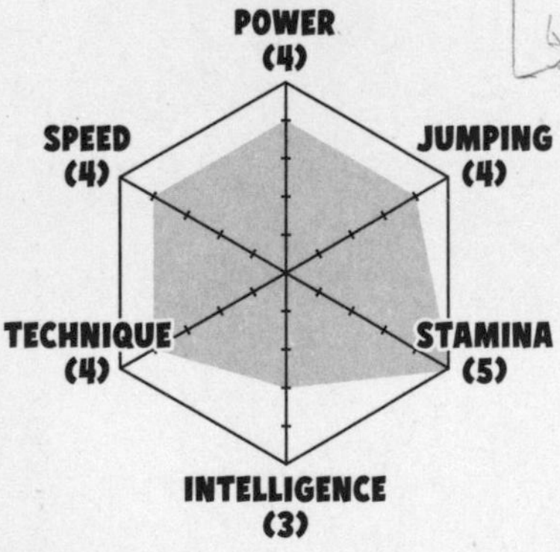
POWER (4)
JUMPING (4)
STAMINA (5)
INTELLIGENCE (3)
TECHNIQUE (4)
SPEED (4)

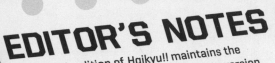

EDITOR'S NOTES

The English edition of Haikyu!! maintains the honorifics used in the original Japanese version. For those of you who are new to these terms, here's a brief explanation to help with your reading experience!

When saying someone's name in Japanese, a suffix is often attached to indicate how familiar the speaker is with the person. Some are more polite and respectful, while others are endearing.

1 *-kun* is often used for young men or boys, usually someone you are familiar with.

2 *-chan* is used for young children and can be used as a term of endearment.

3 *-san* is used for someone you respect or are not close to, or to be polite.

4 *Senpai* is used for someone who is older than you or in a higher position or grade in school.

5 *Kohai* is used for someone who is younger than you or in a lower position or grade in school.

6 *Sensei* means teacher.

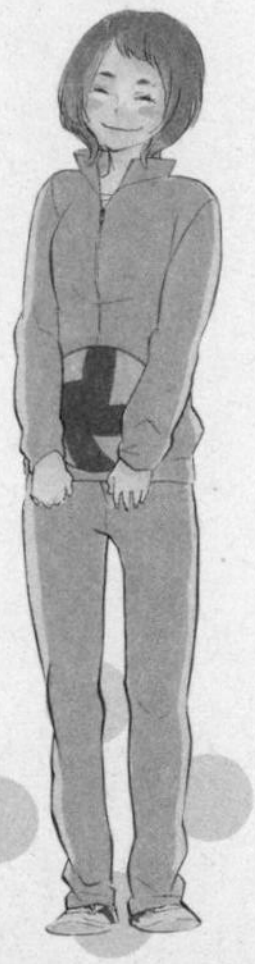

Kuroko's BASKETBALL

TADATOSHI FUJIMAKI

When incoming first-year student Taiga Kagami joins the Seirin High basketball team, he meets Tetsuya Kuroko, a mysterious boy who's plain beyond words. But Kagami's in for the shock of his life when he learns that the practically invisible Kuroko was once a member of "the Miracle Generation"—the undefeated legendary team—and he wants Kagami's help taking down each of his old teammates!

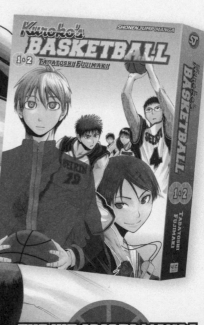

THE HIT SPORTS MANGA FROM _SHONEN JUMP_ IN A 2-IN-1 EDITION!

www.viz.com

KUROKO NO BASUKE © 2008 by Tadatoshi Fujimaki/SHUEISHA Inc.

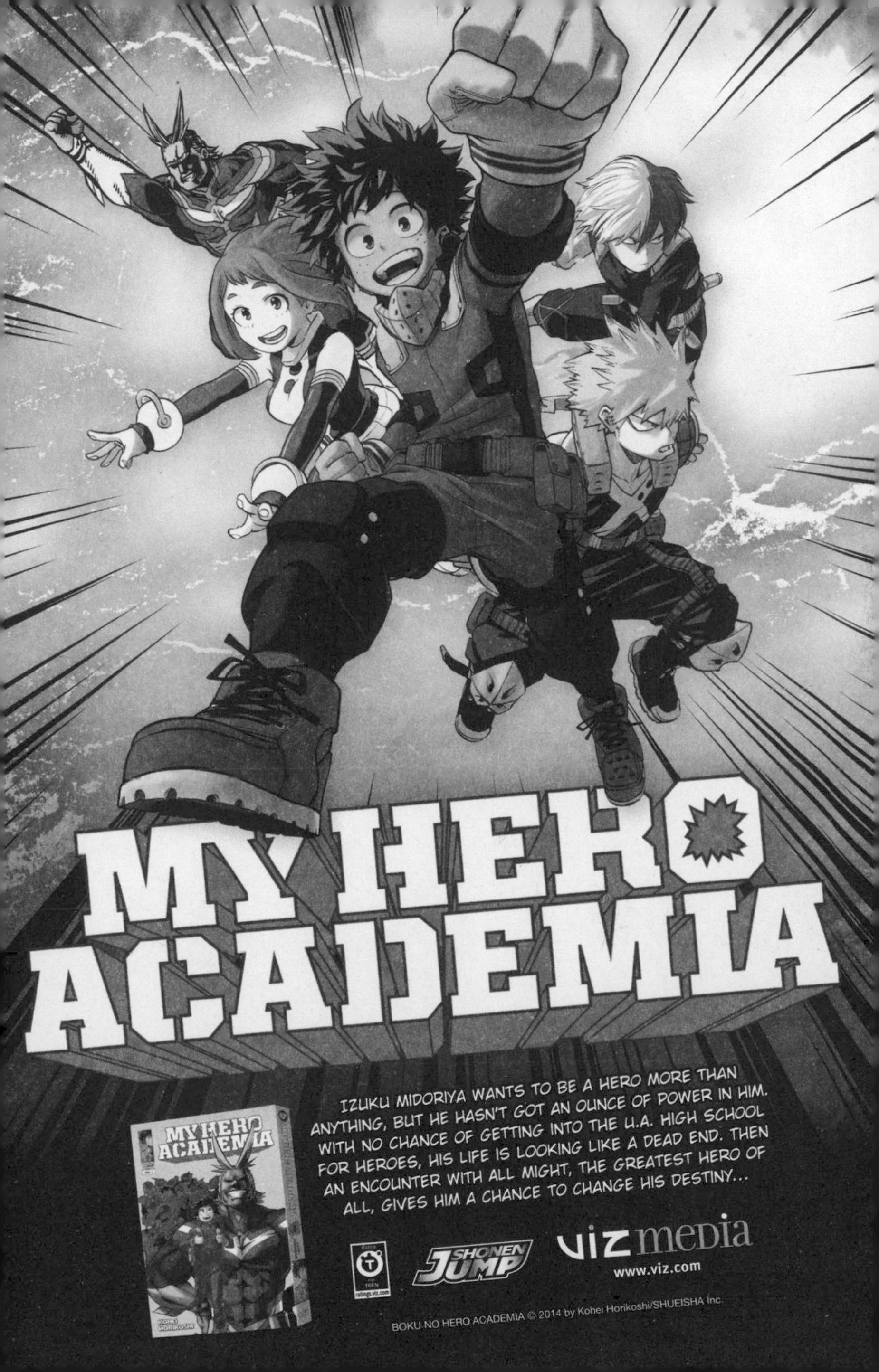

MY HERO ACADEMIA
IZUKU MIDORIYA WANTS TO BE A HERO MORE THAN ANYTHING, BUT HE HASN'T GOT AN OUNCE OF POWER IN HIM. WITH NO CHANCE OF GETTING INTO THE U.A. HIGH SCHOOL FOR HEROES, HIS LIFE IS LOOKING LIKE A DEAD END. THEN AN ENCOUNTER WITH ALL MIGHT, THE GREATEST HERO OF ALL, GIVES HIM A CHANCE TO CHANGE HIS DESTINY...
MY HERO ACADEMIA
KOHEI HORIKOSHI
SHONEN JUMP
viz media
www.viz.com
BOKU NO HERO ACADEMIA © 2014 by Kohei Horikoshi/SHUEISHA Inc.

THE ACTION-PACKED SUPERHERO COMEDY ABOUT ONE MAN'S AMBITION TO BE A HERO FOR FUN!

ONE-PUNCH MAN

STORY BY
ONE

ART BY
YUSUKE MURATA

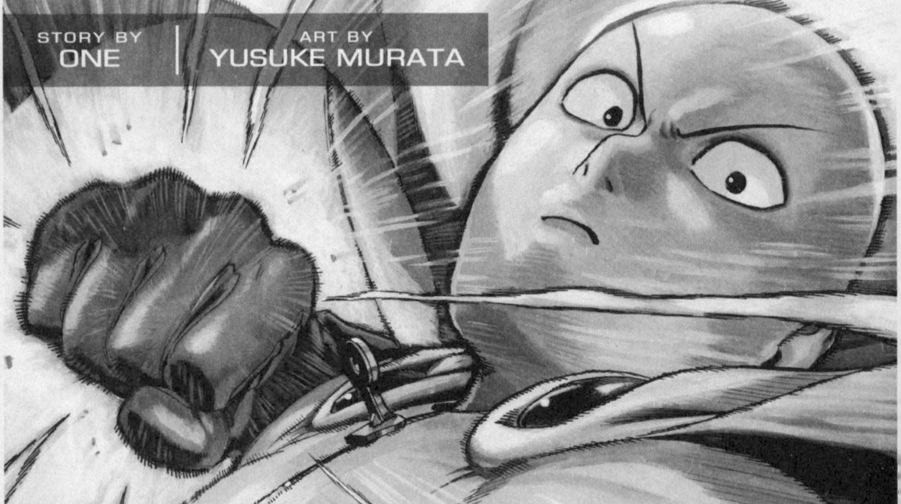

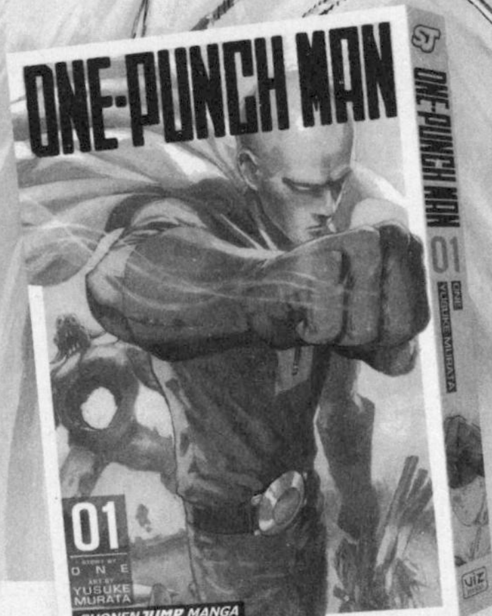

Nothing about Saitama passes the eyeball test when it comes to superheroes, from his lifeless expression to his bald head to his unimpressive physique. However, this average-looking guy has a not-so-average problem—he just can't seem to find an opponent strong enough to take on!

Can he finally find an opponent who can go toe-to-toe with him and give his life some meaning? Or is he doomed to a life of superpowered boredom?

ONE-PUNCH MAN © 2012 by ONE, Yusuke Murata/SHUEISHA Inc.

www.viz.com

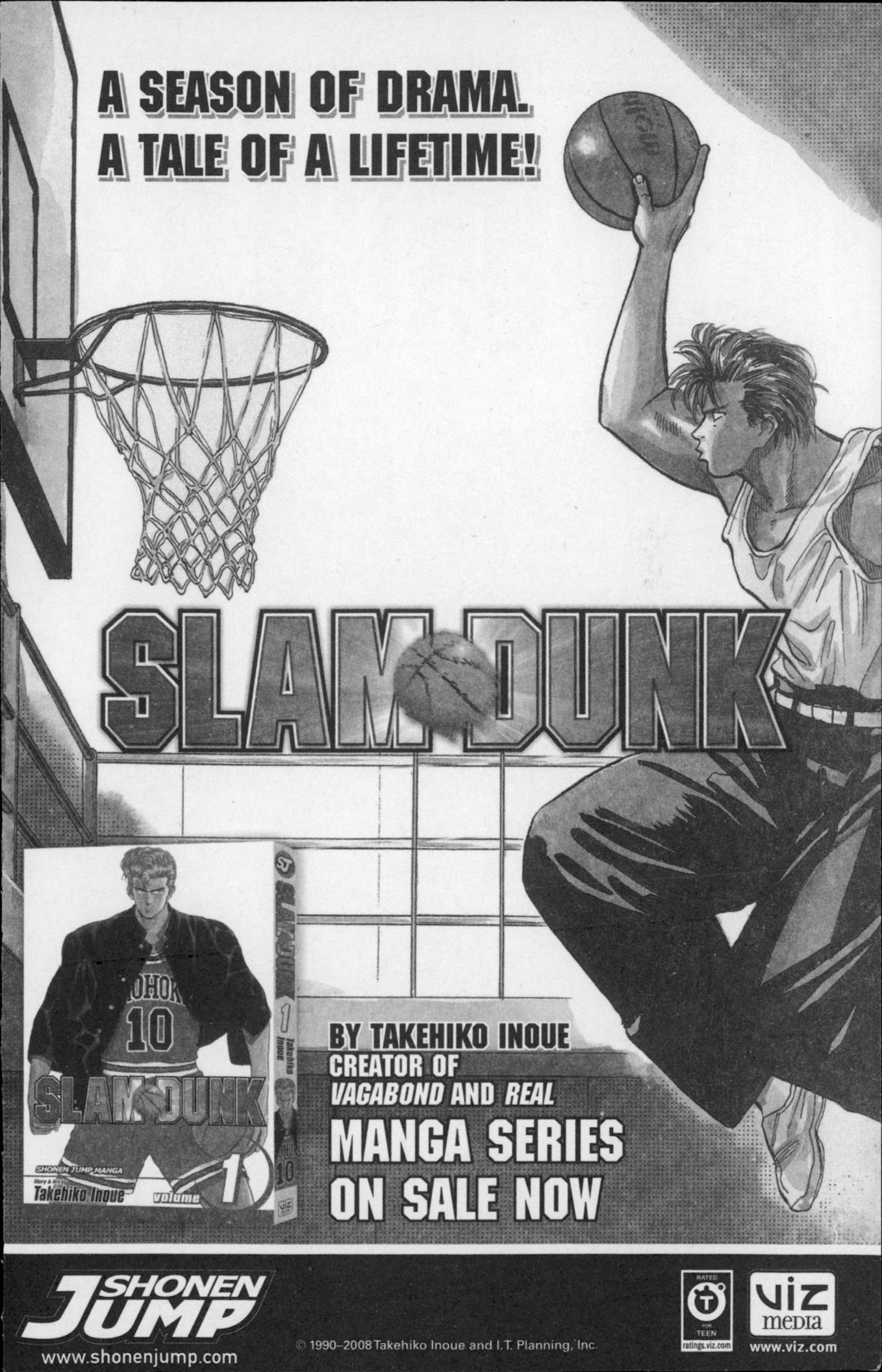
A SEASON OF DRAMA.
A TALE OF A LIFETIME!
SLAM DUNK
SLAM DUNK
SHONEN JUMP MANGA
Story & Art by
Takehiko Inoue
volume 1
BY TAKEHIKO INOUE
CREATOR OF
VAGABOND AND *REAL*
MANGA SERIES
ON SALE NOW
SHONEN JUMP
www.shonenjump.com
© 1990–2008 Takehiko Inoue and I.T. Planning, Inc.
RATED T FOR TEEN
ratings.viz.com
VIZ media
www.viz.com

IN A SAVAGE WORLD RULED BY THE PURSUIT OF THE MOST DELICIOUS FOODS, IT'S EITHER EAT OR BE EATEN!

"The most bizarrely entertaining manga out there on comic shelves. *Toriko* is a great series. If you're looking for a weirdly fun book or a fighting manga with a bizarre take, this is the story for you to read."

—ComicAttack.com

TORIKO

Story and Art by Mitsutoshi Shimabukuro

In an era where the world's gone crazy for increasingly bizarre gourmet foods, only Gourmet Hunter Toriko can hunt down the ferocious ingredients that supply the world's best restaurants. Join Toriko as he tracks and defeats the tastiest and most dangerous animals with his bare hands.

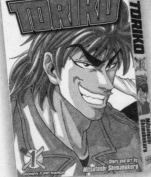

TORIKO © 2008 by Mitsutoshi Shimabukuro/SHUEISHA Inc.

www.shonenjump.com   www.viz.com

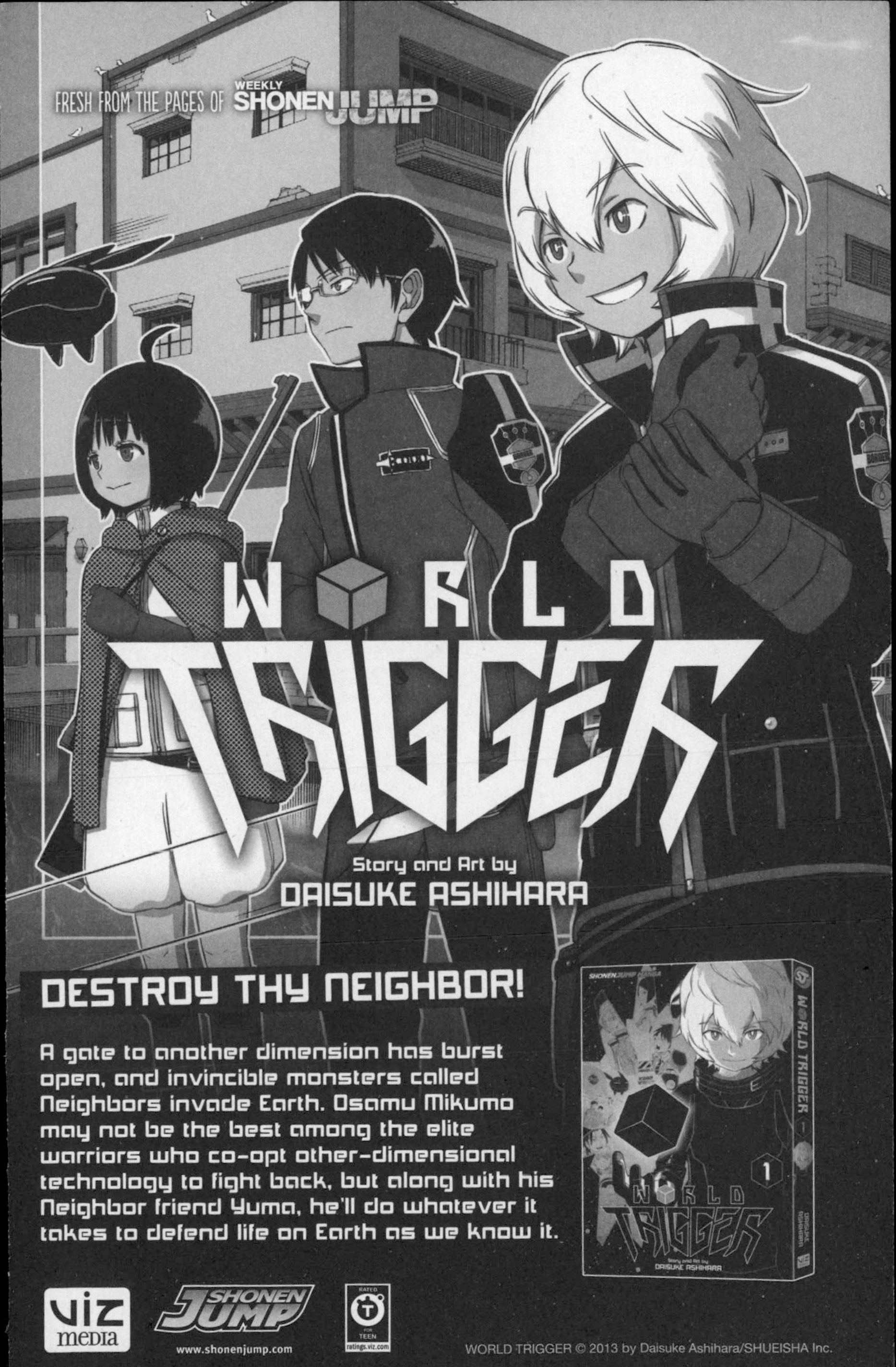

FRESH FROM THE PAGES OF **WEEKLY SHONEN JUMP**

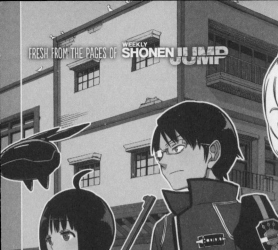

WORLD TRIGGER

Story and Art by
DAISUKE ASHIHARA

DESTROY THY NEIGHBOR!

A gate to another dimension has burst open, and invincible monsters called Neighbors invade Earth. Osamu Mikumo may not be the best among the elite warriors who co-opt other-dimensional technology to fight back, but along with his Neighbor friend Yuma, he'll do whatever it takes to defend life on Earth as we know it.

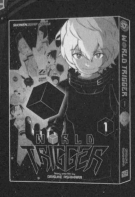

VIZ media

SHONEN JUMP
www.shonenjump.com

RATED T FOR TEEN
ratings.viz.com

WORLD TRIGGER © 2013 by Daisuke Ashihara/SHUEISHA Inc.

EAST MEETS WEST

WHEN TWO GREAT TITANS COME TOGETHER TO CREATE A
GROUNDBREAKING NEW MANGA

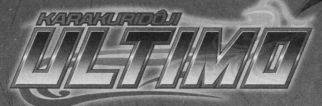

KARAKURIDÔJI ULTIMO

original concept: **STAN LEE** story and art by: **HIROYUKI TAKEI**

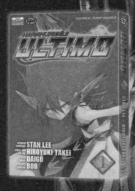

Ultimo and Vice are Karakuri Dôji, the mechanical embodiment of pure good and pure evil, devoid of human emotions that can cloud one's judgment. Their purpose: to battle to the death to prove once and for all whether good or evil is the most powerful force in the universe.

Available at your local bookstore or comic store.

www.shonenjump.com

www.viz.com

KARAKURI DOJI ULTIMO © 2008 by Stan Lee – POW! Entertainment / Dream Ranch, Hiroyuki Takei / SHUEISHA Inc.
* Prices subject to change

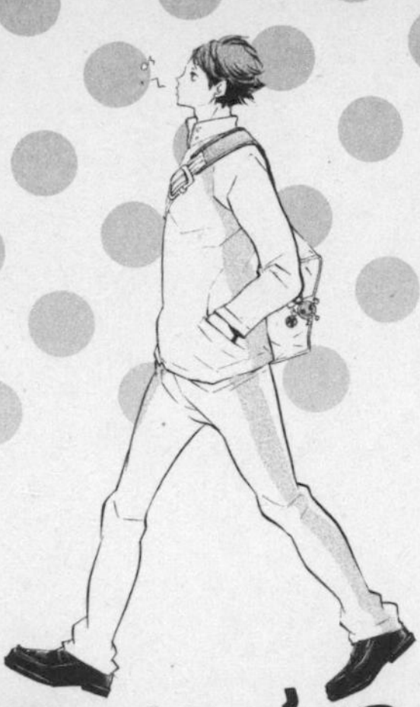

You're Reading the WRONG WAY!

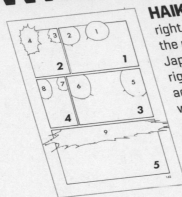

HAIKYU!! reads from right to left, starting in the upper-right corner. Japanese is read from right to left, meaning that action, sound effects and word-balloon order are completely reversed from English order.

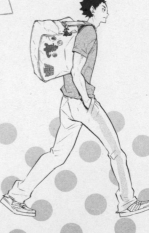